Springer Texts in Business and Economics

Springer Texts in Business and Economics (STBE) delivers high-quality instructional content for undergraduates and graduates in all areas of Business/Management Science and Economics. The series is comprised of self-contained books with a broad and comprehensive coverage that are suitable for class as well as for individual self-study. All texts are authored by established experts in their fields and offer a solid methodological background, often accompanied by problems and exercises.

Naohito Abe

Price Index Numbers

Theory and Application

Springer

Naohito Abe
Institute of Economic Research
Hitotsubashi University
Kunitachi, Tokyo, Japan

ISSN 2192-4333 ISSN 2192-4341 (electronic)
Springer Texts in Business and Economics
ISBN 978-981-97-6307-8 ISBN 978-981-97-6305-4 (eBook)
https://doi.org/10.1007/978-981-97-6305-4

Previously published with NIPPON HYORON SHA CO.,LTD. PUBLISHERS

Translation from the Japanese language edition: "Bukka shisū gairon" by Naohito Abe, © Naohito Abe 2023. Published by NIPPON HYORON SHA CO.,LTD. PUBLISHERS. All Rights Reserved.

This Springer imprint is published by the registered company Springer Nature Singapore Pte Ltd.
The registered company address is: 152 Beach Road, #21-01/04 Gateway East, Singapore 189721, Singapore

Preface

As we enter the twenty-first century, the use of various information sources like scanner data, web scraping, household account management apps, and credit card purchase histories has become common in economic analysis. Unlike traditional economic data such as the Panel Study of Income Dynamics (PSID) or company financial statements, these types of data capture a broader range of behaviors in terms of both quantity and variety.

When analyzing these new data types, aggregation becomes crucial. However, determining how to aggregate such diverse and numerous activity and transaction records is not a straightforward task. Index number theory, with its long history, offers valuable guidelines in addressing this challenge. Centuries ago, European intellectuals faced the challenge of aggregating information on changing prices of various goods. The breakthrough came about three centuries ago, led by William Fleetwood, a bishop who created the world's first price index. In the late nineteenth century, Stanley Jevons initiated modern research into index number theory. Today, economists are actively researching on how to create indices to interpret vast data sources like scanner data in a meaningful way.

Unfortunately, index number theory and the system of national accounts, which are crucial aggregations in macroeconomics, are rarely offered as comprehensive courses at the graduate level. Moreover, finding guidance on cutting-edge aggregation and index number theory typically involves extensive manuals geared towards statistical practitioners, commonly known as CPI manuals, or compact but highly advanced books on index number theory, such as the one by Balk (2008), which requires a solid grasp of mathematics. Self-learning aggregation and index number theory to understand the latest analytical techniques and their challenges often requires reading numerous academic papers, a time-consuming and labor-intensive process. This book seeks to introduce contemporary index number theory and practices to a broader audience.

This book, extensively rewritten for an international audience, is based on an introductory text about price indices originally published in Japan by Nihon-Hyoron-sha. It draws from the author's research and the lecture materials used at Hitotsubashi University. The book introduces recent advancements in index number and aggregation theory, along with practical challenges in the field. Textbooks on economics and statistics typically present discussions on index number theory, including price and quantity indices, at a basic level. Even graduate students specializing in economics or statistics seldom encounter the results of over a century of research in index number theory. It is my hope that this book serves as a gateway to the expanding field of aggregation and index number theory, which has experienced a surge of research activity in recent years.

The Consumer Price Index (CPI) is a crucial measure for economic analysts. When conducting model analysis, real sales, obtained by dividing total sales of an industry by the price index, are treated as total output. Similarly, real consumption, obtained by dividing total household consumption expenditure by the price index, is treated as consumption quantity. The price index transforms nominal variables in accounting, such as sales or total expenditure, into economic variables like production quantity or consumption quantity.

However, many may lack sufficient knowledge about the mechanisms behind this transformation. That is, what conditions and reasoning lead nominal accounting variables to become quantities? One of the aims of this book is to introduce the mechanisms behind this transformation, the price index that aggregates the sales or total expenditure of many products into quantity, and to present the challenges involved, as well as the efforts made by index number researchers and practitioners. It is my hope that readers of this book will gain insights into the world of index number theory and appreciate its potential, especially in aggregating detailed data, often referred to as "Big Data," such as scanner data.

One notable difference between this book and other textbooks like the CPI Manual or Balk (2008) lies in its emphasis on an economic approach. In particular, I have allocated significant space to the Sato–Vartia index. While standard index number theory, as introduced in Chap. 6, classifies the Sato–Vartia index as a quasi-superlative index compared to superlative indices such as the Fisher and Törnqvist indices, in macroeconomics and international trade, the Sato–Vartia index is one of the standard and popular index numbers. Through this book, I hope readers will gain a deeper understanding of this index devised by Sato (1976) and Vartia (1976).

I received valuable feedback from numerous individuals during the preparations of this book. The students who took my Applied Macroeconomics course at the Graduate School of Economics, Hitotsubashi University, significantly improved this manuscript through their questions. Professor Hideyuki Mizobuchi pointed out numerous important errors in the draft of this book. Professor Chihiro Shimizu, who has conducted research on index number theory for many years, provided detailed advice on the entire book. Additionally, Profs. Akiyuki Tonogi, Noriko Inakura, and Hideyasu Sato, with whom I have conducted joint research, provided numerous comments from the early stages of this book. The Price Division of the Statistics Bureau of the Ministry of Internal Affairs and Communications in Japan provided detailed fact-checking during the draft stage of this book. For Chap. 2, Profs. Osamu Saito, Susumu Yamauchi, and Chiaki Yamamoto offered valuable comments and advice from a historian's perspective. Additionally, Profs. Makoto Saito and Kyoji Fukao provided numerous comments on macrohistorical statistics.

Discussions at the workshop held by the Research and Statistics Department of the Bank of Japan were very helpful for Chap. 9.

From Profs. Yoshito Yosizoe, Elwin Diewert, Robert Hill, Marshall Reinsdorf, Robert Feenstra, Tiziana Laureti, and many others, I received valuable discussions at various academic conferences and research meetings, which are reflected throughout this book. In particular, Prof. D. S. Prasada Rao, who introduced me to the world of index number theory and made it fascinating through numerous joint research projects, provided detailed comments on all chapters of this book. I also extend thanks to Prof. Miriam Steuer for her very helpful comments on Chap. 2. I would like to express special gratitude to the market research company INTAGE Inc. for granting permission to use valuable scanner data. Additionally, many of the research outcomes mentioned in this book were supported by Grants-in-Aid for Scientific Research from the Japan Society for the Promotion of Science. This book is a product of the Grant-in-Aid (B)(23K25496) and (S)(24H00012).

Tokyo, Japan Naohito Abe
October 2024

References

Balk, B. M. (2008). *Price and quantity index numbers*. Cambridge University Press.

Sato, K. (1976). The ideal log-change index number. *Review of Economics and Statistics*, *58*(2), 223–228.

Vartia, Y. O. (1976). Ideal log-change index numbers. *Scandinavian Journal of Statistics*, 3, 121–126.

Contents

1 What Are Index Numbers?

Abstract

This chapter introduces the concept of index numbers, particularly in the context of economics. Index numbers are used to measure changes over time or differences between places or individuals, often for quantities that are difficult to measure directly. The chapter begins with a definition from John Maynard Keynes, highlighting that an index number quantifies changes in magnitudes that are otherwise hard to measure accurately. The term "index number" has its origins in the word "index," which initially meant a pointing finger, evolving to signify something that indicates or points out. Its economic application began in the mid-nineteenth century, with significant contributions from economists like William Newmarch and William Stanley Jevons. This chapter explains the structure of the book that includes chapters on the history of index numbers, representative index formulas, advanced index number theory, and practical applications.

1.1 What is Index Number

1.1.1 The Definition of Index Number

There are numerous index numbers in the world. The discomfort index in meteorology, the Human Development Index (HDI) and poverty indices compiled by the United Nations, and even the number of Michelin stars awarded to restaurants can be considered as types of index numbers. This book contemplates index numbers related to prices and quantities.

John Maynard Keynes defined an index number as "in itself no more than the measure of the magnitude of an object at one time or in one place in terms of the magnitude of the same or a similar object at another time or in another place."

N. Abe, *Price Index Numbers*, Springer Texts in Business and Economics,
https://doi.org/10.1007/978-981-97-6305-4_1

(Keynes, 1909, p. 51). Although there are other definitions of an index number,[1] in this book, we adopt the definition by Keynes. That is, we define an index number as "a real number representing the change in something that is difficult to measure over time or between places or individuals."

Column 1: Keynes and Index Number Theory

J. M. Keynes, a prominent figure in the early 20th century, left many contemplations on price indices. In this book, Keynes is primarily introduced as a critic of the stochastic approach, yet his thoughts on price indices are varied. It's challenging to summarize the vast range of points covered in his works and essays, but let us briefly discuss his investigations on price indices here.

Firstly, 'Keynes (1909)', a work he submitted to the University of Cambridge in his mid-20s and for which he won the Adam Smith Prize, is a comprehensive study of price indices, as indicated by its title. Noteworthy points in this work include (1) highlighting the difficulty of calculating the general level/index of prices, (2) a detailed examination of the stochastic approach, and (3) advocating the use of chain indices. He also noted that comparing national income is impossible without comparing the utility levels among different individuals, highlighting the issue of aggregating data from diverse individuals. This point is particularly relevant to current dynamic macroeconomic models that incorporate heterogeneity among individuals.

In his 1930 work 'Treatise on Money' (Keynes, 1930), introduced in this book's second chapter, Keynes launched a comprehensive critique of the stochastic approach. He also revisited and critiqued the chain indices he had supported in 1909, highlighting their inability to include new goods. Additionally, Keynes identified several issues with chain indices, such as path dependency and chain drifts. Notably, his comments on the accumulation of errors indicate a significant potential for chain drift, presaging recent serious concerns:

> In the third place we assume that the successive small errors of approximation – and this is the most serious assumption – are not cumulative so as to add up to a substantial error, when the procedure is repeated a number of times over a succession of positions. (p. 105, Keynes, 1930)

In 'The General Theory' (Keynes, 1930), published in 1936, he discusses price indices in the fourth chapter, stating that determining which of two eras had higher prices is like debating whether Queen Victoria or Queen Elizabeth

[1] In *The New Palgrave Dictionary of Economics, 2nd edition, 2008*, Diewert defines an index number as something "to aggregate detailed information on prices and quantities into scalar measures of price and quantity levels or their growth." On the other hand, Edgeworth, who contributed significantly to the fields of economics and statistics from the late nineteenth to early twentieth centuries, defined an index number as "a number adapted by its variations to indicate the increase or decrease of a magnitude not susceptible of accurate measurement" (Edgeworth, 1925, p. 347).

was happier, thus emphasizing the difficulty of measuring general prices. When discussing prices, Keynes was mindful of the national income deflator, creating indices using not only the prices of consumer goods, as in modern consumer price indices, but also using wages. In the fourth chapter of his 'General Theory', he proposed a deflator using the weighted average of wages. However, the idea of using a wage index as a deflator for the entire economy, similar to the 17th-century thinker Vaughan, seems unconvincing today. Discussions on Keynes's price indices are more about criticizing the prevailing ideas of his time than actively supporting or proposing something. Therefore, it's difficult to evaluate Keynes's contribution to the index number theory, but he might have raised the level of index number research as a formidable opponent to contemporary researchers like Fisher, Edgeworth, and Bowley.

1.2 The Etymology of Index Number

According to the *Oxford English Dictionary*, the term "index number" has its origins in the word "index," which initially meant a pointing finger, and then came to signify something that points out or indicates. The ninth meaning listed under "index" relates to its use in economics as an index number. The use of "index number" in its current sense as an economic term is relatively recent. An 1886 report to the British Parliament suggests that the term was first used in the mid-nineteenth century by William Newmarch (1820–1882), who was also the editor of the enduring economic magazine *The Economist*.[2] However, the use of the term "index" to indicate monetary value was already natural at that time, as seen in David Ricardo's (1772–1823) speech in 1822, where he said, "the price of gold was the index of the depreciation of the currency."[3] William Stanley Jevons (1835–1882), a prominent early index number researcher, only used the term "index number" in his 1884 publication[4] when referring to Newmarch's work. However, by the end of the nineteenth century, numerous papers on index number research were published, and the term "index number" was widely used. Thus, it can be inferred that the term "index number" became rapidly established in the latter half of the nineteenth century.

Moreover, the word "index" also encompasses the meaning of "exponent," which is a superscript denoting a power or root in algebra.[5] Though the use of index number as an exponent may not be common today, it is important to be aware of this when conversing with individuals from different fields.

[2] Refer to Northcote (1886), P. 328.

[3] "..that the price of gold was the index of the depreciation of the currency,.." Ricardo (1822), Speech "RESUMPTION OF CASH PAYMENTS."

[4] Jevons (1884) Investigations in Currency and Finance, MACMILLAN and CO. London.

[5] 8 a. Algebra. A number or other symbol placed above and to the right of a quantity to denote a power or root: = exponent. (Oxford English Library).

1.3 About This Book

1.3.1 Purpose of This Book

This book aims to introduce and discuss theories and practical methods related to index numbers in economics, especially those used in aggregating levels and changes in quantities and prices of commodities. It covers developments in this area up to recent years and discusses various issues that current index number researchers and practitioners face, with the goal of making the world of contemporary index number theory and practices known to a wider audience.

Economic indices, particularly important ones like the consumer price index and the index of industrial production, have become important not just in specialized circles but also in everyday life. In economic analysis, whether micro- or macroeconomics, household and firm models are often built and analyzed using aggregate quantities. For example, category-level expenditure data like food and services expenditures are aggregates. When seeking economically meaningful measure "real consumption," price indices are used as deflators. One of the aims of this book is to clarify various problems in aggregation theory that many researchers use unconsciously, such as the theory and assumptions behind conversions using price indices. In economics coursework programs, including at the graduate level, there is little mention of index numbers. Introductory economics often only covers the Laspeyres and Paasche indices, and occasionally the Fisher index, leaving students with little exposure to advances in index number theory over the last century. Index number theory was also a field of statistics from the nineteenth to the early twentieth century, with Edgeworth even serving as President of the Royal Statistical Society, but it is rarely introduced in current statistics textbooks. For economists and statisticians, as well as researchers, there are only two types of recent specialized books suitable for understanding the entirety of contemporary index number theory: Balk (2008), which requires advanced mathematical knowledge, and the voluminous *CPI Manual*[6] aimed at practitioners from national statistical offices, both of which are challenging reads. While index number theory is scarcely in university curriculum, national statistical offices, international organizations, and index number theory researchers frequently hold research meetings, dedicating significant effort to proposing and validating better aggregation methods and index number formulas.

In index number theory, from its dawn until the mid-twentieth century, the field overflowed with names of talents who contributed significantly to modern economics, such as Jevons, Edgeworth, Marshall, Fisher, Keynes, and Samuelson. Numerous papers were published by renowned researchers such as Deaton, Diewert, Hall, and Jorgenson toward the end of the twentieth century. It appears that the level of interest in index number theory within the economics community today may not be as intense

[6] The CPI Manual, formally titled "Consumer Price Index Manual: Theory and Practice," is a publication by the International Labour Organization (ILO) alongside other international organizations. It offers detailed guidelines and established best practices for constructing Consumer Price Indices (CPIs). The most recent version was released in 2020 by the ILO and its partner organizations

as before. This book hopes to convey salient features of the modern index number theory to a wider audience.

Index number theory uses mathematical methods not typically employed in standard economics, such as functional equations, and different analytical approaches like axiomatic and economic approaches, each with a long history of development, making it difficult to grasp the overall picture. This book makes a conscious effort to interrelate these different approaches.

1.3.2 Structure of This Book

Chapter 2 introduces the history of index numbers and price measurement. Although Balk (1989) and Diewert (1993) provide a detailed history of price index numbers, recent research in the history of economic thought has shed considerable light on the lives of past researchers on index numbers, which were previously not well understood. This book, drawing on these recent research findings, briefly introduces the lives of those who played significant roles in the development of index number theory and methods. It is hoped that the reader will imagine the background against which the field of index number research emerged. Also, there are numerous critical papers written in German and French, like those of Laspeyres, Paasche, and Dutot. Papers on index number theory written in the eighteenth and nineteenth centuries in German and French can be difficult to understand due to differences in mathematical styles. Moreover, misunderstandings like "Laspeyres invented the Laspeyres index," which would not occur if the original papers were read, are still found, likely because many people write without referencing the original works. In writing Chap. 2, we introduce various discussions while consulting the primary sources. Fortunately, the digital library via the Internet and the valuable books stored in the Center for Historical Social Science Literature in Hitotsubashi University, where the author is affiliated, made it possible to obtain copies of most of these historical contributions. This chapter can stand as an independent reading not only for those interested in index number theory but also for those interested in the history of economic thought.

Chapter 3 discusses representative index number formulas, covering what many readers might imagine as "index number theory." This chapter explores the relationships between the Dutot index; the Jevons and Carli indices; the standard Laspeyres, Paasche, Fisher indices; and the increasingly used Törnqvist and Sato–Vartia indices, along with the underlying concepts of averages. With assumed knowledge up to high school mathematics, this chapter should be accessible even without specific economic knowledge.

Chapters 4–6 investigate fully fledged index number theory, assuming intermediate-level knowledge of economics, specifically concepts such as duality and expenditure functions. In Chap. 4, which discusses the axiomatic approach, functional equations, a mathematical method rarely encountered in educational curricula, appear. Although we explain the necessary theorems for functional equations in the mathematical appendix, an introductory book on functional equations may be necessary for serious research in this field. The axiomatic approach in Chap. 4 is central to modern index number theory, marking a groundbreaking approach that gave the index number theory a rigorous logical structure similar to general equilibrium models. This chapter places particular emphasis on the characterization of various indices, i.e., deducing a single index number formula from several axioms.

Chapter 5 discusses the economic approach, focusing on the recently emphasized Constant Elasticity of Substitution (CES)-type utility function. It discusses the concepts and problems of the cost-of-living index. The discussions about the theory and properties of the cost-of-living index presented here are essential for understanding contemporary index number theory. Chapter 6 focuses on the "superlative index," a milestone in index number research in the twentieth century, discussing the relationship between the cost-of-living index and the standard price index number formulas discussed in Chap. 5. Chapter 6 is the most important chapter in this book, connecting the theoretical concept of the cost-of-living index and the standard price index. However, the chapter also discusses recent criticisms of the superlative index, which is no longer considered a universally superior or all-purpose index compared to the time when it was introduced in the 1970s.

Chapter 7 on the Divisia index, once considered an ideal index number formula and still playing an important role in productivity measurement, deals with continuous time, a theoretical concept not suited for practical application but with a strong influence. This chapter should be read in conjunction with Chap. 8 on chain indices, which are used in the system of national account in many countries. Sometimes, chain indices are seen as clearly superior to standard direct indices, but Chap. 8 points out that chain indices are not ideal and have many problems. It details when chain indices are desirable and when they are inappropriate.

Chapter 9 addresses problems encountered when the goods differ between the base and comparison periods. The appearance of new goods, the disappearance of old goods, seasonal products, and differences in culture and environment between regions mean goods differ over time or across regions. This poses significant issues for price and quantity comparisons. While being a major challenge for index number theory, this heterogeneity of goods is also a problem that statistical practitioners face constantly. The heterogeneity of goods across time and regions is a central issue in current index number theory, and Chap. 9 discusses various methods ranging from hedonic estimation to chain indices.

Stochastic approach discussed in Chap. 10 is utilized in the World Bank's purchasing power parity calculations and provides a theory behind core inflation often used in a model of monetary policy. In the stochastic approach, commodity prices are regarded as random variables, enabling the estimation of the price index through the common dynamics of these variables, such as the use of time dummies. This method also facilitates the calculation of standard errors for the price indices. This approach is especially useful when reliability of calculated indices is under discussion. This chapter assumes knowledge of intermediate-level econometrics. Chapter 11 introduces various issues in regional/spatial price comparisons. Regional or spatial price comparisons emphasize transitivity, which is not satisfied by many standard price index numbers. Therefore, various methods have been developed. Active research is ongoing in this area.

Chapter 12 discusses the study of price indices through the lens of Engel curves. Engel curves illustrate how the proportion of income spent on a specific category of goods, especially foods, changes with income. If these curves—the paths showing how spending on foods evolve as income grows—are identical across different countries or time, then any unusual shapes in these curves could indicate errors in measuring data, in particular, price indices. This concept has inspired many significant research articles published in leading economics journals. The chapter goes on to explore the successes and problems encountered in applying this method to study price indices.

Chapter 13 summarizes expectations for the future development of index number theory.

1.3.3 Topics Not Covered in This Book

This book does not address some themes in aggregation theory, such as the separability of preferences and aggregation of different individuals, one of the main topics in general equilibrium theory. Regarding the separability of preferences, I decided not to explain it in this book, as it is thoroughly covered in many graduate-level microeconomics textbooks such as Deaton and Muellbauer (1980). In index number theory, the separability of preferences among categories or different time points is a prerequisite for aggregation, and the separability of preferences is rarely discussed within index number theory. Aggregation among different individuals is also an extremely important issue, but it was difficult to select the content to introduce in this book.

National accounts are closely related to index number theory, with many indices being utilized. Understanding national accounts requires knowledge of commodity flows and input–output tables, which would need many pages just to introduce the basics. Fortunately, many excellent explanatory books on national accounts have been written,[7] so I decided it was unnecessary to discuss them in this book. The price indices of real estate, housing, and rent were also omitted. The theory behind them is based on dynamic models for asset price determination, requiring many pages to discuss in full. Fortunately, excellent explanatory books on indices related to housing and rent, such as Diewert et al. (2020), have been written. Those interested should refer to them.

The most challenging decision was regarding the treatment of monetary theory, which underlies the concept of price indices. Historically, price indices have been emphasized as indicators of monetary value and are still discussed in relation to monetary policy, such as core inflation, which is considered in connection with

[7] A detailed information on System of National Account (SNA) is available in the System of National Accounts (SNA), IMF (2008).

money stock. However, monetary theory is a vast field of research with extensive literature. On the other hand, in modern index number theory, price and quantity indices are constructed based on utility and production functions, without assuming the existence of money. Since there are many excellent specialized books on money and monetary theory, this book limits its discussion of index number theory related to monetary theory to core inflation in Chap. 10.

1.3.4 Target Audience of This Book

This book targets those interested in the theory of various index numbers and methods for aggregating various goods and prices. It is a substantially revised version of lecture notes for advanced undergraduate and master's courses in the Graduate School of Economics at Hitotsubashi University, assuming knowledge of advanced undergraduate-level economic theory. Specifically, basic knowledge on multivariate analysis and linear algebra are required. Basic principles of functional equations are explained in a mathematical appendix. Knowledge of duality, specifically the minimum expenditure function and the indirect utility function, is needed, but as there are many excellent textbooks on this topic, most of the formulas developed in this book can be easily followed with a microeconomics textbook at hand.

References

Balk, B. M. (1989). Changing consumer preferences and the cost-of-living index: Theory and nonparametric expressions. *Journal of Economics, 50*(2), 157–169.

Balk, B. M. (2008). *Price and quantity index numbers*. Cambridge University Press.

Deaton, A., & Muellbauer, J. (1980). An almost ideal demand system. *American Economic Review, 70*(3), 312–326.

Diewert, W. E. (1993). The early history of price index research. In W. E. Diewert, & A. O. Nakamura (Eds.) *Essays in index number theory* (Vol. 1, pp. 33–65).

Diewert, W. E., Nishimura, K., Shimizu, C., & Watanabe, T. (2020) *Property Price Indexes*. Advances in Japanese business and economics series. Springer.

Edgeworth, F. Y. (1925). The plurality of index-numbers. *Economic Journal, 35*(139), 379–388.

Jevons, W. S. (1884). *Investigations in currency and finance*. London: Macmillan and Co.

Keynes, J. M. (1909). The method of index numbers with special reference to the measurement of general exchange value. In *The collected writings of John Maynard Keynes* (pp. 50–156). Macmillan.

Keynes, J. M. (1930). *Treatise on money* (Vol. 1). Macmillan.

Keynes, J. M. (1936). *The general theory of employment, interest, and money*. Macmillan.

Northcote, S. H. (1886) Report of the royal commission appointed to inquire into the depression of trade and industry: Presented to both houses of Parliament by Command of Her Majesty.

Ricardo, D. (1822). Speech on Mr. Western's motion, for a committee to consider the effects produced by the "Resumption of Cash Payments," delivered on the 12th of June, 1822.

History of Making Price Index Numbers

2

Abstract

This chapter traces the history of price index numbers, beginning with early attempts in the sixteenth century and covering key figures such as Bodin, Dutot, Fleetwood, Jevons, and Laspeyres. It highlights how the concept of measuring price changes evolved over time, from the initial empirical efforts by Jean Bodin, who analyzed price fluctuations in sixteenth-century France, to more systematic approaches by later economists. Laspeyres and Paasche are so well-known that their names have become synonymous with price indices. However, this chapter points out that many others have also made significant contributions to this field. It also discusses the theoretical debates and controversies that shaped the development of price index number theory, such as the arguments between Jevons and Laspeyres. The chapter concludes by noting the shift toward more sophisticated methods in the late nineteenth and early twentieth centuries, including the axiomatic and economic approaches that form the foundation of modern index number theory.

Ernst Louis Etienne Laspeyres (1834–1913) and Hermann Paasche (1851–1925), who published papers on price indices in the late nineteenth century, are names that are particularly familiar to those who have studied economics, as their names have been immortalized in index number formulas. However, the history of measurement of price changes, which dates back to the sixteenth century, long predates them. The modern price index as we know it today is the result of a long history and the efforts of many individuals. Among them, while the contributions of the renowned Laspeyres and Paasche cannot be denied, there were quite a few researchers who made far more significant discoveries, embraced new ideas, posed questions, and sought their resolution.

In an era when the term "price index number" did not exist, and the very notion of measuring prices was not yet conceived, who were the people that attempted to measure prices and price changes, for what reasons, and how? Unraveling this history reveals that the seventeenth and eighteenth centuries witnessed the activities

N. Abe, *Price Index Numbers*, Springer Texts in Business and Economics,
https://doi.org/10.1007/978-981-97-6305-4_2

of many talented individuals. Furthermore, today's index number theory has been reached through numerous controversies, and its developmental path has not been smooth. For example, the stochastic approach to index numbers, proposed in the latter half of the nineteenth century, was thoroughly criticized and forgotten in the early twentieth century, only to be rediscovered in the latter half of the twentieth century from a completely different perspective. Fortunately, efforts of researchers who were ahead of their time, and perhaps too far ahead, can now be easily accessed thanks to today's comprehensive digital libraries. In this chapter, we would like to look back on the human history of price measurement and the making of price index numbers.

2.1 The Earliest History of Price Measurement

When money is used in the exchange of goods and services, each item is assigned a price, namely, a rate of exchange with money. If a large quantity of goods can be obtained in exchange for one unit of money, then the value of the money is high; conversely, if the quantity of goods obtained is small, then the value of the money is low. For issuers of money, such as kings or lords, a high value of money means that the real income obtained from issuing one unit of money, that is, the quantity of goods and services, is greater, and this would be desirable. On the other hand, if the value of money fluctuates greatly, such currency would lose its credibility and eventually fall out of use. The fluctuation of monetary value, or, in other words, the fluctuation of prices has been of great interest since the establishment of monetary economies thousands of years ago.

The establishment of a monetary economy is one of the central developments in economic history. While details are left to the expertise of economic and monetary history texts, it is worth noting that in the fourth century BC in Greece, Plato in *The Republic* and Aristotle in *Nicomachean Ethics* each left many contemplations on the value of money.[1] Moreover, in China, *the Guanzi* believed to have been compiled from the Warring States period to the Han Dynasty, around third century BC, contains many considerations on the relationship between money and prices. This indicates that price fluctuations were by no means a minor issue more than 2000 years ago.

Subsequently, in Europe, philosophers and theologians such as Thomas Aquinas in the thirteenth century and Nicole Oresme in the fourteenth century developed theories of money. In Japan, during the Edo period in the seventeenth century, Arai Hakuseki, an influential hatamoto (direct retainer of the shogun), documented observations that prices increased as a result of the recoinage of gold and silver.[2] There are also many discourses that lead to discussions on price fluctuations and the quantity theory of money.[3]

[1] For perspectives on money in ancient and medieval Western history, refer to Gordon (1975).

[2] In the fourth volume of Hakuseki's Proposals.

[3] Among them was the renowned astronomer Nicolaus Copernicus (1473–1543), who, in a report presented to the Prussian parliament in the sixteenth century, highlighted the decline in currency quality and the rise in its quantity as factors contributing to significant price inflation.

The contemplations on prices and money by Aristotle and Arai Hakuseki are normative in nature, addressing how the value of money ought to be. What is missing there is an empirical perspective on what kind of monetary value fluctuations the real society actually experienced. While Copernicus and Arai Hakuseki point out that prices have risen, they did not analyze how much or in what way they have increased with numerical values.

Numerous historical documents show that as dynasties and empires ruling large areas began to decline, the value of their circulating currency decreased, leading to inflation. This scenario is even depicted in *Faust* by Johann Wolfgang von Goethe, a preeminent thinker, poet, and novelist of the seventeenth and eighteenth centuries.[4] The issue of price increases and information on various commodities' market prices were collected by the reigning dynasties or governments of the time. However, no records have been found of aggregating this information and calculating how much the general movement of commodity prices actually changed.

It is curious that not only great thinkers like Aristotle and Copernicus, but also various kingdoms and governments that appeared in world history seemed to place importance on the issue of prices, yet did not show interest in measuring prices. It was not only until the sixteenth century in France that someone became interested not normatively, but also empirically, that is, in how much prices actually rose, and attempted to measure prices.

2.2 Price Revolution in European Countries

The earliest recorded attempt to quantitatively understand price trends was undertaken by the French lawyer Jean Bodin (1530–1596) in the sixteenth century.[5] Before discussing Bodin's price analysis, let's briefly examine the price trends in Europe during that period.

Figure 2.1 illustrates the price trends in southern England.[6] Specifically, it gathers transaction prices of six types of commodities—wheat, meat/fish, butter/cheese, alcohol, fuel, and clothing—primarily from accounting records of institutions such as colleges at the University of Oxford and the University of Cambridge, as well as

[4] See the speech by Jens Weidmann, President of the Deutsche Bundesnank on the episode appeared in part II in Goethe (1833).

[5] Joseph Alois Schumpeter (1883–1950), in his final major work *History of Economic Analysis,* positioned Bodin as a significant figure in early economics and dedicated a considerable amount of space to introduce him. Similarly, William Stanley Jevons (1835–1882), who laid the foundation for modern price index number theory, cited Bodin's work as the oldest book on price research in his book published in 1884. For a detailed exploration of Bodin's economic thought, one can refer to O'Brien (2000).

[6] This price index was created by Phelps-Brown and Hopkins (1956), and the paper includes a long time series up until 1954.

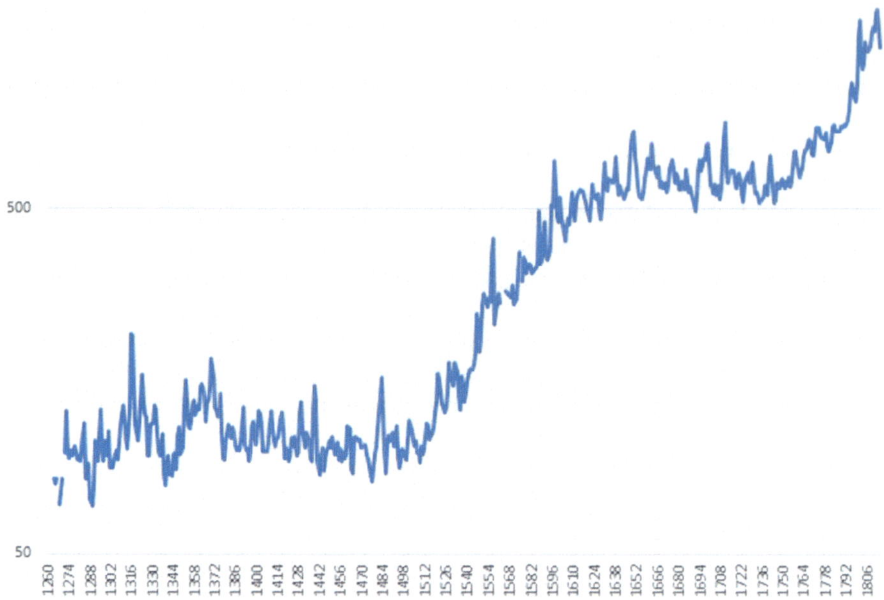

Fig. 2.1 Price Index of Consumption Goods in Southern England. Notes Based on tables in Phelps-Brown and Hopkins (1956). The price index is set at 100 in 1451-

monasteries. The price change rates were then weighted and averaged using household expenditure records from the thirteenth, sixteenth, eighteenth, and twentieth centuries as reference points. In Fig. 2.1, while we can observe price increases that seem to be influenced by the Black Death and various famines in the fourteenth century, the most striking observation is the continuous price increase lasting over a hundred years from the early sixteenth century. This price increase is referred to as the "Price Revolution," and various factors have been considered as its causes, including the influx of gold and silver from overseas, population growth, and more.[7] While there are few regions where medieval European prices have been measured with the precision of Fig. 2.1, similar price increases have been reported in various countries corresponding to present-day Spain, France, and Germany. By the time Bodin published his work on prices in 1568, Europe was already in the middle of a long-term price increase.

[7] The causes of the price revolution have been extensively studied, with Hamilton (1928) being one of the pioneers in this field. For an excellent analysis of the price revolution and the debates in European countries, Outhwaite (1982) is a valuable resource. In terms of more recent quantitative analysis, Edo and Melitz (2019) provide notable contributions.

2.3 Bodin's Price Measurement

According to the Bodin Project at Harvard University,[8] Jean Bodin was born in 1529 or 1530 in Angers, a city in western France, into a middle-class family of a master tailor.[9] Bodin commenced his education at a monastery in Angers and later pursued scholarly studies at the Notre-Dame Monastery in Paris. Despite indications of his remarkable talents, he encountered an inquisition in 1547 that led to his expulsion from Notre-Dame. Subsequently, Bodin studied law at the University of Toulouse and by 1562 had established himself as a lawyer in Paris. However, it was his literary works, rather than his legal career, that earned him acclaim. Operating marginally outside the royal and academic mainstream, Bodin penned his works during a period when inflation was becoming a pressing concern at the French court.

Bodin gained considerable recognition in political history for his treatises on the state and sovereignty, attracting considerable scholarly attention.

In 1566, the court treasurer, Marestroi, released *Paradoxes on the Issue of Currency,* asserting that despite appearances, French prices had remained stable over the previous 300 years. Citing the example of velvet, which in 1566 costed 10 livres, 2.5 times its price in the early fourteenth century, he argued that, when measured in gold coins, its price equated to a consistent 4 écus (unit of gold in France), thereby demonstrating price stability in gold terms.

In response, Bodin (1568) published a rebuttal to Marestroi's thesis. He criticized the selection of velvet as a non-representative commodity. Subsequently, he detailed the price fluctuations of various commodities, including wheat, barley, and wages, over the preceding 60 years across several different French regions such as Champagne. He concluded that most goods had experienced price increases, with rent serving as a barometer for overall price movements, asserting a tenfold price rise over six decades. Furthermore, Bodin (1568) identified the surge in gold and silver supply as the primary inflationary driver, laying the groundwork for the quantity theory of money.

Bodin's 1568 discourse is notable for two reasons. First, he analyzed price trends of multiple commodities across diverse regions to gauge price movements. Second, he synthesized these changes into a singular numerical figure, a precursor to contemporary price indices. This distinguishes him from predecessors like Aristotle and Thomas Aquinas, who lacked both an empirical approach and specific numerical evidence in their discussions.

Nevertheless, it is essential to recognize that Bodin, despite amassing extensive price data, did not synthesize them through methods such as averaging; instead, he employed rents as a proxy without providing a rationale for this choice. Consequently, Bodin is not widely hailed as the "father" of index number and aggregation theory and is rarely cited in price index research discussions.

[8] See https://projects.iq.harvard.edu/bodinproject.

[9] See Kiyosue (1975) for the detail of the life of Bodin.

Column 2: Why Did Price Measurement Not Arise Until the 16th Century in Europe?

It is recorded that severe inflation occurred when empires such as the Roman Empire and ancient Chinese dynasties were in decline. Moreover, the stability of monetary value was one of the significant issues in European Scholastic philosophy. Despite this, why did the measurement of prices not emerge until the 16th century in Europe? Here, I would like to propose a hypothesis. The reasons for rising prices can include a reduction in goods due to wars or disasters, a deterioration in the quality of money, or an increase in the quantity of money. If the cause is temporary, the price increase would also be temporary. In the case of major events such as the collapse of an empire, price increases would merely be one aspect of serious social issues, overshadowed by more critical concerns such as the widespread fatalities or declines in productivity. Measuring prices requires effort. It involves recording or investigating how the prices of various goods have changed. Tracking these changes can be difficult even today when prices fluctuate significantly in a short period due to wars, for example. Additionally, preserving these records for a long time would not have been suitable for clay tablets, wooden strips, or expensive paper. On the other hand, Fig. 2.1 by Phelps-Brown shows the trend of prices in Southern England, indicating that the rise in prices in this region continued for over 100 years from the early 16th to the mid-17th century. This means that over several generations, prices rose gradually but steadily. Under such long-term price increases, investigating changes in commodity prices from records preserved on parchment in monasteries would have been much easier compared to dealing with rapid inflation that settles within a few years. Therefore, the hypothesis is that price measurement was first conducted in the 16th century in Europe because it was the first time humanity experienced a long-term and stable price increase, known as the price revolution. However, verifying this hypothesis is somewhat difficult.

2.4 Vaughan's Price Measurement

The next oldest recorded price measurement after Bodin comes from Rice Vaughan (unknown–1672), an Anglo-Welsh lawyer in the seventeenth century. In his book, Vaughan (1675) analyzed how the influx of silver from Spain and other places influenced prices in England. He adopted wages as a representative measure of prices and argued that between 1346 and the time of his writing,[10] prices had increased by six to eight times.

[10] Vaughan (1675) was published after Vaughan's death, and the actual date of writing is unknown, but it is believed to be around the mid-seventeenth century.

One notable aspect of Vaughan's work is his explanation for choosing wages. He pointed out that commodity prices fluctuate for various reasons, and people's needs and preferences for different goods also change over time. The original text is written as follows:

> But there is only one thing, from whence we may certainly track out the prices, and which carries with it a constant resultance of the Prices of all other things which are necessary for a Mans life: and that is the price of Labourers and Servants Wages, especially those of the meaner sort (Vaughan, 1675, p. 105).

This led him to question the validity of price measurement based on tracking the prices of specific goods. However, he pointed out that only one commodity, labor, remains necessary across eras, justifying the use of wages as an indicator of changes in the value of money, that is, as a measure of prices. This recognition of the various factors affecting commodity prices and the changing preferences of people over time remains an important point in current price index number theory. Especially when analyzing price changes over several centuries, one must take into account that people's behavior patterns evolve. While Vaughan's price measurement crudely aggregates information on many commodity prices, much like Bodin, it is difficult to categorize it as a price index number. Nevertheless, his awareness of these issues connects to present-day considerations.

2.5 The First Price Index: Fleetwood's Price Index

Currently, considered the father of price index number theory is William Fleetwood (1656–1723), a British bishop who was active from the seventeenth to the eighteenth century. Fleetwood was born in London and studied at the University of Cambridge. Later, during a period of political instability due to events like the Glorious Revolution, he led a busy life preaching in various parts of England.[11] However, in 1705, Fleetwood retreated to the small village of Wexham, located to the west of London, immersing himself in historical research. The exact reason for his retreat remains unclear, but during this period, he examined price movements of various commodities in England and published *Chronicon Preciosum* in 1707. It is in Fleetwood (1707)'s work that the world's first price index appeared.

[11] There are numerous records of sermons delivered by Fleetwood.

Fleetwood's work is filled with extensive information about price movements of numerous commodities, but the highlight lies in Chap. 4 of Fleetwood (1707). Here, Fleetwood discusses how during the reign of Henry IV (1399–1413), one could purchase 5 quarters of wheat, 4 barrels of beer, and 6 yards of clothing for 5 pounds. However, in the early eighteenth century, the same items would require 20 pounds.[12] This discussion introduces what is now known as the fixed basket method in index calculation, referred to as the Lowe Index, making it the oldest recorded price index. Let the early fourteenth century be the base, 0 period, the early eighteenth century be the comparison period, 1. Denote p_{it} as the price at period t and q_i as the quantity Fleetwood specified (e.g., 5 quarters of wheat or 4 barrels of beer),[13]

$$\textbf{Price Index}(0, 1) = \frac{\sum_{i=1}^{N} p_{i1} q_i}{\sum_{i=1}^{N} p_{i0} q_i} \tag{2.1}$$

If q_i represents the actual consumption quantity in period 0, then this index aligns with what is now known as the Laspeyres index.[14] On the other hand, if q_i represents the quantity in period 1, it becomes the Paasche index. This index number formula, known as the fixed basket method, serves as the foundation for price index calculations used extensively by statistical agencies worldwide.

[12] 1 quarter (equal to 8 bushels) is approximately 282 L, 1 barrel is about 235 L, and 1 yard is approximately 90 cm. It's worth noting that during the time of Fleetwood, the precise measurements for each commodity were not easily established. For reference, Thirsk (1989) provides useful information on this matter.

[13] The original text is written as follows:

> For, since money is of no other use, than as it is the thing with which we purchase the necessaries and conveniences of life, it is evident, that if 5 £ in H. VI days, would purchase 5 quarters of wheat, 4 hogsheads of beer, and 6 yards of cloth, he who then had 5 £ in his pocket, was full as rich a man as he who has now 20 £ (Fleetwood, 1707, p. 61).

[14] Adam Smith (1723–1790) extensively discusses Fleetwood's work in his famous book, Smith (1776), *The Wealth of Nations*.

Column 3: On Fleetwood's Work, the World's First Theory of Price Indices

The title of Fleetwood's (1707) work is *Chronicon Preciosum*, but it carries the subtitle *"An Account of English Money, the Price of Corn, and Other Commodities, for the Last 600 Years in a Letter to a Student of Oxford University."* This unusual subtitle has the following background.

According to Clark (1936), just before the publication of Fleetwood's work in the early 18th century, an incident occurred at All Souls College, Oxford University, involving a student named William Worth (1677–1742), who protested against the termination of his scholarship. Worth had received an inheritance of six pounds, but there was a rule at All Souls College, dating from the 15th century, that scholarships would be terminated if a student had an income of more than five pounds a year. Worth argued that this old rule was inappropriate in the 18th century, where prices had risen significantly. Although the issue was resolved with Worth retracting his complaint, it seems to have been a well-known incident in England at the time. Fleetwood positioned his work as a response to the scholarship termination issue at the beginning of his book.

It is unclear whether Fleetwood was actually commissioned by Worth. However, by the time the work was published, Worth had withdrawn his complaint, and it did not serve its direct purpose. Moreover, the vast number of commodity price records Fleetwood investigated suggests that the work required years of effort, leading to the speculation that Fleetwood did not have a commitment to resolve Worth's incident, but used it as a marketing strategy for his book. In other words, he used the widely discussed Worth incident as a relatable reason to justify the tedious task of measuring prices. Fleetwood's work was initially published anonymously but quickly gained significant attention.

2.6 Price Index by Dutot

Fleetwood's price index was advanced for its time, but its simplicity in terms of weights and selection of goods does not make it directly applicable to modern index number making. In contrast, the Dutot index and Carli index, devised in the eighteenth century, have been historically used in many countries and are considered practical index number formulas.

In many countries, including Germany, France, Netherlands, and Japan, the most detailed price indices for basic (elementary level) items like apples and oranges in consumer price indices are calculated using the Dutot index formula. This formula, developed by Dutot, was considered to have little value, and was even deemed nearly worthless in the early twentieth century, notably by Irving Fisher (1867–1947)[15] The Dutot index has seen significant variations in its valuation over different periods.[16]

Nicholas Dutot (1684–1741) garnered significant attention during his era, particularly following the release of his work on France's price index, which was subsequently translated into English and published in London the next year. Historically, information on Dutot's life was limited, leading to prolonged uncertainty regarding the correct spelling of his first name—Nicholas or Nicolas—and his surname—Du Tot or Dutot. It was not until 2012, when François R. Velde published a comprehensive study on Dutot, Velde (2012), that more details about his life emerged. This research conclusively established his name as Nicholas Dutot and illuminated his life and contributions.

Dutot was born in 1684 into a family of shipbuilders in Barneville, a small town in the western part of the Normandy Peninsula in France, near the Channel Islands. Unlike many of the price index number researchers introduced in this chapter, who came from affluent or aristocratic backgrounds and received advanced education, Dutot's family was not wealthy, and it seems he did not have formal higher education. However, Dutot moved to larger towns at an early age. By 1708, he was working in the business center of Alsace. In 1717, while working at the Ministry of Justice in Paris, he was arrested for bribery and imprisoned in the Bastille. Then, in 1720, he was working at the bank of John Law (1671–1729).[17]

The year 1720 is significant as it marks the bankruptcy of John Law's bank, leading to a period of rapid inflation in the French economy. It's easy to imagine how this experience profoundly influenced Dutot's thoughts on economics, prices, and currency.

Having amassed wealth through investments, Dutot began to focus on his writing in the late 1720s. In 1734, Jean-François Melon (1675–1738), who had also worked under John Law and served as Law's accountant, published an essay affirming the inflation in France at the time. In response to his former colleague's views, in 1738, Dutot anonymously published *Reflexions Politiques sur les Finances et le Commerce.* This book gained considerable reputation, and the following year, in 1739, it was translated into English and published in London.[18] Because there is an English translation, even those not familiar with eighteenth-century French can easily access

---

[15] The original text is written as follows:

> The simple aggregative index number is usually regarded as almost worthless, Fisher (1922, p. 40).

[16] Diewert (2012) emphasizes that for homogeneous goods, the Dutot index possesses superior properties compared to other indices, and recommends its use in the UK's price index.

[17] The turmoil caused by John Law in the French economy would later be reflected in works like Goethe's *Faust* and others.

[18] In Velde (2012)'s examination of Dutot's preserved diary, it is revealed that, spurred by an English translation, Dutot was invited to London in 1739. During his time in London, he visited numerous bookshops and managed to obtain a book on price index by Fleetwood.

its content. The book is replete with intriguing reflections, including the necessity of stable currency value and the true purpose of the economy lying in consumption, concepts that align closely with modern economic theories.[19]

In his work, Dutot employs calculations that adhere to the French system, which divides units into 12 parts, necessitating careful consideration when replicating these calculations. The methodology, however, is clear-cut. Dutot began by compiling data on prices of various commodities across different regions in the sixteenth century, referencing sources such as Bodin (1568). He then collected data on the prices of the same commodities in the eighteenth century within those regions. This included items like a fat ox, a plump chicken, a dozen eggs, and a yard of linen clothing, among others, to track price changes over a period of 150 years. Subsequently, he analyzed the difference in costs incurred for purchasing these commodities in the sixteenth versus the eighteenth century. Dutot's index methodology can be summarized as follows:

$$\textbf{Price Index}(0, 1) = \frac{\sum_{i=1}^{N} p_{i1}}{\sum_{i=1}^{N} p_{i0}} \tag{2.2}$$

Dividing both numerator and denominator in the right-hand side by N gives:

$$\textbf{Price Index}(0, 1) = \frac{\sum_{i=1}^{N} p_{i1}/N}{\sum_{i=1}^{N} p_{i0}/N} \tag{2.3}$$

Fisher (1922) interprets the Dutot index as a ratio of arithmetic means and criticizes it for having many shortcomings. Balk (2008), a representative advanced textbook in current index number theory, also treats the Dutot index as a ratio of arithmetic means. The problem with using ratio of arithmetic means as the measure of price is that the price index ends up depending on the unit of measurement for commodity prices. Generally, the price of a commodity greatly depends on how the quantity of that commodity is counted. For instance, in Dutot (1738), a unit of 12 eggs is used. However, if we were to use 1 egg as the unit, the price of an egg would become 1/12. In this case, the overall average price would also decrease. Depending on the choice of unit for commodities, the price index can be significantly affected, posing a serious problem for the index number. Did Dutot propose and calculate an index with such inherent issues in mind?

In the English translation of Dutot's work, Dutot (1739), the explanation for aggregation states:

> From the result of these three particulars, I form a general and mean price in this manner: (Dutot 1739, p. 105)

[19] The famous macroeconomist Robert Lucas Jr. (1937–2023), in his Nobel Prize Lecture (Lucas, 1996), introduced David Hume's work as an example of empirical analysis of the non-neutrality of money. He pointed out that the underlying analysis was based on Dutot (Lucas, 1996, p. 664).

Here, the term "mean price" is used, which is consistent with the interpretation of the Dutot index today. On the other hand, in the original French text of Dutot (1738), it reads

> De ces trois résultats particulaiers j'en forme up prix général & common, de cette faon (Dutot, 1738, p. 214)

Here, the term used is "common," referring to a general or shared price. The two terms, common and mean, are similar. Thus, it cannot be considered a mistranslation. However, it is more natural to interpret Dutot's intention as not to examine the changes in the average price of goods, but rather to calculate the changes in the total expenditures when purchasing a specific bundle of goods. In other words, he aimed to calculate a price index using a fixed basket of goods similar to Fleetwood, and extract the common fluctuations among various commodity prices. It should be noted that the unit of goods chosen by Dutot seemed to be a common unit in market transactions at the time, unrelated to household consumption or production quantities. From the perspective of current index number theory, which emphasizes the choice of weights for each commodity price, this approach may seem overly simplistic.

In this regard, it is not possible to evaluate the Dutot index highly as a method to capture general price movements. However, when quantity information is unavailable, the Dutot index, along with the Carli index and the Jevons index introduced later, remains an important index number formula widely used in practical statistics.

2.7 Carli's Index

Gian Rinaldo Carli (1720–1795) was born into an Italian noble family.[20] He showed remarkable talent at a young age, becoming a professor of astronomy and navigation at the University of Padua at the age of 24. In addition to his academic pursuits, he gained fame as a collector of antiquities. In the field of economics, Carli was an early pioneer in studying the value of currency and foreign trade. He particularly analyzed whether the observed decline in the value of currency (price inflation) was due to the increase of gold and silver imported from the Americas or the result of currency recoinage in Italy. He published his findings in Carli (1764). In this extensive work of nearly 600 pages, he calculated the average price changes of wheat, wine, and oil in various Italian cities from 1500 to 1750. He concluded that the cause of price inflation was not the influx of gold from overseas, but rather the currency recoinage

[20] Tusset (2020) provides detailed information about Carli's life and economic thoughts. Carli's works were written in eighteenth-century Italian, they made use of different types of units such as nominal currency, silver coins, and gold coins, making their interpretation challenging. Fortunately, even without reading the original text in eighteenth-century Italian, Sackley (1965) allows for a considerable understanding of the details.

in Italy. His formula can be expressed in modern notation as follows:

$$\textbf{Price Index}(0, 1) = \frac{1}{N} \sum_{i=1}^{N} \left(\frac{p_{i1}}{p_{i0}} \right) \tag{2.4}$$

In other words, it is the simple average of the price change ratios, from the base period, for the three types of commodities. This is now known as the Carli index and has been widely used in many countries. It is still employed as the elementary index in the calculation of the UK Consumer Price Index.[21]

2.8 Price Studies in the Late Eighteenth Century

By the late eighteenth century, the efforts of individuals like Fleetwood, Carli, and Dutot in constructing price indices had become widely known, and endeavors in price measurement were no longer considered unusual. Notable among the price studies of this period were those conducted in the American colony of Massachusetts and the work of the British astronomer George Shuckburgh-Evelyn (1751–1804) in his publication (Shuckburgh-Evelyn, 1798).

During the American Revolutionary War, the United States experienced inflation, and the paper currency issued by various regions rapidly depreciated. In order to compensate for this depreciation, the Massachusetts colony, which was part of the United States at the time, attached a compensation corresponding to the rise in prices to its paper currency. It was during this period that a price index was constructed.[22]

The oldest confirmed price index created by the government of Massachusetts, a former colony, dates back to 1780, after the War of Independence. The Massachusetts state government guaranteed the difference if the total value of 5 bags of corn, 48 and 4/7 pounds of beef, 10 pounds of wool, and 10 pounds of sole leather exceeded 130 pounds. This was based on the fixed basket method of price indexing. Although this initiative in Massachusetts is interesting, it was forgotten for a long time and was only rediscovered by Fisher (1913).[23]

The research on prices conducted by Fleetwood, Dutot, and Carli, with the exception of Dutot who utilized Bodin's data, does not explicitly cite previous literature. It is unclear to what extent they were influenced by earlier studies or used them as references. Their studies appear to have been independently developed.

The first academic study on prices, which is more of a benchmark and directly relevant to modern index number theory, rather than a classical work, can be attributed

[21] In recent years, there has been a tendency to adopt the Dutot index and the later mentioned Jevons index over the Carli index. While a detailed discussion on these three indices will be provided in Chap. 3, Levell (2012) and Białek (2020) are particularly useful references on this matter.

[22] Fisher (1913) asserts that as early as 1747, before the War of Independence, the Massachusetts Colony was already employing a price index based on the fixed basket method. However, it has not been confirmed whether such a price index was actually created or not.

[23] Kendall (1969) provides detailed information on price measurement in Massachusetts.

to Shuckburgh-Evelyn (1798).[24] Following this, especially in Britain, there was a rapid increase in research and calculations regarding prices. Evelyn was a renowned meteorologist and astronomer known for his measurements of atmospheric pressure and observations of celestial bodies using large telescopes.[25] He was elected a Fellow of the Royal Society and was also awarded the prestigious Copley Medal, a recognition reserved for outstanding scientists.[26] His work primarily focused on precise measurements of various phenomena. His published paper, Shuckburgh-Evelyn (1798), "aimed to discuss an invariable and imperishable standard of weight and measure as stated at the beginning of the paper (p. 133)."

While most of Shuckburgh-Evelyn (1798) is devoted to discussions on methods and instruments for measuring weight and atmospheric pressure, toward the end of the paper, he provides insights into the historical changes in various commodity prices, citing Fleetwood (1707) as a reference to illustrate the depreciation of currency value. Although his price index number aggregates a significantly larger number of commodities compared to Fleetwood's, the formula used is a simple arithmetic mean of price relatives, the same as Carli's. In terms of index number theory, it may not be particularly groundbreaking. However, Evelyn's paper is concise, logically clear, and easily understandable for us today. The significance of having prominent scientists of that era conducting price measurements in an accessible manner is substantial. Following Evelyn, price measurement evolved from being the work of individual enthusiasts dedicating immense effort and time to writing extensive treatises into becoming a subject of scientific exploration on par with electricity and weather, rapidly expanding the scope of its analysis.

2.9 Weighted Arithmetic Mean Indices in the Early Nineteenth Century: Index Numbers by Young, Lowe, and Scrope

The nineteenth century experienced a notable increase in research related to price indices, primarily expanding upon the contributions of Evelyn. Key figures in this area included British agriculturalist Arthur Young (1741–1820), Scottish-born political economist Joseph Lowe (unknown–1812), and British geologist George Poulett Scrope (1797–1876). Significantly, each of these individuals championed the idea of applying distinct weights to various goods in the construction of indices.

Young (1812) focused on changes in prices in England from the seventeenth to the eighteenth century. While being aware of Evelyn's research, Young conducted his

[24] Initially, he wrote papers under the name Shuckburgh. However, after marrying a woman from the Evelyn family in 1794, he added Evelyn to his last name. Therefore, while Shuckburgh-Evelyn is the accurate full name, in the context of index number theory, he is often referred to simply as Evelyn. For consistency with convention, I will use Evelyn here.

[25] The refracting telescope he used (Shuckburgh's equatorial refracting) is one of the oldest large equatorial telescopes, and it is currently housed in the Science Museum in London.

[26] The Copley Medal is typically awarded annually to an outstanding scientist. Past recipients include notable figures such as Albert Einstein and Charles Darwin.

own calculations. In contrast to Evelyn, who used a simple arithmetic mean of price changes, Young assigned weights to seven different commodities, such as wheat with a weight of 5, and barley and oats with a weight of 2 (without any specific justification). He then calculated a price index based on this weighted arithmetic mean of price changes. The index now referred to as the Young index is defined as follows[27]:

$$\textbf{Price index}(0, 1) = \sum_{i=1}^{N} \frac{a_i}{\sum_k a_k} \left(\frac{p_{i1}}{p_{i0}}\right) \tag{2.5}$$

Note that a_i is a positive real number. It is worth noting that the inflation rate indicated by Young's price index is considerably smaller than the estimates made by Evelyn.

While Young was one of the pioneers of weighted averages in this context, his method of assigning weights was rather rough, and there isn't a significant difference in weights compared to those used by Fleetwood. In contrast, Joseph Lowe of Scotland conducted a detailed analysis of weights and devised an index number formula that can be considered a standard for current index calculations.

In his work published in 1823, Lowe examines the impact of the loss of colonies due to the American Revolutionary War, as well as the wars with France after the French Revolution and the Napoleonic Wars, on the British economy. Specifically, he considers how much of the increased assets and tax revenues in Britain, both before and after the wars, were merely nominal and how much of it was real in terms of actual value.

The index number formula used by Lowe, now referred to as the Lowe index, is similar to Fleetwood's formula. The key difference lies in the emphasis on the weights, a_i. Lowe argued that appropriate weights should be based on consumption quantities, while acknowledging that changes in consumption quantities may occur due to shifts in population and preferences. However, he noted that such changes are not rapid. Therefore, he proposed fixing the weights for a certain period, specifically suggesting a period of 5 years (Lowe, 1823, Appendix p. 95).

It is worth noting that the current methodology used by statistics bureaus in many countries follows the principle of re-evaluating weights periodically, such as every 5 years. Lowe's proposal continues to be adopted in many countries after two centuries. Lowe's work is a meticulous examination of various crucial aspects of index number theory. It holds significance not only as a historical work but also as a sincere reflection of a researcher, making it relevant and worth serious consideration even today.

As a geologist, Scrope was particularly known for his studies on volcanoes. In 1823, he became a Magistrate in the British Parliament, becoming involved in economic and political issues. After successfully running for and winning a seat in the House of Commons in 1833, he began publishing numerous pamphlets expressing various political opinions. In a pamphlet written in 1833, he coined the term "Tabular

---

[27] For information on the Young index further, it is recommended to refer to Diewert (1993).

Standard" to refer to what is now known as the fixed basket method of aggregation. He argued that weights should be established based on consumption quantities.

Scrope's pamphlet is filled with strong, politically charged assertions that, when read today, may feel lacking in substantial evidence. This stands in stark contrast to the cautious tone taken by Fleetwood, Dutot, and Lowe. However, Scrope's paper had a significant influence as a pamphlet from a member of the British Parliament. The practice of referring to the fixed basket method as the "Tabular Standard" persisted for a long time thereafter.[28]

2.10 Contributions by Jevons

By the mid-nineteenth century, the number of studies on price indices increased significantly. The list of studies on price measurement listed by Jevons (1884) is very long, indicating that numerous studies had been conducted up to that time. Among them, what had a particularly profound impact on later index number studies was the successive discoveries of gold mines in California and Australia, leading to what is known as the Gold Rush. How did this Gold Rush affect European countries? The statistician William Newmarch (1820–1882), who was also a banker, published the price movements of various commodities in London in 1859 in *the Journal of the Statistical Society of London*.[29] This statistical table was subsequently revised almost every year in the same journal, making detailed price data widely available. Collecting historical data on various commodity prices is a very difficult and labor-intensive task when constructing a price index. However, thanks to this statistical table, researchers no longer needed to gather the data themselves. Additionally, *The Economist* magazine began publishing price indices in 1845, and one can find the notation "Index Number," which is the oldest confirmed title for such a table.

Jevons (1863) marks a significant turning point in the history of price index number research. If the origin of price indices can be traced back to Fleetwood (1707), and the practical origin to Lowe (1823), then it is appropriate to say that the theoretical analysis leading to modern index number theory began with Jevons (1863).[30] Following this work, research on price indices rapidly advanced.

Jevons, like Evelyn, initially pursued a career as a natural scientist. While his research spanned various fields, he gained particular renown in meteorology, with the "Jevons effect" (referred to as the "Jevon's Paradox" in modern meteorology),[31] which describes how rainfall measurements are influenced by the wind, a term that remains in use today. In economics, Jevons is best known for his contributions to

[28] Scrope (1833) does not cite Lowe (1822), but Jevons (1884) and Diewert (1992) point out that there is a strong likelihood that Scrope heavily relied on Lowe's work for reference.

[29] This leads to the later establishment of *the Journal of the Royal Statistical Society*, the society's official academic publication.

[30] After Jevons' death, his works on prices were compiled in Jevons (1884), making it a suitable source for comprehensive information on Jevons' research on prices.

[31] See Jevons (1861) for detail.

the concepts of marginal utility and business cycles. However, his influence on price index number research is also immense.

The Jevons index he devised is widely used not only in official statistics of various countries but also extensively in index formulae utilizing scanner data. The Jevons index is a relatively simple formula as follows:

$$\textbf{Price Index}(0, 1) = \prod_{i=1}^{N} \left(\frac{p_{i1}}{p_{i0}} \right)^{1/N} \tag{2.6}$$

That is to say, it is defined as a simple geometric mean of price changes between two points in time. What is noteworthy is the rationale for choosing this index number formula. Jevons' concern lies in measuring the monetary value behind changes in commodity prices. So, when the monetary value fluctuates, how does it affect individual commodity prices? Let's assume there are two commodities: Commodity A priced at \$1000 and Commodity B priced at \$500. Now, let's assume that the monetary value has depreciated to some extent. In this case, how will the two commodities change? Jevons assumes that changes in monetary value will uniformly affect the value of all commodities. Therefore, if due to the depreciation of currency, Commodity A priced at \$1000 becomes \$1100, then Commodity B priced at \$500 should become \$550. However, actual commodity prices can change due to various factors unrelated to monetary value, such as weather. So, how can we determine the fluctuation in monetary value from this information about commodity prices? If the monetary value affects each commodity by a constant proportion, then this impact can be extracted using the simple geometric mean formula in Eq. (2.6).[32] Of course, considering a weighted average is also possible, but assuming that the price of wheat, which has a large consumption proportion, accurately reflects changes in monetary value compared to other commodity prices, is unreasonable. Therefore, the simple geometric mean formula in Eq. (2.6) would be desirable from the perspective of measuring the underlying monetary value.

Jevons' theory of price indices is more aligned with the concept of core inflation, which gained prominence in monetary policy analysis as opposed to the cost-of-living index. It's worth noting that between 1845 and 1862, Jevons pointed out that the UK experienced a price increase of about 9% to 15%, attributing it to the discovery of gold mines in California and Australia.

[32] In order for Eq. (2.6) to be an unbiased estimator of the underlying monetary value fluctuations, it is necessary to assume that factors other than money affecting individual commodity prices are uncorrelated across commodities. However, when aggregating a wide range of different commodities, this assumption may not always hold, and it cannot be considered a very strong one.

2.11 Controversy over Price Indices: Establishment of Laspeyres and Paasche Indices

In 1864, the year following Jevons' introduction of the geometric mean index, Ernst Louis Etienne Laspeyres (1834–1913), a renowned German economist and likely one of the most famous index number researcher, published a critical paper against Jevons. This ignited a famous dispute that significantly advanced index number theory. As a result of this controversy, the widely used Laspeyres index and Paasche index emerged, which form the mainstream of today's index number formulas.

Laspeyres (1864) argued that the simple arithmetic mean, similar to the Carli index, is more appropriate than the geometric mean.[33] He viewed monetary value not as an invisible random variable hidden behind commodity prices, as Jevons envisioned, but rather as the quantity of goods that can be purchased with that money. Consider a scenario where the price of one product increases from \$100 to \$200, while another product's price decreases from \$100 to \$50. Previously, you could buy one unit of each product for \$200 in total, but after the price change, you would need \$250. Calculated with the Carli index, this results in $(2+0.5)/2 = 1.25$, indicating a 25% increase. However, with Jevons index, it becomes $(2 \times 0.5) = 1$, implying no change in prices. Laspeyres contended that since the quantity of goods purchasable with the same amount of money has decreased, the value of money must have depreciated, and prices should have risen. Jevons' rebuttal in Jevons (1865) justified the geometric mean by stating that it lies between the arithmetic mean and the harmonic mean. The dispute between the two, viewed from today's perspective, may not have been particularly fruitful. However, looking back on the controversy from a modern standpoint, we can see the significance lies in the difference between their definitions of monetary value. This, in turn, dictates the corresponding index number formula, highlighting the importance of how we define the value of money.

In 1871, the dynamics of this debate underwent a drastic shift with the entry of two German mathematicians, Moritz Wilhelm Drobisch (1802–1896) and Hermann Paasche (1851–1925).

In his work, Drobisch (1871), Drobisch launched a rigorous critique of both Laspeyres' simple arithmetic mean and Jevons' geometric mean. Drobisch defined monetary value similar to Laspeyres, as the variation in the quantity of goods purchasable with money. Consequently, Jevons' method with the geometric mean was fundamentally outside his evaluation. He argued that in the case of the simple arithmetic mean, important commodities like wheat are treated equally as less significant ones, which is inappropriate. True to his mathematical inclination, his paper is replete with equations. Within it, he introduced the so-called Laspeyres index, which

---

[33] It's important to note that what Laspeyres argued at this time is not what is known today as the Laspeyres index, which is a weighted average.

employs the quantity at the base period, denoted as q_{i0}, as the quantity weight:

$$\textbf{Price Index}(0, 1) = \frac{\sum_{i=1}^{N} p_{i1} q_{i0}}{\sum_{i=1}^{N} p_{i0} q_{i0}} \tag{2.7}$$

If the quantity at the comparison period, q_{i1} is used, we get the following Paasche index:

$$\textbf{Price Index}(0, 1) = \frac{\sum_{i=1}^{N} p_{i1} q_{i1}}{\sum_{i=1}^{N} p_{i0} q_{i1}} \tag{2.8}$$

For Drobisch, the difference between the two formulas, whether to use quantities at the base or comparison period, was equivalent, and there was no reason to favor one over the other. However, the choice between the base and comparison period would lead to different values for the index. Drobisch believed this discrepancy was due to a flaw in the formulas. Therefore, he concluded that the index, known today as the unit value index, defined by the following formula is desirable:[34]

$$\textbf{Price Index}(0, 1) = \frac{\sum_{i=1}^{N} p_{i1} q_{i1} / \sum_{i=1}^{N} q_{i1}}{\sum_{i=1}^{N} p_{i0} q_{i0} / \sum_{i=1}^{N} q_{i0}} \tag{2.9}$$

In response to Drobisch's argument, Laspeyres promptly countered in Laspeyres (1871). He first agreed with Drobisch on the importance of weighting by quantity. However, Laspeyres pointed out that there was little significant difference between the values of the index number obtained using Drobisch's formula and the simple arithmetic mean. He further argued that Drobisch's formula had the property that even if prices remained unchanged, a change in quantity could lead to a change in the price index. Thus, Laspeyres concluded that the formula using quantities at the base period, as expressed in Eq. (2.7), was the preferable one.[35]

In Paasche (1874), Paasche criticized both Laspeyres' simple arithmetic mean and Drobisch's unit value index, asserting that the formula utilizing quantities at the comparison period, as expressed in Eq. (2.8), was the preferable one. Both Laspeyres and Paasche advocated for the use of either base or comparison-period quantities, but neither provided a clear explanation for why one should be chosen over the other, which may seem somewhat puzzling in hindsight. However, they both concurred on the preference for a weighted average over a simple arithmetic mean.

---

[34] Unit value indices garnered significant attention in the nineteenth century. Lehr (1885) devised improvements to Drobisch's unit value index and proposed an index formula that closely resembles the later Geary-Khamis-type index.

[35] The original text is as follows:

> Die Formel von Drobisch genügt nicht, sie kann ad absurdum führen, denn nach derselben kann sich eine durchschnittliche Preissteigerung oder Preissenkung ergeben, während alle einzelnen Waren im Preise gleich geblieben sind. (P. 308, Laspeyres, 1871)

In Edgeworth's (1888) retrospective on the index number controversy involving Jevons, Laspeyres, Drobisch, and Paasche, he remarked

> There are as many kinds of average as there are purposes; and we may almost say in the matter of prices as many purposes as writers. Hence much vain controversy between persons who are literally at cross purposes. To use a metaphor which has been applied to metaphysics, one party makes a good stroke at billiards, and thinks he has scored off another who is playing chess. (Edgeworth, 1888, p. 355).

However, through this controversy, the perspective of using quantities purchasable with currency, rather than a stochastic variable underlying various price changes as Jevons had envisioned, became the standard for index calculation. The necessity of weighted averages also became widely recognized by many.

As pointed out in this section, it was Drobisch who devised the two index formulas known as the Laspeyres index and the Paasche index, and both Laspeyres and Paasche merely argued for the desirability of their respective indices. However, in the early twentieth century, Correa Moylan Walsh (1862–1936), a very influential person in index number research designated Eq. (2.7) as Laspeyres's formula, and Eq. (2.8) as Paasche's formula in his book published in 1901 (Walsh, 1901). From then on, the names Laspeyres and Paasche came to be considered among the most important in index number theory.

2.12 The Onset of the Axiomatic Approach

After the debates between Jevons, Laspeyres, and others concluded, numerous price indices began to be constructed. Among them was the wholesale price index devised by Augustus Sauerbeck.[36] This index, which was updated annually until 1912, exerted significant influence and was cited in numerous studies. Price indices ceased to be a specialized statistical value and became something that caught the attention of many. It was in this context that a new development in index number theory began in the late nineteenth century.

Currently, there are three main pillars in the theory of price indices: the axiomatic approach, the economic approach, and the stochastic approach. The origin of the stochastic approach can be traced back to Jevons (1863), while the economic approach, as we will discuss later, can be attributed to Konüs (1924). However, the most prominent pillar that forms the core of index number theory is the axiomatic approach, also known as the test approach. The starting point for this approach can be found in the paper by Nicolaas Gerard Pierson (1839–1909), who later became the Prime Minister of the Netherlands. In his paper, Pierson (1896), he pointed out significant shortcomings in price indices.

[36] Augustus Sauerbeck (1857–1932) was a British economist known for his work on price indices and economic statistics. The Sauerbeck index, Sauerbeck (1896), was an important early attempt to measure changes in the general price.

Pierson argued that attempts to construct indices should be abandoned in the future. Among Pierson's various points, one known as "time reversal test" became the origin of the axiomatic approach in later years. Pierson (1896) pointed out that at the time, representative price indices did not become their reciprocal when the base period and the comparison period were swapped. For example, in the Laspeyres formula (2.7), when the base period and comparison period are swapped, the Price Index (0, 1) becomes Price Index (0, 1) as follows:

$$\textbf{Price Index}(1,0) = \frac{\sum_{i=1}^{N} p_{i0} q_{i1}}{\sum_{i=1}^{N} p_{i1} q_{i1}} \tag{2.10}$$

However, if we multiply the original Eq. (2.7) by the Price Index (1, 0), which results in

$$\textbf{Price Index}(1,0) \times \textbf{Price Index}(0,1) \neq 1 \tag{2.11}$$

Due to different quantity weights, this product generally does not equal to 1. Therefore, Laspeyres, Paasche, and Carli indices, when the base and comparison periods are swapped, do not generally yield a product of 1. While there were few supporters for Pierson's provocative claim, Edgeworth's response (Edgeworth, 1896) suggested that setting desirable properties that indices should satisfy, and using them as a basis to judge the quality of indices, was a fruitful approach, especially when dealing with numerous indices.[37]

2.13 Development and Limits of the Axiomatic Approach

The perspective introduced by Pierson and Westergaard, concerning the desirable properties that indices should satisfy, was organized and established as the standard approach in index theory by Irving Fisher (1867–1947) in 1922. Fisher (1922) compiled hundreds of price index number formula, which included nearly all known index formulas at the time, and deliberated on what constitutes a desirable index.

A groundbreaking aspect of Fisher's thinking was his emphasis not only on price indices but also on quantity indices. Furthermore, he believed that when multiplied together, quantity and price indices should yield the expenditure ratio for the two periods, creating a value index. Treating quantity and price on equal footing and considering the expenditure amount as the connecting factor between these two indices was a natural approach, especially when dealing with a single good. For instance, if you buy 10 apples for 100 dollars each, the total expenditure would be 100 dollars ×10 = 1,000 dollars.

[37] Prior to Pearson's paper, Harald Ludvig Westergaard (1853–1936) pointed out in Westergaard (1890) that the only index with a property later termed transitivity is the Jevons index. Additionally, Laspeyres' counterargument to Drobisch, as presented in Laspeyres (1871), also aligns closely with such an axiomatic approach.

Similarly, it would be incredibly useful if the product of a price index and a quantity index yielded the expenditure ratio. However, when there are more than two goods, the product of a price index and a quantity index generally does not result in an expenditure ratio. In fact, neither the Laspeyres index nor the Paasche index, nor the Carli index, nor the Jevons index possess this property. However, the index defined as the geometric mean of the Laspeyres and Paasche indices does have this property. Irving Fisher named this the "ideal index", while other indices such as the Walsh index that satisfy almost all desirable properties as the "superlative index." Today, this index, the unweighted geometric mean of the Laspeyres and the Paasche indices is referred to as the Fisher index, and also Fisher's ideal index.

In the axiomatic approach, there are several key properties emphasized for an index. These include

1. **Monotonicity**: The price index should be an increasing function in comparison-period prices.
2. **Identity**: If prices do not change, the index should be equal to 1.
3. **Unit Invariance (Commensurability)**: The value of the index should not depend on the units used to measure prices and quantities (e.g., liters or gallons).

In addition to these, Fisher emphasized "time reversal test," which is also considered desirable for an index number to possess. Currently, there are dozens of properties that are considered desirable for an index number to satisfy. However, it is well known that there is no index that satisfies all of these properties.[38] In the era of Fisher, economists and index number researchers knew which specific properties a particular index might satisfy, but they did not have a clear understanding of whether an index satisfying a given set of properties even existed, and if it did, what it might look like. While it was known what combination of axioms could lead to an index number satisfying certain properties, the necessary conditions for the existence of such an index were not well understood.

In the field of index number theory, it wasn't until the 1970s that such necessary conditions became clear. The groundbreaking work by Eichhorn and Voeller (1976) played a significant role in this regard. They demonstrated that by using functional equations, it was possible to derive specific index number formulas as necessary and sufficient conditions from an axiomatic system. This development marked a substantial leap forward in index number theory.

The 1970s is often considered the golden age of axiomatic approaches in index number theory. However, it also revealed the limits of this approach. This is because it became evident that an index satisfying a crucial property in axioms, known as "circularity" or "transitivity," combined with several other important properties, would result in an extremely limited type of index known as a Cobb–Douglas-type index

[38] Swamy (1965) is a pioneering work on the impossibility of making an index number satisfying several axioms simultaneously.

(Funke et al., 1979). Let us consider a bit deeper into the importance of transitivity, which is a critical axiom.

Let us denote the price index from period s to t as $P(s,t)$. Transitivity is the property where, for any given prices and quantities in periods $s, t, and\ k$.

$$P(s,t) \times P(t,k) = P(s,k) \tag{2.12}$$

Furthermore, Funke et al. (1979) demonstrated that an index number satisfying transitivity, monotonicity, identity, and commensurability simultaneously can only be the following Cobb–Douglas-type Price Index (0, 1)

$$\textbf{Price Index}(0,1) = \prod_{i=1}^{N} \left(\frac{p_{i1}}{p_{i0}}\right)^{w_i}, \sum_i w_i = 1, w_i \geq 0 \tag{2.13}$$

Fisher believed that through axiomatic approaches, it was possible to determine a single ideal index number formula. However, it is now known that there is no universal and ideal index number. As Edgeworth argued in the past, there are as many appropriate index number formulas as there are purposes. Nevertheless, the advancement in axiomatic approaches has been a major achievement, as it allows for the deduction of index number formulas based on the axioms (properties) required for the index number formula.

2.14 Development of the Economic Approach

The foundation of the economic approach to price index number theory can be attributed to Arthur Cecil Pigou (1877–1959), as documented in Pigou (1912), where he sought to integrate the Laspeyres and Paasche indices within a utility maximization framework. Subsequent decades saw contributions from economists like Gottfried Haberler (1900–1995), Ragner Frisch (1895–1973), Sir Roy George Douglas Allen (1906–1983), Abba Lerner (1903–1982), and Wassily Leontief (1906–1999), who explored the interplay between consumer models and index number formulas for prices and quantities.[39] Predating these efforts, in 1924, the Russian economist Alexander Alexandrovich Konüs (1895–1991) published a seminal work (Konüs, 1924) in Russian, significantly influencing the future direction of index number theory.[40] Translated into English and published in *Econometrica* as Konüs (1939), Konüs's paper laid the groundwork for what is now recognized as the economic approach to index number and cost-of-living index theory. His contributions led to the cost-of-living index being known as the Konüs true cost-of-living index, marking a pivotal development in the economic approach to index number theory.

[39] Refer to Haberler (1927), Frisch (1930, 1936), Allen (1933), Lerner (1935), and Leontief (1936) for further insights.

[40] Another notable contribution is a paper by Konüs and Byushgens (1926) on the theory of the cost-of-living index, with its English translation available in Diewert and Zelenyuk (2023).

The concept behind the Konüs cost-of-living index is simple. It compares the minimum expenditure required at the comparison point to secure the same level of utility as in the base period. Unlike the fixed basket approach by Fleetwood and Laspeyres, it assumes that people alter their consumption patterns in response to price changes. In terms of modern microeconomics, the cost-of living index is equivalent to the ratio of the two expenditure functions at two points in time, with utility level held constant at a certain level.

Pollak (1971) provided a clear overview of the discussions by Konüs, Lerner, Leontief, and others, exerting a significant influence on price index research at the time. Additionally, in the 1970s, specialized books on index number theory were published by distinguished economists of the era, including Allen (1975) and Afriat (1977), establishing the golden age of the economic approach in index number theory.

The Konüs cost-of-living index forms the foundation of today's price index number theory based on the economic approach. Most papers relying on the economic approach adhere to the Konüs definition. However, this index comes with several significant practical challenges.

Firstly, to actually calculate a price index using the Konüs cost-of-living index, one must know the shape of the utility or expenditure function. How can one determine a utility or expenditure function that describes the entire economy? How many parameters need to be estimated? Even if estimations are possible, how accurate and reliable are they? Moreover, can a utility or expenditure function that effectively describes the entire economy be assumed to have a specific known functional form?

The theory of the cost-of-living index requires many strong economic assumptions. Criticisms of these assumptions are naturally robust, and even today, various statistics bureau such as that of Japan asserts that the consumption price index is not a cost-of-living index.

The second issue with the cost-of-living index is that the utility functions must be identical across the two points in time or two locations, or between two individuals being compared. In the early discussions of price indices, it was recognized as problematic that people's preferences change over time. Even assuming identical preferences at the same point in time might be unrealistic when considering different countries.

Walter Erwin Diewert (1941–) provided a solution to one of the key issues surrounding the cost-of-living index, namely, the need for specification of the functional form for utility or expenditure functions. In Diewert (1976), he proved that the Fisher index serves as a "second-order approximation" to any cost-of-living index. Results by Diewert (1976), put simply, can be summarized as follows:

Suppose that the observed prices and quantities are consistent with the utility-maximizing (or expenditure-minimizing) behavior of a particular individual, but we do not know the specific functional form. While theoretically correct cost-of-living indices involve complex functions, the Fisher index closely tracks the theoretically correct expenditure function ratio, and thus behaves similarly to the cost-of-living index. Diewert (1976) shows that some classes of the index numbers including the Fisher, Walsh, and Törnqvist indices are good approximations to the true cost-of-living index. Following the terminology by Fisher (1922), Diewert (1976) named the index number formula possessed the above property as the superlative index. This remarkable result garnered significant attention as it overcame a drawback of the economic approach to price indices, which depended on assumptions about unobservable utility or expenditure functions. Based on Diewert's findings, in the United States, the Törnqvist index was published as one type of its Consumer Price Index. However, it is important to note that the premise of Diewert's argument, which assumes that the observed prices and quantities are consistent with the utility-maximizing behavior and a single identical utility function, is a very strong one.

2.15 Divisia Index

Around the same time as Konüs and Fisher, the French economist Francois Divisia (1889–1964) proposed his own unique method for calculating indices that differed from both the axiomatic and economic approaches. In Divisia (1925), he conceptualized the passage of time as continuous and assumed that individual commodity prices and price indices were differentiable functions with respect to time. He then defined the time derivative of the (logarithmic) price index as follows:

$$\frac{d \ln PI^{DV}}{dt} = \sum_{i=1}^{N} \omega_{it} \frac{d \ln p_{it}}{dt} \tag{2.14}$$

Here, ω_{it} represents the expenditure share of commodity i in period t. As a result, the price level from period 0 to period 1 becomes an integral from period 0 to period 1, depending on the entire path of prices over all intervening periods—meaning how prices have changed. This is in stark contrast to nearly all previously constructed price indices, which depended solely on price and quantity information from two points in time. The Divisia index thus exhibits significantly different characteristics.

As introduced in the previous section, there are very few price indices that possess cyclical or transitive properties. However, the absence of transitivity poses significant challenges when analyzing prices over time. For instance, if prices were to increase from 100 to 200 between 1950 and 1975, and then from 200 to 400 between 1975 and 2000, without transitivity, the price level between 1950 and 2000 might not be 100 to 400, but could potentially be various other values like 100 to 1000 or 100 to 50.

The lack of transitivity in price indices is acknowledged as a serious issue by Nobel laureate Paul Anthony Samuelson (1915–2009) in Samuelson and Swamy (1974). In this sense, the Fisher index was not considered ideal. However, the Divisia index defined in Eq. (2.14) not only possesses transitivity but also maintains the coherence between quantity and price indices that Fisher emphasized, which is known as factor reversal property.

The Divisia index possesses many of the desirable properties advocated by the axiomatic approach. Joseph Alois Schumpeter (1883–1950) introduced the Divisia index as a desirable price index in his book, Schumpeter (1939), and as mentioned earlier, Samuelson and Swamy (1974) also discuss the Divisia index as an ideal formula. Furthermore, it is important to note that the Divisia index has played a significant role in the theory of economic growth in the 1950s and in the theory of productivity analysis, which has been actively pursued since the 1970s and continues to be relevant to this day.[41]

While the Divisia index theoretically possesses various desirable properties, there is one fundamental issue with it as an index number. Actual economic data is not created in continuous time, making it impossible to directly compute the Divisia index in its original form. Therefore, many studies have been conducted to explore how the Divisia index can be approximated using discrete data observed on a yearly or monthly basis. One of the most representative approaches is the one devised by Leo Törnqvist (1911–1983), which is now known as the Törnqvist index. Additionally, to address another characteristic of the Divisia index—the dependence on prices and quantities between two points in time—a method involving chain index has been considered. Essentially, by chaining the Törnqvist index, it was believed that a good approximation of the Divisia index could be achieved.

A chain index, when there are more than two points in time, involves changing the base period of the standard two-point price index every period and multiplying the price index accordingly. This allows for the calculation of price indices between time points that are more than one period apart.

The history of chain index dates back to the late nineteenth century, with proposals by figures such as Harald Ludvig Westergaard and Alfred Marshall, who laid the foundation for modern mathematical economics. Today, chain indices are utilized as deflators in system of national accounts, and they are also adopted in many countries. The Törnqvist index is defined as:

$$\ln \mathbf{Price\ Index}(0, 1) = \sum_i \frac{\omega_{i0} + \omega_{i1}}{2} (\ln p_{i1} - \ln p_{i0}) \tag{2.15}$$

Comparing this equation with Eq. (2.14), it can be seen that it provides a natural approximation. The properties of the Törnqvist index, its accuracy as a discrete approximation, and the potential for approximation using other index formulas were extensively studied in the 1960s and 70s.[42] Among these index formulas, the Sato-Vartia index has become particularly important in current index number theory, especially in the economic approach.

Is the discrete approximation of the Divisia index truly a desirable index? Today, with the availability of higher frequency data, such as weekly or daily data, which is closer to continuous time, has the approximation of the Divisia index using indices like the Törnqvist index become closer to the ideal? Unfortunately, as summarized by Diewert (2018), it is known that when high-frequency data is used, the chained version of the Törnqvist index can lead to unrealistic values. For example, the price of a certain daily commodity could be shown to decrease by 500% in 1 year. This

[41] See Solow (1957) and Jorgenson and Griliches (1967).

[42] During that time, representative papers include Theil (1973), Sato (1974, 1976), and Vartia.

phenomenon is known as "chain drift," and avoiding this issue has become one of the most crucial challenges in current index number theory. The fact that in discrete approximation, the ideal index moves far away from the actual ideal formula when continuous time is ideal is a consequence of economic transactions not occurring continuously. The dream of the 1970s, that by shortening the time, we would approach an ideal formula, unfortunately, could not be realized.

2.16 Historical Development of the Stochastic Approach

Modern index number theory traces its origins back to Jevons. The Jevons index remains an important formula for index calculations today. However, the purpose of price index number conceived by Jevons—namely, a method for measuring the value of money—was somewhat overshadowed in subsequent index number theory. For Jevons, commodity prices were determined by two types of factors: macro-factors, which involved the value of money, and individual, commodity-specific fluctuation factors. Under the assumption that when the value of money changes, it uniformly affects all commodities by a certain proportion, Jevons derived his index number formula. Edgeworth further advanced this line of thought.

Edgeworth made significant contributions to economics, particularly in trade theory with concepts like the Edgeworth Box diagram and the Limit Theorem. He also made substantial contributions to statistics, even serving as the President of the Royal Statistical Society. In addition, he wrote numerous papers on price indices, and Fisher's monumental work on the index number theory, Fisher (1922) is dedicated to Edgeworth alongside Walsh. While Edgeworth's research on indices covers a broad spectrum, a unique aspect is his statistical perspective heavily influenced by Jevons. His contributions to economics are encapsulated in Edgeworth (1925), and its essence can be expressed in modern notation as follows.

Like Jevons, Edgeworth posited that the variation in individual commodity prices could be decomposed into the monetary value and specific factors inherent to each commodity, as outlined below:

$$\ln p_{it} - \ln p_{i0} = \pi_t + \varepsilon_{it} \tag{2.16}$$

The purpose of the price index is to estimate the fluctuation in monetary value denoted by π_t. Jevons attempted to estimate the fluctuation in monetary value by the simple arithmetic mean on the left side of Eq. (2.16), which represents the simple geometric mean of price change ratios. However, according to Edgeworth, some goods exhibit significant variations, or, in modern terms, have a large variance in ε_{it}. Edgeworth used the analogy of goods prices being like trees, some swaying vigorously in the wind while others remain stable. He argued that more weight should be given to the information from stable trees (Edgeworth, 1925, p. 246). He further asserted that goods with strong deviations from the mean should be given a smaller weight.

Edgeworth's logic of reducing the weight of variables with high noise in order to extract the desired signal with higher accuracy is nothing short of the essence of modern signal extraction methods. This thinking leads to techniques like factor analysis, Kalman filters, and generalized least squares using the covariance matrix.

The advanced signal extraction concept by Edgeworth and Jevons was subsequently thoroughly rejected in later index number theory. In the extensive work on index number theory published in 1901 by Walsh, which spans nearly 600 pages, Edgeworth and Jevons are positioned as proponents of simple geometric means, and the stochastic aspect of their theory is omitted. In the opening pages of his work (Walsh, 1901, p. 38), Walsh unequivocally equates considering various factors as sources of price variation, akin to adopting Ptolemy's complex geocentric theory in contrast to Copernicus' simple heliocentric theory. Further severe criticism of the stochastic approach comes from John Maynard Keynes (1883–1946). In Keynes (1930), he strongly critiques Edgeworth and Jevons' price indices for separating between the overall price level and relative prices, effectively dismissing the significance of relative price movements. According to Keynes, changes in relative prices influence not only the price level but also render meaningless the very concept of the price level when relative prices are constant (Keynes, 1930, p. 87).[43]

While Keynes' argument is vehement, it is also heavily abridged, making it not easily traceable for the author. If one were to summarize Keynes' assertion, it would be as follows: relative price movements are not independent stochastic events from prices and are instead endogenous variables connected through various channels with prices and quantities of other goods. Discarding this information is a mistake.[44] The stochastic perspective on index theory, emphasized by economic giants like Jevons and Edgeworth, is temporarily interrupted by the critiques from Keynes and his contemporaries.

In the latter half of the twentieth century, the stochastic approach saw a resurgence in two main ways. One was through the proposition by Otto Eckstein (1927–), who introduced the concept of core inflation (Eckstein, 1981), which is now considered important in current macroeconomic policy. The other was the construction of regional and national price indices, namely, purchasing power parity, using regression analysis by Robert Summers (1922–2012) and his colleagues in the 1970s.[45] Initially, when their analyses began, the connection between core inflation, regression analysis, and the studies of Jevons and Edgeworth was not consciously acknowledged, and their pioneering research was conducted independently.

2.17 History of the Official Price Index

As previously mentioned, by the mid-nineteenth century, *The Economist* magazine was regularly publishing price indices, and in 1886, a price index calculated by

[43] In his 1909 work that won the Adam Smith, Keynes (1909), Keynes examined price indices based on a stochastic approach and discussed various methods of averaging to minimize error.

[44] Keynes further intensifies his tone, stating that "Jevons is pursuing a mirage (p. 76)" and summarizing that he is "root-and-branch erroneous (p. 85)."

[45] See Summers (1973) for example.

Sauberbeck began, which was continued in *The Statist* magazine. In Germany, Adolf Soetbeer initiated publishing the price index of the city of Hamburg annually from 1885 until his death in 1895 (Soetbeer, 1885). In the United States, *Bradstreet's* index was initiated in 1897, followed by similar price index publications in *Dun's Review*.[46] In France, *La Réforme économique*, a weekly journal on social and political economy edited by Jules Domergue started publishing the French price index began in 1893.

Contrastingly, the development of what are termed official price indices, regularly and systematically compiled by government agencies, began in the twentieth century across many nations.[47] While some trials of making of price indices by governmental bodies can be observed in the nineteenth century such as Horatio C. Burchard in the United States,[48] in many countries, the compilation of official price indices began in the twentieth century. The U.S. Bureau of Labor Statistics initiated the publication of the wholesale price index in 1902. Subsequently, the United Kingdom followed in 1903, with the Board of Trade taking charge, France in 1904 under the auspices of Statistique Générale de France, and Germany in 1905, where the Kaiserliche Statistische Amt spearheaded the effort. These initiatives marked the beginning of systematic governmental compilation of price indices. By the early 1920s, numerous countries including Australia, Bulgaria, Canada, Denmark, Egypt, Hungary, Italy, the Netherlands, New Zealand, Norway, Peru, Romania, Russia, South Africa, and Sweden had commenced the compilation of governmental price indices.[49] Japan and India were ahead in this endeavor, with the Bank of Japan and Fred. J. Atkinson, the Accountant General of the United Provinces in India, initiating the publication of official price indices in 1897 (Atkinson, 1897). This marked a pioneering move in Japan and India toward the establishment of regular official price indices at a time when no private entities, such as *The Economist* and *The Bradstreet's*, had yet ventured into price index publication.

2.18 Concluding Remarks

This chapter provides an overview of the history of attempts to measure trends of changes in prices. Since the introduction of money into human society, price stability has remained a significant issue for economic and social systems. It is not difficult to find references to the value of money, or prices, in the writings of ancient thinkers like Aristotle in Greece and Guanzi in China. However, the earliest record of an attempt to quantitatively grasp how much prices had changed comes from Bodin in sixteenth-century France, with systematic measurement of prices beginning in the early eighteenth century in the United Kingdom by Fleetwood, and academic

[46] The two companies later merged, forming what is today known as Dun and Bradstreet.

[47] For an extensive review of the evolution of official price indices in various countries, refer to BLS (1921). For insights into the United States' history of the official price index, consult (Shiskin, 1974).

[48] See Department of Mint (1881). Laughlin (1887a, b) for the detail of the price index by Burchard.

[49] For detailed accounts of the development of official price indices in these nations, see BLS (1921).

research starting in the mid-nineteenth century with Jevons. All of these efforts were in the context of price increases faced by European countries and the exploration of the effects of gold inflows. The debates among Jevons, Laspeyres, Drobisch, and Paasche led to the development of index number formulas that are the precursors to those used today, and by the 1920s, official price indices began to be compiled in various countries. Since the 1930s, index number theory has been analyzed under various methodologies, including axiomatic approaches, economic approaches, and the stochastic approach. Today, the role of price indices has significantly expanded from the initial measurement of the value of money. Particularly within the theory of price indices based on the economic approach, prices serve as crucial information for measuring household welfare, and price indices are used in many economic analyses, often without explicit reference to index number theory. While price indices have become commonplace, comprehending the entire scope of index number theory has become increasingly challenging. Moreover, nearly 150 years after Jevons' writings, debates continue over what constitutes an "appropriate" price index number formula, especially in the context of measuring prices using high-frequency scanner data. With the expanding scope of price index number theory today, understanding what its creators thought and what objectives they had in mind when developing the current index formulas is by no means a waste, as it helps to organize the discussion.

References

Afriat, S. N. (1977). *The price index*. Cambridge University Press.

Allen, R. G. D. (1933). On the marginal utility of money and its application. *Economica,40*, 186–209.

Allen, R. G. D. (1975). *Index numbers in economic theory and practice*. Routledge.

Atkinson, F. J. (1897). Silver prices in India. *Journal of the Royal Statistical Society, 60*(1), 84–147.

Balk, B. M. (2008). *Price and quantity index numbers*. Cambridge University Press.

Białek, J. (2020). Basic statistics of Jevons and Carli indices under the GBM price model. *Journal of Official Statistics, 36*(4), 737–761.

Bodin, J. (1568). La Response de Maistre Jean Bodin Advocat en la Cour au Paradoxe de Monsieur de Malestroit, Touchant l'encherissement de ToutesChoses, & Le Moyen d'y Remedier. A Monsieur Prevost, Seigneur de Morsan, President pour le Roy en sa Cour de Parlemennt, Martin le Jeune. Paris, English Translation by Tudor, H., Dyson, W. W., & O'Briedn, D. P. (1997). Response to the paradoxes of Malestroit. Primary sources in political thought, 2. Bloomsbury Publishing Plc.

Bureau of Labor Statistics (BLS) (1921) Index Numbers of Wholesale Prices in the United States and Foreign Countries, Bulletin of the United States Bureau of Labor Statistics, 284.

Carli, G.A. (1764) Del Valore e della Proporzione dei Metallic Monetati con i Generi in Italia Prima delle Scoperte dell'Indie col Confronto del Valore e della Proporzione de' Tempi Nostri, Lucca, Reprinted in a Series Dedicated to the Italian Economists in 1804.

Clark, G. N. (1936). The occasion of Fleetwood's 'Chronicon Preciosum'. *English Historical Review, 51*(204), 686–690.

Deartment of Mint. (1881). Report of the director of the Mint on the production of the precious metals.

Diewert, W. E. (1976). Exact and superlative index numbers. *Journal of Econometrics, 4*(2), 115–145.

Diewert, W. E. (1992). Fisher ideal output, input, and productivity indexes revisited. *Journal of Productivity Analysis, 3*(3), 211–248.

Diewert, W. E. (1993). The early history of price index research. In W. E. Diewert, & A. O. Nakamura (Eds.) *Essays in index number theory* (Vol. 1, pp. 33–65).

Diewert, W. E. (2012) Consumer price statistics in the UK. Office for National Statistics, the Government Statistical Agency for the UK.

Diewert, W. E. (2018). *Scanner data, elementary price indexes and the chain drift problem. Discussion Paper 18–06*. Vancouver School of Economics: University of British Columbia.

Diewert, W. E., & Zelenyuk, V. (2023). On the problem of the purchasing power of money by A. A. Konus and S. S. Byushgens: Translation and Commentary. *Journal of Productivity Analysis*. https://doi.org/10.1007/s11123-023-00696-x

Divisia, F. (1925). L'indice Monétaire et la Théorie de la Monnaie. *Revue d'Économie Politique,XXXIX*(4, 5, 6), 842–61, 980–1008, 1121–1151.

Drobisch, M. W. (1871). Über Mittelgrossen und die Anwendbarkeit derselben auf die Berechnung des Steigens und Sinkens des Geldwerths. Berichte über die Verhandlungen der Königlich Sächsischen Gesellschaft der Wissebschaften zu Leipzig, Bd. XXIII, pp. 25–48.

Dutot, N. (1738). Reflexions Politiques sur les Finances et le Commerce, A La Haye: Vaillant and Nicolas Prévost, English Translation: Political reflections upon the finances and commerce of France, A. Millar, 1739.

Eckstein, O. (1981). *Core inflation*. Prentice Hall.

Edgeworth, F. Y. (1888). Some new methods of measuring variation in general prices. *Journal of the Royal Statistical Society, 51*(2), 346–368.

Edgeworth, F. Y. (1896). A defense of index-numbers. *Economic Journal, 6*(21), 132–142.

Edgeworth, F. Y. (1925). *Papers relating to political economy* (Vol. 1). London: Macmillan and Co. Ltd

Edo, A., & Melitz, J. (2019). The primary cause of European inflation in 1500-1700: Precious metals or population? The English Evidence. CEPII Working Paper 2019-10.

Eichhorn, W., & Voeller, J. (1976). *Theory of the price index: Fisher's test approach and generalizations*. Lecture notes in economics and mathematical systems (Vol. 140). Springer.

Fisher, I. (1922). The making of index numbers. Houghton Mifflin Company.

Fisher, W. C. (1913). The tabular standard in Massachusetts history. *Quarterly Journal of Economics, 27*(3), 417–454.

Fleetwood, W. (1707). Chronicon Preciosum: Or, an account of english money, the price of corn, and other commodities, for the last 600 years: In a letter to a student in the University of Oxford. Printed for Charles Harper.

Frisch, R. (1930). Necessary and sufficient conditions regarding the form of an index number which shall meet certain of Fisher's tests. *American Statistical Association Journal, 25*(172), 397–406.

Frisch, R. (1936). Annual survey of general economic theory: The problem of index numbers. *Econometrica, 4*(1), 1–38.

Funke, H., Hacker, G., & Voeller, J. (1979). Fisher's circular test reconsidered. Schweizerische Zeitschrift fur Volkswirtschaft and Statistik, 1979-IV-2, pp. 677–688.

Goethe, J. W. V. (1833) Faust. Eine Tragödie. Zweyter Theil in fünf Acten. Stuttgart and Tübingen: J.G. Cotta.

Haberler,G. (1927). Der Sinn der Indexzahlen: eine Untersuchung uber den Begriff des Preisniveaus und die Methoden seiner Messung, 134 S. Tübingen: J. C. B. Mohr (Paul Siebeck).

Hamilton, E. J. (1928). American treasure and Andalusian prices, 1503–1660: A study in the Spanish price revolution. *Journal of Economic and Business History, 1*, 1–35.

Jevons, W. S. (1861). LIV. On the deficiency of rain in an elevated Rain-gauge, as caused by wind. *London, Edinburgh, and Dublin Philosophical Magazine and Journal of Science,22*(149), 421–433.

Jevons, W. S. (1863). *A serious fall in the value of gold ascertained and its social effects set forth*. Edward Stanford.

Jevons, W. S. (1865). On the variation of prices and the value of currency since 1728. *Journal of the Royal Statistical Society,28*, 294–320 (+1-4).

Jevons, W. S. (1884). *Investigations in currency and finance*. London: Macmillan and Co.

Jorgenson, D. W., & Griliches, Z. (1967). The explanation of productivity change. *Review of Economic Studies, 34*(3), 249–283.
Kendall, M. G. (1969). Studies in the history of probability and statistics, XXI. The early history of index numbers. *Revue de l'Institut International de Statistique/Review of the International Statistical Institute, 37*(1), 1–12.
Keynes, J. M. (1909) The Method of Index Numbers with Special Reference to the Measurement of General Exchange Value, In: *The Collected Writings of John Maynard Keynes*. Macmillan. pp. 50–156.
Keynes, J. M. (1930). *Treatise on money* (Vol. 1). Macmillan.
Kiyosue, T. (1975). The life of Bodin (1) (Bodan no Shogai 1) in Japanese). *Hokudai Hougaku Ronshu, 03–26,25*(4), 65–148.
Konüs, A. A., & Byushgens, S. S. (1926). K probleme pokupatelnoi sily deneg. *Voprosy Konyunktury, 2*(1), 151–172. (English translation of Russian title: On the problem of the purchasing power of money)
Konüs , A. A. (1939). The problem of the true index of the cost of living, Translated from the Russian 1924. *Econometrica, 7*(1), 10–29.
Laspeyres, E. (1864). Hamburger Waarenpreise 1850-1863 und die Kalifornisch-Australischen Geldentdeckung Seit 1848. *Jahrbücher für Nationalökonomie. Statistik,3*, 81–118, 209–236.
Laspeyres, E. (1871). Die Berechnung einer mittleren Waarenpreissteigerung. *Jahrbucher für Nationalökonomie und Statistik, 16*, 296–315.
Laughlin, J. L. (1887a). Gold and prices since 1873. *The Quarterly Journal of Economics, 1*(3), 319–355.
Laughlin, J. L. (1887b). Prices in the United States. *The Quarterly Journal of Economics, 1*(3), 397–399.
Lehr, J. (1885). *Beitrage zur Statistik der Preise: Insbesondere des Geldes und des Holzes*. Frankfurt a. M.: J. D. Sauerlander Verlag.
Leontief, W. (1936). Composite commodities and the problem of index numbers. *Econometrica, 4*(1), 39–59.
Lerner, A. P. (1935). A note on the theory of price index numbers. *Review of Economic Studies, 3*(1), 50–56.
Levell, P. (2012). A winning formula? Elementary indices in the retail prices index. IFS Working Paper, W12/22.
Lowe, J. (1823). *The present State of England in regard to agriculture, trade and finance; with a comparison of the prospects of England and France* (2nd ed.). Hurst, Rees, Orme and Brown: Longman.
Lucas, R. E., Jr. (1996). Nobel lecture: Monetary neutrality. *Journal of Political Economy, 104*(4), 661–682.
O'Brien, D. P. (2000). Bodin's analysis of inflation. *History of Political Economy, 32*(2), 267–292.
Outhwaite, R. B. (1982). Inflation in tudor and early Stuart England: Studies in economic and social history series (2nd edn.) Macmillan.
Paasche, H. (1874). Über die Preisentwicklung der Letzten Jahre Nach den Hamburger Börsennotirungen. *Jahrbücher für Nationalökonomie und Statistik, 12*, 168–178.
Phelps-Brown, E. H., & Hopkins, S. V. (1956). Seven centuries of the prices of consumables, compared with builders' wage-rates. *Economica, 23*(92), 296–314.
Pierson, N. G. (1896). Further considerations on index-numbers. *Economic Journal, 6*(21), 127–131.
Pigou, A. C. (1912). *The economics of welfare*. London: Macmillan.
Pollak, R. A. (1971). The theory of the cost of living index. Research discussion paper no. 11, Research Division, Office of Prices and Living Conditions, U. S. Bureau of Labor Statistics.
Sackley, A. (1965). Coinage, commodities, and count Carli: An account of the inventor and the computation of the original index numbers. *Monthly Labor Review, 88*(7), 817–821.
Samuelson, P. A., & Swamy, S. (1974). Invariant economic index numbers and canonical duality: Survey and synthesis. *American Economic Review, 64*(4), 566–593.

Sato, K. (1974). Ideal index numbers that almost satisfy factor reversal test. *Review of Economics and Statistics, 56*(4), 549–552.

Sato, K. (1976). The ideal log-change index number. *Review of Economics and Statistics, 58*(2), 223–228.

Sauerbeck, A. (1896) Prices of commodities and the precious metals. *Journal of the Statistical Society of London, 49*(3), 581–648

Schumpeter, J. A. (1939). *Business cycles: A theoretical, historical, and statistical analysis of the capitalist process*, McGraw-Hill Book Co.

Scrope, G. P. (1833). *Principles of political economy*. Longman, Rees, Orme, Brown, Green, & Longman.

Shiskin, J. (1974). Updating the consumer price index? An overview. *Monthly Labor Review,97*(7), 3–20.

Shuckburgh-Evelyn, G. (1798). An account of some endeavours to ascertain a standard of weight and measure. *Philosophical Transactions of the Royal Society of London,88*, 133–182.

Smith, A. (1776). An inquiry into the nature and causes of the wealth of nations, W. Strahan and T. Cadell.

Solow, R. (1957). Technical change and the aggregate production function. *Review of Economics and Statistics, 39*(3), 312–320.

Summers, R. (1973). International price comparisons based upon incomplete data. *Review of Income and Wealth, 19*(1), 1–16.

Swamy, S. (1965). Consistency of Fisher's tests. *Econometrica, 33*(3), 619–623.

Theil, H. (1973). A new index number formula. *Review of Economics and Statistics, 55*(4), 498–502.

Thirsk, J. (Ed.). (1989). *The Agrarian history of England and Wales* (Vol. VI, pp. 1750–1850). Cambridge University Press.

Tusset, G. (2020). Gian Rinaldo Carli (1720–1795): Diagnosis and treatment of a monetary plague. *History of Economic Thought and Policy, 9*(2), 39–65.

Vaughan, R. (1675). A discourse of coin and coinage. Th. Basset.

Velde, F. (2012) The life and tines of Nicolas Dutot. *Journal of the History of Economic Thought, 34*(1), 67–107.

Walsh, C. M. (1901). *The measurement of general exchange value*. Macmillan.

Westergaard, H. (1890) *Die Grundzüge der Theorie der Statistik, Gustav Fischer.*

Young, A. (1812). An enquiry into the progressive value of money in England, as marked by the price of agricultural products: with observations upon Sir G. Shuckburgh's table of appreciation: The whole deduced from a great variety of authorities, not before collected, McMillan.

Introduction to Standard Indices

3

Abstract

This chapter introduces standard indices used by statistical agencies and in academic research. It covers widely used price indices like the Laspeyres and Paasche indices, which rely on price and quantity data of various commodities over time. The construction of price indices typically involves a two-stage aggregation process: lower level (elementary) and upper level aggregates. Widely used index number formulas for elementary price indices include the Carli, Dutot, and Jevons indices. The chapter discusses their mathematical properties and practical applications, noting that the choice of formula significantly impacts the final index value. The Laspeyres and Paasche indices are introduced for upper level aggregation, where the Laspeyres index uses base-period weights and the Paasche index uses comparison-period weights. The chapter also covers quantity indices and their calculation methods, emphasizing the importance of the factor reversal test. The chapter concludes with a discussion on alternative index formulas like the Fisher, Walsh, Marshall–Edgeworth, Törnqvist, Sato–Vartia, Theil, and Young indices, highlighting their theoretical properties and practical implications. The Fisher index, in particular, is noted for its theoretical advantages but is less commonly used due to data collection difficulties.

Before entering into full-fledged index number theory in the next chapter and beyond, this chapter discusses the characteristics of typical indices that are widely used by statistical agencies and academic research. Standard price indices, such as the Laspeyres index and the Paasche index, are a function of the price and quantity of various commodities or the amount of expenditure at two points in time. However, in the field of statistical compilation, there are many cases where there is no information on the quantity or amount of expenditure. For example, in web scraping, which has become frequently used in recent years, it is impossible in principle to know how much has been sold at the observed price in a method of searching for and collecting

N. Abe, *Price Index Numbers*, Springer Texts in Business and Economics,
https://doi.org/10.1007/978-981-97-6305-4_3

product prices displayed on Internet websites. Also, when it comes to fresh food, many retailers only record the amount of sales, and do not record detailed quantity information, such as how many or kilograms of mandarin oranges are in a bag.

In the traditional price survey, statistical enumerators visit supermarkets and other stores every month and record the prices sold there as basic data for price statistics. Usually, quantities and sales amounts are not collected. The price survey and the quantity and expenditure survey are conducted separately, and the latter is created by household budget surveys such as the "Family Expenditure Survey (FES)" in the United States, or the "Family Income and Expenditure Survey" in Japan for each product category such as mandarin oranges and salmon. In a price survey, the price of a specific brand or commodity, for example, two sockeye salmon fillets, is examined, and the amount of expenditure directly corresponding to it is not only the fillet, but also the amount of spending on various salmon will be used.[1]

In many cases, price indices are calculated in two stages: lower (or elementary) level aggregate and upper level aggregate. The lower level aggregate refers to creating price indices based on prices of relatively homogeneous goods within a fine product category, such as mandarin oranges or salman. On the other hand, the upper level aggregate involves using quantity and expenditure information from other surveys, such as the FES, to create a comprehensive index based on the fine category price indices calculated at the lower level. In constructing a price index, the most labor-intensive part is not the upper level but the lower level aggregate. The lower level aggregate has a significant impact on the final index value. The Bureau of Labor Statistics (BLS) in the United States reported a 0.2% annual decrease in the overall value of the price index when it changed the lower level aggregate index formula from the arithmetic mean (Carli) index to the geometric mean (Jevons) index in 1999 (BLS, 2001).[2] A 0.2 percentage point decrease in the annual rate of change is not a small value and has a significant long-term impact.

3.1 Elementary Level Aggregation: The Carli, Dutot, and Jevons Indices

The choice of formula for the lower level aggregate is a crucial issue that significantly affects the overall value of the index, and much research has been progressing on this topic in recent years. In this section, we will introduce the nature of index number formulas used for lower level aggregation and related recent discussions.

[1] An exception is the sales records at supermarket registers, which are widely used today. At the register, data is recorded on a transaction basis, hence it is also referred to as Point-of-Sales (POS) data. POS includes both quantity and price information, but for fresh food items, it is very difficult to obtain price and quantity data with sufficient accuracy for fresh foods because very often, no product code such as the Universal Product Code (UPC), European Article Number (EAN), or Japanese Article Number (JAN) are assigned.

[2] Gábor-Tóth and Vermeulen (2019) found that using the Fisher index as the reference, the biases caused by the choice of the elementary index are quantitatively bigger than the biases caused by the upper level substitution.

One of the historically famous index number formulae for lower level aggregation is the Carli index, introduced in Chap. 2, which is defined by the simple arithmetic average of price ratios (price relatives) at two points in time,[3] as shown below:

$$\textbf{Carli Index}\ (0, 1) = \frac{1}{N}\sum_{i=1}^{N}\left(\frac{p_{i1}}{p_{i0}}\right) \tag{3.1}$$

where p_{it} denotes the price of the commodity i at time $t(=0\ or\ 1)$. N is the number of the commodities. While the Carli index was commonly used in the past, the Dutot index and the Jevons indices, defined below, have become more commonly used in recent years:

$$\textbf{Dutot Index}\quad (0, 1) = \frac{\sum_{i=1}^{N} p_{i1}}{\sum_{i=1}^{N} p_{i0}} \tag{3.2}$$

$$\textbf{Jevons Index}\quad (0, 1) = \left(\prod_{i=1}^{N}\frac{p_{i1}}{p_{i0}}\right)^{\frac{1}{N}} \tag{3.3}$$

The price indices used in lower level aggregation are also referred to as elementary price indices. The mathematical characteristics of these three elementary price indices are well known. The Carli index is very straightforward and has a long history. However, as introduced in Chap. 2, it has the disadvantage of not satisfying "time reversal test." If a price index has passed the time reversal test, multiplying the index from period 0 to 1 by the index from period 1 to 0 would result in 1, implying no changes in general prices. However, this is generally not the case with the Carli index. On the other hand, the Jevons and Dutot indices are one of those few indices that satisfy not only the time reversal test but also transitivity test.

The Dutot index has the drawback of being dependent on the unit of measurement of the products. For example, the index value changes depending on whether one apple and 1 liter of milk or one apple and 100 milliliters of milk are considered as one unit when calculating the price of apples and milk. Therefore, when using the Dutot index, it is necessary to limit the aggregation to a narrow range of similar products, such as only milk or only apples.[4]

The Jevons index has the disadvantage that if one of the prices in the comparison period is zero, the value of the index number becomes zero. If one of the prices in the base period is zero, the index is undefined involving division by zero. One might think that there are no products with a price of zero, but in June 2020, during

[3] The base and comparison periods are denoted by 0 and 1, respectively.

[4] However, even with a product like milk, there is a significant price difference between premium and non-premium milk, suggesting that they are not homogeneous. The degree of homogeneity suitable for using the Dutot index is something that should be seriously discussed in principle, but unfortunately, there is not enough accumulated research on the topic. Those interested may refer to von Auer (2008).

the COVID-19 pandemic in Japan, the water and sewage fees in Aomori City were free for 1 month, resulting in a price survey value of zero. While this is an extreme case, services provided by governments such as primary education, childcare, and emergency medical services are often provided for free of charge in many countries. In this regard, when the fees for such services change from positive to zero or zero to positive, the Dutot index has the advantage of not becoming zero or undefined, even if there are products with a price of zero.

From the above discussion, it can be seen that each of these three indices has its own advantages and disadvantages, and that no one index is superior or inferior across the board. However, in index number theory, the Dutot and Jevons indices are considered preferable to the Carli index when limiting the aggregation range to relatively homogeneous commodities. Fisher even wrote in his magnum opus, Fisher (1922), that:

> But we shall see that the simple arithmetic average produces one of the very worst of index numbers. And if this book has no other effect than to lead to the total abandonment of the simple arithmetic type of index number, it will have served a useful purpose. (Fisher, 1922; pp. 29–30)

Why is the Carli index not desirable? On the other hand, why are there still countries using the Carli index? In the next section, we will briefly explain the characteristics of these three basic price indices, following Silver and Heravi (2007) and Diewert (2012).

3.2 Relationship Between Elementary Price Indices

First, let us examine the relationship between the Dutot and Jevons indices. Define p_t^* as the unweighted arithmetic mean of prices at time t, and e_{it} as the deviation from the mean. That is, we have

$$p_t^* = \frac{1}{N}\sum_{i=1}^{N} p_{it} \tag{3.4}$$

$$p_{it} = p_t^* (1 + e_{it}) = p_t^* + p_t^* e_{it} \tag{3.5}$$

Then, the mean of e_{it} is zero. The Dutot and Jevons indices can be written as follows:

$$\sum_{i=1}^{N} e_{it} = 0 \tag{3.6}$$

$$\text{Dutot Index } (0, 1) = \frac{p_1^*}{p_0^*} \tag{3.7}$$

$$\textbf{Jevons Index}\,(0,1) = \prod_{i=1}^{N}\left(\frac{p_{i1}}{p_{i0}}\right)^{1/N} \tag{3.8}$$

$$= \frac{p_1^*}{p_0^*}\prod_{i=1}^{N}\left(\frac{(1+e_{i1})}{(1+e_{i0})}\right)^{1/N} \tag{3.9}$$

The right-hand side of Eq. (3.9) can be simplified by taking the second-order approximation at e_{it}=0. The numerator of the direct product part on the right side of equation (3.9) can be simplified using the law of large numbers, provided that N is sufficiently large and e_{it} is independent across different commodities. That is, we can get the following expressions:

$$\prod_{i=1}^{N}(1+e_{i1})^{1/N} \tag{3.10}$$

$$= 1 + \frac{1}{N}\sum e_{i1} + \frac{1-N}{2N^2}\sum {e^2}_{i1} + o \tag{3.11}$$

$$\approx 1 - \frac{1}{2N}\sum {e^2}_{i1} \tag{3.12}$$

$$= 1 - \frac{1}{2}Var\,(e_{i1}) \tag{3.13}$$

where $Var\,(e_{it})$ is the variance of the deviation from the mean at time t. Therefore, we can derive the following relationships:

$$\textbf{Jevons Index}(0,1) = \frac{p_1^*}{p_0^*}\prod_{i=1}^{N}\left(\frac{(1+e_{i1})}{(1+e_{i0})}\right)^{1/N} \approx \left(\frac{p_1^*}{p_0^*}\right)\left(1 + \frac{1}{2}\mathrm{Var}(e_{i0}) - \frac{1}{2}\mathrm{Var}(e_{i1})\right) \tag{3.14}$$

Therefore, the relative magnitude of the Jevons and Dutot indices depends on the variance of prices at the base and comparison periods. If the variance is almost the same in periods 0 and 1, then the Jevons and Dutot indices will also be nearly the same.

As for the Carli and Jevons indices, since it is a comparison between the geometric and arithmetic means, it's always true that the following equation holds.[5]

$$\prod_{i=1}^{N}\left(\frac{p_{i1}}{p_{i0}}\right)^{1/N} \leq \frac{1}{N}\sum_{i=1}^{N}\left(\frac{p_{i1}}{p_{i0}}\right) \tag{3.15}$$

In other words, the Carli index tends to be higher compared to the Jevons index and the Dutot index. Moreover, the difference between the Carli index and the Jevons

[5] Please see Mathematical Appendix A for the derivation.

index, that is, the difference between the arithmetic mean and the geometric mean, depends on the variance of the price ratios. Let's verify this. Firstly, let the price ratio at two points in time be r_i, its arithmetic mean be r^*, and the deviation rate of the price ratio from its arithmetic mean be e_i. Then, the following holds:

$$r_i = \frac{p_{i1}}{p_{i0}} \tag{3.16}$$

$$r^* = \frac{1}{N} \sum_{i=1}^{N} \frac{p_{i1}}{p_{i0}} \tag{3.17}$$

$$r_i = r^* (1 + e_i) \tag{3.18}$$

$$\sum_{i=1}^{N} e_i = 0 \tag{3.19}$$

Substituting this into the Jevons index, and, as before, using the second-order approximation in the neighborhoods of $e_i = 0$, and then using the law of large numbers,

$$\textbf{Jevons Index (0,1)} = \prod_{i=1}^{N} \left(\frac{p_{i1}}{p_{i0}} \right)^{1/N} \tag{3.20}$$

$$= \prod_{i=1}^{N} (r_i)^{1/N} \tag{3.21}$$

$$= \prod_{i=1}^{N} \left(r^* (1 + e_i)\right)^{1/N} \tag{3.22}$$

$$\approx r^* \left(1 - \frac{1}{2} \mathrm{Var}(e_i) \right) \tag{3.23}$$

Now, it should be clear that the Carli index is

$$\textbf{Carli Index}(0, 1) = \frac{1}{N} \sum_{i=1}^{N} \frac{p_{i1}}{p_{i0}} = r^* \tag{3.24}$$

Therefore, when the variance of the price ratios is zero, the Jevons index and the Carli index coincide. The larger the variance, the greater the Carli index becomes compared to the Jevons index.

Diewert (2012) refers to the tendency of the Carli index to assume larger values compared to other elementary price indices as the upward bias of the Carli index, and considers it one of the drawbacks of the Carli index. However, the author questions the judgment that the Jevons index and the Dutot index are "more correct" than the Carli index just because they yield similar numbers. If the Carli index is considered undesirable for lower level aggregation, it would be due to lack of transitivity and time reversal in the Carli index. The Eurostat (2018) manual on price indices of the European Union Statistical Office recommends either the Dutot index or the Jevons index for lower level aggregation, advising against the use of the Carli index, citing its lack of transitivity as the reason.

One reason why the Carli index is still used in some countries, including the UK, can be found in the CPI Manual (2020). When conducting price surveys at the lower level, it is necessary to decide in advance which products to survey and in which stores. It is known that if, at the time of this product-store selection, sampling based on quantity share is possible, then calculating the Carli index with the prices obtained from this sampling results in an unbiased estimator of the Laspeyres index. Of course, it is difficult to fully accept this justification from the CPI Manual as is, because elementary price index formulas are used precisely because quantity information is not available. However, when conducting a price survey, for instance, for oranges, it is possible to survey more of the popular oranges and less of the less popular ones. In cases where there is heterogeneity in the types of oranges, the Dutot index would be inappropriate, and the choice would be between the Jevons index and the Carli index. The Jevons index calculates the overall change in prices by multiplying the price changes of individual products together. This means if the price of just one product drops significantly, it can cause the entire price index to decrease sharply. When the variance of the price relatives, p_{i1}/p_{i0}, is very large, statistical offices may find the Carli index more attractive than the potentially unstable Jevons index.

3.3 Price Indices for Upper Level Aggregation

Historically, significant number index number formulas used for upper level aggregation in the calculation of the consumer price include the Laspeyres index, the Paasche index, the Fisher index, the Törnqvist index, and the less commonly used Walsh index.

3.3.1 Basics of the Laspeyres Index and the Paasche Index

The Laspeyres and the Paasche indices are representative index number formulas that often appear in introductory macroeconomics textbooks. They are also used in important economic indices produced by many national statistical offices. In this subsection, we will introduce the basic properties of these two representative index number formulas.

First, let us consider the quantity of good i in period t as q_{it} and its price as p_{it}. Then, the total expenditure for period t can be expressed as $\sum_i p_{it}q_{it}$. The ratio of total expenditures between period 0 and period 1 is called the value index. Unless otherwise specified, it is assumed that all prices and quantities are positive real numbers.[6] The value index between time 0 and 1 can be represented as follows, using the inner product. The value index can be described as follows by the inner product of prices and quantities:

$$V_{01} = \frac{\mathbf{p}_1^{'}\mathbf{q}_1}{\mathbf{p}_0^{'}\mathbf{q}_0} \tag{3.25}$$

Here, bold $\mathbf{p_0}$ is the vector of prices, $\mathbf{p_0} = (p_{i0}, p_{10}, p_{20}, \dots p_{N0})$, and its transposed is $\mathbf{p}_0^{'}$. The value index is closely related to the price index. It can also be represented as weighted sum of price ratios, as illustrated below:

$$V_{01} = \sum_i w_{i1}^* \frac{p_{i1}}{p_{i0}},\ w_{i1}^* = \frac{p_{i0}q_{i1}}{\sum_i p_{i0}q_{i0}} \tag{3.26}$$

However, the weights, w_{i1}^*, are not summed up to unity because the periods for quantities differ between the numerator and the denominator. In order for the sum to become unity, it is necessary to standardize the period for evaluating quantities. Specifically, this involves removing the time index from the quantities.

$$P_{01} = \frac{\sum_i p_{i1}q_i}{\sum_i p_{i0}q_i} = \frac{\mathbf{p}_1^{'}\mathbf{q}}{\mathbf{p}_0^{'}\mathbf{q}} = \sum_i w_i \frac{p_{i1}}{p_{i0}} \tag{3.27}$$

$$w_i = \frac{p_{i0}q_i}{\sum_i p_{i0}q_i},\ \sum_i w_i = 1 \tag{3.28}$$

When the reference quantity vector is set as the base period, here being period 0, it results in the Laspeyres price index. That is,

$$P_{01}^L = \frac{\sum_i p_{i1}q_{i0}}{\sum_i p_{i0}q_{i0}} \tag{3.29}$$

On the other hand, if the period for the quantity is set to the comparison period, period 1, it yields the Paasche price index:

$$P_{01}^P = \frac{\sum_i p_{i1}q_{i1}}{\sum_i p_{i0}q_{i1}} \tag{3.30}$$

[6] The exclusion of zero quantity presents a significant issue when examining household-level consumption behavior. Nonetheless, this becomes less problematic when analyzing the aggregate consumption behavior of the entire economy. This assumption is made for simplicity's sake. In the axiomatic approach, prices are typically assumed to be positive, and quantities non-negative. For more detailed treatment, please see the following chapter.

The above are the definitional formulas for the Laspeyres and Paasche indices. However, typically, both indices are often calculated in the following form:

$$P_{01}^{L}=\frac{\sum_i p_{i1}q_{i0}}{\sum_i p_{i0}q_{i0}}=\sum_i \frac{p_{i1}}{p_{i0}}\left(\frac{p_{i0}q_{i0}}{\sum_i p_{i0}q_{i0}}\right)=\sum_i w_{i0}\frac{p_{i1}}{p_{i0}} \tag{3.31}$$

where $w_{i0}=p_{i0}q_{i0}/\sum_i p_{i0}q_{i0}$ is the expenditure share at the base period (0 period). The Paasche index can be written as

$$\left(P_{01}^{P}\right)^{-1}=\sum_i \frac{p_{i0}}{p_{i1}}\left(\frac{p_{i1}q_{i1}}{\sum_i p_{i1}q_{i1}}\right)=\sum_i w_{i1}\frac{p_{i0}}{p_{i1}} \tag{3.32}$$

or

$$P_{01}^{P}=\frac{1}{\sum_i w_{i1}\left(\frac{p_{i1}}{p_{i0}}\right)^{-1}} \tag{3.33}$$

where w_{i1} is the expenditure share at the time 1 (comparison period). In other words, the Laspeyres index is a weighted arithmetic average of the price relatives by the share of expenditure at the base period, while the Paasche index is the weighted harmonic mean of the price relatives by the share of expenditure at the time of comparison.

The index number formulas given by Eqs. (3.31) and (3.33) are much more user-friendly than the definitional formulas (3.29) and (3.30). In upper level aggregation, we compile data across different categories such as ice cream, bread, and clothing. The equivalent of individual product prices in lower level aggregation becomes the elementary price index at this level. Using the formulas for Laspeyres and Paasche indices at this stage is very challenging because the price information we have only covers changes between the base and comparison periods. Furthermore, even though we need to aggregate various types of ice cream and bread, there's a lack of specific quantity information at the lower level, meaning there's no quantity data at the upper level either. However, if it's possible to calculate the index as a function of expenditure shares and price relatives, then information on total expenditures for ice cream, clothing, and bread can be easily obtained from household surveys. By substituting elementary price indices for price relatives, aggregation at the upper level can be performed quite straightforwardly. In fact, in many countries, the statistics bureaus calculate the Laspeyres and Paasche indices using expenditure shares as per Eqs. (3.31) and (3.33), rather than the definitional formulas like Eqs. (3.29) and (3.30).

3.3.2 Quantity Index

To obtain the quantity index, prices and quantities in the price index formula are interchanged. If the quantity index is denoted as Q, then the quantity indices of Laspeyres and Paasche, respectively, are

$$Q_{01}^{L}=\frac{\sum_i p_{i0}q_{i1}}{\sum_i p_{i0}q_{i0}}=\frac{\mathbf{p}_0^{\prime}\mathbf{q}_1}{\mathbf{p}_0^{\prime}\mathbf{q}_0} \tag{3.34}$$

$$Q_{01}^{P} = \frac{\sum_i p_{i1}q_{i1}}{\sum_i p_{i1}q_{i0}} = \frac{\mathbf{p}_1^{\prime}\mathbf{q}_1}{\mathbf{p}_1^{\prime}\mathbf{q}_0} \tag{3.35}$$

The quantity index has the same mathematical structure as the price index.[7] The Laspeyres quantity index can be expressed as a weighted arithmetic average of the quantity ratio at two time points using the expenditure weights at the base period and the Paasche quantity index is a weighted harmonic mean of the quantity ratio using the expenditure shares at the comparison periods as the weights. However, as discussed in the previous section, it is often difficult to obtain detailed product quantity information, and it is rare to calculate the quantity index in using Eqs. (3.34) and (3.35).[8]

If there is only one type of good, the product of its quantity and price becomes the expenditure amount. Conversely, if the price and expenditure are known, the quantity can be easily determined. It would be convenient if a similar operation could be applied to index numbers. Specifically, if the product of a quantity index and a price index becomes a value index, it would be easy to derive the quantity index from the value index and the price index. This is a property called factor reversal test, which was emphasized by Fisher in the early twentieth century. Unfortunately, neither the Laspeyres index nor the Paasche index possesses this property. For example, the product of the Paasche price index and the Paasche quantity index would result in the following:

$$Q_{01}^{P} P_{01}^{P} = \frac{\mathbf{p}_1^{\prime}\mathbf{q}_1}{\mathbf{p}_1^{\prime}\mathbf{q}_0} \frac{\mathbf{p}_1^{\prime}\mathbf{q}_1}{\mathbf{p}_0^{\prime}\mathbf{q}_1} \tag{3.36}$$

Unfortunately, the above index is incomprehensible. Laspeyres price index together with Paasche quantity index, and vice versa, satisfies this property. That is, we get the following:

$$Q_{01}^{L} P_{01}^{P} = \frac{\mathbf{p}_0^{\prime}\mathbf{q}_1}{\mathbf{p}_0^{\prime}\mathbf{q}_0} \frac{\mathbf{p}_1^{\prime}\mathbf{q}_1}{\mathbf{p}_0^{\prime}\mathbf{q}_1} = \frac{\mathbf{p}_1^{\prime}\mathbf{q}_1}{\mathbf{p}_0^{\prime}\mathbf{q}_0} = V_{01} \tag{3.37}$$

$$Q_{01}^{P} P_{01}^{L} = \frac{\mathbf{p}_1^{\prime}\mathbf{q}_1}{\mathbf{p}_1^{\prime}\mathbf{q}_0} \frac{\mathbf{p}_1^{\prime}\mathbf{q}_0}{\mathbf{p}_0^{\prime}\mathbf{q}_0} = \frac{\mathbf{p}_1^{\prime}\mathbf{q}_1}{\mathbf{p}_0^{\prime}\mathbf{q}_0} = V_{01} \tag{3.38}$$

---

[7] Economic interpretation of quantity indices is very different from that of price index. Chapter 5 discusses the economic interpretation of quantity indices in detail.

[8] As recommended by the United Nations in 2010, United Nations (2010), many countries employ industrial production indices targeting manufacturers. These indices are based on a Laspeyres-type quantity index that is created using information on production quantities. In the system of national accounts, real production and consumption quantities are calculated by dividing the nominal gross production and total expenditure values by the price index, specifically at the detailed classification unit of commodity flow. Subsequently, these real quantities are utilized to construct a Laspeyres-type quantity index.

That is, multiplying the Paasche price (quantity) index and the Laspeyres quantity (price) index results in the value index. Therefore, if one has the value index and the Laspeyres price index at hand, it is possible to obtain the Paasche quantity index even without information on quantities. In many countries, when compiling the national accounts, the Paasche price index (strictly speaking, the chain Paasche price index) is used. This is because an implicit price index (implicit deflator) is obtained by dividing the value index (nominal values such as nominal Gross Domestic Products (GDP)) by the Laspeyres-type quantity index (real values such as real GDP). The indirect quantity index obtained by dividing the value index by the price index is referred to as the cofactor of the price index. The Laspeyres quantity index, Q_{01}^{L}, is a cofactor of the Paasche price index, P_{01}^{P}.

The Industrial Production Index and the real GDP are typical examples of quantity indices. In many countries, both are Laspeyres quantity indices using the weights at the base period, but in terms of real gross domestic product, the base period is revised every year, which leads to the chain index.[9] The industrial production index is published with values like 95 or 110, based on a base-period set at 100, whereas real GDP is expressed in monetary units, such as $26.950 trillion. This is because real GDP (constant price GDP) is defined as the nominal value at the base period multiplied by the quantity index, as follows:

$$Q_{01}^{L} \times \sum_{i} p_{i0}q_{i0} = \frac{\sum_{i} p_{i0}q_{i1}}{\sum_{i} p_{i0}q_{i0}} \times \sum_{i} p_{i0}q_{i0} = \sum_{i} p_{i0}q_{i1} \tag{3.39}$$

The purchasing cost of quantities at the comparison period, evaluated using the price vector at the base period, is used as the real value. This method of calculation has the advantage of being easy to understand, as it can be used without needing to be aware that real GDP (constant price GDP) is an index number. However, there is a risk of forgetting that real GDP is an index number and has various characteristics inherent to index number formulas. For values like 110 or 140, it's clear that the importance lies in which year is normalized to 100, but for a value like $30 trillion, the fact that this figure is an index number with various properties of Laspeyres indices can be hidden. It's important to note that real values of GDP or national income are essentially Laspeyres quantity indices, not just mere monetary amounts.[10] Note that the current value GDP, or nominal GDP, can be obtained by multiplying the amount of the expenditure in the base period by the Value index.

$$Nominal\ GDP = \frac{\sum p_{i1}q_{i1}}{\sum p_{i0}q_{i0}} \times \sum p_{i0}q_{i0} = \sum p_{i1}q_{i1} \tag{3.40}$$

It is easy to verify that the real GDP can be obtained by dividing the nominal GDP by the GDP deflator, the Paasche price index.

[9] The chain index will be discussed in detail in Chap. 8.

[10] In the United States, the Fisher quantity index is used for the real GDP.

3.3.3 Relationship Between Laspeyres and Paasche Indices

An indicator of the rate of divergence between the Laspeyres index and the Paasche index, in particular, the rate of discrepancies defined below

$$g = \frac{P_{01}^P - P_{01}^L}{P_{01}^L} \tag{3.41}$$

is called the Laspeyres–Paasche gap. g can be decomposed as follows[11]:

$$g = \frac{\sum_i w_{i0}\left(\frac{p_{i1}}{p_{i0}} - P_{01}^L\right)\left(\frac{q_{i1}}{q_{i0}} - Q_{01}^L\right)}{P_{01}^L Q_{01}^L} \tag{3.42}$$

The numerator in the definitional formula of the Laspeyres–Paasche gap (3.42) can be viewed as the covariance of the deviations of the price and quantity relatives from Laspeyres price and quantity indices, respectively. When the covariance between price and quantity changes is negative, meaning there is a relationship where quantities decrease when prices are high, the Laspeyres–Paasche gap is negative. Consequently, the Paasche price index will be lower than the Laspeyres price index. Note that if the covariance is zero, the Laspeyres and Paasche indices become identical. This relationship, first derived by Ladislaus von Bortkiewicz (1868–1931) and noted in Bortkiewicz (1923), is also referred to in honor of him as the Bortkiewicz decomposition.

From the discussion in Mathematical Appendix B, we can derive the following relationships:

$$\sum_i w_{i0}\left(\frac{p_{i1}}{p_{i0}} - P_{01}^L\right)\left(\frac{q_{i1}}{q_{i0}} - Q_{01}^L\right) = COV = V_{01} - P_{01}^L Q_{01}^L = P_{01}^L Q_{01}^P - P_{01}^L Q_{01}^L \tag{3.43}$$

$$= P_{01}^L\left(Q_{01}^P - Q_{01}^L\right) \tag{3.44}$$

Therefore, it can be seen that when the covariance is negative, the Paasche quantity index is smaller than the Laspeyres quantity index.

Drawing from introductory-level microeconomics textbooks, one might initially assume that this covariance is typically negative, leading to the conclusion that "g" would also be negative. However, a deeper understanding gained from intermediate-level econometrics reveals that prices and quantities are determined by market equilibrium. Therefore, if fluctuations arise from demand-side factors, it's possible that prices and quantities may reflect movements along the supply curve. Furthermore, if

[11] See Mathematical Appendix B for proofs.

preferences are not homothetic, the shape of the demand curve depends on income levels, making it unclear what the sign of the aggregated Laspeyres–Paasche gap for the whole economy would be. Therefore, it's important to note that a non-negative Laspeyres–Paasche gap does not immediately imply inconsistency between economic theory and data.

3.3.4 Fisher Index

The Fisher index, which is the geometric mean of the Laspeyres and Paasche indices as shown below, was not only considered by Fisher as an ideal formula, but is still regarded today as superior to both the Laspeyres and Paasche indices.

$$\textbf{Fisher Index}\ (0,1) = \sqrt{P_{01}^L P_{01}^P} = \sqrt{\left(\frac{\sum_i p_{i1}q_{i0}}{\sum_i p_{i0}q_{i0}}\right)\left(\frac{\sum_i p_{i1}q_{i1}}{\sum_i p_{i0}q_{i1}}\right)} \tag{3.45}$$

This index possesses several important properties. First, it is easy to see that if the base and comparison periods are interchanged, the price index becomes its reciprocal, passing time reversal test. Next, the Fisher index has the factor reversal property, meaning that multiplying the Fisher quantity index by the Fisher price index results in the value index. Additionally, as discussed in Chap. 6, the Fisher index is known to have high affinity with economic theory. Although the Fisher index is known to be an "ideal" index, many countries still use the Laspeyres index for their consumer price index number formulas.[12] To calculate the Fisher index, one needs data on quantities or expenditures for both the base and comparison periods. However, acquiring this information for the comparison period can be difficult. This difficulty often prevents many countries from adopting the Fisher index for compiling monthly or quarterly indices.

Figure 3.1 compares monthly price indices computed using different formulas and using the Family Income and Expenditure Survey of Japan and the Consumer Price Index by item. The base period is set in January 2018. The Laspeyres index is consistently higher than the Paasche index, while the Fischer index falls in between. Notably, the Paasche index saw a significant drop in April 2021 due to the impact of reduced mobile phone usage charges. In that month, the itemized price index for mobile phone charges decreased by nearly 40% compared to the previous month. However, since spending on mobile phones did not drop sharply, the real expenditure on mobile phones, or the "quantity" of mobile phone consumption, increased in the calculation. This resulted in a substantial decrease in the Paasche index due to the higher weight of mobile phones in its calculation. In contrast, the Jevons index, which is not influenced by volume or spending, shows no effect from the changes in mobile phone prices.

[12] A rare exception is Japan after the end of World War II. At that time, Japan used the Fisher index for a while as the formula for its consumer price index.

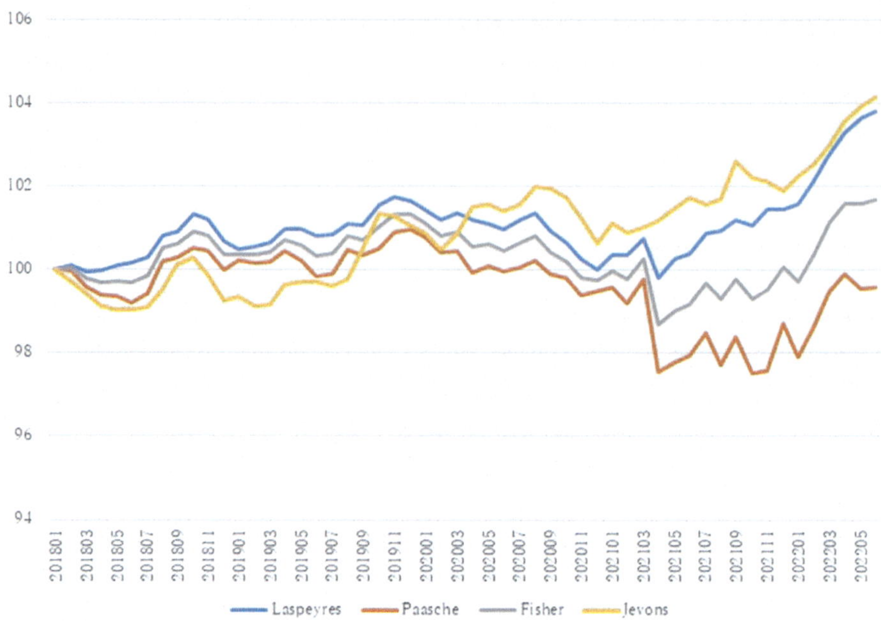

Fig. 3.1 Differences among Price Index Number Formula Notes: Data Household Income and Expenditure Survey of Japan, and CPI

3.3.5 Fixed Basket Method

The Laspeyres and Paasche indices belong to the class of fixed basket method index numbers. The fixed basket method compares the ratio of the total amounts spent at these times. Given a quantity vector, $q^* = (q^*{}_1, q^*{}_2, \ldots, q^*{}_N)$, the fixed basket price index number formula is expressed by the following equation:

$$\textbf{Price Index}(0,1) = \frac{\sum_{i=1}^{N} p_{i1} q^*{}_i}{\sum_{i=1}^{N} p_{i0} q^*{}_i} \tag{3.46}$$

This formula was used by Fleetwood in the early eighteenth century, Fleetwood (1707) as an indicator of the value of money, and is still widely used in price statistics in various countries, and is a very important formula. If the quantity vector, q^*, is the quantity from the base period, it becomes the Laspeyres index, and if the quantity vector is from the time of comparison, it becomes the Paasche index. If this quantity vector does not depend on the information at the base nor comparison periods, it is called a Lowe index.

As discussed in Chap. 2, the Laspeyres index and the Paasche index do not have time reversal property. In other words, if the price index from the 0th to the 1st period is P(0,1), the relationship with the price change from the 1st to the 0th period, P(1,0), is generally as follows:

$$P(0,1) \times P(1,0) \neq 1 \tag{3.47}$$

As mentioned in Chap. 2, this issue was raised by Pearson at the end of the nineteenth century as a serious problem. Indeed, it can become a significant issue when using price indices in dynamic economic analysis. For example, suppose the economy is in a steady state in 2020, then a certain commodity price changes in 2021, and in 2022, the prices return to the steady-state level. If the price index lacks time reversal property, the price index from 2020 to 2022 will not be 1. That is, the price index in a steady state will change. To satisfy the time reversal property using the fixed basket method, there are two ways: (1) use a fixed quantity vector that is independent and does not depend on the base or comparison time or (2) ensure symmetry in the base and comparison time (the quantity vector does not change when the base and comparison times are swapped). An example of the first method is the Lowe index, but it is difficult to justify using quantities unrelated to the information of both 2020 and 2021 when comparing prices between these years.

As for the second method, two famous indices have been devised. Firstly, an index that adopts the geometric mean of the quantities at two time points, respectfully named the Walsh index in honor of the proposer (Walsh, 1901).[13]

$$\textbf{Walsh Index (0,1)} = \frac{\sum_{i=1}^{N} p_{i1}\sqrt{q_{i1}q_{i0}}}{\sum_{i=1}^{N} p_{i0}\sqrt{q_{i1}q_{i0}}} \tag{3.48}$$

The second index number formula using a symmetric weights is called the Marshall–Edgeworth index that uses the arithmetic mean of the quantities:

$$\textbf{Marshall–Edgeworth Index}\ (0,1) = \frac{\sum_{i=1}^{N} p_{i1}\left(\frac{q_{i1}+q_{i0}}{2}\right)}{\sum_{i=1}^{N} p_{i0}\left(\frac{q_{i1}+q_{i0}}{2}\right)} \tag{3.49}$$

The Walsh index has a problem where, if the quantity is zero at either the base or comparison period, the weight of that commodity becomes zero as well, making it difficult to use with data that includes zero quantities. However, in index number theory based on the axiomatic and economic approaches, the Walsh index is often argued to be more desirable than the Marshall–Edgeworth index.[14] While both indices are less frequently used compared to the Fisher index and the Törnqvist index mentioned later, they are valuable options for indices.

[13] The Walsh index can be expressed as functions of price relatives and expenditure share, as in, $PI(0,1)^W = \sum_i w_{i1}^{WAL}\left(\frac{p_{i1}}{p_{i0}}\right),\ w_{i1}^{WAL} = \frac{\sqrt{(w_{i0}\times w_{i1})/\left(\frac{p_{i1}}{p_{i0}}\right)}}{\sum_i \sqrt{(w_{i0}\times w_{i1})/\left(\frac{p_{i1}}{p_{i0}}\right)}}$.

[14] See Chapter 6 for details.

3.3.6 Logarithmic Difference (Geometric Mean) Index

As mentioned in Chap. 2, under continuous time, the price index defined by taking the natural logarithm of prices and then calculating the weighted average of the changes between two points in time is known as the Divisia index:

$$\frac{d \ln PI^{DV}}{dt} = \sum_{i=1}^{N} \omega_{it} \frac{d \ln p_{it}}{dt} \tag{3.50}$$

The Divisia index is known to have a number of theoretically desirable properties. The details of the Divisia index are left to Chap. 11, but if the index is to be used in practice, it must be approximated in discrete time. A simple discrete approximation of Eq. (3.50) is

$$\ln \left(\text{Price Index } (0, 1)\right) = \sum_i \omega_i \left(\ln p_{i1} - \ln p_{i0}\right) \tag{3.51}$$

A lot of research has focused on that weight, ω_i. If we use identical weights (no weights), it will be the Jevons index. If we take the simple arithmetic average of the expenditure shares at two points in time as the weights, it is the Törnqvist index introduced in Chap. 2:

$$\ln \textbf{Törnqvist Index } (0, 1) = \sum_i \frac{\omega_{i0} + \omega_{i1}}{2} \left(\ln p_{i1} - \ln p_{i0}\right) \tag{3.52}$$

The Törnqvist index is a typical index number formula that is considered to be a desirable index along with the Fisher index. It was used in the United States and is also widely used in academic research.[15] In logarithmic difference-type index number formulas, when weights are taken as logarithmic averages, it becomes what is known as the Sato–Vartia index. This index is defined as follows, provided that the expenditure shares take positive values:

$$\ln \textbf{Sato–Vartia Index}(0.1) = \sum_i s_i \left(\ln p_{i1} - \ln p_{i0}\right) \tag{3.53}$$

$$s_i = \frac{L\left(w_{i0}, w_{i1}\right)}{\sum_i L\left(w_{i0}, w_{i1}\right)} \tag{3.54}$$

[15] The axiomatic nature of the Törnqvist index is discussed in Chap. 4, and the characteristics of the Törnqvist index in economic approaches are discussed in detail in Chap. 6.

$$L\left(w_{i0}, w_{i1}\right) = \frac{w_{i1} - w_{i0}}{\ln\left(w_{i1}\right) - \ln\left(w_{i0}\right)} \quad \text{if } w_{i0} \neq w_{i1} \tag{3.55}$$

$$L\left(w_{i0}, w_{i1}\right) = w_{i0} \quad \text{if} \quad w_{i0} = w_{i1} \tag{3.56}$$

$L(x, y)$ represents a positive value known as the logarithmic mean of x and y. It might be a less familiar concept of averaging, but it is often used in the field of index number theory. The logarithmic mean is the ratio of the ordinary difference to the logarithmic difference, and it is known that the following inequality holds.[16]

$$\sqrt{x \times y} \leq L\left(x, y\right) \leq \frac{x + y}{2} \tag{3.57}$$

In general, there is the following relationship between the harmonic mean, the geometric mean, and the arithmetic mean.

$$\frac{N}{\sum_{i=1}^{N}\left(\frac{1}{x_i}\right)} \leq \prod_{i=1}^{N}\left(x_i\right)^{1/N} \leq \frac{1}{N}\sum_{i=1}^{N} x_i \tag{3.58}$$

Thus, in the case of two variables, the logarithmic mean falls into the above inequality as follows[17]:

$$\frac{2}{\frac{1}{x} + \frac{1}{y}} \leq \sqrt{x \times y} \leq L\left(x, y\right) \leq \frac{x + y}{2} \tag{3.59}$$

The Sato–Vartia index, which uses the logarithmic mean as a weight, has a high affinity with economic theory and has been frequently used in macroeconomics and international trade theory in recent years. In addition, the Sato–Vartia index has the factor reversal property, that is, the product of the Sato–Vartia price and quantity indices becomes the value index. This index will be discussed in more detail in Chap. 6.

The Jevons index, the Törnqvist index, and the Sato–Vartia index all share a common drawback. In each of them, if the price of even one of the products being compared drops to zero, the index itself will also drop to zero. It's not impossible for the price of certain goods, like services provided by government, to become zero. It is a serious problem that the entire index drops to zero even if this happens with just a less important product.

[16] The logarithmic mean is discussed in detail by Törnqvist et al. (1985).

[17] The derivation of the above two inequalities is presented in Mathematical Appendix A. Note that the geometric mean, the arithmetic mean, and the harmonic mean can be calculated even in the case of three or more variables, while the logarithmic mean is, in principle, limited to only the case of two variables.

Then, consider the following index, where the weight is the geometric mean of the expenditure shares at two points in time. This is known as the Theil index.

$$\ln \textbf{Theil Index}\ (0,1)) = \sum_i \sqrt{w_{i0} \times w_{i1}}\ (\ln p_{i1} - \ln p_{i0}) \tag{3.60}$$

In the Theil index, the speed at which weights decrease to zero is faster than the rate at which the logarithmic prices diverge to negative infinity. As a result, when the price becomes zero, it doesn't affect the overall value of the price index, leading to the exact opposite extreme outcome. Among logarithmic change-type indices, the following formula known as Vartia I index, proposed by Yrjö Vartia, has distinct properties compared to other logarithmic difference-type indices.

$$\ln \textbf{Vartia I Index}(0,1)) = \sum_i s_i\ (\ln p_{i1} - \ln p_{i0}) \tag{3.61}$$

$$s_i = \frac{L\left(v_{i0}, v_{i1}\right)}{L\left(\sum_i v_{i0}, \sum_i v_{i1}\right)},\ v_{i1} = p_{i1} \times q_{i1} \tag{3.62}$$

Vartia (1976) notes that when the price of good i at time 1 becomes zero, the logarithmic mean in the numerator of the weight in Eq. (3.62) converges to zero, resulting in$s_i \to 0$. Furthermore, when setting $p_i \to 0$, it is possible to derive the following from a simple transformation:

$$\begin{aligned} L\left(v_{i0}, v_{i1}\right)(\ln p_{i1} - \ln p_{i0}) &= \frac{v_{i1} - v_{i0}}{\ln v_{i1} - \ln v_{i0}}(\ln p_{i1} - \ln p_{i0}) \\ &= \frac{v_{i1} - v_{i0}}{\frac{\ln p_{i1}}{\ln p_{i1}} - \frac{\ln p_{i0}}{\ln p_{i1}} + \frac{1}{\ln p_{i1}}(\ln q_{i1} - \ln q_{i0})}\left(1 - \frac{\ln p_{i0}}{\ln p_{i1}}\right) \to -v_{i0} \end{aligned}$$

Therefore, when $p_i \to 0$, the Vartia I index will fall by $-v_{i0}/L\left(\sum_i v_{i0}, \sum_i v_{i1}\right)$. This represents a significant difference from the Törnqvist, Sato–Vartia, and Jevons indices, where the overall price level becomes zero if the price of a single product drops to zero, and from the Theil index, where the price index is unaffected if a price becomes zero. Unfortunately, the Vartia I index has the property that if all prices are multiplied by K, the price index does not multiply by K, meaning it is not a first-degree homogeneous function with respect to the prices at the comparison point. Consequently, the practical application of the Vartia I index is limited.

Column 4: Geometric Mean

The geometric mean, also known as the multiplicative mean, is one of the most important averages in the index number theory. While many people are familiar with the arithmetic mean, which is widely used in everyday life, the geometric mean might be less well-known. As its name suggests, the geometric mean is closely linked to geometry.

Consider a rectangle with sides of length a and b. What would be the side length of a square that has the same area as this rectangle? Since the area of the rectangle is $a \times b$, the answer would be a square with a side length of $\sqrt{a \times b}$, which is the geometric mean of the two sides.

The geometric mean is particularly useful when considering economic growth. Suppose Japan's GDP is assumed to be 100 trillion yen. If it increases by 100% (doubling) in the first year and then by 50% (1.5 times) in the next year, what would be the average growth rate per year over these two years? The GDP grows from 100 trillion to 200 trillion, then to 300 trillion yen, tripling over two years. Therefore, the growth rate that triples the GDP over two years is $\sqrt{a \times b} = \sqrt{3} \cong 1.73205$, which is the geometric mean of the growth rates for each year. In contrast, the arithmetic mean of the annual growth rates, 1.75, does not match the average growth rate over the two years.

While the geometric mean is useful for economic analysis, it is important to note that if even one of the numbers is zero, the geometric mean of them will always be zero, regardless of the other values. For example, when calculating the average score for a math test in a class, if even one student scores zero, the class's average score becomes zero, even if all the other students score 100. When there is extreme variability in the numbers, the geometric mean can be significantly lower than the arithmetic mean, potentially resulting in values that do not align with intuition.

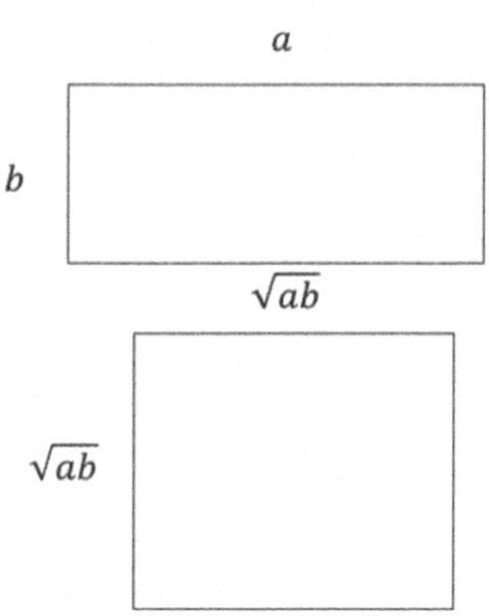

3.3.7 Other Index Number Formulas

Among the index number formulas that are neither fixed basket nor logarithmic differences, the Young index defined below is particularly noteworthy:

$$\textbf{Young Index } (0,1) = \sum_{i=1}^{N} \frac{a_i}{\sum_k a_k} \left(\frac{p_{i1}}{p_{i0}}\right) \tag{3.63}$$

The Young index is not directly related to the share of expenditure at the base period or comparison period. The Young index is actually used in various national statistics offices in some occasions. When COVID-19 pandemic occurred, the consumption pattern at that time became very different from that in pre-Pandemic period. In many countries, the average of the expenditures in 2019 and 2020 is used to compute the weights, which leads to the Young index number.

The Laspeyres index is a weighted arithmetic average of price ratios using the expenditure shares at the base period. By analogy, quite a few people consider the Paasche index as a weighted average using the expenditure shares, w_{i1}, at the comparison period, as follows:

$$\textbf{Price Index}(0,1) = \sum_{i=1}^{N} w_{i1} \left(\frac{p_{i1}}{p_{i0}}\right) \tag{3.64}$$

The Paasche index is a harmonic mean of the price ratios using the expenditure shares at the comparison period as the weights, which is different from Eq. (3.33). The formula in (3.64) was used by Sir Robert Harry Inglis Palgrave, an Editor of *The Economist* and the Compiler of the still-continuing *Palgrave's Dictionary of Economics*, hence it is called the Palgrave index.[18]

[18] The price index by Palgrave is featured in the substantial work of nearly 500 pages, Great Britain, Royal Commission to Inquire into the Depression of Trade and Industry (1886).

Column 5: Harmonic Mean

The simple harmonic mean of a vector of positive real numbers, $(x_1, x_2, .., x_n)$ is defined in a somewhat cumbersome form as the reciprocal of the average of the reciprocals:

$$\frac{n}{h} = \frac{1}{x_1} + \frac{1}{x_2} + \ldots + \frac{1}{x_n}$$

$$h = \frac{n}{\left(\frac{1}{x_1} + \frac{1}{x_2} + \ldots + \frac{1}{x_n}\right)}$$

A well-known application of the harmonic mean is in calculating the average speed. For instance, consider traveling to a destination 100 km/h away, using an express train at 100 km/h for the outbound journey and a special express at 200 km/h for the return. To find the average speed for the round trip, note that the outbound journey takes 1 hour and the return 30 min. Covering 200 km in 1 hour and 30 min results in an average speed of 133.33 km/h. This matches the harmonic mean of the two speeds. Similar to the geometric mean, the harmonic mean is not useful when any of the numbers are zero or close to zero. As seen in the definition of h, if any x_i approaches zero, the denominator becomes very large, leading the harmonic mean to converge to zero as long as the other values are finite.

A geometric mean version of the Laspeyres index, i.e., formula (3.51) with weights set to the expenditure shares at the base period, is called the Geometric Laspeyres index. On the other hand, when the weights in formula (3.51) are set to the expenditure shares at the comparison period, it is not called the Geometric Palgrave but, somewhat expectedly, the Geometric Paasche index. The simple geometric mean of the Geometric Laspeyres and the Geometric Paasche is the Törnqvist index. The Geometric Laspeyres and Geometric Paasche do not have a consistent size relationship like the standard Laspeyres–Paasche indices. In fact, the Geometric Paasche index often takes on a larger value than the Geometric Laspeyres index.

To determine the size of the index by analyzing the demand curve's shape, consider the following scenarios based on the elasticity of substitution in quantity to price:

1. **Elasticity of 1 (Cobb–Douglas Utility Function):** In this case, price changes do not alter the expenditure share, which remains constant. Consequently, the Geometric Laspeyres index and the Geometric Paasche index will coincide and will equal the Törnqvist index.
2. **Elasticity Greater Than 1**: Here, a 1% increase in price results in a decrease in quantity by more than 1%, leading to a reduced expenditure share. As a result, the Geometric Laspeyres index will exceed the Geometric Paasche index.

3. **Elasticity Less Than 1**: In this scenario, the quantity decrease due to a price increase is relatively small, causing the expenditure share to increase. Therefore, the Geometric Paasche index will be larger than the Geometric Laspeyres index.

Therefore, if the aggregation scope for calculating the index consists of homogeneous goods, it can be assumed that the elasticity of substitution is high, and the Geometric Paasche index will likely be smaller than the Geometric Laspeyres index. Conversely, if the aggregation scope includes significantly different goods categories like fresh food and clothing, the Geometric Paasche index will likely be larger than the Geometric Laspeyres index. Note that the Geometric Laspeyres index naturally emerges as the index number formula for price changes from the steady state when constructing a macro-model with multiple commodities and applying a logarithmic linear approximation in the steady state. However, it is important to note that since the geometric mean is always smaller than the logarithmic mean, the official consumer price index, often calculated with the arithmetic mean, will always be larger than the predictions of a macro-model based on the geometric mean.

Other famous price indices include the Stuvel index, which is conceived from a completely different idea than fixed baskets or geometric means; the Geary-Khamis index used in inter-regional price indices; and the Lloyd–Moulton index, which assumes a utility function with constant elasticity of substitution. In this book, the Stuvel index is discussed in the supplementary section of Chap. 4, the Geary-Khamis index in Chap. 11, and the Lloyd–Moulton index in Chap. 7.

3.4 Conclusions

This chapter explains the characteristics of various well-known index formulas. In recent years, many papers have been published on the Dutot, Jevons, and Carli indices, which are used for lower level aggregation. Particularly in the UK, where the Carli index is utilized, there have been numerous studies on the validity of the Carli index.[19] Besides Silver and Heravi (2007), the topic is also vigorously debated in works like Levell (2012) and Białek (2020). The Törnqvist and Sato–Vartia indices have been increasingly used in recent years for price measurement based on scanner data. For more details on the scanner data and the elementary price indices, refer to Chapter 10 of the CPI Manual (2020), Białek and Berżsewicz (2021) and Gábor-Tóth and Vermeulen (2019).

[19] See, for example: https://publications.parliament.uk/pa/ld201719/ldselect/ldeconaf/246/24605.htm.

3.5 Mathematical Appendix A: Several Inequalities

It is known that the following inequality holds between the geometric mean, arithmetic mean, and harmonic mean with respect to positive real numbers, $x_i > 0, i = 1, 2, ..., N$.

$$\frac{N}{\sum_{i=1}^{N}\left(\frac{1}{x_i}\right)} \le \prod_{i=1}^{N}(x_i)^{1/N} \le \frac{1}{N}\sum_{i=1}^{N}x_i$$

In addition, in the case of two positive variables, the logarithmic mean can be placed as follows:

$$\frac{2}{\frac{1}{x}+\frac{1}{y}} \le \sqrt{xy} \le \frac{x-y}{\ln(x)-\ln(y)} \le \frac{x+y}{2}$$

At first, let's show the following inequality:

$$\prod_{i=1}^{N}(x_i)^{1/N} \le \frac{1}{N}\sum_{i=1}^{N}x_i$$

First of all, as a preparation, we will show the following:

$$e^x - 1 - x \ge 0$$

Define a function on one-dimensional real space, *f*, as follows:

$$f(x) = e^x - 1 - x$$

Then, we can get the following characteristics:

$$f^{'}(x) > 0 \quad if \quad x > 0$$

$$f^{'}(x) < 0\, if\, x < 0$$

$$f^{'}(0) = 0,\, f(0) = 0$$

Consider the area of $x > 0$. Because

$$f^{'}(x) > 0, \text{and } f(0) = 0$$

we get the following:

$$f(x) > 0$$

Next, given the area of $x < 0$, we get

$$f^{'}(x) < 0$$

The function, f, becomes a monotonic decreasing function of x. Because $f(0) = 0$ holds, when x is smaller than zero, $f(x)$ must be greater than 0. Consequently, we get

$$f(x) > 0$$

This is

$$e^x - 1 - x > 0 \quad if\ x \neq 0$$

$$= 0\ if\ x = 0$$

Next define v as

$$v = \frac{1}{N}\sum_{i=1}^{N} m_i$$

where m_i is a real number. And set x as

$$x = \frac{m_i}{v} - 1$$

By substituting x into the inequality just shown, we get

$$\exp\left(\frac{m_i}{v} - 1\right) - \left(\frac{m_i}{v} - 1\right) - 1 \geq 0$$

$$\exp\left(\frac{m_i}{v} - 1\right) \geq \frac{m_i}{v}$$

Multiplying this for each $i = 1, , , N$ as follows:

$$\exp\left(\sum_{i=1}^{N}\left(\frac{m_i}{v} - 1\right)\right) \geq \prod_{i=1}^{N}\frac{m_i}{v}$$

$$\exp\left(\sum_{i=1}^{N}\left(\frac{m_i}{v}\right) - n\right) \geq \frac{\prod_{i=1}^{N} m_i}{v^N}$$

Note that by definition,

$$v = \frac{1}{N}\sum_{i=1}^{N} m_i$$

Therefore,

$$\exp\left(\sum_{i=1}^{N}\left(\frac{m_i}{v}\right) - n\right) = 1$$

Consequently

$$\prod_{i=1}^{N} m_i \le v^N$$

$$\prod_{i=1}^{N} m_i^{1/N} \le v$$

$$\prod_{i=1}^{N} m_i^{1/N} \le \frac{1}{N}\sum_{i=1}^{N} m_i$$

Thus, the derivation of the desired inequality has been completed.
Next, let's show the following inequality:

$$\frac{N}{\sum_{i=1}^{N}\left(\frac{1}{x_i}\right)} \le \prod_{i=1}^{N}(x_i)^{1/N}$$

This is actually simple. Consider the inequality shown earlier,

$$\prod_{i=1}^{N}(x_i)^{1/N} \le \frac{1}{N}\frac{N}{\sum_{i=1}^{N}\left(\frac{1}{x_i}\right)} \le \prod_{i=1}^{N}(x_i)^{1/N}$$

Then set m_i as

$$m_i = \frac{1}{x_i}$$

Substitute x_i into the above inequality, we get

$$\prod_{i=1}^{N}\left(\frac{1}{x_i}\right)^{1/N} \le \frac{1}{N}\sum_{i=1}^{N}\frac{1}{x_i}$$

If we take the reciprocal, we get

$$\frac{1}{\frac{1}{N}\sum_{i=1}^{N}\frac{1}{x_i}} \le \frac{1}{\prod_{i=1}^{N}\left(\frac{1}{x_i}\right)^{1/N}}$$

By arranging the above, we obtain the following inequality:

$$\frac{N}{\sum_{i=1}^{n}\frac{1}{x_i}} \le \prod_{i=1}^{N}(x_i)^{1/N}$$

Next, let's show the following inequality:

$$\sqrt{xy} \leq \frac{x-y}{\ln(x)-\ln(y)}, \quad if \ x>0, y>0$$

When $x=y$, from the definition of the logarithmic mean, we get

$$\frac{x-y}{\ln(x)-\ln(y)}=x$$

Therefore, the above equation is established. Then, suppose $x>y$ and define m as

$$x/y=m$$

A simple calculation leads us to

$$x/y-1=\frac{x-y}{y}$$

$$=m-1$$

Then, it is easy to show the following:

$$\frac{x-y}{\ln(x)-\ln(y)}=y\frac{m-1}{\ln(m)},$$
$$\frac{1}{y}\sqrt{xy}=\sqrt{\frac{x}{y}}$$

Using the above equations, the inequality becomes

$$\sqrt{m} \leq \frac{m-1}{\ln(m)}, \quad if \ m>1$$

In addition, define z as

$$z^2=m$$

Then, if $z>1$, that is, $\ln(z)>0$ the inequality becomes

$$z \leq \frac{z^2-1}{2\ln(z)}$$

$$2\ln(z) \leq \frac{z^2-1}{z}$$

In addition, define functions f and g as follows:

$$f(z)=2\ln(z),$$
$$g(z)=\frac{z^2-1}{z}$$

Then

$$f(1) = g(1) = 0$$

$$f^{'}(z) = \frac{2}{z}$$

$$g^{'}(z) = \frac{2z^2 - z^2 + 1}{z^2}$$

$$= \frac{z^2 + 1}{z^2}$$

$$= 1 + \frac{1}{z^2}$$

By the way, we can get the following:

$$g^{'}(z) - f^{'}(z) = 1 + \frac{1}{z^2} - \frac{2}{z}$$

$$= \frac{1}{z^2}\left(z^2 - 2z + 1\right)$$

$$= \frac{1}{z^2}(z - 1)^2$$

This is positive if $z \neq 1$. That is, we get

$$f(1) = g(1) = 0,$$

$$f^{'}(z) < g^{'}(z) \quad if \quad z > 1$$

Consequently

$$2\ln(z) \leq \frac{z^2 - 1}{z}$$

is established. Thus, we have shown that the following inequality holds:

$$\sqrt{xy} \leq \frac{x - y}{\ln(x) - \ln(y)}$$

Finally, let's show the following inequality:

$$\frac{x - y}{\ln(x) - \ln(y)} \leq \frac{x + y}{2}$$

As before, we transform the R.H.S. using m,

$$\frac{x-y}{\ln(x)-\ln(y)}=y\frac{m-1}{\ln(m)}$$

Then, we get

$$\frac{x+y}{2}=y\left(\frac{x/y+1}{2}\right)$$

$$=y\left(\frac{m+1}{2}\right)$$

Consequently

$$\frac{x-y}{\ln(x)-\ln(y)}\leq\frac{x+y}{2}$$

$$y\frac{m-1}{\ln(m)}\leq y\left(\frac{m+1}{2}\right)$$

$$\frac{m-1}{\ln(m)}\leq\frac{m+1}{2}$$

$$\frac{m-1}{m+1}\leq\frac{\ln(m)}{2}\quad if\ m>1$$

As before, set the following functions:

$$f(m)=\frac{m-1}{m+1},\ g(m)=\frac{\ln(m)}{2}$$

Then, we get

$$f(1)=g(1)=0$$

$$f^{'}(m)=\frac{m+1-m+1}{(m+1)^2}$$

$$=\frac{2}{(m+1)^2}$$

$$g^{'}(m)=\frac{1}{2m}$$

Therefore,

$$g^{'}(m)-f^{'}(m)$$

$$= \frac{(m+1)^2 - 4m}{2m\,(m+1)^2}$$

$$= \frac{(m-1)^2}{2m\,(m+1)^2} > 0 \quad if\ m > 1$$

Consequently, we can show the following inequalities:

$$\frac{m-1}{\ln(m)} \le \frac{m+1}{2}$$

$$\frac{x-y}{\ln(x) - \ln(y)} \le \frac{x+y}{2}$$

(End of Proof)

3.6 Mathematical Appendix B: Derivation of the Laspeyres–Paasche Gap

By expanding the numerator of Eq. (3.42), we get

$$\sum_i w_{i0}\left(\frac{p_{i1}}{p_{i0}} - P_{01}^L\right)\left(\frac{q_{i1}}{q_{i0}} - Q_{01}^L\right) = \sum_i w_{i0}\frac{p_{i1}}{p_{i0}}\frac{q_{i1}}{q_{i0}} - \sum_i w_{i0}\frac{p_{i1}}{p_{i0}}Q_{01}^L - \sum_i w_{i0}\frac{q_{i1}}{q_{i0}}P_{01}^L + \sum_i w_{i0}P_{01}^L Q_{01}^L$$

From the definition formula of each index, it is possible to obtain the following equations:

$$\sum_i w_{i0} = 1,\ \sum_i w_{i0}\frac{p_{i1}}{p_{i0}}Q_{01}^L = P_{01}^L Q_{01}^L$$

$$\sum_i w_{i0}\frac{q_{i1}}{q_{i0}}P_{01}^L = P_{01}^L Q_{01}^L$$

$$w_{i0} = \frac{p_{i0}q_{i0}}{\sum_i p_{i0}q_{i0}}$$

$$\sum_i w_{i0}\frac{p_{i1}}{p_{i0}}\frac{q_{i1}}{q_{i0}} = \sum_i \frac{p_{i1}q_{i1}}{\sum_i p_{i0}q_{i0}} = V_{01}$$

Therefore, the equation is simplified as follows:

$$\sum_i w_{i0}\left(\frac{p_{i1}}{p_{i0}} - P_{01}^L\right)\left(\frac{q_{i1}}{q_{i0}} - Q_{01}^L\right) = V_{01} - P_{01}^L Q_{01}^L = P_{01}^P Q_{01}^L - P_{01}^L Q_{01}^L$$

If we multiply the numerator/denominator of the definition formula of g by the Laspeyres quantity index, we get

$$g \equiv \frac{P_{01}^{P} - P_{01}^{L}}{P_{01}^{L}} = \frac{P_{01}^{P} Q_{01}^{L} - P_{01}^{L} Q_{01}^{L}}{P_{01}^{L} Q_{01}^{L}}$$

Thus, we get the following formula:

$$g = \frac{\sum_i w_{i0} \left(\frac{p_{i1}}{p_{i0}} - P_{01}^{L} \right) \left(\frac{q_{i1}}{q_{i0}} - Q_{01}^{L} \right)}{P_{01}^{L} Q_{01}^{L}}.$$

(End of Proof)

References

Białek, J. (2020). Basic statistics of Jevons and Carli indices under the GBM price model. *Journal of Official Statistics, 36*(4), 737–761.

Białek, J., & Beręsewicz, M. (2021). Scanner data in inflation measurement: from raw data to price indices. *The Statistical Journal of the IAOS, 37*, 1315–1336.

Bortkiewicz, L. V. (1923). Zweck und Struktur einer Preisindexzahl. *Nordisk Statistisk Tidsskrift, 2*, 369–408.

Bureau of Labor Statistics (BLS). (2001). The Experimental CPI using Geometric Means (CPI-U-XG). Retrieved October 16, 2001, from https://web.archive.org/web/20081128080159/http://www.bls.gov/cpi/cpigmrp.htm

Diewert, W. E. (2012). Consumer price statistics in the UK. Office for National Statistics, the Government Statistical Agency for the UK.

Eurostat (2018). Harmonised Index of Consumer Prices (HICP) methodological manual.

Fisher, I. (1922). *The making of index numbers*. Houghton Mifflin Company.

Fleetwood, W. (1707). Chronicon Preciosum: or, an Account of English Money, the Price of Corn, and Other Commodities, for the Last 600 Years: in a Letter to a Student in the University of Oxford, Printed for Charles Harper.

Gábor-Tóth, E., & Vermeulen, P. (2019). Elementary index bias: Evidence for the Euro area from a large scanner dataset. *German Economic Review, 20*(4), e618–e656.

International Monetary Fund (IMF), Eurostat, United Nations, OECD, and World Bank (2020) *Consumer Price Index Manual: Concepts and Methods. (CPI Manual).*

Levell, P. (2012). A winning formula? Elementary indices in the retail prices index. IFS Working Paper, W12/22.

Silver, M., & Heravi, S. (2007). Why elementary price index number formulas differ: Evidence on price dispersion. *Journal of Econometrics, 140*(2), 874–883.

Törnqvist, L., Vartia, P., & Vartia, Y. O. (1985). How should relative changes be measured? *American Statistician, 39*(1), 43–46.

United Nations (2010) International Recommendations for the Index of Industrial Production 2010, *Department of Economic and Social Affairs Statistics Division Statistical Papers*, Series F, 107.

Vartia, Y. O. (1976). Ideal log-change index numbers. *Scandinavian Journal of Statistics, 3*, 121–126.

von Auer, L. (2008). *Questioning some general wisdom in axiomatic index theory*. mimeo.

Walsh, C. M. (1901). *The measurement of general exchange value*. Macmillan.

4 Axiomatic Approach

Abstract

This chapter investigates the axiomatic approach in index number theory. This approach, also known as the test approach, aims to determine the most appropriate index number formula by listing and satisfying various axioms or tests. The chapter begins by addressing the multitude of existing index number formulas and emphasizes the importance of selecting one based on specific objectives. Edgeworth's view, which advocated for choosing an index number formula according to its purpose, contrasts with the opinions of contemporaries like Walsh and Fisher. The axiomatic approach is central to modern index number theory, narrowing down desirable indices through axioms such as transitivity, monotonicity, linear homogeneity, identity, and independence from the measurement unit. The chapter introduces some basic axioms, elaborating on their significance and the only index number formula (the Cobb–Douglas-type index) that satisfies all these axioms. It also discusses the implications of abandoning certain axioms, such as transitivity, leading to a variety of index formulas that meet other criteria. Further, the chapter explores indices like the Walsh, Fisher, Törnqvist, and Sato–Vartia indices, highlighting their axiomatic properties and practical applications. It explains the concept of characterization, where an index number is defined through its foundational axioms, identifying specific index number formulas that uniquely fulfill these conditions. The chapter concludes by presenting the characterization of well-known index number formulas within the axiomatic framework, discussing various debates related to them, and emphasizing the ongoing importance and centrality of the axiomatic approach in current index number theory.

4.1 What is Axiomatic Approach?

When numerous index number formulas, like the Laspeyres, Paasche, Fisher, and Törnqvist, coexist, it's natural to question which one is preferable. From the dawn of index number theory, detailed in Chap. 2, Edgeworth argued that the selection of an

N. Abe, *Price Index Numbers*, Springer Texts in Business and Economics,
https://doi.org/10.1007/978-981-97-6305-4_4

index number formula should hinge on the specific goals it is meant to serve. This viewpoint, however, did not find general agreement among the prominent economists and index number theorists of that period, such as Walsh and Fisher.[1] Recognizing that no single formula can fulfill all objectives, various index number formulas are utilized for distinct purposes, including basic aggregation, international comparisons, and assessments of welfare. The subsequent challenge lies in identifying the best fitting index number formula for each specific aim. A crucial approach, formulated between the early- and mid-twentieth century and still remains central to index number theory today, is the axiomatic approach.

The axiomatic approach, also known as the test approach in index number theory, narrows down the range of desirable indices by listing the tests (axioms) that an index number should pass (satisfy).[2] For example, let us assume that the price index is a positive continuous function that depends only on the quantity and price vector at two points in time. Also imagine we're looking at data that stretches over a long period, like several decades. We're interested in seeing how things have changed not just from 1 year to another, but over many years. For instance, if we're examining how prices have changed in the 1980s, 1990s, and 2000s, we'd want to make sure our calculations can connect those periods together smoothly. So, if we want to compare the year 1980–2000 directly, our method should let us do this by combining the changes from 1980 to 1990 with the changes from 1990 to 2000. This idea that you can link different periods together by multiplications of the index numbers is known as transitivity. It helps ensure that our comparisons over time are consistent, no matter where we begin. In addition to the transitivity, as axioms, it would be desirable if monotonicity, linear homogeneity, identity, and independence from the unit of measurement regarding prices at the time of comparison are satisfied. What kind of price index number satisfies these axioms? As introduced in Chap. 2, the only price index that satisfies these axioms is the Cobb–Douglas-type index. When there are many characteristics that an index should have, an axiomatic approach makes it possible to narrow down the choice of index number formula to a considerable degree.

Unfortunately, in the Cobb–Douglas-type index, the weight of each commodity is constant, which makes it difficult for us to apply the index number to the cases where expenditure shares of commodities keep changing. What would happen if we abandoned transitivity? There are countless price indices that satisfy the other four axioms besides transitivity. What happens if we constrain our choice of index number formula to the straightforward and comprehensible fixed basket method, while also requiring invariance to the proportional changes in the quantities at current periods, and possessing time reversal property? This chapter reveals that the Walsh index emerges as the sole index number meeting these criteria. Furthermore, there

[1] Fisher (1922) pursued the concept of an ideal formula, coining the term "Superlative Index" for an exemplary index formula (p. 247). He specifically referred to the Fisher index, his own creation, as the "Ideal Index" (pp. 220–221).

[2] Fisher (1922) ranks indices according to the number of axioms they satisfy. However, this requires the difficult task of equating all axioms or determining the relative importance of each axiom.

are known sets of axioms leading to the Fisher, Törnqvist, and Marshall–Edgeworth indices. The objective is to pinpoint the essential axioms that a price index number should adhere to, frame a price index as a measure that aligns with these axioms, and identify a specific index number formula by demonstrating that it uniquely fulfills these conditions. This approach to defining a price index through its foundational principles is referred to as the "Characterization" of a price index. Regrettably, besides the characterization of the Cobb–Douglas-type index, many such characterizations often involve somewhat unnatural axioms, indicating potential areas for refinement. In this chapter, we aim to present the characterization of well-known index number formulas within the axiomatic framework and explore various debates related to them.

4.2 Basic Axioms

There are numerous properties that a price index should satisfy, properties considered desirable to fulfill. However, the five properties or axioms introduced below have been particularly regarded as important for a long time. In the seminal work on the axiomatic approach by Eichhorn and Voeller (1976), these are positioned as basic axioms.

The price indices and quantity indices considered in this chapter are defined on strictly positive real-valued price vectors $\mathbf{p}_t = (p_{1t}, p_{2t}, ..., p_{Nt})'$ and quantity vectors, $\mathbf{q}_t = (q_{1t}, q_{2t}, ..., q_{Nt})'$ at two points in time. In other words, the price index PI and the quantity index QI that measure changes in prices or quantities between time 0 and 1 are defined as functions from $(\mathbf{q}_0, \mathbf{p}_0, \mathbf{q}_1, \mathbf{p}_1)$ to strictly positive real space, $PI : \mathbb{R}^{4N}_{++} \to \mathbb{R}_{++}$, $QI : \mathbb{R}^{4N}_{++} \to \mathbb{R}_{++}$.[3]

(A-1) Monotonicity
PI is a strictly increasing function with respect to $\mathbf{p}_1$, and a strictly decreasing function with respect to $\mathbf{p}_0$, i.e., the following should hold:

$$PI(\mathbf{q}_0, \mathbf{p}_0, \mathbf{q}_1, \mathbf{p}_1) > PI(\mathbf{q}_0, \mathbf{p}_0, \mathbf{q}_1, \mathbf{p}) \text{ if } \mathbf{p}_1 \geq \mathbf{p}$$
$$PI(\mathbf{q}_0, \mathbf{p}_0, \mathbf{q}_1, \mathbf{p}_1) < PI(\mathbf{q}_0, \mathbf{p}, \mathbf{q}_1, \mathbf{p}_1) \text{ if } \mathbf{p}_0 \geq \mathbf{p}$$

Monotonicity is a property that requires the price index to increase with a rise in commodity prices. It is one of the basic properties that a price index should satisfy. However, the Törnqvist index and the Sato–Vartia index do not satisfy monotonicity. Additionally, the Gini–Eltető–Köves–Szulc (GEKS) index, which is often used with high-frequency scanner data (discussed in Chap. 8 of this book) and purchasing power parity (discussed in Chap. 11), does not satisfy monotonicity, either. There remains a debate about how necessary monotonicity is.

[3] The inequality sign between two vectors, $\geq$, indicates that if $\mathbf{p}_1 \geq \mathbf{p}$, then all the variables in the vector $\mathbf{p}_1$ are equal to or greater than the corresponding variables in the vector $\mathbf{p}$, and at least one of them is strictly greater.

(A-2) Linear Homogeneity
When the price vector at the comparison period, p_1*, is multiplied by a positive real value,* λ*, PI also becomes multiplied by* λ*, i.e.,*

$$PI\left(\mathbf{q_0}, \mathbf{p_0}, \mathbf{q_1}, \lambda\mathbf{p_1}\right) = \lambda PI\left(\mathbf{q_0}, \mathbf{p_0}, \mathbf{q_1}, \mathbf{p_1}\right) \quad \text{for } \forall\ \lambda \in \mathbb{R}_{++}$$

It is a natural requirement for a price index that if all prices double, the price index should also double. Very few indices fail to satisfy this property of homogeneity of degree one, and among the well-known formulas, only the Vartia I and Stuvel indices, which are introduced in the supplementary section of this chapter, do not meet this criterion.

(A-3) Identity
If all prices are the same between two points in time, PI is 1, independent of the quantity level, $\mathbf{q_0}, \mathbf{q_1}$*, i.e., for any positive vector* $\mathbf{p}$*, the following equation holds:*

$$PI\left(\mathbf{q_0}, \mathbf{p}, \mathbf{q_1}, \mathbf{p}\right) = 1$$

Identity is particularly important among the basic axioms, and most indices satisfy this property. However, like monotonicity, chain indices and the GEKS formula do not possess this property.[4] Moreover, it is recognized that even when prices remain constant, the price index may not necessarily equal unity if preferences vary across different time periods or regions. This notion has been recently highlighted by Redding and Weinstein (2020), who introduced a price index that deviates from the identity property.[5] This development has sparked renewed interest in re-evaluating the importance and applicability of this axiom in price index number theory.

(A-3') Strong Identity
If all prices and quantities are the same between two points in time, then PI is 1, i.e., for any positive vector $\mathbf{p}, \mathbf{q}$*, the following equation holds:*

$$PI\left(\mathbf{q}, \mathbf{p}, \mathbf{q}, \mathbf{p}\right) = 1$$

Strong identity imposes a more relaxed constraint on price indices than identity does. That is, if an index satisfies identity, it always satisfies strong identity, but an index that meets strong identity does not necessarily satisfy identity. To my best knowledge, almost all index number formulas, including GEKS and the index by Redding and Weinstein (2020), which do not satisfy identity, do meet the criteria for strong identity.

[4] Chapter 8 discusses the property of chain indices.

[5] Chapter 5 discusses the index by Redding and Weinstein (2020) in detail.

(A-4) Dimensionality

Changes in currency units do not affect prices, i.e., for any price and quantity vectors, the following equation holds:

$$PI(\mathbf{q_0}, \lambda\mathbf{p_0}, \mathbf{q_1}, \lambda\mathbf{p_1}) = PI(\mathbf{q_0}, \mathbf{p_0}, \mathbf{q_1}, \mathbf{p_1}) \quad \text{for } \forall\, \lambda \in \mathbb{R}_{++}$$

Dimensionality is also an important property, and all major price indices satisfy this. Furthermore, if the index number formula satisfies the linear homogeneity, the dimensionality implies that the price index is a negative first-degree homogeneous function with respect to the base price, that is, if the base price increases by 10 times, the price index becomes 1/10.

(A-5) Independence from Measurement Unit (commensurability)

Changing the unit of measurement for a product does not affect price index numbers. Specifically, suppose the unit of quantity of good i is multiplied by a strictly positive real value, λ_i, and the price is multiplied by $1/\lambda_i$ (amount of spending on good i remains unchanged). That is, let
$\Lambda = \text{diag}^{6}\ (\lambda_1, \lambda_2, ..., \lambda_N)$, $\Omega = \text{diag}\left(\frac{1}{\lambda_1}, \frac{1}{\lambda_2}, ..., \frac{1}{\lambda_N}\right)$, $\lambda_i > 0$ *for any i, and compute* $PI(\Lambda\mathbf{q_0}, \Omega\mathbf{p_0}, \Lambda\mathbf{q_1}, \Omega\mathbf{p_1})$. *Then the price index number is unchanged:*

$$PI(\Lambda\mathbf{q_0}, \Omega\mathbf{p_0}, \Lambda\mathbf{q_1}, \Omega\mathbf{p_1}) = PI(\mathbf{q_0}, \mathbf{p_0}, \mathbf{q_1}, \mathbf{p_1})$$

The axiom of independence from the measurement unit, also known as commensurability, is a fundamental requirement for price and quantity index numbers. However, from a mathematical perspective, this requirement is rather stringent, imposing significant restrictions on the functional form of the index number. For instance, a utility function, which depends on the quantity consumed, varies significantly with the unit of measurement, such as measuring water in liters versus gallons. Consequently, many microeconomic concepts, including the marginal rate of substitution, typically do not conform to this principle of unit indifference. Consider, for example, the following Cobb–Douglas utility function for two commodities, a quantity of orange juice measured in liters, x, and a quantity of meat measured in kilograms, y:

$$U(x, y) = x^{0.5}y^{0.5}$$

The marginal rate of substitution (MRS) between the two products is given by

$$MRS(x, y) = \frac{\partial U/\partial x}{\partial U/\partial y} = \frac{x^{0.5-1}y^{0.5}}{x^{0.5}y^{0.5-1}} = \frac{y}{x}$$

[6] A square matrix in which all elements except those on the diagonal are zero is called a *diagonal matrix*. It can be represented as $\text{diag}\{a_1, \ldots, a_n\}$, where the diagonal elements from the top left to the bottom right are $a_1, \ldots, a_n$.

If $x = y = 1$, the MRS, $MRS(1, 1)$, equals one. Now, assume we change the measurement unit of x from liters to milliliters, resulting in $x = 1000$ and $y = 1$, which leads to $MRS(1000, 1) = 1/1000$. Note that while the MRS in the Cobb–Douglas example depends on the choice of measurement units, the ratio of utilities under different consumption vectors remains invariant to the unit of measurement. Let the consumption quantity of goods x at time t be denoted as x_t. Then, the ratio of utilities between times 0 and 1 is given by

$$\frac{U(x_1, y_1)}{U(x_0, y_0)} = \frac{x_1^{0.5} y_1^{0.5}}{x_0^{0.5} y_0^{0.5}}$$

It is evident that even if we change the measurement units of the consumption goods, such that the variables are multiplied by some strictly positive real numbers, the effect disappears due to cancellation between the numerator and the denominator.[7]

In the realm of index number theory, nearly all indices conform to this axiom of unit independence, with the notable exception being the Dutot index, which is essentially a ratio of average prices.[8]

Commensurability, along with identity, is particularly crucial among the axioms of price indices. Its validity allows for the adjustment of commodity units so that prices at the base time are set to 1 when calculating the price index. Consider a scenario where only the information about the ratio of prices at two points in time, rather than the prices themselves, is available. If the price index is commensurable, changing all base-time prices to 1 will not alter the value of the price index. Therefore, even without the level information of individual prices at two points, as long as the percentage change in prices from the base time is known, it is possible to compute the price index.

These basic axioms (A-1), (A-2), (A-3), (A-4), and (A-5) do not contradict each other, nor does one encompass the other. In other words, each of these five axioms has indices that do not satisfy that particular axiom but do satisfy the other four. There are also indices that satisfy all the axioms. When this occurs, the set of axioms is called independent. In other words, the five basic axioms are mutually independent. Eichhorn and Voeller (1976) introduced the following theorem.

Theorem 4.2.1 *Axioms (A-1), (A-2), (A-3), (A-4), and (A-5) are mutually independent.*

Proof (sketch)

[7] The property that the utility ratio between two points in time becomes commensurable reflects a characteristic of the Cobb–Douglas utility function and does not hold for more general utility functions.

[8] Additionally, the index number by Redding and Weinstein (2020), which is a cost-of-living index with changes in preferences, does not satisfy commensurability when using functional forms other than the geometric mean type, as per its normalization condition. For more details, see Abe and Rao (2024a,b).

For each axiom, the proof is completed by finding a function that does not satisfy that axiom but satisfies all other axioms. It is easy to find such functions for monotonicity, linear homogeneity, identity, and commensurability, but dimensionality is difficult. An example provided by Eichhorn and Voeller (1976) that does not satisfy only dimensionality is

$$PI(\mathbf{q}_0, \mathbf{p}_0, \mathbf{q}_1, \mathbf{p}_1) = \frac{\mathbf{q}_0'\mathbf{p}_0}{\mathbf{q}_0'\mathbf{p}_0 + 1}\frac{1}{N} \times \sum \frac{p_{i1}}{p_{i0}} + \frac{1}{\mathbf{q}_0'\mathbf{p}_0 + 1} \max\left[\frac{p_{11}}{p_{10}}, \frac{p_{11}}{p_{10}}, \dots, \frac{p_{N1}}{p_{N0}}\right]$$

It is not difficult to show that this index number formula satisfies the other four axioms, but does not satisfy dimensionality. (End of Proof)

Many of the famous formulas, such as the Laspeyres, Paasche, and Fisher indices, satisfy all of the five axioms above. One of the axioms derived from the above axioms is the following intermediate value property.

(A-6) Mean Value

The value of the price index (PI) lies between the minimum and maximum values of the price relatives of its components, i.e.,

$$\min\left(\frac{p_{11}}{p_{10}}, \frac{p_{21}}{p_{20}}, \dots, \frac{p_{N1}}{p_{N0}}\right) \le PI(\mathbf{q}_0, \mathbf{p}_0, \mathbf{q}_1, \mathbf{p}_1) \le \max\left(\frac{p_{11}}{p_{10}}, \frac{p_{21}}{p_{20}}, \dots, \frac{p_{N1}}{p_{N0}}\right)$$

Theorem 4.2.2 *Suppose there is a price index, $PI(\mathbf{q}_0, \mathbf{p}_0, \mathbf{q}_1, \mathbf{p}_1)$, that satisfies axioms (A-1), (A-2), and (A-3). Then, $PI(\mathbf{q}_0, \mathbf{p}_0, \mathbf{q}_1, \mathbf{p}_1)$ possesses the mean value property.*

Refer to page 10 in Eichhorn and Voeller (1976) for proof.

Column 6: "Axiom" in the Theory of Price Indices

The axiomatic approach to index number theory was established by Irving Fisher, but the axiomatic index number theory developed there differs significantly from today's axiomatic mathematical economics. In Fisher (1922), while the properties that an index should satisfy are listed and the functional properties of the index are emphasized, the use of mathematics is very casual. It lacks the rigor found in the axiomatic frameworks used in general equilibrium models by Abraham Wald or Gérard Debreu. The formal axiomatization of index number theory, akin to that in general equilibrium models, had to wait for a series of studies by Wolfgang Eichhorn and his co-authors after 1970, putting it about 20 years behind mathematical economics. Looking at the research on index number theory from the 1950s to the early 1970s, it is evident that the focus was on index number theory based on economic approaches, particularly the analysis of logarithmic price indices and Divisia indices by Henri Theil and others. The emphasis was on the practical issue of how to easily calculate indices against the context of general utility functions. At that time, index number theory was predominantly characterized as an applied theory with a strong emphasis on practice. Therefore, the research by Eichhorn and others, which separated economics and index number theory to focus solely on the mathematical structure of indices without assuming any relationship between prices and quantities, likely provided a new perspective that revolutionized the existing theories of index numbers.

4.3 Other Axioms and Cobb–Douglas Price Index

In addition to the basic axioms above, the following axioms are also emphasized in index number theory.

(A-7) Proportionality

If the prices in the comparison period are λ times those at the base period, the value of the price index becomes λ, regardless of the values in the quantity vector, i.e.,

$$PI\left(\mathbf{q}_0, \mathbf{p}_0, \mathbf{q}_1, \lambda\mathbf{p}_0\right) = \lambda$$

Proportionality is automatically satisfied if identity and linear homogeneity are satisfied.

(A-7') Strong Proportionality

If the quantities are the same at the base time and the time of comparison, and if the prices at the time of comparison are λ times those at the base time, then the value of the price index will be λ.[9]

$$PI\left(\mathbf{q}_0, \mathbf{p}_0, \mathbf{q}_0, \lambda\mathbf{p}_0\right) = \lambda$$

(A-8) Transitivity
Suppose there are three time points: 0, 1, and 2. For any price and quantity vectors, the following equation holds:

$$PI\left(\mathbf{q}_0, \mathbf{p}_0, \mathbf{q}_1, \mathbf{p}_1\right) PI\left(\mathbf{q}_1, \mathbf{p}_1, \mathbf{q}_2, \mathbf{p}_2\right) = PI\left(\mathbf{q}_0, \mathbf{p}_0, \mathbf{q}_2, \mathbf{p}_2\right)$$

This axiom has stirred the most debate among all the axioms presented so far. Transitivity is crucial for comparing price indices over time or between countries. For instance, consider a scenario where the price index from 2000 to 2010 is 110, and from 2010 to 2020 is also 110. With transitivity, the price index from 2000 to 2020 would be 1.1 × 1.1 = 1.21. This means if the price level in 2000 was 100, it would be 121 in 2020. Without transitivity, however, the 2020 value could diverge significantly from this, potentially being any numbers that are very different from 121. The absence of transitivity, especially when using scanner data increasingly utilized in recent years, poses a significant problem. Few indices satisfy transitivity, with notable ones like the Fisher index and Törnqvist index not meeting this criterion. Recognizing the lack of transitivity has been a critical issue since the early development of the axiomatic approach. In light of this, the following theorem holds special significance.

Theorem 4.3.1 *Funke et al. (1979)*
Suppose the price index, $PI : R_{++}^{4N} \to R_{++}$, possesses monotonicity (A -1), linear homogeneity (A-2), identity (A-3), commensurability (A-5), and transitivity (A-8). Then, the price index must be the following Cobb–Douglas type:

$$PI\left(\mathbf{q}_0, \mathbf{p}_0, \mathbf{q}_1, \mathbf{p}_1\right) = \prod_{i=1}^{N} \left(\frac{p_{i1}}{p_{i0}}\right)^{\alpha_i}, \alpha_i > 0, \sum \alpha_i = 1.$$

The original proof provided by Funke et al. (1979) was complex. However, Balk (2008) introduced a more straightforward proof. Therefore, in this discussion, we will focus on Balk's (2008) version of the proof, incorporating additional equations to elucidate the specifics. While the proof of this theorem is somewhat technical, its significance in contemporary index number theory justifies the effort.

Proof

[9] Eichhorn and Voeller (1976) call this axiom Weak Proportionality.

If transitivity (A-8) holds, the following holds for any quantity and price vector:

$$PI(\mathbf{q_1}, \mathbf{p_1}, \mathbf{q_2}, \mathbf{p_2}) = \frac{PI(\mathbf{q_0}, \mathbf{p_0}, \mathbf{q_2}, \mathbf{p_2})}{PI(\mathbf{q_0}, \mathbf{p_0}, \mathbf{q_1}, \mathbf{p_1})} \tag{4.1}$$

Since the left side of Eq. (4.1) does not depend on the information from period 0, it follows that the right side is not a function of period 0, either. Therefore, we can get the following equation:

$$PI(\mathbf{q_1}, \mathbf{p_1}, \mathbf{q_2}, \mathbf{p_2}) = \frac{g(\mathbf{q_2}, \mathbf{p_2})}{g(\mathbf{q_1}, \mathbf{p_1})} \tag{4.2}$$

Using identity axiom (A-3) and by setting prices in both periods at the same level, we have

$$PI(\mathbf{q_1}, \mathbf{p_1}, \mathbf{q_2}, \mathbf{p_1}) = \frac{g(\mathbf{q_2}, \mathbf{p_1})}{g(\mathbf{q_1}, \mathbf{p_1})} = 1 \tag{4.3}$$

$$g(\mathbf{q_2}, \mathbf{p_1}) = g(\mathbf{q_1}, \mathbf{p_1}) \tag{4.4}$$

Equation (4.4) is an identity with respect to $\mathbf{q_1}, \mathbf{q_2}$, thus, must hold for any quantity vectors. That implies that the function g does not depend on quantity vector. Therefore, we can rewrite the above as

$$g(\mathbf{q_2}, \mathbf{p_1}) = k(\mathbf{p_1}) \tag{4.5}$$

Using Eq. (4.5), we can rewrite Eq. (4.2) as

$$PI(\mathbf{q_1}, \mathbf{p_1}, \mathbf{q_2}, \mathbf{p_2}) = \frac{k(\mathbf{p_2})}{k(\mathbf{p_1})} \tag{4.6}$$

Note that the price index in (4.6) does not depend on quantity vectors. This suggests that the bilateral transitive price index must not be determined by quantities or expenditures. Next, upon applying the principle of commensurability (A-5), the price index remains unchanged even when the price vector is multiplied by any positive scalar. Here, as a positive vector that multiplies the price, consider the following:

$$\Delta = \operatorname{diag}\left(\frac{1}{p_{11}}, \frac{1}{p_{21}}, \ldots, \frac{1}{p_{N1}}\right) \tag{4.7}$$

Thus, we get

$$\frac{k(\Lambda\mathbf{p_2})}{k(\Lambda\mathbf{p_1})} = \frac{k(\mathbf{p_2})}{k(\mathbf{p_1})} \tag{4.8}$$

Using the notation:

$$\frac{\mathbf{p_2}}{\mathbf{p_1}} = \left(\frac{p_{12}}{p_{11}}, \frac{p_{22}}{p_{21}}, \ldots, \frac{p_{N2}}{p_{N1}}\right) \tag{4.9}$$

we can write Eq. (4.8) as follows:

$$\frac{k\left(\frac{\mathbf{p_2}}{\mathbf{p_1}}\right)}{k\left(\mathbf{1_N}\right)} = \frac{k\left(\mathbf{p_2}\right)}{k\left(\mathbf{p_1}\right)} \tag{4.10}$$

Consider the following function:

$$h\left(\mathbf{p}\right) = k\left(\mathbf{p}\right)/k\left(\mathbf{1_N}\right) \tag{4.11}$$

For any price vector $\mathbf{p_1}, \mathbf{p_2}$, we get the following functional equations:

$$h\left(\mathbf{p_2}/\mathbf{p_1}\right) = h\left(\mathbf{p_2}\right)/h\left(\mathbf{p_1}\right) \tag{4.12}$$

Note that, by setting $\mathbf{p_1} = (1, 1, ..., 1)$, we can show that $h\,(1, 1, ..., 1) = 1$.
Furthermore, by setting $\mathbf{x} = p_2, \mathbf{y} = 1/p_1$, and $k\left(\mathbf{y}\right) = 1/h\left(\mathbf{1}/\mathbf{y}\right)$, it is possible to rewrite Eq. (4.12) as follows:

$$h\left(\mathbf{xy}\right) = h\left(\mathbf{x}\right) k\left(\mathbf{y}\right) \tag{4.13}$$

for any positive vectors **x** and **y**. Also from monotonicity (A-1), we know that a function h is also an increasing function. From the Generalized Cauchy Functional Equation 3 in **Mathematics Appendix C**, we can see that the general solution to this functional equation is of the Cobb–Douglas type. Finally, the linear homogeneity (A-2) leads to the adding up condition on the parameters. (End of Proof)

This theorem can be considered a landmark in axiomatic index number theory, and the result that imposing transitivity on a general price index function leads to a Cobb–Douglas form is indeed striking. The Cobb–Douglas type is not desirable as a price index number in general, as it does not utilize information on quantity information or expenditure shares. Of course, it's possible to compute some parameters in the index using quantity- or expenditure-share information. For instance, calculating parameters like in the Törnqvist or Sato–Vartia indices and fixing them at these values would make the Cobb–Douglas index behave similarly to these indices in practice. However, in that case, it becomes necessary to separately determine how long and for what reasons to fix these weights. This is because having fixed weights is not desirable in a world where prices, incomes, and expenditure shares change.

(A-9) Determinateness
If one of the elements of the price vector converges to zero, then PI converges to a certain positive real value.

Determinateness becomes an issue when prices approach zero closely. In practical scenarios, prices may drop to zero, for instance, due to policies rendering certain goods or services free. Should the price of even a single product become nearly zero, price indices, such as the Törnqvist index, which rely on the geometric mean, will similarly approach zero, thus failing to uphold determinateness.

(A-10) Factor Reversal Test
A price index satisfies the factor reversal test if the product of the price index and the quantity index obtained by switching prices and quantities in the price index formula equals the value index. That is,

$$PI\left(\mathbf{q}_0, \mathbf{p}_0, \mathbf{q}_1, \mathbf{p}_1\right) PI\left(\mathbf{p}_0, \mathbf{q}_0, \mathbf{p}_1, \mathbf{q}_1\right) = \frac{\mathbf{q}_1^{\prime}\mathbf{p}_1}{\mathbf{q}_0^{\prime}\mathbf{p}_0}$$

The factor reversal test, alongside transitivity, constitutes an axiom that has sparked considerable debate. In the simple case of a single type of good, multiplying the price by the quantity yields the total expenditure. The factor reversal property endows both the price and quantity indices with a similar characteristic, necessitating that they share the exact same functional form. If factor reversal property is not imposed, it becomes difficult to assign a meaningful interpretation to the quantity index in terms of real consumption derived from deflating the value index. Factor reversal property has been emphasized in index number theory since Fisher in the early twentieth century. The great advantage of the Stuvel index and Sato–Vartia index is that they possess factor reversal property. On the other hand, there is no particular reason why the quantity index and the price index should have exactly the same functional form other than simplicity. Therefore, the following axiom is proposed.

(A-10') Weak Factor Reversal Test
There exists a quantity index that satisfies $QI : \mathbb{R}_{++}^{-4N} \to \mathbb{R}_{++}$ (A-1), (A-2), (A-3), (A-4), (A-5) and satisfies the following:

$$PI\left(\mathbf{q}_0, \mathbf{p}_0, \mathbf{q}_1, \mathbf{p}_1\right) QI\left(\mathbf{q}_0, \mathbf{p}_0, \mathbf{q}_1, \mathbf{p}_1\right) = \frac{\mathbf{q}_1^{\prime}\mathbf{p}_1}{\mathbf{q}_0^{\prime}\mathbf{p}_0}$$

Factor reversal property requires that the quantity index and price index share the same functional form. However, weak factor reversal test only demands that the quantity index adheres to basic axioms (A-1) to (A-5). Essentially, it upholds the notion that there should exist a quantity index with desirable properties as an index number, and that multiplying quantity by price yields value index. If the weak factor reversal test is satisfied, it becomes possible to determine the quantity index as the value index divided by the price index. Moreover, this will also correspond to the real expenditure, which is the expenditure of the first period divided by the price index. Additionally, when the weak factor reversal test is met, practitioners in index calculation gain two options: they can either aggregate various commodities' quantities to directly construct a quantity index and then indirectly obtain the price index by dividing the value index by it, or they can first directly create a price index and then indirectly derive the quantity index from the value index.[10]

Fisher's strongly emphasized concept of factor reversal property, however, is incompatible with transitivity. The inconsistency between transitivity and the factor reversal property was initially highlighted by Frisch (1930) and next by Wald (1937). Eichhorn and Funke, in their 1976 work, formulated a theorem demonstrating that no index number formula can simultaneously meet the criteria of weak factor reversal test, transitivity, and proportionality, with proportionality being an extended form of factor reversal property. Moreover, Eichhorn and Funke's 1976 publication includes several results that illustrate the inconsistencies between factor reversal property and transitivity.

Theorem 4.3.2 *Let $N > 1$. There is no function $PI : \mathbb{R}_{++}^{4N} \to \mathbb{R}_{++}$ that simultaneously satisfies proportionality (A-7), transitivity (A-8), and weak factor reversal test.*

See Balk (2008) for the proof.

When identity is required instead of proportionality, transitivity and factor reversal test become contradictory demands.

Theorem 4.3.3 *Let $N > 1$. There is no function $PI : \mathbb{R}_{++}^{-4N} \to \mathbb{R}_{++}$ that simultaneously satisfies identity (A-3), transitivity (A-8), and factor reversal test (A-10).*

Proof See Mathematical Appendix A.

From Theorems 4.3.2 and 4.3.3, it becomes clear that as long as we need identity or proportionality, factor reversal property or weak factor reversal test and transitivity are mutually exclusive, and index makers must choose one over the other. If the purpose of creating a price index is to deflate nominal series, then factor reversal test or strong factor reversal property becomes very important, as it allows "real" expenditures to be interpreted as a quantity index. On the other hand, if a price index is used to grasp long-term price trends or for comparisons across many countries and regions, it is preferable to use an index number with transitivity. Often, we need an index number that possesses both axioms. In such cases, a different type of price index, a multilateral index, becomes necessary. This will be discussed in more detail in Chap. 11.

4.4 Characterization of the Walsh Index

The Walsh index by Walsh (1901) introduced in Chap. 3 is considered to be one of the desirable indices in index number theory, along with the Fisher index and Törnqvist

---

[10] Allen and Diewert (1981) have extensively discussed these indirect indices, or implicit indices.

index, and in recent years, research using this index has been increasing.[11] The Walsh index was defined as follows:

$$\textbf{Walsh Index (0,1)} = \frac{\sum_{i=1}^{N} p_{i1}\sqrt{q_{i1}q_{i0}}}{\sum_{i=1}^{N} p_{i0}\sqrt{q_{i1}q_{i0}}}$$

The Walsh index belongs to a group of indices known as the fixed basket method. Let us consider a more general fixed basket index number formula like the one below:

$$\textbf{Linear Mean Index}(0, 1) = \frac{\sum_{i=1}^{N} p_{i1} m\left(q_{i1}, q_{i0}\right)}{\sum_{i=1}^{N} p_{i0} m\left(q_{i1}, q_{i0}\right)}$$

Here, $m\left(q_{i1}, q_{i0}\right)$ is called a mean function, and is a continuous and increasing function defined on a positive quantity vector, which satisfies the following properties:

$$m : \mathbb{R}_{++}^{2\mathrm{N}} \to \mathbb{R}_{++}, m\left(x, x\right) = x$$

Before we provide a characterization of the Walsh index, we introduce two axioms.

(A-11) Time Reversal Test

If 0 and period 1 are swapped, the price index becomes the reciprocal.

$$PI\left(\mathbf{q_0}, \mathbf{p_0}, \mathbf{q_1}, \mathbf{p_1}\right) = \frac{1}{PI\left(\mathbf{q_1}, \mathbf{p_1}, \mathbf{q_0}, \mathbf{p_0}\right)}.$$

This axiom was devised by Fisher (1922) to address the lack of transitivity in the Fisher index. For instance, consider that the price index from period 0 to period 1 is 1.2. If, in period 2, prices and quantities revert to their period 0 levels, and assuming the price index upholds the time reversal property, then the price index from period 1 back to period 0 must be $1/1.2$. In other words, the product of the two price indices, first from period 0 to 1 and then from 1 to 2, should equal one. Fulfillment of transitivity inherently ensures time reversal test. While the Laspeyres, Paasche, and Carli indices do not meet the time reversal criterion, both the Fisher and Törnqvist indices do.

(A-8') Circularity

When the combination of price and quantity changes as $\left(\mathbf{q_0}, \mathbf{p_0}\right) \to \left(\mathbf{q_1}, \mathbf{p_1}\right) \to \left(\mathbf{q_2}, \mathbf{p_2}\right) \to \left(\mathbf{q_0}, \mathbf{p_0}\right)$, *the following equation holds:*

$$PI\left(\mathbf{q_0}, \mathbf{p_0}, \mathbf{q_1}, \mathbf{p_1}\right) PI\left(\mathbf{q_1}, \mathbf{p_1}, \mathbf{q_2}, \mathbf{p_2}\right) PI\left(\mathbf{q_2}, \mathbf{p_2}, \mathbf{q_0}, \mathbf{p_0}\right) = 1$$

There are varying definitions of the axiom "Circularity" among researchers. Balk (1980) and Eichhorn and Voeller (1976) treat it as synonymous with transitivity

[11] See Mizobuchi and Zelenyuk (2021) and Abe (2022), for example.

(A-8). On the other hand, Walsh (1901) employs the definition introduced in this book, (A-8'). To avoid confusion, this book distinguishes between, transitivity and circularity.

Obviously, if transitivity (A-8) is satisfied, circularity (A-8') is also met. The following theorem shows the relationship between circularity and transitivity.

Theorem 4.4.1 *If PI satisfies time reversal test (A-11) and circularity (A-8'), transitivity (A-8) is also satisfied.*

Proof
From (A-8'), we get

$$PI\left(\mathbf{q}_0, \mathbf{p}_0, \mathbf{q}_1, \mathbf{p}_1\right) PI\left(\mathbf{q}_1, \mathbf{p}_1, \mathbf{q}_2, \mathbf{p}_2\right) = \frac{1}{PI\left(\mathbf{q}_2, \mathbf{p}_2, \mathbf{q}_0, \mathbf{p}_0\right)} \tag{4.14}$$

Suppose time reversal test holds, then, we get

$$PI\left(\mathbf{q}_2, \mathbf{p}_2, \mathbf{q}_0, \mathbf{p}_0\right) PI\left(\mathbf{q}_0, \mathbf{p}_0, \mathbf{q}_2, \mathbf{p}_2\right) = 1 \tag{4.15}$$

Therefore, we get

$$\frac{1}{PI\left(\mathbf{q}_2, \mathbf{p}_2, \mathbf{q}_0, \mathbf{p}_0\right)} = PI\left(\mathbf{q}_0, \mathbf{p}_0, \mathbf{q}_2, \mathbf{p}_2\right)$$

Thus, we get

$$PI\left(\mathbf{q}_0, \mathbf{p}_0, \mathbf{q}_1, \mathbf{p}_1\right) PI\left(\mathbf{q}_1, \mathbf{p}_1, \mathbf{q}_2, \mathbf{p}_2\right) = PI\left(\mathbf{q}_0, \mathbf{p}_0, \mathbf{q}_2, \mathbf{p}_2\right) \tag{4.16}$$

This is transitivity, (A-8). (End of Proof)

(A-12) Invariance to Proportional Changes in Current Quantities
Even if the size of the quantity at the comparison changes proportionally, the price index does not change.

$$PI\left(\mathbf{q}_0, \mathbf{p}_0, \lambda\mathbf{q}_1, \mathbf{p}_1\right) = PI\left(\mathbf{q}_0, \mathbf{p}_0, \mathbf{q}_1, \mathbf{p}_1\right) \quad \text{for } \forall\, \lambda \in \mathbb{R}_{++}$$

This axiom is considered crucial when comparing price levels across countries. For instance, let us imagine a scenario where Germany is the reference country, and we are comparing it with multiple countries, like the United Kingdom and Ireland. Suppose the prices of all goods are identical in Ireland and England. If the economic scale of the England is larger than Ireland, with the quantity in England being exactly double that of Ireland, then axiom (A-12) dictates that the price indices between Germany and England, and Germany and Ireland, should be equal. This neutralizes the effect of size on price indices, which is particularly vital in international price comparisons.

In the context of time series data, seasonal fluctuations are observed, such as increased spending around Christmas and year-end. However, even in months with significantly higher expenditures due to seasonal variations, it's essential that the magnitude of these expenditures does not influence the index number.

The Walsh index can be characterized using the two axioms, (A-11) and (A-12). In other words, we can show the Walsh index is the only fixed basket index number formula that satisfies (A-11) and (A-12).

Theorem 4.4.2 *The Walsh index is the only linear mean index that satisfies the time reversal test of the price index and the invariance to the proportional changes in the quantity at the comparison point.*

Please see Mathematics Appendix B for the proof. The characterization of the Walsh index was first established by Diewert (2001). In his paper, Diewert allowed for prices to be zero, which excluded the geometric mean index such as Jevons index, Törnqvist index, and Sato–Vartia index from consideration. Abe and Rao (2022a, 2022b) provided a characterization of the multilateral Walsh index even when the price index is defined over strictly positive values. The proof presented in Mathematical Appendix B is the bilateral case of the more general theorem by Abe and Rao (2022a, 2022b).

The problem with the Walsh index lies in the fact that when the quantity of a product drops to zero at either the comparison or base, the product's weight becomes zero, which means disregarding its price information. Consequently, it can be asserted that the Walsh index is appropriate for products or aggregated category units where the quantity does not become to zero. However, for high-frequency scanner data, where zero quantity occurrences are common, the Walsh index proves to be of limited applicability.

4.5 Characterization of the Fisher Index

In modern index number theory, special focus is given to the Fisher and Törnqvist indices. Numerous efforts have been made to derive these two indices based on axioms. However, unlike the derivation of the Cobb–Douglas and Walsh indices, formulating these two indices as necessary and sufficient conditions from multiple axioms has not always been fruitful. While it is feasible to enumerate the characteristics of functions that result in these two indices, considering these characteristics as axioms—inherently correct or desirable—incorporates some unnatural aspects. In this section, we will examine the characterization of the Fisher index. Various sets of axioms that lead to the Fisher index have been proposed. To begin, let us introduce the following "axioms."

(A-13) Value Dependence

There is a function $f : \mathbb{R}_{++}^{4n} \to \mathbb{R}_{++}$ that satisfies the following:

$$PI\left(\mathbf{q_0}, \mathbf{p_0}, \mathbf{q_1}, \mathbf{p_1}\right) = f\left(\mathbf{p_0^{'}q_0}, \mathbf{p_0^{'}q_1}, \mathbf{p_1^{'}q_0}, \mathbf{p_1^{'}q_1}\right)$$

This property suggests that the price index can be represented as a function of the total expenditures in periods 0 and 1, and the hypothetical expenditure amounts when purchasing the quantities of period 1 at period 0 prices, and vice versa. The idea of shifting the time periods of prices and quantities resonates with the Laspeyres and Paasche formulas. It is difficult to argue that an index number that does not satisfy this axiom is flawed. However, imposing this axiom allows us to easily derive the Fisher index, as per the following theorem.

Theorem 4.5.1 *The only index,* $PI : \mathbb{R}_{++}^{4n} \to \mathbb{R}_{++}$*, that satisfies linear homogeneity (A-2), factor reversal test (A-10), and value dependence (A-13) is the following Fisher index.*

$$PI\left(\mathbf{q_0}, \mathbf{p_0}, \mathbf{q_1}, \mathbf{p_1}\right) = \sqrt{\left(\frac{\sum p_{i1}q_{i0}}{\sum p_{i0}q_{i0}}\right)\left(\frac{\sum p_{i1}q_{i1}}{\sum p_{i0}q_{1}}\right)} \tag{4.17}$$

See Balk (1995) for the proof.

Furthermore, we will introduce two more theorems for characterizing the Fisher index.[12]

Theorem 4.5.2 *Among functions,* $PI : \mathbb{R}_{++}^{4N} \to \mathbb{R}_{++}$*, only the Fisher index satisfies factor reversal test (A-10), time reversal test (A- 11), and the following functional equation.*

$$PI\left(\mathbf{q_0}, \mathbf{p_0}, \mathbf{q_1}, \mathbf{p_1}\right) = \frac{1}{PI\left(\mathbf{q_0}, \mathbf{p_1}, \mathbf{q_1}, \mathbf{p_0}\right)}$$

Theorem 4.5.3 *Among functions,* $PI : \mathbb{R}_{++}^{4N} \to \mathbb{R}_{++}$*, only the Fisher index satisfies identity (A-3), factor reversal test (A-10), and the following functional equation:*

$$\frac{PI\left(\mathbf{q_0}, \mathbf{p_0}, \mathbf{q_1}, \mathbf{p_1}\right)}{PI\left(\mathbf{q_0}, \mathbf{p_0}, \mathbf{q_0}, \mathbf{p_1}\right)} = \frac{PI\left(\mathbf{q_0}, \mathbf{p_0}, \mathbf{q_1}, \mathbf{p_1}\right)}{PI\left(\mathbf{q_0}, \mathbf{p_0}, \mathbf{q_1}, \mathbf{p_0}\right)}.$$

Several more different characterizations of the Fisher index have been carried out based on various axioms.[13] However, in addition to factor reversal test and time reversal test, there is always some unnatural axiom imposed. These appear to be axioms or properties devised specifically to derive the Fisher index. Nonetheless, such characterizations are very useful for understanding the mathematical structure of the Fisher index. Those interested should refer to the CPI Manual for more details.

[12] For the proof of these theorems, refer to Balk (2008).

[13] See Balk (2008) and Eichhorn and Voeller (1976) for more discussions.

4.6 Characterization of the Sato–Vartia and the Törnqvist Indices

Several characterizations have been established for the Törnqvist index and the Sato–Vartia index, both of which represent types of geometric mean indices. Particularly in cases involving just two variables, Abe and Rao (2019) showed that the Sato–Vartia index can be derived exclusively through the application of factor reversal and linear homogeneity to geometric mean-type indices.

Theorem 4.6.1 *Let $N = 2$. Then, the Sato–Vartia is the only index that belongs to the class of the following geometric mean price index:*

$$PI\left(\mathbf{q_0}, \mathbf{p_0}, \mathbf{q_1}, \mathbf{p_1}\right) = \prod_{i=1}^{2} \left(\frac{p_{i1}}{p_{i0}}\right)^{\phi_i}, 0 \leq \phi_i, \sum_i \phi_i = 1$$

and satisfies factor reversal test (A-10).

Proof
Applying the factor reversal property to the geometric mean index, we get

$$\ln\left(\frac{p_{11}q_{11} + p_{21}q_{21}}{p_{10}q_{10} + p_{20}q_{20}}\right) - \phi_1 \ln \frac{p_{11}}{p_{10}} - \phi_2 \ln \frac{p_{21}}{p_{20}} - \phi_1 \ln \frac{q_{11}}{q_{10}} - \phi_2 \ln \frac{q_{21}}{q_{20}} = 0 \tag{4.18}$$

We can rewrite the above as

$$\phi_1 \ln \frac{w_{11}}{w_{10}} + \phi_2 \ln \frac{w_{21}}{w_{20}} = 0 \tag{4.19}$$

Therefore, by solving the simultaneous equations, $\phi_1 + \phi_2 = 1$ and (4.19), ϕ_i becomes the weight of the Sato–Vartia index, that is, the logarithmic average of the expenditure shares scaled so that the sum is 1. (End of Proof)

When the number of products is 3 or more, there is a price index that is a linearly homogeneous geometric mean index that satisfies factor reversal, but is not a Sato–Vartia index.[14] Fattore (2010) characterizes the Sato–Vartia index by restricting it to a class of functional forms called geo-Logarithms price indices.[15]

Several characterizations of the Törnqvist index have been presented, but here we will introduce a simple one by Balk and Diewert (2001).

---

[14] Abe and Rao (2019) introduce an example of a geometric mean-type index that is not a Sato–Vartia index but satisfies factor reversal test when the number of commodities is greater than or equal to 3.

[15] See Białek (2019) for more discussion on geo-logarithmic price indices.

Theorem 4.6.2 *Consider the following geometric mean-type index.*

$$PI(\mathbf{q_0}, \mathbf{p_0}, \mathbf{q_1}, \mathbf{p_1}) = \prod_{i=1}^{N} \left(\frac{p_{i1}}{p_{i0}}\right)^{\phi_i(w_{i0}, w_{i1})}, 0 \leq \phi_i(w_{i0}, w_{i1}), \sum_{i}^{N} \phi_i(w_{i0}, w_{i1}) = 1$$

Then, the only geometric mean-type index number that satisfies the time reversal test (A-11) is the Törnqvist index. Note that w_{it} is the share of spending on good i in period t.

For the proof, see Balk and Diewert (2001).

Theorem 4.6.2 necessitates only linear homogeneity and time reversal properties. While the Sato–Vartia index, a geometric mean-type index, satisfies linear homogeneity and time reversal, it does not qualify under Theorem 4.6.2 due to its weights not adhering to the theorem's specified functional form. The weights in the Sato–Vartia index are normalized to ensure their sum equals one. Specifically, the weight for commodity i in the Sato–Vartia index is defined as $s_i = \frac{L(w_{i0}, w_{i1})}{\sum_i L(w_{i0}, w_{i1})}$, where $L(w_{i0}, w_{i1}) = \frac{w_{i1} - w_{i0}}{\ln(w_{i1}) - \ln(w_{i0})}$ if $w_{i0} \neq w_{i1}$. The denominator of the weights, $\sum_i L(w_{i0}, w_{i1})$, incorporates information from commodities other than i. Theorem 4.6.2 states that the weight of good i in the price index depends only on the expenditure share of good *i,* which excludes the Sato–Vartia index from this assumption.

Diewert (2021) found a way to characterize the Törnqvist index without assuming the geometric mean type in advance. There, the price index is defined as a function of the amount of expenditure and price for each product instead of the quantity, $PI(\mathbf{v_0}, \mathbf{p_0}, \mathbf{v_1}, \mathbf{p_1})$, and is based on time reversal, identity, commensurability, and the independence from the size of quantities at the comparison period that is used for characterization of the Walsh index. He then proves that the Törnqvist index can be characterized by 17 axioms. At first glance, this characterization seems very natural, but the problem lies in the definition of the price index. For example, Diewert (2021) describes linear homogeneity for any positive real number λ,

$$PI(\mathbf{v_0}, \mathbf{p_0}, \mathbf{v_1}, \lambda\mathbf{p_1}) = \lambda PI(\mathbf{v_0}, \mathbf{p_0}, \mathbf{v_1}, \mathbf{p_1}), \lambda \in \mathbb{R}_{++}$$

That is, it is assumed that even if all commodity prices in the first period are multiplied by λ, the amount of expenditure in the first period will not change at all. When considering a price index that depends on a standard quantity vector, a very special case is assumed in which the price is multiplied by λ and the quantity is multiplied by $1/\lambda$ at the same time. As with the characterization of the Fisher index, no axioms imposing strong and unnatural constraints on the function form are used here. However, the very definition of the price index assumes a function form where quantities and prices move in tandem, which in itself might not be considered a convincing specification.

4.7 Summary Regarding the Axiomatic Approach

The axiomatic approach involves enumerating "axioms" or "tests" that an index number formula must fulfill and identifying a formula that possesses these properties. When only one index satisfies these criteria, we say that the index number formula is characterized by the set of axioms. Regrettably, every known specification of the index number formula includes at least one axiom that seems unnatural, except for Theorem 4.3.1, which deduces the Cobb–Douglas-type formula. While Theorem 4.3.2, which defines the Walsh index, does not feature any unnatural axioms, it restricts the index number formula to a fixed basket type.[16] Although the fixed basket type is straightforward and historically prevalent, it is not necessary to confine the index number formula to this category.

As will be explored in Chap. 6, the Törnqvist index and the Fisher index are closely aligned with economic theory and are often referred to as the superlative indices. The Fisher index, in particular, is highly esteemed among index number formulas and is known as the ideal formula or Fisher's ideal index. For instance, the CPI manual suggests that the Fisher index is superior because it fulfills 20 axioms, in contrast to the Törnqvist index, which meets only 11. Indeed, it is accurate that both the Törnqvist index and the Sato–Vartia index do not satisfy the monotonicity axiom, that is, both indices are not monotonically increasing with respect to the prices at comparison periods.[17] Additionally, the Törnqvist index and the Walsh index fail to meet the criterion of factor reversal test. In this regard, the Fisher index is indeed a preferable choice. However, of the 20 axioms referenced in the CPI manual, the ones known as quantity reversal test and price reversal test are included.

(AA-1) Quantity Reversal Test
The price index does not change even if the quantity vectors at the base time and comparison time are exchanged, i.e.,

$$PI(\mathbf{q}_0, \mathbf{p}_0, \mathbf{q}_1, \mathbf{p}_1) = PI(\mathbf{q}_1, \mathbf{p}_0, \mathbf{q}_0, \mathbf{p}_1)$$

(AA-2) Price Reversal test
The implicit quantity index does not change even if the price vectors at the base time and the comparison time are exchanged, i.e.,

$$\frac{\mathbf{q}_1'\mathbf{p}_1}{\mathbf{q}_0'\mathbf{p}_0 \times PI(\mathbf{q}_0, \mathbf{p}_0, \mathbf{q}_1, \mathbf{p}_1)} = \frac{\mathbf{q}_1'\mathbf{p}_0}{\mathbf{q}_0'\mathbf{p}_1 \times PI(\mathbf{q}_0, \mathbf{p}_1, \mathbf{q}_1, \mathbf{p}_0)}.$$

Imposing these two reversal conditions on the price index would exclude the Törnqvist and Sato–Vartia indices. Utilizing these axioms also facilitates the charac-

[16] Krtscha (1984) gave us a characterization of the Marshall–Edgeworth index, another famous fixed basket index number.

[17] The fact that both indices do not satisfy monotonicity will be discussed in detail in Chap. 6.

terization of the Fisher index.[18] However, the significance of enforcing such reversal conditions is not immediately clear. Some may find it challenging to interpret the Törnqvist index as inferior to the Fisher index just because it doesn't satisfy these two axioms.

In the axiomatic approach, the results are distinctly binary in that: axioms are either fulfilled or not. Take the Törnqvist index, for example, which fails to satisfy the monotonicity axiom. However, it is quite rare for the Törnqvist index to become a decreasing function with respect to comparison point price. Therefore, even if it does not meet the axiom, as long as this infrequency does not lead to significant practical problems, the non-compliance with the axiom might not be a major flaw.

The domain of the function is crucial in the axiomatic approach. In this chapter, the price index is conceptualized as a function that depends on the price and quantity vectors from both the base and comparison periods. This conceptualization hinders the price index from reflecting disparities in the amount of information between these periods. To demonstrate this, consider the Lowe index, like the one mentioned below, where the weighting is based on a quantity from a different time point (such as the average quantity over the last 5 years) within a fixed basket framework.

$$\textbf{Lowe Price Index}\,(0, 1) = \frac{\sum_i p_{it} q_i^*}{\sum_i p_{i0} q_i^*}$$

Does this Lowe index satisfy commensurability? In this chapter's definition (A-5), the price and quantity are multiplied by a parameter to change the unit of measurement of the product. Since q_i^* is not a quantity at base or comparison periods, it cannot be multiplied by parameters to change the unit of measurement according to the definition of the commensurability. Therefore, the Lowe index does not satisfy commensurability. However, most likely, statistical practitioners who create Lowe indices would change the units of their weights when the units of measurement change. This means that the functional form of the Lowe index does not belong to the class of price index functions considered in this chapter. For example, in this chapter, indices with transitivity are limited to Cobb–Douglas and Jevons indices. However, it is possible to create an index number that satisfies transitivity by changing the domain of the function. For example, in the above Lowe index, if we allow the weights, q_i^*, to change as the unit of measurement changes, the Lowe index will have the properties of transitivity, monotonicity, identity, and linear homogeneity required by Theorem 4.3.1. This example suggests that by broadening the domain of the price index, there is considerable scope for further exploration within the axiomatic approach. In Chap. 8, we will discuss multilateral index numbers that have broader domains than the bilateral price index numbers in this chapter.

In the realm of price index number theory, the contribution of the axiomatic approach has been significant in clarifying the mathematical characteristics of index numbers and enhancing the analytical capabilities of index researchers by introducing

[18] For the proof, see Funke and Voeller (1978).

them to the method of functional equations. Some of the various hypotheses that Walsh and Frisch intuitively held at the beginning of the twentieth century have become provable in mathematics through the use of functional equations. While the economic approach discussed in the next chapter imposes strong constraints on the domain of the index, the axiomatic approach, which places minimal restrictions on the domain, possesses a generality. If clear conclusions can be drawn using this approach, it would be more significant compared to other approaches. Given its discussion in a general function space, it can be said that the axiomatic approach continues to hold a central position in current index number theory.

4.8 Supplement 1: Aggregation Consistency

4.8.1 What is Aggregation Consistency?

The concept of "Aggregation Consistency" also referred to as additive consistency, presented in this supplement, has gained significant emphasis in index number research, particularly in the context of national accounts.[19] Research on prices and national aggregates, such as gross domestic products, often concentrates on identifying which products, groups, or items have had a substantial impact on the overall change in price (or production volume). For instance, when the overall price index increases by 10%, the nature of corresponding policies and their impact will vary, depending on whether this increase is due to a rise in fresh food and energy prices, or if there's a uniform increase across all products. Aggregation consistency is an axiom that demands the division of products into various groups, ensuring that the prices calculated for each group collectively correspond to the total. Without aggregation consistency in the price index, in an extreme scenario, a 10% increase in food item prices and a 5% increase in non-food item prices could result in an overall price rise that doesn't fall between 5% and 10%; it could be as high as 12% or as low as 3%. The same principle applies to quantity indices; when the gross domestic product, a quantity index, changes by 10%, the rate of change in its components may not align with the overall rate of change in the gross domestic product.

Let's define the concept of "Aggregation Consistency" here, in line with Balk (2008). First, let A represent the set of goods. For example, if the price index consists of 500 types of goods, the number of elements in A will be 500. Then, this set of goods A is partitioned into mutually exclusive and exhaustive groups. Specifically,

[19] There exist several interpretations of aggregation consistency. In this case, we have adopted the approach of Balk (2008), but von Auer and Wengenroth (2021) have recently endeavored to express it in a more generalized form. Pertaining to this attribute, Kurabayashi and Sakuma 1990) have devised a distinct formulation employing matrices, proving beneficial for the comparison of international prices.

consider the following division:

$$A = \bigcup_{k=1}^{K} A_k, \; A_k \cap A_l = \phi \quad \text{if} \quad k \neq l \tag{4.20}$$

For example, let's categorize the 500 types of products into groups like fresh foods, processed foods, and clothing. It is feasible to construct a price index exclusively for fresh foods using data from dozens of fresh food types, or, alternatively, to calculate a price index that omits fresh foods. Indeed, in monetary policy decision-making, the core inflation index, which excludes fresh food, is deemed significant. Aggregation consistency falls into two scenarios: one where the price index is calculated at once using information on all products, and another where the price index for each group is computed first, then each group's index is treated as a price for the category for further calculations. When constructing a composite price index based on these indices, it's necessary that both price indices yield identical values. The challenge here is that a standard price index is based on price and quantity information at two time points, but when building a second-stage price index, its elements are not derived from prices at two time points, but rather from price indices that spans two time points.

Let us take the price index, $PI_{Nk}(\mathbf{q_{k0}}, \mathbf{p_{k0}}, \mathbf{q_{k1}}, \mathbf{p_{k1}})$, for a group of goods k. The elements of this index are vectors of prices and quantities in good group k. Next, let V_{kt} be the total expenditure on goods group k at time t. The second-stage price index is defined as a function of the total expenditure for each group and the price index for each group. Specifically, the second-stage price index is defined as follows:

$$PI_N(\mathbf{q_0}, \mathbf{p_0}, \mathbf{q_1}, \mathbf{p_1}) = PI_K\left(PI_{Nk}(\mathbf{q_{k0}}, \mathbf{p_{k0}}, \mathbf{q_{k1}}, \mathbf{p_{k1}}), V_{k0}, V_{k1}\right); k = 1, ..., K \tag{4.21}$$

For example, in many countries, consumer price index, the Dutot or the Jevons index is used in the lower aggregation, i.e., goods group k, and the Laspeyres index is used in the second level, i.e., the higher aggregation. The Laspeyres index used in the second stage is a function of the expenditure share and price ratio for each good group at the time of comparison, so if we write the two-stage process all at once, it becomes as follows:

$$\begin{aligned} PI_N^*(\mathbf{q_0}, \mathbf{p_0}, \mathbf{q_1}, \mathbf{p_1}) &= \sum_k \frac{V_{k0}}{\sum_s V_{s0}} PI_{Nk}(\mathbf{q_{k0}}, \mathbf{p_{k0}}, \mathbf{q_{k1}}, \mathbf{p_{k1}}) \\ &= \sum_k \frac{V_{k0}}{\sum_s V_{s0}} \left(\frac{\sum_s p_{s1}}{\sum_s p_{s0}}\right) \end{aligned} \tag{4.22}$$

Th problem is that this second-stage index PI^*_N can depend on the method of dividing goods used in the first stage. In other words, the value of the overall price index depends on whether fresh food and processed food are separated as different food groups, or whether they are combined into a food category, or whether clothing is separated into men's and women's clothing.

Is there really a two-stage aggregation method that does not depend on the category division method, that is, aggregation consistent? In fact, the well-known Laspeyres index and Paasche index are known to be independent of the aggregation method. If you use the Laspeyres index for both upper and lower level aggregations, we get the following equations:

$$\sum_k \frac{V_{k0}}{\sum_s V_{s0}} \left(\frac{\sum_s p_{s1}}{\sum_s p_{s0}} \right) = \sum_k \frac{V_{k0}}{\sum_s V_{s0}} PI_{Nk} \left(\mathbf{q_{k0}}, \mathbf{p_{k0}}, \mathbf{q_{k0}}, \mathbf{p_{k1}} \right) \tag{4.23}$$

$$= \sum_k \frac{V_{k0}}{\sum_s V_{s0}} \frac{\sum_i p_{i0} q_{i0}}{V_{k0}} \frac{p_{i1}}{p_{i0}} \tag{4.24}$$

$$= \sum_i \frac{p_{i0} q_{i0}}{\sum_s V_{s0}} \frac{p_{i1}}{p_{i0}} \tag{4.25}$$

The outcome is the weighted average of price ratios, calculated using the share of expenditure at the base time, namely, the Laspeyres index. The value of the price index at the second stage is independent of the grouping method used at the first stage. By applying the Paasche index at both the upper and lower levels, it can be demonstrated that the index's value is unaffected by the method of division. However, for the Fisher index, Törnqvist index, Sato–Vartia index, Walsh index, Jevons index, Dutot index, and Carli index, if the same formula is applied at both levels, the index value will vary depending on the division method. Among index number formulas that are not influenced by the division method, the Lowe index is recognized as an alternative to the Laspeyres–Paasche index. Additionally, the Vartia Type I index and the Stuvel index are also known to satisfy the aggregation consistency. The logarithm value of Vartia I was given below:

$$\ln PI = \sum_i \frac{L \left(p_{i0} q_{i0}, p_{i1} q_{i1} \right)}{L \left(\sum_i p_{i0} q_{i0}, \sum_i p_{i1} q_{i1} \right)} \left(\ln p_{i1} - \ln p_{i0} \right) \tag{4.26}$$

Or, we can write (4.26) as follows:

$$L \left(\sum_i p_{i0} q_{i0}, \sum_i p_{i1} q_{i1} \right) \ln PI = \sum_i L \left(p_{i0} q_{i0}, p_{i1} q_{i1} \right) \left(\ln p_{i1} - \ln p_{i0} \right) \tag{4.27}$$

Here, if we replace the log price differences on the right side with the first-stage price index,

$$L\left(\sum_i p_{i0}q_{i0}, \sum_i p_{i1}q_{i1}\right) \ln PI^* \tag{4.28}$$

$$= \sum_k L\left(V_{k0}, V_{k1}\right)\left(\ln PI_k\right) \tag{4.29}$$

$$= \sum_k L\left(V_{k0}, V_{k1}\right)\left(\frac{1}{L\left(V_{k0}, V_{k1}\right)} \sum_i L\left(V_{i0}, V_{i1}\right)\left(\ln p_{i1} - \ln p_{i0}\right)\right) \tag{4.30}$$

$$= \sum_i L\left(V_{i0}, V_{i1}\right) n \left(\ln p_{i1} - \ln p_{i0}\right) \tag{4.31}$$

This shows that, like the Laspeyres index, the second-stage price Vartia I index does not depend on the first-stage grouping.

The Stuvel index exists as a rare index that satisfies both factor reversal and aggregation consistency. This index formula is complex, and the price index number formula is given as follows:

$$PI^{SV} = \frac{PI^L - QI^L}{2} + \sqrt{\left(\frac{QI^L - PI^L}{2}\right)^2 + \frac{V_1}{V_0}} \tag{4.32}$$

The quantity index is

$$QI^{SV} = \frac{QI^L - PI^L}{2} + \sqrt{\left(\frac{QI^L - PI^L}{2}\right)^2 + \frac{V_1}{V_0}} \tag{4.33}$$

where QI^L, PI^L, and V_1/V_0 are the Laspeyres quantity index, Paasche price index, and value index, respectively. In essence, despite its complex form, the Stuvel index can be easily computed using Laspeyres and Paasche's price/quantity indices. For a detailed proof that this index adheres to factor reversal and aggregation consistency, refer to Stuvel (1989) and Vogt (1981), and for its characterization, see Balk (1996). A notable issue with this index, apart from its complexity, is its lack of linear homogeneity in terms of quantity and price. This means that even if all prices double, the price index does not necessarily double. The same applies to the Vartia I index.

At a glance, Eq. (4.33) might not resemble a traditional price, but in practice, its value often aligns closely with the Fisher index. Table 4.1 presents the consumer price index, excluding imputed rent, calculated using various index formulas based on the Japanese Household Survey and item-specific price indices. Stuvel index is almost identical up to one decimal place to the Fisher and Törnqvist indices.

Table 4.1 Comparison of price indices

	Laspeyres	Paasche	Jevons	Fisher	Törnqvist	SV	Stuvel
2018	100.00	100.00	100.00	100.00	100.00	100.00	100.00
2019	100.49	100.25	99.37	100.37	100.38	100.39	100.37
2020	101.44	100.80	100.87	101.12	101.15	101.17	101.12
2021	100.38	99.60	101.14	99.99	100.02	100.00	100.00
2022	101.58	97.90	102.28	99.72	100.06	100.04	99.72

Note This table is based on the consumer price index at the elementary level and the Family Income and Expenditure Survey provided by the Statistics Bureau of Japan. Calculations were performed by the author. The base period for this data is January 2018. The index values represent the figures for each January of the respective years.

4.8.2 Some Issues on Aggregation Consistency

It is difficult to formulate aggregate consistency like other axioms. Vartia (1976), who pointed out the importance of aggregate consistency half a century ago, defined aggregate consistency as follows.

(A-14) Aggregation Consistency (p. 124 Vartia, 1976)
First the price indices (and possibly the volume indices) are calculated for every subset A_k of the partition. Thereafter the total index for A is calculated, using the subindices and the same index formula, from the aggregate data for the subsets. An index formula is consistent in aggregation if the value of the index as calculated in two stages necessarily coincides with the value of the index as calculated in an ordinary way.

Regrettably, this definition of aggregate consistency includes ambiguous elements when compared to other axioms. The first- and second-stage price indices differ in their domains and typically involve a varying number of variables. This raises the question of how to define the "same index formula" in such cases. Additionally, while the first stage price index is defined by quantity and price vectors, the second-stage price index is a function of expenditure amounts and prices, indicating a fundamental difference in the nature of the variables. von Auer and Wengenroth (2021) attempt to provide a precise, unambiguous definition of aggregate consistency, but this definition is quite complex and challenging to handle in the same manner as other axioms. The reason this section is an appendix to the axiomatic approach is due to the ambiguous nature of the "axiom" definition for aggregate consistency and the ongoing debate over the axiom's importance or the necessity for aggregate consistency. For instance, the CPI Manual published in 2004 (ILO et al. 2004) despite being over 500 pages long, offers only a brief discussion on aggregate consistency, even suggesting that "aggregate consistency may not be important."[20] It has an added negative connotation. On the other hand, in national accounts, the importance of aggregation consistency has been strongly emphasized.[21] The requirement for aggregation consistency, like the requirement for transitivity, is an extremely strong requirement for index number formulas, and there are only a few indices that satisfy this requirement. When actually creating the consumer price index, different index formulas are used for lower level and higher level aggregations, and there is no consideration for consistency in aggregation. Therefore, the lack of aggregation consistency in the higher level aggregation might not be a big problem.

However, when analyzing the consumer price index by categorizing it into segments like food, durable goods, and services, the absence of aggregation consistency can lead to discrepancies between the category-specific price index and the overall index. This potential inconsistency should always be considered. Additionally, as discussed in Chap. 7, even the Laspeyres and Paasche indices lack aggregation consistency in the context of chain indices. Nowadays, chained indices are extensively utilized in many countries for price indices, suggesting that in such nations, there is an absence of aggregation consistency in both the gross domestic product and the price index. On the flip side, quantifying the extent of inconsistency caused by a lack of aggregation consistency is not straightforward. Defining aggregate consistency precisely is challenging in itself, and it remains an area fraught with numerous unresolved issues.

4.9 Supplement 2: Other Axioms

Here we introduce axioms that were introduced in the C PI Manual (2020) but were not discussed in this chapter.

(AA-3) Positive Sign

The price index takes a strictly positive value

$$PI\left(\mathbf{q}_0, \mathbf{p}_0, \mathbf{q}_1, \mathbf{p}_1\right) > 0$$

(AA-4) Fixed Basket

If the quantity is the same between two points in time, the price index must be consistent with the fixed basket method.

$$PI\left(\mathbf{q}_0, \mathbf{p}_0, \mathbf{q}_0, \mathbf{p}_1\right) = \frac{\sum_i p_{i1} q_i}{\sum_i p_{i0} q_i}$$

[20] It may be argued, however, that consistency in aggregation is not necessarily an important or even appropriate criterion, or that it is unachievable when the amount of information available on quantities and expenditures is not the same at the different levels of aggregation (p. 160).

[21] See Kurabayashi and Sakuma (1990) on the consistency of aggregation in System of National Account.

Note that if we adopt (AA-4), indices that use the geometric mean will be eliminated.

(AA-5) Negative Linear Homogeneity Regarding Base Price

$$PI(\mathbf{q}_0, \lambda\mathbf{p}_0, \mathbf{q}_1, \mathbf{p}_1) = \frac{1}{\lambda} PI(\mathbf{q}_0, \mathbf{p}_0, \mathbf{q}_1, \mathbf{p}_1) \quad \text{for } \forall\lambda \in \mathbb{R}_{++}$$

(AA-6) Invariance Regarding Quantity during Comparison

$$PI(\lambda\mathbf{q}_0, \mathbf{p}_0, \mathbf{q}_1, \mathbf{p}_1) = PI(\mathbf{q}_0, \mathbf{p}_0, \mathbf{q}_1, \mathbf{p}_1) \quad \text{for } \forall\lambda \in \mathbb{R}_{++}$$

(AA-7) Intermediateness Regarding Quantity

$$\min\left(\frac{q_{11}}{q_{10}}, \frac{q_{21}}{q_{20}}, \ldots, \frac{q_{N1}}{q_{N0}}\right) \leq \frac{\mathbf{q}_1'\mathbf{p}_1}{\mathbf{q}_0'\mathbf{p}_0 \times PI(\mathbf{q}_0, \mathbf{p}_0, \mathbf{q}_1, \mathbf{p}_1)} \leq \max\left(\frac{q_{11}}{q_{10}}, \frac{q_{21}}{q_{20}}, \ldots, \frac{q_{N1}}{q_{N0}}\right)$$

(AA-8) Laspeyres–Paasche Boundedness
The price index lies between the Laspeyres price index and the Paasche price index.

In general, geometric mean-type indices do not satisfy the above axiom. Instead of (AA-8), if we impose that the index must be between Geometric Laspeyres and Geometric Paasche indices, then the Fisher index does not satisfy such an axiom, while the Törnqvist index does.

(AA-9) Monotonicity Regarding Quantity
The implicit quantity index is a strictly increasing function with respect to $\mathbf{q}_1$ *while it is a strictly decreasing function with respect to* $\mathbf{q}_0$, *i.e.,*

$$\frac{\mathbf{q}'\mathbf{p}_1}{\mathbf{q}_0'\mathbf{p}_0 \times PI(\mathbf{q}_0, \mathbf{p}_0, \mathbf{q}, \mathbf{p}_1)} > \frac{\mathbf{q}_1'\mathbf{p}_1}{\mathbf{q}_0'\mathbf{p}_0 \times PI(\mathbf{q}_0, \mathbf{p}_0, \mathbf{q}_1, \mathbf{p}_1)} \quad \text{if } \mathbf{q} \geq \mathbf{q}_1$$

$$\frac{\mathbf{q}_1'\mathbf{p}_1}{\mathbf{q}_0'\mathbf{p}_0 \times PI(\mathbf{q}_0, \mathbf{p}_0, \mathbf{q}_1, \mathbf{p}_1)} < \frac{\mathbf{q}_1'\mathbf{p}_1}{\mathbf{q}_0'\mathbf{p}_0 \times PI(\mathbf{q}_0, \mathbf{p}_0, \mathbf{q}_1, \mathbf{p}_1)} \quad \text{if } \mathbf{q} \leq \mathbf{q}_0$$

(AA-10) Goods Reversal Test
Let $\boldsymbol{p}^*$ *represent a reordering of goods in* $\boldsymbol{p}$, *and* $\boldsymbol{q}^*$ *denote a reordering of goods in* $\boldsymbol{q}$ *that is consistent with the prices. Under these circumstances, the following relation is maintained:*

$$PI(\mathbf{q}_0^*, \mathbf{p}_0^*, \mathbf{q}_1^*, \mathbf{p}_1^*) = PI(\mathbf{q}_0, \mathbf{p}_0, \mathbf{q}_1, \mathbf{p}_1)$$

This implies all the goods must be treated symmetrically in the index number formula. For instance, if there's a need to assign a greater weight to a specific good compared to others, it can be accomplished by basing it solely on the quantity or (and) price information of that good at either the base time or the comparison time. When considering a Cobb–Douglas index, only the Jevons index fulfills the criterion of (AA-10).

4.10 Mathematics Appendix A: Proof of Theorem 4.3.3

Theorem 4.3.3 *Let $N > 1$. There is no function, $PI : \mathbb{R}_{++}^{4N} \to \mathbb{R}_{++}$, that simultaneously satisfies identity (A-3), transitivity (A-8), and factor reversal (A-10).*

Proof

This proof is based on Balk (2008), but a few additional equations have been added to clarify the derivation process of several formula.

If transitivity holds, the following equation must hold:

$$PI\left(\mathbf{q}_0, \mathbf{p}_0, \mathbf{q}_1, \mathbf{p}_1\right) PI\left(\mathbf{q}_1, \mathbf{p}_1, \mathbf{q}_2, \mathbf{p}_2\right) = PI\left(\mathbf{q}_0, \mathbf{p}_0, \mathbf{q}_2, \mathbf{p}_2\right)$$

Thus, we get

$$PI\left(\mathbf{q}_0, \mathbf{p}_0, \mathbf{q}_1, \mathbf{p}_1\right) = \frac{PI\left(\mathbf{q}_0, \mathbf{p}_0, \mathbf{q}_2, \mathbf{p}_2\right)}{PI\left(\mathbf{q}_1, \mathbf{p}_1, \mathbf{q}_2, \mathbf{p}_2\right)} \tag{4A.1}$$

The left-hand side of (4A.1) does not depend on the information from the second period. Therefore, we can write

$$PI\left(\mathbf{q}_0, \mathbf{p}_0, \mathbf{q}_1, \mathbf{p}_1\right) = \frac{g\left(\mathbf{q}_1, \mathbf{p}_1\right)}{g\left(\mathbf{q}_0, \mathbf{p}_0\right)} \tag{4A.2}$$

$$PI\left(\mathbf{q}_0, \mathbf{p}_0, \mathbf{q}_1, \mathbf{p}_1\right) = \frac{g\left(\mathbf{q}_1, \mathbf{p}_1\right)}{g\left(\mathbf{q}_0, \mathbf{p}_0\right)} \tag{4A.3}$$

Since identity is satisfied, we can get

$$PI\left(\mathbf{q}_0, \mathbf{p}_0, \mathbf{q}_1, \mathbf{p}_1\right) = \frac{g\left(\mathbf{q}_1, \mathbf{p}_0\right)}{g\left(\mathbf{q}_0, \mathbf{p}_0\right)} = 1 \tag{4A.4}$$

$$g\left(\mathbf{q}_1, \mathbf{p}_0\right) = g\left(\mathbf{q}_0, \mathbf{p}_0\right) \tag{4A.5}$$

Equation (4A.5) holds true for any $(\mathbf{q}_1, \mathbf{q}_0)$. Thus, the function g does not depend on the quantity vector. Therefore, we can introduce a new function h such that

$$g\left(\mathbf{p}, \mathbf{x}\right) = h\left(\mathbf{p}\right) \tag{4A.6}$$

Therefore, we get

$$PI(\mathbf{q_0}, \mathbf{p_0}, \mathbf{q_1}, \mathbf{p_1}) = \frac{h(\mathbf{p_1})}{h(\mathbf{p_0})} \tag{4A.7}$$

Here, if factor reversal test holds, then

$$\frac{h(\mathbf{p_1})}{h(\mathbf{p_0})}\frac{h(\mathbf{q_1})}{h(\mathbf{q_0})} = \frac{\mathbf{p}_1'\mathbf{q_1}}{\mathbf{p}_0'\mathbf{q_0}} \tag{4A.8}$$

Therefore,

$$h(\mathbf{p_1})\,h(\mathbf{q_1}) = h(\mathbf{p_0})\,h(\mathbf{q_0}) \times \frac{\mathbf{p}_1'\mathbf{q_1}}{\mathbf{p}_0'\mathbf{q_0}}$$

$$= b \times \mathbf{p}_1'\mathbf{q_1}$$

where b can be any positive value. Let's assume $h(\mathbf{1_n}) = \alpha > 0$. At this time, if price and quantity are all 1, then, we get

$$h(\mathbf{p_1}) = b \times \mathbf{p}_1'\mathbf{1_n}\frac{1}{\alpha} \tag{4A.9}$$

Substituting this into $h(\mathbf{p_1})\,h(\mathbf{q_1}) = b \times \mathbf{p}_1'\mathbf{q_1}$

$$h(\mathbf{p_1})\,h(\mathbf{q_1}) = b \times \mathbf{p}_1'\mathbf{1_n}\frac{1}{\alpha} \times \left(b \times \mathbf{1}_\mathbf{n}'\mathbf{q_1}\frac{1}{\alpha}\right)$$

$$= \frac{b^2}{\alpha^2}\left(\mathbf{p}_1'\mathbf{1_n}\right) \times \left(\mathbf{1}_\mathbf{n}'\mathbf{q_1}\right)$$

$$= b \times \mathbf{p}_1'\mathbf{q_1}$$

We can rearrange the above as

$$\begin{aligned}\frac{b^2}{\alpha^2}\left(\mathbf{p_1}'\mathbf{1_n}\right) \times \left(\mathbf{1_n}'\mathbf{q_1}\right) &= \frac{b^2}{\alpha^2}\left(\sum p_{1i}\right) \times \left(\sum q_{1i}\right)\\ &= b \times \mathbf{p_1}'\mathbf{q_1}\end{aligned}$$

Therefore, we get

$$\frac{b}{\alpha^2}\left(\sum p_{1i}\right) \times \left(\sum q_{1i}\right) = \mathbf{p}_1'\mathbf{q_1}$$

This generally does not hold when $N \geq 2$. (End of Proof)

4.11 Mathematics Appendix B: Proof of Theorem 4.4.2

Theorem 4.4.2 *The Walsh index is the only linear mean index that satisfies time reversal test and invariance with respect to the size of the comparison point quantity.*

Proof
Consider the following fixed basket index number.

$$PI(\mathbf{q_0}, \mathbf{p_0}, \mathbf{q_1}, \mathbf{p_1}) = \frac{\sum_{i=1}^{N} p_{i1} q_{if}}{\sum_{i=1}^{N} p_{i0} q_{if}} \tag{4B.1}$$

We consider the case when the quantity basket vector, $\mathbf{q_f} = (q_1, q_2, \ldots, q_N)$, is a function of observed quantity vectors. Consider the following functional form for $\mathbf{q_f}$:

$$q_{if} = m_i(q_{i0}, q_{i1}) \quad \text{for } i = 1, \ldots, N \text{ where } m_i^{st} : \mathbb{R}_{++}^2 \to \mathbb{R}_{++}$$

$$m_i(a, a) = a \quad \text{for any } a \in \mathbb{R}_{++} \text{ for } i = 1, \ldots, N$$

where M is the number of locations or times. q_{ji} is the quantity of commodity i at time j.

Without loss of generality, let us change quantities of country a multiple λ. Then invariance of the fixed basket index implies

$$\frac{\sum_{i=1}^{N} p_{i1} m_i(q_{i0}, q_{i1})}{\sum_{i=1}^{N} p_{i0} m_i(q_{i0}, q_{i1})} = \frac{\sum_{i=1}^{N} p_{i1} m_i(\lambda q_{i0}, q_{i1})}{\sum_{i=1}^{N} p_{i0} m_i(\lambda q_{i0}, q_{i1})} \tag{4B.2}$$

Rearranging (4B.2) as

$$\frac{\sum_{i=1}^{N} p_{i0} m_i(\lambda q_{i0}, q_{i1})}{\sum_{i=1}^{N} p_{i0} m_i(q_{i0}, q_{i1})} = \frac{\sum_{i=1}^{N} p_{i1} m_i(\lambda q_{i0}, q_{i1})}{\sum_{i=1}^{N} p_{i1} m_i(q_{i0}, q_{i1})} = G(\lambda, \mathbf{q}) \tag{4B.3}$$

where $\mathbf{q}$ is a quantity vector Note that the left-hand side of the equation above does not include prices at time 1. Additionally, the middle part of the equation does not include prices at time 0. Since this is an identity with respect to prices, the right-hand side should not include prices either. Rearranging (4B.3), we obtain

$$\sum_{i=1}^{N} p_{it} m_i(\lambda q_{i0}, q_{i1}) = G(\lambda, \mathbf{q}) \sum_{i=1}^{N} p_{it} m_i(q_{i0}, q_{i1}) \tag{4B.4}$$

Because (4B.4) is an identity with respect to p_{it}, the following equation must hold for each i,

$$m_i(\lambda q_{i0}, q_{i1}) = G(\lambda, \mathbf{q})\, m_i(q_{i0}, q_{i1}) \tag{4B.5}$$

The L.H.S. does not depend on the quantity vector other than that for the ith goods. Therefore, the R.H.S. should depend only on the ith quantity vector and λ.

By applying the same arguments for other commodities, we can show that G does not depend on the quantity vector. Thus, we get the following functional equation:

$$m_i(\lambda q_{i0}, q_{i1}) = G(\lambda) m_i(q_{i0}, q_{i1}) \tag{4B.6}$$

From the Generalized Cauchy Function Equation 3 in Mathematical Appendix C, if the function, m_i, is a continuous function, the general solution of the functional equation is given by

$$m_i(q_{i0}, q_{i1}) = \prod_{m=0}^{1} q_{im}^{c_m} \tag{4B.7}$$

Because we have

$$m(a, a) = a^{c_0 + c_1} = a \tag{4B.8}$$

$$c_0 + c_1 = 1. \tag{4B.9}$$

Finally, because the price index possesses time reversal property, we have

$$\frac{\sum_{i=1}^{N} p_{i1} m_i(q_{i0}, q_{i1})}{\sum_{i=1}^{N} p_{i0} m_i(q_{i0}, q_{i1})} = \frac{\sum_{i=1}^{N} p_{i1} m_i(q_{i1}, q_{i0})}{\sum_{i=1}^{N} p_{i0} m_i(q_{i1}, q_{i0})} \tag{4B.10}$$

Rearranging the above, we get

$$\frac{\sum_{i=1}^{N} p_{i1} m_i(q_{i0}, q_{i1})}{\sum_{i=1}^{N} p_{i1} m_i(q_{i1}, q_{i0})} = \frac{\sum_{i=1}^{N} p_{i0} m_i(q_{i0}, q_{i1})}{\sum_{i=1}^{N} p_{i0} m_i(q_{i1}, q_{i0})} \tag{4B.11}$$

Suppose we have

$$m_i(q_{i0}, q_{i1}) \neq m_i(q_{i1}, q_{i0}) \tag{4B.12}$$

Then, there exists $X(\neq 1)$ such that

$$\frac{\sum_{i=1}^{N} p_{i1} m_i(q_{i0}, q_{i1})}{\sum_{i=1}^{N} p_{i1} m_i(q_{i1}, q_{i0})} = X \neq 1 \tag{4B.13}$$

Further, if $m_i(q_{i0}, q_{i1}) \neq m_i(q_{i1}, q_{i0})$, because the price vector at time zero can take any positive numbers, it is possible to have

$$\frac{\sum_{i=1}^{N} p_{i0} m_i(q_{i0}, q_{i1})}{\sum_{i=1}^{N} p_{i0} m_i(q_{i1}, q_{i0})} \neq X \tag{4B.14}$$

This is a contradiction. Therefore, we must have $m_i(q_{i0}, q_{i1}) = m_i(q_{i1}, q_{i0})$, which indicates $c_0 = c_1 = \frac{1}{2}$.

(End of Proof)

4.12 Mathematics Appendix C: Cauchy's Functional Equation

The problem of finding the shape of a function that satisfies certain properties is an old problem called a functional equation. The goal is to find a function $f(x)$ that always holds a certain relationship for arbitrary real numbers x and y. Specifically, there are known solutions for the function $f(x)$ that always satisfy each of the following four equations called Cauchy's functional equations.

$$f(x+y) = f(x) + f(y) \tag{4C.1}$$

$$f(x+y) = f(x)f(y) \tag{4C.2}$$

$$f(xy) = f(x)f(y) \tag{4C.3}$$

$$f(xy) = f(x) + f(y) \tag{4C.4}$$

Equation (4C.3) is often used in index number theory. For a rigorous proof of the general case, refer to Aczél (1966; 1987), where we limit the domain to $x > 0$, $y > 0$, and we consider continuous functions f from $\mathbb{R}^2_{++} \to \mathbb{R}_{++}$. Alternatively, we can assume that f is a monotonically increasing or decreasing function with positive value. For any given value, $x, y > 0$ the function that always holds (4C.1), that is, the solution to (4C.1) is limited to

$$f(x) = cx, c \in \mathbb{R}$$

Let's show the only part. If (4C.1) holds, then by mathematical induction for $x_i > 0$, we have

$$f(x_1 + x_2 + \ldots + x_n) = f(x_1) + f(x_2) + \ldots + f(x_n)$$

holds true. Here, $x_1 = x_2 = \ldots = x_N$ for any positive integer n and positive real number, x

$$f(nx) = nf(x)$$

holds true. Here, again using positive integers m and positive real numbers, t

$$x = (m/n)t$$

Then, for any positive real number t, the following holds:

$$f(nx) = f(mt)$$

$$nf(x) = mf(t)$$

$$f\left(\frac{m}{n}t\right) = \frac{m}{n}f(t)$$

Now, set c as

$$\frac{m}{n} = c$$

Then, we can get the following:

$$f(1) = \frac{n}{m} f\left(\frac{m}{n}\right) = c$$

$$f\left(\frac{m}{n}\right) = c\frac{m}{n}$$

Therefore, for any positive rational number$x$, the following holds:

$$f(x) = cx \tag{4C.5}$$

Furthermore, if f is a continuous or monotonic function, then (4C.5) holds true for any positive real number x.[22]

Thus, we have just shown that the function that satisfies (4C.2) is

$$f(x) = e^{cx}$$

only. Assume that for any $x, y > 0$, f always takes a positive value. Then, it is possible to take the logarithm of both sides of (4C.2), which leads to

$$\ln f(x + y) = \ln f(x) + \ln f(y)$$

Since this is (4C.1),

$$\ln f(x) = cx$$

is the solution. Therefore, we get

$$f(x) = e^{cx}$$

Finally, let's show that the solution to (4C.3) is given by

$$f(x) = x^c$$

Set $x = e^u$, $y = e^v$, then

$$f\left(e^{u+v}\right) = f\left(e^u\right) f\left(e^u\right)$$

[22] This theorem can be generalized in terms of continuity, domain range, etc., but general solutions that do not assume continuity or monotonicity include complex solutions. The interested reader is referred to Aczél (1966, 1987).

Set a function g as

$$g(x) = f\left(e^{x}\right)$$

Then, we get

$$g(x + y) = g(x)\, g(y)$$

The solution for this functional equation is given by

$$g(x) = e^{cx}$$

Therefore, we get

$$\begin{aligned} g(\ln x) &= e^{c \ln(x)} \\ &= x^{c} \\ &= f(x) \end{aligned}$$

The results of somewhat generalizing Cauchy's functional equation are known. We will limit the introduction to those frequently used in index theory.

Theorem 4.12.1 *Aczél (1966)*
For any positive real numbers, $x, y > 0$, there are positive continuous functions f, g, and h such that

$$f(xy) = g(x)\, h(y)$$

Then the functional forms of the functions are given by

$$f(x) = abx^{c}$$

$$g(x) = ax^{c}$$

$$h(x) = bx^{c}$$

where a, b, c are real numbers.

For the proof, see Aczél (1966, 1987). When applying Cauchy's functional equation to index number theory and economics, it is often desirable to secure a domain of two or more variables. Fortunately, the following theorem is known.

Theorem 4.12.2 *Generalized Cauchy Function Equation 1*
A function $F(x_1, x_2, ..., x_n) = c_1x_1 + c_2x_2 +, ..., +c_nx_n$ is a general solution of the following functional equation:

$$F(x_1 + y_1, x_2 + y_2, ..., x_n + y_n) = F(x_1, x_2, ..., x_n) + F(y_1, y_2, ..., y_n)$$

where F is a continuous or monotonic function.

This proof can be easily achieved using mathematical induction. Similarly, by using mathematical induction, it is also possible to derive the following theorem.

Theorem 4.12.3 *Generalized Cauchy Function Equation 2*
A function

$$F(x_1, x_2, ..., x_n) = x_1^{C1} x_2^{C2}, ..., x_n^{Cn}$$

is a general solution of the following functional equations:

$$F(x_1 y_1, x_2 y_2, ..., x_n y_n) = F(x_1, x_2, ..., x_n) F(y_1, y_2, ..., y_n)$$

where F *is a continuous or monotonic function.*

The above proof can be carried out based on the theorem for the one-dimensional case, using mathematical induction.

Theorem 4.12.4 *Generalized Cauchy Function Equation 3*

$$F_1(x_1, x_2, ..., x_n) = ABx_1^{C1} x_2^{C2}, ..., x_n^{Cn}, \tag{4C.6}$$

$$F_2(x_1, x_2, ..., x_n) = Ax_1^{C1} x_2^{C2}, ..., x_n^{Cn}, \tag{4C.7}$$

$$F_2(x_1, x_2, ..., x_n) = Bx_1^{C1} x_2^{C2}, ..., x_n^{Cn} \tag{4C.8}$$

are the general solutions of the following functional equations:

$$F_1(x_1 y_1, x_2 y_2, ..., x_n y_n) = F_2(x_1, x_2, ..., x_n) F_3(y_1, y_2, ..., y_n)$$

where F_1*,* F_2*, and* F_3 *are continuous or monotonic functions.*

For the proof, see Luce (1964), Eichhorn (1978), or Aczél (1987).

For those who are interested in functional equations further, Aczél (1966) is a classical textbook. Luce (1964) also provides us with a very nice explanation on various functional equations. When it comes to applications in economics, Eichhorn (1978) is a good reference as it applies it to production functions, price index numbers, etc.

References

Abe, N. (2022). Measuring inflation under pandemic conditions': A comment. *Journal of Official Statistics, 38*(1), 295–300.

Abe, N., & Rao, D. S. P. (2019). Multilateral Sato-Vartia index for international comparisons of prices and real expenditures. *Economics Letters, 183*, 108535.

Abe, N., & Rao, D. S. P. (2022a). Transitivity, substitution bias and the fixed basket multilateral Walsh index for international price and real expenditure comparisons. RCESR Discussion Paper Series, DP22-1.

Abe, N., & Rao, D. S. P. (2022b). The fixed basket multilateral Walsh index for international price and real expenditure comparisons. *Economics Letters, 220*, 110857.

Abe, N., & Rao, D. S. P. (2024a). Generalized logarithmic index numbers with demand shocks: Bridging the gap between theory and practice. RCESR Discussion Paper Series, DP20-1.

Abe, N., & Rao, D. S. P. (2024b) Commensurability and characterization of normalization conditions for cost-of-living comparisons under time-varying CES preferences. *Economics Letters, 244*, 112018.

Aczél, J. (1966). *Lectures on functional equations and their applications, 19*. Academic.

Aczél, J. (1987). *A short course for the functional equation*. Springer.

Allen, R. C., & Diewert, W. E. (1981). Direct versus implicit superlative index number formulae. *The Review of Economics and Statistics, 63*(3), 430–435.

Balk, B. M. (1980). A method for constructing price indices for seasonal commodities. *Journal of the Royal Statistical Society A: General, 143*(1), 68–75.

Balk, B. M. (1995). Axiomatic price index theory: A survey. *International Statistical Review / Revue Internationale de Statistique, 63*(1), 69–93.

Balk, B. M. (1996). Consistency-in-aggregation and Stuvel indices. *Review of Income and Wealth, 42*(3), 353–363.

Balk, B. M. (2008). *Price and quantity index numbers*. Cambridge University Press.

Balk, B. M., & Diewert, W. E. (2001). A characterization of the Törnqvist price index. *Economics Letters, 72*(3), 279–281.

Białek, J. (2019). Remarks on Geo-logarithmic price indices. *Journal of Official Statistics, 35*(2), 287–317.

Diewert, W. E. (2001). The consumer price index and index number purpose. *Journal of Economic and Social Measurement, 27*(3–4), 167–248.

Diewert, W. E. (2021). The Axiomatic or Test Approach to Index Number Theory. *Consumer Price Index Theory*, Chapter 3.

Eichhorn, W. (1978). Functional equations in economics. Series Applied mathematics and computation (No. 11). London: Addison-Wesley Publishing Co.

Eichhorn, W., & Voeller, J. (1976). *Theory of the price index: Fisher's Test approach and generalizations*. Lecture notes in economics and mathematical systems (Vol. 140). Springer.

Fattore, M. (2010). Axiomatic properties of Geo-logarithmic price indices. *Journal of Econometrics, 156*(2), 344–353.

Fisher, I. (1922). *The Making of index numbers*. Houghton Mifflin Company.

Frisch, R. (1930). Necessary and sufficient conditions regarding the form of an index number which shall meet certain of Fisher's Tests. *American Statistical Association Journal, 25*(172), 397–406.

Funke, H., & Voeller, J. (1978). A note on the characterization of Fisher's 'Ideal Index'. In W. Eichhorn, R. Henn, O. Opitz, & R. W. Shephard (Eds.), *Theory and applications of economic indices* (pp. 177–181). Physica-Verlag HD.

Funke, H., Hacker,G., & Voeller, J. (1979). Fisher's circular test reconsidered. Schweizerische Zeitschrift fur Volkswirtschaft and Statistik, 1979-IV-2 (pp. 677–688).

Krtscha, M. (1984). A characterization of the Edgeworth-Marshall index. *Methods of Operations Research, 48*, 127–135.

Kurabayashi, Y., & Sakuma, I. (1990). *Studies in international comparisons of real product and prices*. Kinokuniya Company, LTD.

Luce, R. D. (1964). A generalization of a theorem of dimensional analysis. *Journal of Mathematical Psychology, 1*(2), 278–284.

Mizobuchi, H., & Zelenyuk, V. (2021). Quadratic-mean-of-order-r indexes of output, input and productivity. *Journal of Productivity Analysis, 56*(2–3), 133–138.

Redding, S. J., & Weinstein, D. E. (2020). Measuring aggregate price indices with taste shocks: Theory and evidence for CES preferences. *Quarterly Journal of Economics, 135*(1), 503–560.

Stuvel, G. (1989). *The index-number problem and its solution*. Intl Specialized Book Services, Inc.

Vartia, Y. O. (1976). Ideal log-change index numbers. *Scandinavian Journal of Statistics, 3*, 121–126.

von Auer, L., & Wengenroth, J. (2021). Consistent aggregation with superlative and other price indices. *Journal of the Royal Statistical Society Series A: Statistics in Society, 184*(2), 589–615.

Wald, A. (1937). Zur Theorie der Preisindexziffern. *Zeitschrift für Nationalökonomie, 8*(2), 179–219.

Walsh, C. M. (1901). *The measurement of general exchange value*. Macmillan.

Economic Approach

5

Abstract

This chapter explores the economic approach to index numbers, specifically focusing on the cost-of-the living (COLI). This approach conceptualizes price indices based on utility levels and prices, differentiating from axiomatic and stochastic approaches which rely purely on price and quantity data. The chapter discusses the theoretical basis of the COLI, which measures the expenditure required to maintain a constant level of utility over time. It investigates the assumptions underlying the COLI, such as homothetic preferences, and the mathematical simplicity of computing the index through expenditure functions. However, it also addresses the practical challenges and limitations of applying COLI, especially the difficulty in estimating necessary economic parameters and adapting the model to real-world data where consumer preferences and conditions vary. The discussion highlights the need for robust economic models to accurately reflect consumer behaviours emphasizing the gap between theoretical ideal and practical application.

5.1 What Is the Economic Approach?

The economic approach to index numbers, alongside the axiomatic approach in Chap. 4 and the stochastic approach in Chap. 10, stands as a pivotal framework within the discipline. Unlike the axiomatic and stochastic approaches, which define price indices as functions of non-negative (or positive) real number spaces of prices and quantities, the economic approach conceptualizes price indices as functions of prices and utility levels. In this approach, quantities are assumed to be determined as functions of prices and utility (or production) levels, consistent with a posited economic model. This means that the domain of definition and handling of quantity information

N. Abe, *Price Index Numbers*, Springer Texts in Business and Economics,
https://doi.org/10.1007/978-981-97-6305-4_5

in the economic approach differs significantly from the other two approaches. This chapter discusses the consumer theory-based economic approach to price indices.[1]

A standard method for price indices based on economic theory is to compute the cost-of-living index (COLI). The COLI represents the change in the minimum amount of expenditures required to maintain a constant level of utility at prices prevailing in two periods. The term "cost of living" whereas COLI in the economic approach, also known as the "True Cost-of-Living Index (TCOLI)", is defined as the ratio of expenditure functions at two different time points or locations, given a specific preference or utility as well as the prices at each time or location. Here, quantities are assumed to be on the compensated demand function, which is the solution to the problem of minimizing the cost of attaining a certain utility level at a given set of prices. The premise is that there is a certain economic relationship between quantities and prices. For example, if a Cobb–Douglas utility function is assumed, the expenditure share of each good remains constant regardless of the prices and incomes. If preferences are homothetic, meaning the utility function is a monotonically increasing transformation of a first-degree homogeneous function, the income elasticity of each good becomes 1, and their expenditure shares become independent of the income level. These properties are strong assumptions at the individual or product level and rarely observed in real-world data on consumption quantities, prices, and income. Consequently, there have been attempts to generalize the utility functions underlying the COLI.

Not just for the COLI, but in any economic analysis, models are necessary. Even large economic models with many variables and parameters cannot explain all observed phenomena. Assuming a specific model, i.e., viewing economic phenomena through the filter of model constraints, is standard in economic analysis. However, the empirical aspect of whether the assumed utility function or preferences is consistent with real data or not has not been emphasized in the theory of price index number. The economic approach in price index number theory, particularly in the field of COLI research, has focused on how easily computable COLIs can be derived from very general utility or expenditure function forms. One reason for the limited interest in the empirical aspect among index number researchers is the difficulty of estimating structural parameters, such as elasticities of substitution, required for monthly official statistics. Other reasons include the existence of "superlative indices", discussed in the next chapter. According to the theory of superlative indices, representative price indices like the Fisher, Walsh, and Törnqvist indices are all good approximations of the COLI under very general utility or expenditure functions. Therefore, there is little need for the arduous task of estimating general utility or expenditure functions; simply computing one of these three indices will yield a result almost identical to the COLI, assuming consistency between economic assumptions and observed price and quantity data.

[1] For price indices based on producer theory, the Producer Price Index Manual (ILO et al., 2004b) is the most comprehensive reference.

The definition of the COLI as the ratio of expenditure functions is mathematically simple. However, the relationship between the COLI and representative bilateral price indices like the Fisher index, as well as their interpretation, is often misunderstood. There is a frequent misperception that the Törnqvist index always equals the COLI. In reality, the Fisher, Walsh, Törnqvist, and Sato–Vartia indices do not always coincide with the COLI. This and the next chapters focus on the economic approach, particularly examining the Sato–Vartia index, to explore issues of the economic approach to the index number theory.

5.2 Konüs Cost-of-Living Index Under Homothetic Preferences

Consider a household utility function $u(\mathbf{q}) \in \mathbb{R}_{+}$ under a goods vector $\mathbf{q} \in \mathbb{R}^{N}_{++}$. The expenditure function is defined as follows, assuming that the household does not perform dynamic optimization and has no savings[2]:

$$C\left(\mathbf{p}_t, u_t\right) = \min_{\{q_i\}} \left\{ \sum_{i=1}^{N} p_{it} q_i : u(\mathbf{q}) \geq u_t \right\} \tag{5.1}$$

$$= \sum_{i=1}^{N} p_{it} q_{it}^{*} \tag{5.2}$$

where $u(\mathbf{q})$ is a utility function while $\mathbf{q}$ is a vector of consumption quantities. q_{it}^{*} is the solution to the cost minimization problem.

The cost-of-living index by Konüs indicates how much the minimum consumption expenditure required to achieve a certain utility level differs between two points in time.[3] Like the expenditure function, the cost-of-living index generally depends on the utility level at which the minimum cost is evaluated. The COLI in Konüs' framework evaluated at the utility level of the base period's quantity vector is defined as

$$PI_k\left(\mathbf{p}_0, \mathbf{p}_t, \mathbf{q}_0\right) = \frac{C\left(\mathbf{p}_t, u\left(\mathbf{q}_0\right)\right)}{C\left(\mathbf{p}_0, u\left(\mathbf{q}_0\right)\right)} \tag{5.3}$$

$$= \frac{C\left(\mathbf{p}_t, u_0\right)}{\sum_{i=1}^{N} p_{i0} q_{i0}} \tag{5.4}$$

Note that, in deriving equation (5.4), we assume the observed quantities and prices are consistent with consumers' optimal behavior.

[2] Incorporating savings makes calculating the cost-of-living index very difficult, as the household's utility level would depend on future consumption. However, if preferences are separable over time, sub-utility functions can be defined at each point in time, and the discussion here applies. For the cost-of-living index with savings, see Osborne (2018).

[3] An important assumption when comparing the expenditure function between two points in time is that the utility function, and therefore the shape of the expenditure function does not change. The cost-of-living index for changing preferences is discussed in the latter part of this chapter.

On the other hand, the cost-of-living index at which utility is being evaluated at the quantity vector of the comparison period is

$$PI_k(\mathbf{p}_0, \mathbf{p}_t, q_t) = \frac{C(\mathbf{p}_t, u(\mathbf{q}_t))}{C(\mathbf{p}_0, u(\mathbf{q}_t))} \tag{5.5}$$

$$= \frac{\sum_{i=1}^{N} p_{it} q_{it}}{C(\mathbf{p}_0, u(\mathbf{q}_t))} \tag{5.6}$$

Thus, the COLI can vary depending on the quantity vector at which utility is being evaluated, which is somewhat problematic property. Therefore, in the theory of COLI, the shape of the utility function is often assumed such that it does not depend on the utility level at which it is evaluated. Preferences are called homothetic when the utility function is a homogeneous function of the first degree, or its monotonic increasing transformation. Homothetic functions, such as Cobb–Douglas and CES (Constant Elasticity of Substitution) types, frequently appear in analyses of household consumption and production technologies.[4] Let us consider the expenditure function $C\left(\mathbf{p}_t, \overline{u}\right)$ when the utility function $u\left(\mathbf{q}_t\right)$ is homogeneous of degree one with respect to the consumption vector $\mathbf{q_t}$. In this case, the expenditure function can be expanded as follows:

$$C\left(\mathbf{p}_t, \overline{u}\right) = \min_{\{q_i\}} \left\{ \sum_{i=1}^{N} p_{it} q_{it} : u\left(\mathbf{q_t}\right) \geq \overline{u} \right\} \tag{5.7}$$

$$= \min_{\{q_i\}} \left\{ \sum_{i=1}^{N} p_{it} q_{it} : u\left(\frac{\mathbf{q_t}}{\overline{u}}\right) \geq \frac{1}{\overline{u}} \overline{u} \right\}$$

$$= \min_{\{q_i\}} \left\{ \sum_{i=1}^{N} \overline{u} p_{it} \frac{q_{it}}{\overline{u}} : u\left(\frac{\mathbf{q_t}}{\overline{u}}\right) \geq 1 \right\}$$

$$= \overline{u} \times \min_{\left\{\frac{q_i}{\overline{u}}\right\}} \left\{ \sum_{i=1}^{N} p_{it} \frac{q_{it}}{\overline{u}} : u\left(\frac{\mathbf{q_t}}{\overline{u}}\right) \geq 1 \right\}$$

$$= \overline{u} \times C\left(\mathbf{p}_t, 1\right) \tag{5.8}$$

Writing the unit cost function corresponding to one unit of utility as $C\left(\mathbf{p}_t, 1\right) = c\left(\mathbf{p}_t\right)$, we get

$$C\left(\mathbf{p}_t, \overline{u}\right) = \overline{u} c\left(\mathbf{p}_t\right) \tag{5.9}$$

In other words, when preferences are homothetic, the expenditure function is proportional to the utility level. In this case, the COLI, which is the ratio of expenditure

[4] Analysis of cost-of-living indices under non-homothetic situations has also been conducted in recent years. For example, see Handbury (2021).

functions under different price vectors, is independent of the utility levels. That is, the COLI becomes the ratio of the two unit cost functions as follows:

$$PI_k\left(\mathbf{p}_0, \mathbf{p}_t, \overline{u}\right) = \frac{c\left(\mathbf{p}_t\right)}{c\left(\mathbf{p}_0\right)} \tag{5.10}$$

When utility function is homothetic, the COLI or price index becomes independent of utility level, making it much more user-friendly. For example, consider two individuals with identical preferences but different incomes. If we consider the COLI using the quantity vector at the base period, in the case of non-homothetic preferences, the COLI for the two individuals will be different, implying that the index depends on income level. However, if preferences are homothetic, the COLI becomes independent of income, and the indices for both individuals will be the same.

5.2.1 Cobb–Douglas Utility Function

Let us consider the Cobb–Douglas utility function:

$$u(\mathbf{q}) = \prod_{i=1}^{N} q_i^{\alpha_i}, \quad \alpha_i \geq 0 \tag{5.11}$$

The expenditure function becomes

$$C(\mathbf{p}, \overline{u}) = \left(\sum_{i=1}^{N} \alpha_i\right)\left(\overline{u}\prod_{i=1}^{N}\left(\frac{p_i}{\alpha_i}\right)^{\alpha_i}\right)^{\left(1/\sum_{i=1}^{N}\alpha_i\right)}$$

If we impose the following adding up condition:

$$\sum_{i=1}^{N} \alpha_i = 1$$

then α_i becomes the expenditure share of commodity i. In this case, the expenditure function simplifies to

$$c(\mathbf{p}, \overline{u}) = \overline{u}\prod_{i=1}^{N}\left(\frac{p_i}{\alpha_i}\right)^{\alpha_i}$$

Under these conditions, the COLI becomes

$$PI(\mathbf{p}_0, \mathbf{p}_t) = \prod_{i=1}^{N}\left(\frac{p_{it}}{p_{i0}}\right)^{\alpha_i} \tag{5.12}$$

which is the expenditure-share weighted geometric mean of the price relatives.

5.2.2 CES Utility Function and Its Cost-of-Living Index

Consider a utility function of the form of constant elasticity of substitution (CES) given by

$$u(\mathbf{q}) = \left(\sum_{i=1}^{N} (a_i q_i)^{\frac{\sigma-1}{\sigma}} \right)^{\frac{\sigma}{\sigma-1}} \tag{5.13}$$

$$\sigma > 1, a_i > 0, \sum_{i=1}^{N} a_i = 1$$

In this case, the compensated demand function and (unit) expenditure function, P, are as follows:

$$q_i = (a_i)^{\sigma-1} \left(\frac{p_i}{P} \right)^{-\sigma} u \tag{5.14}$$

$$C(\mathbf{p}, 1) = P = c(\mathbf{p}) = \left(\sum_{i=1}^{N} \left(\frac{p_i}{a_i} \right)^{1-\sigma} \right)^{\frac{1}{1-\sigma}} \tag{5.15}$$

Hence, the COLI becomes

$$\begin{aligned} PI(\mathbf{p}_0, \mathbf{p}_t) &= \frac{\left(\sum_{i=1}^{N} (p_{it}/a_i)^{1-\sigma} \right)^{\frac{1}{1-\sigma}}}{\left(\sum_{i=1}^{N} (p_{i0}/a_i)^{1-\sigma} \right)^{\frac{1}{1-\sigma}}} \\ &= \left(\frac{\sum_{i=1}^{N} (p_{it}/a_i)^{1-\sigma}}{\sum_{i=1}^{N} (p_{i0}/a_i)^{1-\sigma}} \right)^{\frac{1}{1-\sigma}} \end{aligned} \tag{5.16}$$

If we introduce the parameter a_i in the utility function as

$$u(\mathbf{q}) = \left(\sum_{i=1}^{N} a_i (q_i)^{\frac{\sigma-1}{\sigma}} \right)^{\frac{\sigma}{\sigma-1}} \tag{5.17}$$

then a_i becomes known as the share parameter. The compensated demand function and (unit) expenditure function in this case are

$$q_i = \left(\frac{p_i}{a_i P} \right)^{-\sigma} u \tag{5.18}$$

$$P = \left(\sum_{i=1}^{N} a_i^{\sigma} (p_i)^{1-\sigma} \right)^{\frac{1}{1-\sigma}} \tag{5.19}$$

The cost-of-living index simplifies to

$$PI\left(\mathbf{p}_0, \mathbf{p}_t\right) = \left(\frac{\sum_{i=1}^{N} a_i^{\sigma} p_{it}^{1-\sigma}}{\sum_{i=1}^{N} a_i^{\sigma} p_{i0}^{1-\sigma}}\right)^{\frac{1}{1-\sigma}} \tag{5.20}$$

The difference between (5.16) and (5.20) is just a matter of formulation, and there is no substantial difference as long as $\sigma > 1$ is assumed. However, for the case where the elasticity of substitution is $0 < \sigma < 1$, a significant difference arises when considering a_i approaching zero. Specifically, for $\sigma > 1$:

$$\lim_{a_i \to 0} q_i = \lim_{a_i \to 0} (a_i)^{\sigma-1} \left(\frac{p_i}{P}\right)^{-\sigma} u = \lim_{a_i \to 0} \left(\frac{p_i}{a_i P}\right)^{-\sigma} u = 0$$

but for $0 < \sigma < 1$:

$$\lim_{a_i \to 0} q_i = \lim_{a_i \to 0} \left(\frac{p_i}{a_i P}\right)^{-\sigma} u = 0$$

$$\lim_{a_i \to 0} q_i = \lim_{a_i \to 0} (a_i)^{\sigma-1} \left(\frac{p_i}{P}\right)^{-\sigma} u = \infty$$

When $\sigma = 1$, the distinction between the two parameterizations becomes clearer. The CES function defined as (5.17) converges to the Cobb–Douglas utility function, where the expenditure share for commodity i is given by a_i[5]:

$$\lim_{\sigma \to 1} \left(\sum_{i=1}^{N} a_i q_i^{\frac{\sigma-1}{\sigma}}\right)^{\frac{\sigma}{\sigma-1}} = \prod_{i=1}^{N} q_i^{a_i} \tag{5.21}$$

However, the CES function defined as (5.13) approaches the unweighted geometric mean, which is a special case of the Cobb–Douglas utility function[6]:

$$\lim_{\sigma \to 1} \left(\sum_{i=1}^{N} (a_i q_i)^{\frac{\sigma-1}{\sigma}}\right)^{\frac{\sigma}{\sigma-1}} \cdot 2^{\frac{1-\sigma}{\sigma}} = \prod_{i=1}^{N} \left(\frac{q_i}{a_i}\right)^{\frac{1}{N}} \tag{5.22}$$

In macroeconomics, it is common to assume $\sigma > 1$, but the elasticity of substitution being less than 1 is conceivable, i.e., quantity ratios do not change much even with changes in relative prices. If we consider large categories of goods, such as food and clothing, the elasticity of substitution between them would typically be equal or

[5] By taking the natural logarithm of the utility function and applying L'Hôpital's rule, it is possible to determine the function's limit. Note that we use the adding up condition, $\sum_{i=1}^{N} a_i = 1$.

[6] Note that the left-hand side of (5.22) includes $2^{\frac{1-\sigma}{\sigma}}$ that is necessary for the function to converge to the Cobb–Douglas function.

less than 1, as they are not considered strong substitutes. In such cases, formulating the model as in (5.13) can cause significant problems when a_i is very small or zero, or the elasticity of substitution is unity. Therefore, when using the CES utility function, it is necessary to consider the possible value of the elasticity of substitution. If the elasticity can take value of unity or smaller, the parametrization in (5.17) might be more appropriate than in (5.13).

5.2.3 Quantity Index

The implicit quantity index is defined as the ratio between the value index and the price index. When preferences are homothetic, the following equation holds:

$$\sum_{i=1}^{N} p_{it}q_{it} = C\left(\mathbf{p}_t, u\left(\mathbf{q}_t\right)\right) \tag{5.23}$$

$$= u\left(\mathbf{q}_t\right) \times c\left(\mathbf{p}_t\right) \tag{5.24}$$

Therefore, by dividing the Value Index by the COLI, i.e., deflating the change in expenditure by the COLI, we get

$$\frac{c\left(\mathbf{p}_0\right)}{c\left(\mathbf{p}_t\right)} \frac{\sum_{i=1}^{N} p_{it}q_{it}}{\sum_{i=1}^{N} p_{i0}q_{i0}} = \frac{c\left(\mathbf{p}_0\right)}{c\left(\mathbf{p}_t\right)} \frac{u\left(\mathbf{q}_t\right) \times c\left(\mathbf{p}_t\right)}{u\left(\mathbf{q}_0\right) \times c\left(\mathbf{p}_0\right)} \tag{5.25}$$

$$= \frac{u\left(\mathbf{q}_t\right)}{u\left(\mathbf{q}_0\right)}$$

$$= QI_k\left(\mathbf{q}_0, \mathbf{q}_t\right) \tag{5.26}$$

This means that when preferences are homothetic, the implicit quantity index obtained by deflating the value index by the COLI equals the ratio of utility functions. This property is very important for welfare comparisons using the COLI. For example, by dividing the nominal income ratio between two points in time by the COLI, i.e., calculating the real income, it is possible to measure changes in welfare. This is one of the biggest advantages of the cost-of-living index. As mentioned at the beginning of this chapter, the economic approach does not harbor much skepticism about the correctness of assumptions regarding preferences, partly because the cost-of-living index is a tool for welfare analysis. When analyzing welfare, the choice of preferences and utility functions is more of a normative issue for analysts, i.e., it concerns how and under what value criteria economic welfare is measured.

As evident from (5.10), the COLI under homothetic preferences is a function that depends only on the prices at two points in time and is independent of quantities. This will be repeatedly emphasized throughout this chapter; in the theory of the COLI, quantities are assumed to be functions of price and utility levels, so there is no need to use quantity information. That is, the COLI is essentially a kind of welfare indicator, assuming that quantities move according to economic theory.

5.2.4 COLI and Its Relationship with Laspeyres and Paasche Indices

When preferences are homothetic, it is well known that there is a clear relationship between the COLI and the Laspeyres and Paasche indices. Let us first consider the relationship between COLI and the Paasche index. Under the price vector of period 0, the cost of maintaining utility obtained with quantity $\mathbf{q}_1$ from period 1 is not greater than $\mathbf{p}_0'\mathbf{q}_1$. Therefore, the value of the unit cost function in period 0 is not greater than $\mathbf{p}_0'\mathbf{q}_1$. Hence, we get the following relationships:

$$\frac{\mathbf{p}_1'\mathbf{q}_1}{\mathbf{p}_0'\mathbf{q}_1} \leq \frac{c(\mathbf{p}_1)}{c(\mathbf{p}_0)} \tag{5.27}$$

Similarly, the minimum cost of maintaining utility obtained with the quantity vector $\mathbf{q}_0$ from period 0 under the price vector of period 1 is not greater than $\mathbf{p}_1'\mathbf{q}_0$. Therefore, the unit cost function in the denominator of COLI is not greater than $\mathbf{p}_1'\mathbf{q}_0$. Thus, we derive that

$$\frac{c(\mathbf{p}_1)}{c(\mathbf{p}_0)} \leq \frac{\mathbf{p}_1\mathbf{q}_0}{\mathbf{p}_0\mathbf{q}_0} \tag{5.28}$$

5.3 Axiomatic Properties of the Cost-of-Living Index

The Cost-of-Living Index (COLI) is a price index that depends only on prices and utility levels, defined as the ratio of expenditure functions. When preferences are homothetic, the COLI simplifies to the ratio of the unit cost functions (expenditure functions when utility level is fixed at one), as follows:

$$COLI\left(\mathbf{p}_0, \mathbf{p}_t\right) = \frac{c\left(\mathbf{p}_t\right)}{c\left(\mathbf{p}_0\right)} \tag{5.29}$$

When considering this COLI as a price index like those discussed in previous chapters, several points need attention. Being the ratio of expenditure functions, the COLI possesses most of the properties of expenditure functions. For details, refer to intermediate-level microeconomics textbooks, and note that expenditure functions are (1) monotonically increasing, (2) homogeneous of degree one, and (3) concave with respect to the price vector. Therefore, the COLI also possesses these three properties with respect to current prices (comparison point prices). That is, the COLI satisfies (A-1) monotonicity and (A-2) homogeneity of degree one. Additionally, if all prices are the same at the comparison and base points, then:

$$COLI\left(\mathbf{p}, \mathbf{p}\right) = \frac{c\left(\mathbf{p}\right)}{c\left(\mathbf{p}\right)} = 1 \tag{5.30}$$

Therefore, the COLI satisfies (A-3) identity. Further, due to homogeneity of degree one, using any positive real number λ, we have

$$COLI\left(\lambda\mathbf{p}_0, \lambda\mathbf{p}_t\right) = \frac{c\left(\lambda\mathbf{p}_t\right)}{c\left(\lambda\mathbf{p}_0\right)} = \frac{\lambda c\left(\mathbf{p}_t\right)}{\lambda c\left(\mathbf{p}_0\right)} = \frac{c\left(\mathbf{p}_t\right)}{c\left(\mathbf{p}_0\right)} = COLI\left(\mathbf{p}_0, \mathbf{p}_t\right) \quad (5.31)$$

Thus, it satisfies (A-4) dimensionality. Regarding (A-8) transitivity, we have

$$COLI\left(\mathbf{p}_0, \mathbf{p}_s\right) \times COLI\left(\mathbf{p}_s, \mathbf{p}_t\right) = \frac{c\left(\mathbf{p}_s\right)}{c\left(\mathbf{p}_0\right)} \times \frac{c\left(\mathbf{p}_t\right)}{c\left(\mathbf{p}_s\right)} = \frac{c\left(\mathbf{p}_t\right)}{c\left(\mathbf{p}_0\right)} = COLI\left(\mathbf{p}_0, \mathbf{p}_t\right) \quad (5.32)$$

Therefore, it also satisfies transitivity. But what about (A-5) commensurability, i.e., independence from the measurement units?

Let's consider a case with CES preferences. The COLI under CES preferences is given as follows:

$$PI\left(\mathbf{p}_0, \mathbf{p}_t\right) = \left(\frac{\sum_{i=1}^{N}\left(\frac{p_{it}}{a_i}\right)^{1-\sigma}}{\sum_{i=1}^{N}\left(\frac{p_{i0}}{a_i}\right)^{1-\sigma}}\right)^{\frac{1}{1-\sigma}} \quad (5.33)$$

Assume there are only two goods with $\alpha_1 = \alpha_2 = 0.5$, $\sigma = 2$. In Table 5.1, for Case 1, the value of the CES-type COLI is 0.375. Changing the unit of measurement for Good 2 in Case 2 results in a COLI value of 0.471. According to Theorem 3 in Chap. 4, to satisfy transitivity, monotonicity, homogeneity of degree one, identity, and commensurability, we are limited to the Cobb–Douglas type, i.e., $\sigma = 1$. If $\sigma = 2$, some of the axioms in Theorem 3 in Chap. 4 must be violated.

This phenomenon arises when considering the cost-of-living index purely as a function of prices. Let's return to the definition of the expenditure function:

$$C\left(\mathbf{p}_t, u_t\right) = \min_{\{q_i\}}\left\{\sum_{i=1}^{N} p_{it}q_i : u\left(\mathbf{q}\right) \geq u_t\right\} \quad (5.34)$$

Consider changing the measurement units of quantities and adjusting the utility function accordingly to reflect the new units. The solution to the above expenditure minimization problem, i.e., the minimum cost, should remain unchanged. Therefore, if we return to the very definition of the COLI, it must satisfy independence from the

Table 5.1 An example of a change in the measurement units of Good 2 affecting its price

	Case 1		Case 2	
Periods	0	1	0	1
Good 1	10	5	10	5
Good 2	10	3	100	30

measurement units. In the case of the CES utility function, adjusting the parameters α_i for each good to match the change in measurement units is equivalent. In Table 5.1, when changing from Case 1 to Case 2, adjusting the parameter α_2 associated with Good 2 from 1 to 10 makes Case 2 effectively identical to Case 1, and the value of the COLI will also match. Therefore, by adjusting the utility and expenditure function parameters to match the change in measurement units, the value of the COLI remains constant. The COLI's independence from measurement units, similar to the Lowe Index, is due to the price index depending on parameters that are changed when the changes in the measurement unit occur. In other words, when discussing the commensurability, we need to treat the parameters in the COLI such as α_i in (5.33) as variables that change when the measurement unit changes.

One property of the COLI is that it becomes a concave function with respect to the price vector at the comparison point, which imparts an interesting characteristic to the price index. If the COLI is concave with respect to comparison time prices, the COLI value is smaller when prices are scattered rather than concentrated at one level. For instance, consider the case of (5.20) with $\alpha_1 = \alpha_2 = 1/2$ and $\sigma = 2$. Calculating the price indices for Cases 3 and 4 shown in Table 5.2, we find that the COLI for Case 3 is 0.5 and for Case 4, it is 0.18. In both cases, the simple arithmetic average of price ratios, i.e., the Carli index, is 0.5, and the simple geometric average, i.e., the Jevons index, is 0.5 for Case 3 and 0.3 for Case 4, both higher than the COLI.

To understand the mechanism behind the concavity of the expenditure function, let us consider a hypothetical expenditure maximization problem:

$$\text{Max} \quad C\left(p_1, p_2, \ldots, p_N, u\right) \quad \text{s.t.} \sum_{i=1}^{N} p_i = 1 \tag{5.35}$$

The first-order condition, with the Lagrange multiplier λ, is

$$\frac{\partial C}{\partial p_i} = \lambda \quad \text{for all } i.$$

Using the Shepherd–McKenzie Lemma, the first derivative of the expenditure function becomes the compensated demand function, h_i, satisfying:

$$h_i = \lambda \quad \text{for all } i \tag{5.36}$$

Table 5.2 An example of a change in price concentration

	Case 3		Case 4	
Periods	0	1	0	1
Good 1	10	5	10	9
Good 2	10	5	10	1

Thus, the expenditure function achieves its maximum value when all compensated demand quantities are equal. Assuming homothetic preferences and that heterogeneity between goods is represented by parameters a_i, the compensated demand function can be written as

$$h_i = h_i\left(\frac{p_1}{a_1}, \frac{p_2}{a_2}, ..., \frac{p_N}{a_N}\right) \times u \tag{5.37}$$

where all prices p_i/a_i enter the function symmetrically. Under this assumption, when all p_i/a_i are equal, it becomes a solution to (5.36), maximizing the expenditure function.

The concavity of the expenditure function arises from the assumption of expenditure minimization (definition of the expenditure function) and is independent of the underlying preferences or utility function. Thus, the decrease in COLI due to price dispersion is unrelated to consumption smoothing often discussed in macroeconomics. The intuition behind the concavity of the expenditure function is as follows: if there is a spread in prices, relatively cheaper goods will always be available compared to when prices are concentrated at one point. By purchasing more of such goods, a household can achieve higher utility. In other words, for a given level of utility, it becomes possible to ensure it with a smaller amount of expenditure. This mechanism becomes important in the discussion of the COLI when preferences change, which we will discuss next.

5.4 Cases Where Konüs' Cost-of-Living Index Is Inappropriate

While Konüs' COLI is based on standard microeconomic theory, it relies on a significant assumption: that preference, or utility functions, remains the same between two points in time or space. This implies that when comparing price levels between two places, such as between the United States and Japan, we must assume that preferences are identical in both countries. For instance, when measuring the cost of living in two different countries such as the United States and India, how meaningful is it to assume the same preferences between a country where beef is not consumed and one where it is favored? It is very difficult to assess the prices in a country that does not consume beef based on the preferences of a beef-eating country, and vice versa. Assuming preference homogeneity over time means that prices and quantities are always on the same demand curve, implying that the demand curve itself does not change, or, in other words, there are no demand shocks. However, is it because the prices of ice cream or hot pot change in summer and winter, respectively, that their demands increase during these seasons? Should we assume that the marginal rate of substitution derived from chocolate or cakes remains the same before Christmas or Valentine's Day? Under Konüs' cost-of-living index, phenomena seen as an increase in demand would be attributed solely to supply-side factors (and income variations). Furthermore, the surge in demand for face masks and sanitizers during the COVID-19 pandemic would be non-existent under Konüs' COLI. Analyzing the price trends of masks and sanitizers during the pandemic using Konüs' COLI might yield unrealistic results. Konüs' COLI reflects actual price movements only under the assumption that the demand function does not shift and that preferences remain constant. Otherwise, it remains a hypothetical exercise based on the assumption of constant preferences and should be treated with caution.

5.5 Changes in Preferences

Until now, it has been assumed that preferences remain the same over time, which is a very strong assumption. Even for the same brand of ice cream, the utility derived from it may differ between summer and winter, and over a decade, even for the same individual, the utility from dining out or traveling is likely to change. Moreover, assuming identical preferences between different countries is quite a stretch. Attempts to depict changes in preferences within standard consumption models, starting with Ichimura (1951), have been made by introducing simple parameters. Subsequently, in the study of the cost-of-living index, with the exception of Philps (1971), instead of analyzing the impact of preference changes on the cost of living, the approach of Fisher and Shell (1971)—calculating the cost of living under two different sets of preferences and comparing the difference—became the standard. This lack of direct analysis of preference differences in the cost-of-living index theory is because the definition of the index itself, as the ratio of expenditure functions under constant utility, does not hold when preferences differ. However, it is clear that people's behavior differs over time and place, and continuing to calculate the cost-of-living index while completely ignoring this fact risks becoming detached from reality.

Two types of cost-of-living indices for cases where preferences differ between two points in time have been proposed. Let U_t, U_s represent the utility functions at times t and s, respectively. The first index, assuming cardinal utility comparability, is defined as

$$\frac{C_t\left(\mathbf{p}_t, U_t\left(\mathbf{q}_t\right) = U\right)}{C_s\left(\mathbf{p}_s, U_s\left(\mathbf{q}_s\right) = U\right)} \tag{5.38}$$

This index, advocated by Redding and Weinstein (2020), becomes the ratio of unit cost functions under homothetic preferences, the index becomes simple as follows:

$$\begin{aligned} \frac{C_t\left(\mathbf{p}_t, U_t\left(\mathbf{q}_t\right) = U\right)}{C_s\left(\mathbf{p}_s, U_s\left(\mathbf{q}_s\right) = U\right)} &= \frac{C_t\left(\mathbf{p}_t, 1\right) U}{C_s\left(\mathbf{p}_s, 1\right) U} \\ &= \frac{c_t\left(\mathbf{p}_t\right)}{c_s\left(\mathbf{p}_s\right)} \end{aligned} \tag{5.39}$$

They named this index for the CES utility function as CUPI (CES Unified Price Index) and used it as the basis for subsequent analysis.

The second index, proposed by Balk (1989), does not assume interpersonal comparability and is ordinal. It is defined as

$$\frac{C_t\left(\mathbf{p}_t, U_t\left(\mathbf{q}_R\right)\right)}{C_s\left(\mathbf{p}_s, U_s\left(\mathbf{q}_R\right)\right)} \tag{5.40}$$

using a standard quantity vector $\mathbf{q}_R$. The issue with using cardinal utility is that it deviates from the ordinal utility theory tradition of Hicks and Allen (1934) and attempts to compare levels of different utility functions. Normalization of each utility function is required to make such comparisons, but specifying this normalization from the observed demand system is impossible. Redding and Weinstein (2020) introduce preference shocks to the CES utility function, following Ichimura (1951), and add the condition that the simple geometric mean of these preference shocks always equals zero. The problem arises if an arithmetic mean is set to zero instead, altering the value of the index.[7] Using the CES utility function, Redding and Weinstein (2020) derived following CUPI (CES Unified Price Index) as the COLI under variable preferences:

$$\ln \text{CUPI}\,(s,t) = \frac{1}{N}\sum_{k=1}^{N}\left(\ln p_{it} - \ln p_{is}\right) - \frac{1}{1-\sigma}\frac{1}{N}\sum_{k=1}^{N}\left(\ln w_{it} - \ln w_{is}\right), \tag{5.41}$$

where w_{it} is the expenditure share of good i in period t.[8] Consider a decrease in the price of a good. If the elasticity of substitution for the good is greater than 1, the expenditure share of the cheaper good will increase. Thus, the expenditure share w_{it} rises, partially offsetting the effect of the price decrease in the right-hand side of Equation (5.41). The first term on the right-hand side of Equation (5.41) is the logarithmic value of the Jevons index (simple geometric mean of price ratios). Thus, the difference between the Jevons index and the cost-of-living index in Equation (5.41) arises due to changes in the expenditure share. An important feature of Equation (5.41) is that even if the relative prices do not change at all, the cost-of-living index changes as the expenditure shares vary. Even if $\sum w_{it} = \sum w_{is} = 1$, $(1/N)\sum \ln w_{it} \neq (1/N)\sum \ln w_{is}$, and the second term on the right-hand side is generally not zero if the expenditure shares change. Furthermore, the logarithm function is concave, so the more dispersed the expenditure shares w_{it} are, the smaller the value of $(1/N)\sum \ln w_{it}$ becomes. Therefore, if the dispersion of expenditure shares

---

[7] Abe and Rao (2024) have characterized this normalization condition, deriving axioms that uniquely determine it.

[8] For details, see Redding and Weinstein (2020).

at the comparison point is larger than at the base period, the cost-of-living index decreases for a substitution elasticity greater than 1 and increases for a substitution elasticity less than 1.[9]

There are some issues with the practical application of CUPI. First, the index becomes infinite when the elasticity of substitution, σ, is 1, and values near 1 become unstable. When the aggregation target is a large category, the elasticity of substitution is expected to be near or less than 1. Therefore, CUPI is suitable for very detailed levels, like at the product level, where the elasticity of substitution is high, but not for category-level aggregations. The second issue is the dependence of the index value on an exogenous condition, the normalization condition. CUPI has desirable properties both axiomatically and economically, but it also has many drawbacks, including consistency issues with standard economic theory when using cardinal utility. Redding and Weinstein (2020) avoid the elasticity issue by using product-level data, where the elasticity of substitution is presumed to be high.

Abe et al. (2022) used CUPI to report that during the COVID-19 pandemic in Japan, there was a significant demand shock for masks, resulting in a markedly different outcome for CUPI compared to the Fisher and Sato–Vartia indices. Specifically, the chained CCV depicted in Fig. 5.1, corresponding to the CUPI of Redding and Weinstein (2020) for the case where the number of goods does not change (CES Exact Price Index for Common Varieties, CCV), shows a sharp increase during the summer of 2020, unlike the Jevons, Fisher, and Sato–Vartia indices, which all show a decline. This reflects the fact that during this period, the demand for masks changed significantly, increasing the variance of a_{it}, the preference parameter, and consequently raising the cost of living.[10] Despite growing interest in the relationship between preference differences or changes and the cost-of-living index, CUPI has not been widely accepted in the official statistical bureaus due to its use of a different definition from traditional cost-of-living indices and its dependence on the normalization condition. The ordinal utility-based cost-of-living index proposed by Balk (1989), which does not require a normalization condition, adheres more closely to standard economic theory than Redding and Weinstein's index, but its axiomatic properties are not yet fully understood, and further developments are anticipated.

5.6 Conclusions: The Konüs' Cost-of-Living Index as the CPI

This chapter discusses the economic approach to the index number theory. The current standard economic approach is the cost-of-living index by Konüs. When we try to use the cost-of-living index, we need to specify many parameters during its

[9] Note, for a substitution elasticity of 1, the utility function becomes Cobb–Douglas, and the expenditure share is always constant. However, this case cannot be analyzed with the above CES formulation. To handle the Cobb–Douglas case, a formulation like $u(\mathbf{q}) = \left(\sum_{i=1}^{N} a_i (q_i)^{\frac{\sigma-1}{\sigma}}\right)^{\frac{\sigma}{\sigma-1}}$ is necessary.

[10] For more details, see Abe et al. (2022)

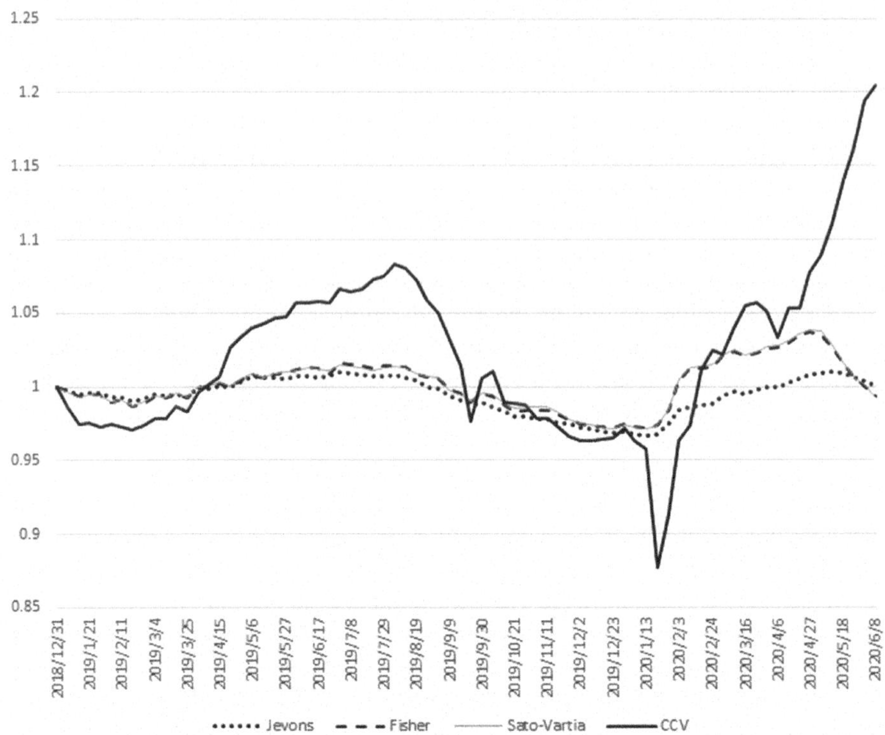

Fig. 5.1 COVID pandemic and price index of face masks in Japan. *Note* based on SRI data provided by INTAGE Inc.

calculation. Even assuming a simple CES utility function for N goods, there is a need to estimate N parameters. If we use more general functional forms such as the Almost Ideal Demand System, the number of parameters that need to be estimated increases in proportion to the square of the number of goods categories. Recent CPI manual (IMF et al., 2020) pointed out that "In practice, it is not possible to compile a true COLI. (p. 38, 2.91, IMF et al., 2020)" Several[11] academic papers have attempted to estimate Konüs COLI. Notably, as highlighted by Redding and Weinstein (2020) and Hottman et al. (2016), the availability of high-frequency data, such as scanner data, significantly aids research in this area. Despite this, from what has been observed, the process of estimating the COLI tends to be more complex and challenging than the hedonic model estimation methods that will be discussed in Chap. 9. While the Boskin Report (Boskin et al., 1996) has advocated the use of

[11] Oulton (2008) has shown that the Konüs' COLI based on AIDS requires an order of magnitude only several times the number of goods categories, not the square of the number of categories. Using information on 70 goods categories from the UK, he has calculated the Konüs' cost-of-living index over a period of 30 years.

the COLI for the Consumer Price Index in the United States, Eurostat has declined the adoption of the COLI framework in their statistical methodologies.[12] Cost-of-living indices, which are based on economic theory, pose several challenges when being adopted by national statistical offices for their monthly index compilations. In statistical practice and many empirical analyses, standard price indices, often known as "exact" indices that will be introduced in Chap. 6, are commonly used instead of the COLI in this chapter. These standard indices coincide with the cost-of-living index under certain conditions. For example, the Fisher index aligns with the cost-of-living index when a specific utility function is applied. The next chapter will investigate the relationship between standard price indices and the cost-of-living index, with a particular focus on the exact indices and the "superlative" index proposed by Diewert (1976).

References

Abe, N., Inoue, T., & Sato, H. (2022). Price index numbers under large-scale demand shocks: The Japanese experience of the COVID-19 pandemic. *Journal of Official Statistics, Sciendo, 38*(1), 301–317.

Abe, N., & Rao, D. S. P. (2024) Commensurability and characterization of normalization conditions for cost-of-living comparisons under time-varying CES preferences. *Economics Letters, 244*, 112018.

Balk, B. M. (1989). Changing consumer preferences and the cost-of-living index: Theory and nonparametric expressions. *Journal of Economics, 50*(2), 157–169.

Boskin, M. J., Dulberger, E., Gordon, R., Griliches, Z., & Jorgenson, D. (1996) Toward a more accurate measure of the cost of living. Final Report to the Senate Finance Committee, December 4.

Diewert, W. E. (1976). Exact and superlative index numbers. *Journal of Econometrics, 4*(2), 115–145.

Eurostat. (1999). Compendium of HICP Reference Documents: Harmonisation of Price Indices, Eurostat, January.

Fisher, F. M., & Shell, K. (1971). Taste and quality change in the pure theory of the true cost of-living index. In Z. Griliches (Ed.), *Price indexes and quality change.* Harvard University Press.

Handbury, J. (2021). Are poor cities cheap for everyone? Non-homotheticity and the cost of living across US cities. *Econometrica, 89*(6), 2679–2715.

Hicks, J. R., & Allen, R. G. D. (1934). A reconsideration of the theory of value: Part I. *Economica, 1*(1), 52–76.

Hottman, C. J., Redding, S. J., & Weinstein, D. E. (2016). Quantifying the sources of firm heterogeneity. *Quarterly Journal of Economics, 131*(3), 1291–1364.

Ichimura, S. (1951). A critical note on the definition of related goods. *Review of Economic Studies, 18*(3), 179–183.

International Labour Organization (ILO), Eurostat, IMF, OECD, World Bank, UN (2004b)Producer Price Index Manual: Theory and Practice. International Monetary Fund.

International Monetary Fund (IMF), Eurostat, United Nations, OECD, and World Bank. (2020). Consumer Price Index Manual: Concepts and Methods.

Osborne, M. (2018). Approximating the cost-of-living index for a storable good. *American Economic Journal: Microeconomics, 10*(2), 286–331.

[12] See Eurostat (1999) and Triplett (1985) for detail.

Oulton, N. (2008). Chain indices of the cost-of-living and the path-dependence problem: An empirical solution. *Journal of Econometrics, 144*(1), 306–324.
Redding, S. J., & Weinstein, D. E. (2020). Measuring aggregate price indices with taste shocks: Theory and evidence for CES preferences. *Quarterly Journal of Economics, 135*(1), 503–560.
Triplett, J. E. (2001). Should the cost-of-living index provide the conceptual framework for a consumer price index? *The Economic Journal, 111*(472), F311–F334.

Exact and Superlative Index

6

Abstract

This chapter discusses superlative indices, exploring their relationship with the cost-of-living index (COLI) and how they can provide a good approximation without precise knowledge of the utility and expenditure functions. It explains the concept of "exact" indices, such as the Sato–Vartia index, which aligns perfectly with the COLI under specific utility functions like the Constant Elasticity of Substitution (CES). The chapter also introduces the theory of superlative indices, which simplifies the computation of exact indices by using standard indices like Fisher, Walsh, and Törnqvist without identifying the underling expenditure function. Key examples are given to illustrate how these indices correspond to the COLI under various assumptions, showing how superlative indices can be computed easily and how they approximate the true COLI effectively. The discussion highlights their practical significance in simplifying complex economic measurements and their impact on theoretical and practical economics, making them pivotal in modern index number research.

6.1 Introduction

The cost-of-living index (COLI) discussed in Chap. 5 is defined as the ratio of expenditure functions and it requires the estimation of structural parameters contained in the expenditure function for its calculation. While this is a valuable academic endeavor, it is not suitable for the daily task of compiling prices and quantities. Furthermore, the assumption that quantities always lie on the demand curve is a strong one, and observed quantities can significantly differ from the assumed ones.

The potential of the COLI expands considerably when we treat the information on quantities more flexibly. Standard price indices, such as the Laspeyres and Fisher indices, have a domain that covers all positive real values of prices and quantities. On the other hand, the COLI is defined in a much narrower range due to the constraint

N. Abe, *Price Index Numbers*, Springer Texts in Business and Economics,
https://doi.org/10.1007/978-981-97-6305-4_6

that "quantities and prices must lie on the demand curve." This means that standard bilateral price indices have larger domains than the COLI. The concept that comes into play here is an "exact" index. A bilateral price index that depends on prices and quantities is called an exact index if it matches the COLI when the quantities and prices lie on a specific demand function. As we will show in this chapter, the Sato–Vartia index becomes identical to the Constant Elasticity of Substitution (CES)-type COLI when the quantities and prices are on the demand curve derived from a CES-type utility function. In this case, the Sato–Vartia index is called "exact" with respect to the CES utility function. To be more precise, first consider a specific preference relation, or utility/expenditure function. Then, if a price index is "exact" with respect to that utility function, it means that the index coincides with the true COLI by Konüs when the quantities are on the demand function derived from that of the preference. In other words, when the observed quantities and prices are consistent with the assumed preference relation, and a price index coincides with the COLI, such an index is called "exact."

That the Sato–Vartia index is "exact" with respect to the CES-type utility function means that when there is a CES-type demand curve relationship between quantities and prices, the Sato–Vartia index acquires the properties of the COLI. Similar properties can also be obtained for the Fisher, Walsh, and Törnqvist indices. While each corresponds to different utility and expenditure functions, all become the COLI when quantities are on their respective demand curves. One might think that these exact price indices are useless without knowing the relationship between quantities and prices, namely, the shape of the demand curve. However, the superlative index by Diewert (1976) solves this problem. The superlative index is an exact index that corresponds to an expenditure (utility) function with many free parameters, allowing it to approximate any twice continuously differentiable expenditure (utility) function to the second order. The Fisher, Walsh, and Törnqvist indices are known as superlative indices. This means that, as long as we use either the Fisher, Walsh, or Törnqvist index, we can treat it as a very good approximation of the exact index for a broad class of preferences. In other words, the theory of the superlative index enables us to obtain a good approximation of the exact index without the need to identify or assume the demand function, underlying preferences, or the expenditure function. This represents a significant turning point in the history of index number theory. In this chapter, we will discuss in detail the superlative index, focusing on the relationship between standard price indices and the COLI.

6.2 Examples of Correspondence Between COLI and Price Index (CES Type)

As in Chap. 5, let's assume a CES-type homothetic utility function with observed quantities lying on the corresponding demand function:

$$u(\mathbf{q}) = \left(\sum_{i=1}^{N} (a_i q_i)^{\frac{\sigma-1}{\sigma}} \right)^{\frac{\sigma}{\sigma-1}} \tag{6.1}$$

$$\sigma > 1, a_i > 0, \sum_{i=1}^{N} a_i = 1$$

The compensated demand function, the unit expenditure function, and the COLI are then given by

$$q_i = (a_i)^{\sigma-1} \left(\frac{p_i}{P} \right)^{-\sigma} u \tag{6.2}$$

$$P = \left(\sum_{i=1}^{N} \left(\frac{p_i}{a_i} \right)^{1-\sigma} \right)^{\frac{1}{1-\sigma}} \tag{6.3}$$

$$COLI(P_0, P_t) = \left(\frac{\sum_{i=1}^{N} (a_i)^{\sigma-1} (p_{it})^{1-\sigma}}{\sum_{i=1}^{N} (a_i)^{\sigma-1} (p_{i0})^{1-\sigma}} \right)^{\frac{1}{1-\sigma}} \tag{6.4}$$

Transforming the COLI results in

$$\begin{aligned} COLI(P_0, P_t) &= \left(\frac{\sum_{i=1}^{N} (a_i)^{\sigma-1} (p_{it})^{1-\sigma}}{\sum_{k=1}^{N} (a_k)^{\sigma-1} (p_{k0})^{1-\sigma}} \right)^{\frac{1}{1-\sigma}} \\ &= \left(\frac{\sum_{i=1}^{N} (a_i)^{\sigma-1} (p_{i0})^{1-\sigma}}{\sum_{k=1}^{N} (a_k)^{\sigma-1} (p_{k0})^{1-\sigma}} \left(\frac{p_{it}}{p_{i0}} \right)^{1-\sigma} \right)^{\frac{1}{1-\sigma}} \end{aligned} \tag{6.5}$$

Transforming the demand function yields

$$p_{i0} q_{i0} = (a_i)^{\sigma-1} (p_{i0})^{1-\sigma} u P_0^{\sigma}$$

Considering Y as the nominal total consumption expenditure and using the homogeneity of (6.1), we get

$$Y = C(\mathbf{p}, u) = uP \tag{6.6}$$

Hence

$$\frac{p_i q_i}{P_0} = (a_i)^{\sigma-1} (p_{i0})^{1-\sigma} P_0^{\sigma-1} = w_{i0} \tag{6.7}$$

Organizing this leads to

$$(a_i)^{\sigma-1}(p_{i0})^{1-\sigma} = w_{i0}P_0^{1-\sigma} \tag{6.8}$$

$$\sum_{i=1}^{N}(a_i)^{\sigma-1}(p_{i0})^{1-\sigma} = \sum_{i=1}^{N} w_{i0}P_0^{1-\sigma} = P_0^{1-\sigma} \tag{6.9}$$

Substituting these into (6.5), we get

$$\begin{aligned}
COLI(P_0, P_t) &= \left(\frac{\sum_{i=1}^{N}(a_i)^{\sigma-1}(p_{i0})^{1-\sigma}}{\sum_{k=1}^{N}(a_k)^{\sigma-1}(p_{k0})^{1-\sigma}}\left(\frac{p_{i1}}{p_{i0}}\right)^{1-\sigma}\right)^{\frac{1}{1-\sigma}} \\
&= \left(\frac{\sum_{i=1}^{N} w_{i0}P_0^{1-\sigma}}{P_0^{1-\sigma}}\left(\frac{p_{i1}}{p_{i0}}\right)^{1-\sigma}\right)^{\frac{1}{1-\sigma}} \\
&= \left(\sum_{i=1}^{N} w_{i0}\left(\frac{p_{it}}{p_{i0}}\right)^{1-\sigma}\right)^{\frac{1}{1-\sigma}}
\end{aligned} \tag{6.10}$$

This is the renowned Lloyd and Moulton index number formula, representing the CES-type price index based on price ratios.[1] Essentially, when quantities align with the demand function, the COLI matches the CES-type price index weighted by the base-period expenditure shares. This means that the Lloyd- and Moulton-type price index is an exact index in relation to the CES-type utility function.

It is noteworthy that, besides the Lloyd and Moulton indices, there exists a range of exact price indices that align with the CES-type COLI. Let Y denote the nominal total expenditure, then the demand function is as follows:

$$q_i = (a_i)^{\sigma-1}\left(\frac{p_i}{P}\right)^{-\sigma}\frac{Y}{P} \tag{6.11}$$

Transforming this equation, we have

$$\frac{p_i q_i}{Y} = (a_i)^{\sigma-1}\left(\frac{p_i}{P}\right)^{1-\sigma}$$

The left side represents the expenditure share. Denoting the expenditure share for good i in period t as w_{it}, we can write

$$w_{it} = (a_i)^{\sigma-1}\left(\frac{p_{it}}{P_t}\right)^{1-\sigma} \tag{6.12}$$

[1] For further details, refer to Lloyd (1975), Moulton (1996), and Shapiro and Wilcox (1997). Additional recent studies on this index include Lent and Dorfman (2009).

Taking the logarithmic difference between periods 0 and t in (6.12), and since the preference parameter a_i is constant over time, we get

$$\ln w_{it} - \ln w_{i0} = (1-\sigma)(\ln p_{it} - \ln p_{i0}) - (1-\sigma)(\ln P_t - \ln P_0)$$

Organizing this, we find

$$\ln P_t - \ln P_0 = (\ln p_{it} - \ln p_{i0}) - \frac{1}{(1-\sigma)}(\ln w_{it} - \ln w_{i0}) \tag{6.13}$$

The left side of (6.13) is equal to the natural logarithm of the COLI. Therefore, the COLI becomes a function of the price ratio and the expenditure share ratio for good i only, and can be expressed as

$$\frac{P_t}{P_0} = \frac{p_{it}}{p_{i0}}\left(\frac{w_{it}}{w_{i0}}\right)^{\frac{1}{\sigma-1}} \tag{6.14}$$

Normally, to compute a price index, it is necessary to aggregate prices and quantities for many goods. However, if quantities are on the demand function, we can obtain the COLI by observing only the changes in price and expenditure share of any single good. The left side of (6.13) does not depend on the type of good i, and the right side holds for any i. This means that we have numerous options for representing the COLI. For example:

$$\frac{P_t}{P_0} = \frac{p_{1t}}{p_{10}}\left(\frac{w_{1t}}{w_{10}}\right)^{\frac{1}{\sigma-1}} \tag{6.15}$$

$$= \frac{p_{2t}}{p_{20}}\left(\frac{w_{2t}}{w_{20}}\right)^{\frac{1}{\sigma-1}} \tag{6.16}$$

$$= \frac{1}{2}\frac{p_{1t}}{p_{10}}\left(\frac{w_{1t}}{w_{10}}\right)^{\frac{1}{\sigma-1}} + \frac{1}{2}\frac{p_{2t}}{p_{20}}\left(\frac{w_{2t}}{w_{20}}\right)^{\frac{1}{\sigma-1}} \tag{6.17}$$

$$= \left(\frac{p_{1t}}{p_{10}}\left(\frac{w_{1t}}{w_{10}}\right)^{\frac{1}{\sigma-1}}\right)^{1/2}\left(\frac{p_{2t}}{p_{20}}\left(\frac{w_{2t}}{w_{20}}\right)^{\frac{1}{\sigma-1}}\right)^{1/2} \tag{6.18}$$

As such, the relationship between the prices and expenditure shares of any good, and their various "averages," all coincide, meaning that (6.15)–(6.18) are all exact with respect to the CES-type utility function, i.e., they coincide with the COLI when quantities and prices are on the CES-type demand function.[2] The right side of (6.13) is a function of prices and expenditure shares and represents a type of (logarithmic difference) price index. Therefore, it can be considered a standard bilateral price index number formula.

---

[2] For more details on the COLI corresponding to the CES-type utility function, see de Haan (2020).

Let's take the simple arithmetic average of each good in the right side of (6.13):

$$\ln P_t - \ln P_0 = \frac{1}{N}\sum(\ln p_{it} - \ln p_{i0}) + \frac{1}{N}\sum\frac{1}{(\sigma-1)}(\ln w_{it} - \ln w_{i0}) \tag{6.19}$$

This equation is identical to the CUPI formula by Redding and Weinstein (2020) discussed in Chap. 5, which is a COLI when preferences change. If preferences do not change, and quantities are always on the demand curve corresponding to the CES-type utility function, then (6.19) coincides with the CES-type COLI. In other words, (6.19) is exact for the CES-type utility function under the assumption of constant preferences. The CUPI, or the COLI when preferences change, imposes no constraints on quantities and prices, so (6.19) always coincides with the COLI when preferences change.

When using exact indices without directly computing the COLI, it is essential that these exact indices have desirable properties as index number formulas. In this regard, (6.19) does not satisfy identity, and the Lloyd and Moulton type (6.10) requires the estimation of substitution elasticity, which is not a trivial task. Then, taking the logarithmic average of each good in the right side of (6.13), we get

$$\ln P_t - \ln P_0 = \sum_{i=1}^{N}\beta_i\left((\ln p_{it} - \ln p_{i0}) - \frac{1}{(1-\sigma)}(\ln \omega_{it} - \ln \omega_{i0})\right)$$

$$\beta_i = \frac{\omega_{it}-\omega_{i0}}{\ln\omega_{it}-\ln\omega_{i0}} \Big/ \sum_{i=1}^{N}\left(\frac{\omega_{it}-\omega_{i0}}{\ln\omega_{it}-\ln\omega_{i0}}\right)$$

Organizing this, we find

$$\ln P_t - \ln P_0 = \sum_{i=1}^{N}\beta_i\left((\ln p_{it} - \ln p_{i0})\right) - \frac{1}{(1-\sigma)}\sum_{i=1}^{N}\beta_i(\ln \omega_{it} - \ln \omega_{i0})$$

$$\begin{aligned}\sum_{i=1}^{N}\beta_i(\ln\omega_{it}-\ln\omega_{i0}) &= \sum_{i=1}^{N}\frac{(\omega_{it}-\omega_{i0})(\ln\omega_{it}-\ln\omega_{i0})}{\ln\omega_{it}-\ln\omega_{i0}} \Big/ \sum_{i=1}^{N}\left(\frac{\omega_{it}-\omega_{i0}}{\ln\omega_{it}-\ln\omega_{i0}}\right)\\ &= \sum_{i=1}^{N}(\omega_{it}-\omega_{i0}) \Big/ \sum_{i=1}^{N}\left(\frac{\omega_{it}-\omega_{i0}}{\ln\omega_{it}-\ln\omega_{i0}}\right)\end{aligned}$$

Using the fact that

$$\sum_{i=1}^{N}\omega_{it} = \sum_{i=1}^{N}\omega_{i0} = 1$$

the terms involving substitution elasticity disappear, resulting in

$$\ln P_t - \ln P_0 = \sum_{i=1}^{N} \beta_i \left(\ln p_{it} - \ln p_{i0}\right)$$

$$\beta_i = \frac{\omega_{it} - \omega_{i0}}{\ln \omega_{it} - \ln \omega_{i0}} \Big/ \sum_{i=1}^{N} \left(\frac{\omega_{it} - \omega_{i0}}{\ln \omega_{it} - \ln \omega_{i0}} \right)$$

This results in the Sato–Vartia index, which can be computed easily from observed price and expenditure share information without the need to estimate elasticities of substitution. The Sato–Vartia index satisfies commensurability, identity, and homogeneity of degree one properties. As seen in Chap. 4, it also possesses the rare property of the factor reversal. Furthermore, if quantities are on the demand curve, it may appear to be an ideal index formula, satisfying other important axiomatic properties such as monotonicity and transitivity. It is important to note that monotonicity and transitivity only hold when quantities are on the demand curve; generally, the Sato–Vartia index does not satisfy even monotonicity, let alone transitivity.[3] The fact that monotonicity does not generally hold may be surprising. The reason is as follows.

The Sato–Vartia and Törnqvist indices use expenditure share information as weights. When prices change while quantities remain constant, the weights also change. Depending on this change, in extreme cases, the Sato–Vartia and Törnqvist indices may fail to satisfy monotonicity. Below, let's consider an example by Lippe (2007). In a two-good two-period model, consider the case where the price of the second good $p_{12} = x$ in the first period (comparison time) takes on three different values: 1, 5, and 10 as in Table 6.1.

Then, the index number values are reported in Table 6.2.

Table 6.1 An example by Lippe: Data

Time	p_0	p_1	q_0	q_1
1	30	40	50	20
2	80	x	4	40

Table 6.2 An example by Lippe: index numbers

p_{12}	Laspeyres	Paasche	Törnqvist	Sato–Vartia
1	1.101	0.221	0.791	0.837
5	1.110	0.263	0.750	0.751
10	1.121	0.316	0.730	0.740

[3] Not only the Sato–Vartia index but also the Törnqvist index does not satisfy monotonicity. For more details, see Reinsdorf and Dorfman (1999).

Laspeyres and Paasche indices satisfy monotonicity, so as prices, p_{12}, increase, the values of these indices also increase. However, as shown in Table 6.2, the Törnqvist index and the Sato–Vartia index decrease as prices rise.

The Sato-Vartia index becomes a COLI when quantities and prices lie on the demand functions derived from a CES utility function. In such cases, the quantity ratio of two goods, i and j, is expressed as follows:

$$\frac{q_i}{q_j} = \left(\frac{a_j p_i}{a_i p_j}\right)^{-\sigma} \tag{6.20}$$

which becomes a function of the price ratio of the two goods. For example, the quantity ratio of apples to oranges is independent of the price of bananas. This is because it assumes that the elasticities of substitution between apples and oranges, and oranges and another good, are the same, which is quite a strong assumption and not always valid. Therefore, a more general demand function, that is, a price index formula corresponding to preference relations, would be desirable. This is the idea behind Diewert's superlative index (Diewert 1976), where the following "Flexible Function" plays an important role.

6.3 Flexible Function

A flexible function is a function with numerous parameters that can approximate any complex shape (continuously differentiable) function by adjusting its parameters. Assuming there are N goods, consider two functions f and $f^* : \mathbb{R}^N_{++} \to \mathbb{R}_{++}$ in the N-dimensional positive real number space. Assuming both are twice differentiable, for their second-order approximations to match at $x^* \in \mathbb{R}^N_{++}$, it is required that

$$f\left(\mathbf{x}^*\right) = f^*\left(\mathbf{x}^*\right) \tag{6.21}$$

$$\nabla f\left(\mathbf{x}^*\right) = \nabla f^*\left(\mathbf{x}^*\right) \tag{6.22}$$

$$\nabla^2 f\left(\mathbf{x}^*\right) = \nabla^2 f^*\left(\mathbf{x}^*\right) \tag{6.23}$$

The number of equations imposed by each condition are one for (6.21), N for (6.22) since it's N-dimensional, and N^2 for (6.23). Considering continuous twice differentiability of both f and f^*, by Young's theorem, $\nabla^2 f\left(x^*\right)$ becomes a symmetric matrix. Therefore, the number of constraints from (6.23) is $N(N+1)/2$. The total number of constraints is then $1 + N + N(N+1)/2$.

For instance, consider the function $f(\mathbf{x})$ as

$$f(\mathbf{x}) = a_0 + a'\mathbf{x} + \frac{1}{2}\mathbf{x}'A\mathbf{x} \tag{6.24}$$

The number of free parameters is $1 + N + N(N+1)/2$. Additionally, by solving the following three equations:

$$a_0 + a'\mathbf{x}^* + \frac{1}{2}\mathbf{x}^{*\prime}A\mathbf{x}^* = f^*\left(\mathbf{x}^*\right)$$
$$a + \mathbf{x}^* = \nabla f^*\left(\mathbf{x}^*\right)$$
$$A = \nabla^2 f^*\left(\mathbf{x}^*\right)$$

we can obtain A, a, and a_0. Thus, any twice continuously differentiable function $f^*(\mathbf{x})$ can be approximated to the second order by the function $f(\mathbf{x})$ defined in (6.24). In economic models, it is common to assume homogeneity in functions such as expenditure functions, cost functions, or production functions. For instance, consider an expenditure function denoted as $f^*(\mathbf{x})$. When calculating its cost-of-living index (COLI) approximation, it is not necessary to consider all twice continuously differentiable functions. Instead, it suffices to restrict the scope to functions that are both twice continuously differentiable and homogenous of degree one. In other words, the function $f(\mathbf{x})$ that needs to approximate can be limited to homogeneous functions of degree one.

However, finding a function $f(\mathbf{x})$ that approximates up to the second order and satisfies homogeneity is not trivial. For example, imposing first-degree homogeneity on (6.24) leads to

$$a_0 = 0, \quad A = 0,$$
$$f(\mathbf{x}) = a'\mathbf{x}.$$

However, this form fails to satisfy both (6.23) and (6.21), meaning that (6.24) does not provide a meaningful approximation in economics.

When the function $f(\mathbf{x})$ is homogeneous of degree one, constraints can be imposed on the first and second derivatives for any $\mathbf{x} \in \mathbb{R}^N_{++}$ as follows:

$$x'\nabla f(\mathbf{x}) = f(\mathbf{x}) \tag{6.25}$$

$$\nabla^2 f(\mathbf{x})\,\mathbf{x} = 0 \tag{6.26}$$

$$\nabla^2 f(\mathbf{x}) = \left[\nabla^2 f(\mathbf{x})\right]' \tag{6.27}$$

Note that, by Euler's theorem, the first derivative of an Nth degree homogeneous function becomes an $(N-1)$th degree homogeneous function. The number of constraints for each are 1, N, and $N(N-1)/2$, respectively.

Now, consider twice continuously differentiable first-degree homogeneous functions, f and $f^* : \mathbb{R}^N_{++} \to \mathbb{R}_{++}$. Then, both functions satisfy (6.25)–(6.27). Furthermore, for f to be a second-order approximation of f^*, the following conditions must be met:

$$\nabla f\left(\mathbf{x}^*\right) = \nabla f^*\left(\mathbf{x}^*\right) \tag{6.28}$$

$$\frac{\partial^2 f(\mathbf{x}^*)}{\partial x_i \partial x_j} = \frac{\partial^2 f^*(\mathbf{x}^*)}{\partial x_i \partial x_j} \quad \text{for } 1 \le i < j \le n \tag{6.29}$$

The required number of constraints are N and $N(N-1)/2$, which total to $N(N+1)/2$. Note that if $\nabla f(\mathbf{x}^*) = \nabla f^*(\mathbf{x}^*)$, then both functions being first-degree homogeneous imply $\nabla f(\mathbf{x}^*)\mathbf{x}^* = \nabla f^*(\mathbf{x}^*)\mathbf{x}^* = f(\mathbf{x}^*) = f^*(\mathbf{x}^*)$. Also, (6.29) excludes diagonal components. This is because, if the off-diagonal components are determined and $\nabla^2 f(\mathbf{x}^*)\mathbf{x}^* = \nabla^2 f(\mathbf{x}^*)\mathbf{x}^* = 0$ holds, then the diagonal components are also determined from there.

6.4 Quadratic Mean of Order r

In the theory of price indices, a frequently used functional form is the Quadratic Mean of Order r, given by

$$f(\mathbf{p}) = \left(\sum_{i=1}^{N} \sum_{k=1}^{N} a_{ik} p_i^{r/2} p_k^{r/2} \right)^{1/r}$$
$$a_{ij} = a_{ji}, \quad r \neq 0$$

This function is twice continuously differentiable and first-degree homogeneous. Now, can this function serve as a second-order approximation for any continuously twice differentiable function, $f^*(\mathbf{x})$? Diewert (1976) demonstrates that this function indeed approximates $f^*(\mathbf{x})$ up to the second order. Fixing r and allowing a_{ij} to vary freely, the number of parameters becomes $N(N+1)/2$. Therefore, there are enough parameters. Thus, it needs to be shown that

$$\frac{\partial^2 f}{\partial p_i \partial p_j} = \frac{\partial^2 f^*}{\partial p_i \partial p_j} \quad \text{for } 1 \leq i < j \leq n$$
$$\nabla f(\mathbf{x}^*) = \nabla f^*(\mathbf{x}^*)$$

This can be proven by brute force, arranging (6.28) and (6.29), solving the resulting system of $N(N+1)/2$ equations for a_{ij}, and showing that a solution exists. The proof is quite involved, so for details, refer to Diewert (1976). As shown below, the Walsh index becomes an (implicit) COLI when $r = 1$, and the Fisher index becomes a COLI when $r = 2$. That is, both the Fisher and Walsh indices correspond to cost-of-living indices for flexible functions. A flexible function is a twice continuously differentiable and can approximate any such function to the second order, meaning it can be considered a COLI without specifying an underlying utility or expenditure function. In contrast, the CES-type utility function introduced at the beginning of this chapter has only $N+1$ parameters, far fewer than the Quadratic Mean of Order r, and cannot achieve a second-order approximation. Diewert (1978) classifies the Sato–Vartia index, derived from a CES-type utility function, as a pseudo-superlative index because it lacks the flexibility to yield a second-order approximation and remains only a first-order approximation.[4]

6.5 Walsh Index and Superlative Index as Cost-of-Living Indices

This section demonstrates that the Walsh index serves as an (indirect) COLI. Assume a Quadratic Mean of Order r type utility function as follows:[5]

$$u(\mathbf{q}) = \left(\sum_{i=1}^{N} \sum_{k=1}^{N} a_{ik} q_i^{r/2} q_k^{r/2} \right)^{1/r} \tag{6.30}$$

$$a_{ij} = a_{ji}, \quad r \neq 0$$

where $0 < r$. Consider the following quantity index:

$$QI^r = \frac{\left(\sum_{i=1}^{N} w_{i0} (q_{i1}/q_{i0})^{r/2} \right)^{1/r}}{\left(\sum_{i=1}^{N} w_{i1} (q_{i0}/q_{i1})^{r/2} \right)^{1/r}} \tag{6.31}$$

$$w_{it} = \frac{p_{it} q_{it}}{\sum_{i=1}^{N} p_{it} q_{it}}$$

This quantity index matches the ratio of utility functions defined in (6.30) when $r = 1$.[6] Now consider the implicit price index that acts as the cofactor to this quantity index, i.e., the value index deflated by the quantity index. Assuming $r = 1$, we have

$$PI^r = \frac{\sum_{i=1}^{N} p_{i1} q_{i1}}{QI^r \sum_{i=1}^{N} p_{i0} q_{i0}} \tag{6.32}$$

$$= \frac{\sum_{i=1}^{N} w_{i1} (q_{i0}/q_{i1})^{1/2} \sum_{i=1}^{N} p_{i1} q_{i1}}{\sum_{i=1}^{N} w_{i0} (q_{i1}/q_{i0})^{1/2} \sum_{i=1}^{N} p_{i0} q_{i0}}$$

$$= \frac{\sum_{i=1}^{N} p_{i1} q_{i1} (q_{i0}/q_{i1})^{1/2}}{\sum_{i=1}^{N} p_{i0} q_{i0} (q_{i1}/q_{i0})^{1/2}} \tag{6.33}$$

$$= \frac{\sum_{i=1}^{N} p_{i1} (q_{i0} q_{i1})^{1/2}}{\sum_{i=1}^{N} p_{i0} (q_{i1} q_{i0})^{1/2}} \tag{6.34}$$

[4] On the other hand, Barnett and Choi (2008) relax the definition of a "flexible function" and, according to their unique definition, demonstrate that the Sato–Vartia index can also be a COLI for a flexible function, approximating any expenditure function to the second order like a superlative index. Whether the Sato–Vartia index can truly provide a good approximation remains unsettled.

[5] The proof that the Walsh, Fisher, and Törnqvist indices (Walsh index in an implicit manner) serve as cost-of-living indices is covered in Diewert (1976).

[6] For the proof, refer to Mathematical Appendix A.

which becomes the Walsh index. In other words, the Walsh index coincides with the implicitly defined COLI for the Quadratic Mean of Order r, where $r = 1$. Broadly speaking, the Walsh index is exact for the Quadratic Mean of Order r case when $r = 1$.

What does it mean that the Walsh index is (implicitly) exact for a flexible utility function? Suppose actual quantities and prices are determined by unknown preference relations. We calculate the COLI using (6.30). This utility function includes many parameters. To calculate the COLI, these parameters must be estimated. Normally, this estimation is done using regression analysis or various moments to fit the data and model. Then, the derived the COLI from (6.30) is identical to the Walsh index! That is, we can obtain the COLI simply from the information on quantities and prices at two points in time without having to estimate numerous parameters. How is this possible? The Walsh index is a COLI derived from the flexible function (6.30). This function can be a second-order approximation to any twice continuously differentiable utility function. By calculating the Walsh index, we effectively specify the vast parameters, which can be interpreted as providing a second-order approximation of the true utility function. Diewert called such indices superlative indices. We need not struggle to estimate the true COLI or the complex parameters of a utility function structure. Simply calculating a Walsh-type price index gives us a good approximation of the true COLI. Of course, this assumes a certain constant relationship between quantities and prices, but the theory of the superlative index is one of the greatest achievements in index number theory in the late twentieth century.

6.6 Fisher Index as a Cost-of-Living Index

The Fisher index, like the Walsh index, is also a superlative index. This is demonstrated below.

Let's assume a flexible function for the expenditure function instead of the utility function. Taking the natural logarithm of the expenditure function and differentiating it with respect to logarithmic prices, we get

$$\frac{\partial \ln C(\mathbf{p}, u)}{\partial \ln p_i} = \frac{p_i}{C(\mathbf{p}, u)} \frac{\partial C(\mathbf{p}, u)}{\partial p_i}$$

From the Shephard-McKenzie's lemma, the partial derivative of the expenditure function with respect to the price of good i becomes the compensated demand for that good:

$$\frac{\partial C(\mathbf{p}, u)}{\partial p_i} = h_i(\mathbf{p}, u)$$

Thus,

$$\frac{\partial \ln C(\mathbf{p}, u)}{\partial \ln p_i} = \frac{p_i h_i(\mathbf{p}, u)}{C(\mathbf{p}, u)}$$

becomes the expenditure share. Assuming homothetic preferences, the expenditure function is separable into a unit cost function and utility level:

$$C(\mathbf{p}, u) = c(\mathbf{p})\, u.$$

Now, let's assume the following Quadratic Mean of Order r function for the expenditure function:

$$c(\mathbf{p}) = \left(\sum_{i=1}^{N} \sum_{k=1}^{N} b_{ik} p_i^{r/2} p_k^{r/2} \right)^{1/r} \tag{6.35}$$

$$b_{ik} = b_{ki}$$

Expanding the expression, we get

$$c^r = \sum_{i=1}^{N} \sum_{k=1}^{N} b_{ik} p_i^{r/2} p_k^{r/2}$$

$$r c^{r-1} c' = \frac{r}{2} \sum_{k=1}^{N} b_{ik} p_i^{(r-2)/2} p_k^{r/2}$$

$$\frac{p_i c'}{c} = w_i = c^{-r} \frac{r}{2} \sum_{k=1}^{N} b_{ik} p_i^{r/2} p_k^{r/2}$$

Differentiating this expenditure function with respect to the price of good i, we obtain

$$\frac{p_i}{c(\mathbf{p})} \frac{\partial c(\mathbf{p})}{\partial p_i} = \frac{p_i^{(r-2)/2} \sum_{k=1}^{N} b_{ik} p_k^{r/2}}{c(\mathbf{p})^r} \tag{6.36}$$

$$= \frac{\sum_{k=1}^{N} b_{ik} p_i^{r/2} p_k^{r/2}}{c(\mathbf{p})^r} \tag{6.37}$$

$$= w_i \tag{6.38}$$

Consider the following price index:

$$PI^r = \frac{\sqrt[r]{\sum_{i=1}^{N} w_{i0} (p_{i1}/p_{i0})^{r/2}}}{\sqrt[r]{\sum_{i=1}^{N} w_{i1} (p_{i0}/p_{i1})^{r/2}}} \tag{6.39}$$

Eliminating expenditure shares and using the symmetry of the function, we have

$$PI^r = \frac{c(\mathbf{p}_1)\sqrt[r]{\sum_{i=1}^{N}(p_{i1}/p_{i0})^{r/2}\left(\sum_{k=1}^{N} b_{ik}p_{i0}^{r/2}p_{k0}^{r/2}\right)}}{c(\mathbf{p}_0)\sqrt[r]{\sum_{i=1}^{N}(p_{i0}/p_{i1})^{r/2}\left(\sum_{k=1}^{N} b_{ik}p_{i1}^{r/2}p_{k1}^{r/2}\right)}} \tag{6.40}$$

$$= \frac{c(\mathbf{p}_1)\sqrt[r]{\sum_{i=1}^{N}(p_{i1})^{r/2}\left(\sum_{k=1}^{N} b_{ik}p_{k0}^{r/2}\right)}}{c(\mathbf{p}_0)\sqrt[r]{\sum_{i=1}^{N}(p_{i0})^{r/2}\left(\sum_{k=1}^{N} b_{ik}p_{k1}^{r/2}\right)}} \tag{6.41}$$

$$= \frac{c(\mathbf{p}_1)\sqrt[r]{\sum_{i=1}^{N}\sum_{k=1}^{N}\left(b_{ik}p_{k0}^{r/2}p_{i1}^{r/2}\right)}}{c(\mathbf{p}_0)\sqrt[r]{\sum_{i=1}^{N}\sum_{k=1}^{N}\left(b_{ik}p_{k1}^{r/2}p_{i0}^{r/2}\right)}} \tag{6.42}$$

$$= \frac{c(\mathbf{p}_1)}{c(\mathbf{p}_0)}. \tag{6.43}$$

Therefore, this price index is exact for the Quadratic Mean of Order r expenditure function. When $r = 2$, this price index is

$$PI^2 = \frac{\sqrt{\sum_{i=1}^{N} w_i^0 (p_{i1}/p_{i0})}}{\sqrt{\sum_{i=1}^{N} w_i^1 (p_{i0}/p_{i1})}} \tag{6.44}$$

$$= \sqrt{\sum_{i=1}^{N} w_i^0 (p_{i1}/p_{i0}) \times \frac{1}{\sqrt{\sum_{i=1}^{N} w_i^1 (p_{i0}/p_{i1})}}} \tag{6.45}$$

This equates to the Fisher index. In other words, the Fisher index is exact for the quadratic mean function order r when $r = 2$.

6.7 Translog Function and Törnqvist Index

Another flexible function, other than the Quadratic Mean of Order r, is the translog function. Specifically, if we define the expenditure function in the translog form and impose homogeneity of degree one in prices, it becomes

$$\ln C(\mathbf{p}, u) = a_0 + \sum_{i=1}^{N} a_i \ln p_i + \frac{1}{2}\sum_{i=1}^{N}\sum_{k=1}^{N} a_{ik} \ln p_i \ln p_k + b_0 \ln u$$
$$+ \sum_{i=1}^{N} b_i \ln p_i \ln u + \frac{1}{2} b_{00} (\ln u)^2$$
$$a_{ik} = a_{ki}, \sum_{i=1}^{N} a_i = 1, \sum_{k=1}^{N} a_{ik} = 0, \sum_{i=1}^{N} b_i = 0$$

Dropping the utility-related terms and renaming variables, we get

$$\ln f(\mathbf{x}) = a_0 + \sum_{i=1}^{N} a_i \ln x_i + \frac{1}{2}\sum_{i=1}^{N}\sum_{k=1}^{N} a_{ik} \ln x_i \ln x_k$$
$$a_{ik} = a_{ki}, \sum_{i=1}^{N} a_i = 1, \sum_{k=1}^{N} a_{ik} = 0$$

This function can be shown to be a second-order approximation of any arbitrary function $f^*(\mathbf{x})$, similar to before, by matching the gradients and Hessians of the two functions and selecting a_{ik}, a_i, a_0 accordingly.[7] Thus, the translog function is also a flexible function. The number of parameters includes 1 for a_0, N for a_i (reduced to $N - 1$ due to the sum constraint), and N^2 for a_{ik} (reduced to $N(N-1)/2$ due to symmetry and sum constraints). Ultimately, there are $1 + N - 1 + N(N-1)/2 = N(N+1)/2$ parameters, sufficient for a second-order approximation. The Törnqvist index is exact for this translog-type expenditure function. Note that, in general, the translog-type expenditure function does not impose homothetic preferences. When preferences are non-homothetic, the COLI depends on the utility level. The COLI evaluated at the simple geometric mean of utility levels in periods 0 and 1, $u^* \left(= \sqrt{u_0 u_1}\right)$, can be derived as the Törnqvist index. Those interested can refer to the proof written in Mathematical Appendix B:

$$\begin{aligned}
&\ln C\left(\mathbf{p}_1, u^*\right) - \ln C\left(\mathbf{p}_0, u^*\right) \\
&= \frac{1}{2}\sum_{i=1}^{N}\left[\frac{\partial \ln C\left(\mathbf{p}_1, u^*\right)}{\partial \ln p_i} + \frac{\partial \ln C\left(\mathbf{p}_0, u^*\right)}{\partial \ln p_i}\right](\ln p_{i1} - \ln p_{i0}) \\
&= \frac{1}{2}\sum_{i=1}^{N}\left[w_{i0} + w_{i1}\right](\ln p_{i1} - \ln p_{i0}) \qquad (6.46)
\end{aligned}$$

The Törnqvist index is a price index that is exact when the expenditure function is of the translog type. Moreover, since the translog-type expenditure function is

[7] This proof is provided by Christensen et al. (1971).

flexible, the Törnqvist index qualifies as a superlative index. It is particularly noteworthy that, unlike the Fisher and Walsh indices, it does not restrict preferences to being homothetic. Under homothetic preferences, the expenditure function becomes a linear function of the utility level, and the income elasticity equals 1. However, the Törnqvist price index matches the COLI in a simple form without such strong assumptions, making it applicable to a broader class of utility functions than the Fisher and Walsh indices.

6.8 Translog Function and Quadratic Mean of Order r Function

Both the Fisher and Walsh indices are known to correspond to the cost-of-living indices for the Quadratic Mean of Order r function. Depending on the value of r, different cost-of-living indices correspond. Diewert (1980) showed that under the assumptions $\sum_{k=1}^{N} b_{ik} = 0$, $\sum_{i=1}^{N} b_i = 1$, and $b_{ik} = b_{ki}$, a slightly modified Quadratic Mean of Order r function is given by

$$\lim_{r\to 0}\left(\sum_{i=1}^{N} b_i p_i^{r/2} + \frac{2}{r}\sum_{i=1}^{N}\sum_{k=1}^{N} b_{ik} p_i^{r/2} p_k^{r/2}\right)^{1/r} = \sum_{i=1}^{N} b_i \ln p_i + \frac{1}{2}\sum_{i=1}^{N}\sum_{k=1}^{N} b_{ik}\ln p_i \ln p_k \tag{6.47}$$

Thus, the Törnqvist index can be considered as a COLI corresponding to the Quadratic Mean of Order r function for $r = 0$. The proof is straightforward. Using $\sum_{k=1}^{N} b_{ik} = 0$, the following transformations allow the quadratic mean function to be converted into a translog form:

$$y = \left(\sum_{i=1}^{N} b_i p_i^{r/2} + \frac{2}{r}\sum_{i=1}^{N}\sum_{k=1}^{N} b_{ik} p_i^{r/2} p_k^{r/2}\right)^{1/r} \tag{6.48}$$

$$y^r = \sum_{i=1}^{N} b_i p_i^{r/2} + \frac{2}{r}\sum_{i=1}^{N}\sum_{k=1}^{N} b_{ik} p_i^{r/2} p_k^{r/2} \tag{6.49}$$

$$\frac{y^r - 1}{r} = \frac{\sum_{i=1}^{N} b_i p_i^{r/2} - 1}{r} + \frac{\left(2\sum_{i=1}^{N}\sum_{k=1}^{N} b_{ik} p_i^{r/2} p_k^{r/2}\right)}{r^2} \tag{6.50}$$

$$= \frac{\sum_{i=1}^{N} b_i p_i^{r/2} - 1}{r} + \frac{1}{2}\sum_{i=1}^{N}\sum_{k=1}^{N} b_{ik}\frac{\left(p_i^{r/2} - 1\right)}{r/2}\frac{\left(p_k^{r/2} - 1\right)}{r/2} \tag{6.51}$$

Using the definition of the natural logarithm as r approaches zero, we get

$$\lim_{r \to 0} \frac{y^r - 1}{r} = \ln y \tag{6.52}$$

$$= \sum_{i=1}^{N} b_i \ln p_i + \frac{1}{2} \sum_{i=1}^{N} \sum_{k=1}^{N} b_{ik} \ln p_i \ln p_k \tag{6.53}$$

Therefore, by setting parameters in the Quadratic Mean of Order r function to $r = 0, 1, 2$, we can obtain preferences for which Törnqvist, Walsh, and Fisher indices (implicit in the case of Walsh) are exact. It is noted that the Marshall–Edgeworth index is not considered a superlative index as no flexible function has been found that makes it exact.

6.9 Some Criticism: Are Superlative Indices Really the Superlative?

Diewert's theory of superlative indices, which posits that good approximations of the COLI can be obtained by simply calculating Walsh, Fisher, or Törnqvist indexes without imposing strong assumptions on the shape of utility or expenditure functions or estimating structural parameters, has garnered significant attention. Paul Anthony Samuelson, a foundational figure in modern economics and Nobel Laureate, hailed the superlative index as the single greatest advancement in index number research since his "Foundations of Economic Analysis" nearly 40 years earlier.[8] Moreover, the Boskin Report, submitted to the U.S. government in the mid-1990s, advocated the adoption of superlative indices as the official measure of inflation. The United States had published price indices based on the TÃ¶rnqvist index formula from 2002 until 2024. Törnqvist Consumer Price Index (C-CPI-U), a chained index based on the Törnqvist formula.[9]

Fisher, Walsh, and Törnqvist indices are all superlative indices. What relationship does this commonality create among them? Diewert (1978)[10] reached a clear conclusion: "all superlative indices closely approximate each other" (Diewert 1978 p. 884), meaning any two superlative indices are second-order approximations of each other when price and quantity changes between two periods are minimal, i.e., $p_0 = p_1, q_0 = q_1$. While the proof is complex, interested readers are encouraged to consult Diewert (1978). However, it's important to note that just because all superlative indices approximate each other locally does not mean they always yield close values in practice. The superlative property is inherently local, not global, and may remain confined to a very limited domain, differing significantly over the ranges covered in actual data. Indeed, Hill (2006) utilized the Quadratic Mean of Order r

[8] See p.xx in the introduction of Samuelson (1983).

[9] More precisely, it is a chained index based on the Törnqvist formula.

[10] See Diewert (1978).

function to create and compare cost-of-living indices for U.S. GDP data from 1977 to 1994, varying r across a range of values. Remarkably, when r was set to negative and positive infinity, the maximum difference between the resulting indices exceeded that between Laspeyres and Paasche indices in 146 out of 153 items. Even when limiting r between -5 and 5, the indices often surpassed the Laspeyres–Paasche difference. Hill (2006) discovered that as r diverges to infinity, the COLI satisfies

$$\lim_{r\to\infty} PI^r = \lim_{r\to-\infty} PI^r = \sqrt{\min\left(\frac{p_{i1}}{p_{i0}}\right) \times \max\left(\frac{p_{i1}}{p_{i0}}\right)}$$

This right-hand side represents a very special index: the geometric mean of the maximum and minimum price changes among N goods.

Recall that the cost-of-living indices corresponding to the Quadratic Mean of Order r function at $r = 0, 1, 2$ were the Törnqvist, Walsh, and Fisher indices, respectively. Hill (2006) reported that superlative indices generated within $r = 0$ to 2 yield almost identical values. Moreover, using U.S. data and international price comparisons among OECD countries, he noted that the differences were minimal, significantly smaller than those between Laspeyres and Paasche, and at most a few percentage points. However, as the absolute value of r increases, the differences between superlative indices also grow, sometimes exceeding 100%. Thus, even though an index may be superlative, it does not necessarily provide a good approximation in reality.

6.10 Conclusion

The superlative index bridges the gap between standard bilateral price indices such as the Fisher index, and the COLI based on economic theory. It also clearly demonstrates the significance of the Fisher, Törnqvist, and Walsh indices over other indices, significantly influencing subsequent index number theory research and the practice of index compilation. In December 1996, the Consumer Price Index Advisory Committee of the United States Senate presented its final report, "Toward a More Accurate Measure of the Cost of Living," commonly known as the Boskin Report, advocating for the adoption of the superlative index. The United States had published price indices based on the Törnqvist index formula from 2002 until 2024. However, it is also true that, despite being based on the theory of flexible functions, the superlative index relies on strong assumptions. The theory of the superlative index heavily relies on assumption that utility or expenditure functions remain identical across time and locations. To apply superlative index theory to regional price indices, one must assume, for instance, that preferences in the U.S. and Japan, or China and Germany, are identical, as well as between the US in the 1980s and 2000s. In other words, prices and quantities must "always" exist on a specific common demand curve. This is an extreme assumption and difficult to empirically support. When preferences vary across regions and time, or when demand shocks shift demand curves, can an economic approach to calculating price indices still be viable? This remains a frontier in the index number theory, to be explored in detail in Chap. 10.

6.11 Mathematical Appendix A: Derivation of the Walsh Quantity Index

Since the utility function $u(\mathbf{q})$ in Eq. (6.30) is homogeneous of degree one, the preferences underlying it are homothetic. In this case, using the Shephard-McKenzie lemma and setting $C(\mathbf{p}, 1) = c(\mathbf{p})$), we have

$$q_i = u(\mathbf{q})\frac{\partial c(\mathbf{p})}{\partial p_i} \tag{6.54}$$

From the definition of the expenditure function, we get

$$\sum_{i=1}^{N} p_i q_i = u(\mathbf{q})c(\mathbf{p}) \tag{6.55}$$

Therefore,

$$\frac{q_i}{\sum_{i=1}^{N} p_i q_i} = \frac{1}{c(\mathbf{p})}\frac{\partial c(\mathbf{p})}{\partial p_i}$$

Now, using the Lagrange multiplier λ in the first-order condition of expenditure minimization:

$$p_i = \lambda \frac{\partial u(\mathbf{q})}{\partial q_i} \tag{6.56}$$

$$\sum_{i=1}^{N} p_i q_i = \lambda \sum_{i=1}^{N} \frac{\partial u(\mathbf{q})}{\partial q_i} q_i$$

Thus,

$$\lambda = \frac{\sum_{i=1}^{N} p_i q_i}{\sum_{i=1}^{N} \frac{\partial u(\mathbf{q})}{\partial q_i} q_i} \tag{6.57}$$

Therefore,

$$\frac{p_i}{\sum_{i=1}^{N} p_i q_i} = \frac{1}{\sum_{i=1}^{N} \frac{\partial u(\mathbf{q})}{\partial q_i} q_i}\frac{\partial u(\mathbf{q})}{\partial q_i} \tag{6.58}$$

Since the utility function is homogeneous of degree one, Euler's theorem gives us

$$\sum_{i=1}^{N} \frac{\partial u(\mathbf{q})}{\partial q_i} q_i = u(\mathbf{q}) \tag{6.59}$$

Substituting this into Eq. (6.58):

$$\frac{p_i}{\sum_{i=1}^{N} p_i q_i} = \frac{1}{u(\mathbf{q})}\frac{\partial u(\mathbf{q})}{\partial q_i} \tag{6.60}$$

Thus, we have

$$w_{it} = \frac{q_{it}}{u(\mathbf{q}_t)}\frac{\partial u(\mathbf{q}_t)}{\partial q_i}$$

Consider the following derivation:

$$\frac{\partial u(\mathbf{q}_0)}{\partial q_{i0}}\frac{1}{u(\mathbf{q}_0)} = \frac{q_{i0}^{(r-2)/2}\sum_{k=1}^{N} a_{ik} q_{k0}^{r/2}}{u(\mathbf{q}_0)^r} \tag{6.61}$$

$$= \frac{q_{i0}^{-1}\sum_{k=1}^{N} a_{ik} q_{i0}^{r/2} q_{k0}^{r/2}}{u(\mathbf{q}_0)^r} \tag{6.62}$$

Using this, we have

$$w_{it} = \frac{q_{it}}{u(\mathbf{q}_t)}\frac{\partial u(q_t)}{\partial q_i} \tag{6.63}$$

$$= \frac{q_{it} q_{it}^{-1}\sum_{k=1}^{N} a_{ik} q_{it}^{r/2} q_{kt}^{r/2}}{u(\mathbf{q}_t)^r}$$

$$= \frac{\sum_{k=1}^{N} a_{ik} q_{it}^{r/2} q_{kt}^{r/2}}{u(\mathbf{q}_t)^r} \tag{6.64}$$

Setting $r = 1$, we get

$$w_{it} = \frac{\sum_{k=1}^{N} a_{ik} q_{it}^{1/2} q_{kt}^{1/2}}{u(\mathbf{q}_t)}$$

Now, consider the quantity index QI^r:

$$QI^r = \frac{\left(\sum_{i=1}^{N} w_{i0}\,(q_{i1}/q_{i0})^{r/2}\right)^{1/r}}{\left(\sum_{i=1}^{N} w_{i1}\,(q_{i0}/q_{i1})^{r/2}\right)^{1/r}} \tag{6.65}$$

$$= \frac{\frac{1}{u(\mathbf{q}_0)}\sum_{i=1}^{N}\left(\sum_{k=1}^{N} a_{ik} q_{i0}^{1/2} q_{k0}^{1/2}\right)(q_{i1}/q_{i0})^{1/2}}{\frac{1}{u(\mathbf{q}_1)}\sum_{i=1}^{N}\left(\sum_{k=1}^{N} a_{ik} q_{i1}^{1/2} q_{k1}^{1/2}\right)(q_{i0}/q_{i1})^{1/2}} \tag{6.66}$$

$$= \frac{u(\mathbf{q}_1)\sum_{i=1}^{N}\left(\sum_{k=1}^{N} a_{ik} q_{i1}^{1/2} q_{k0}^{1/2}\right)}{u(\mathbf{q}_0)\sum_{i=1}^{N}\left(\sum_{k=1}^{N} a_{ik} q_{i0}^{1/2} q_{k1}^{1/2}\right)} \tag{6.67}$$

Given that $a_{ik} = a_{ki}$, we have

$$\sum_{i=1}^{N}\sum_{k=1}^{N} a_{ik} q_{i1}^{1/2} q_{k0}^{1/2} = \sum_{i=1}^{N}\sum_{k=1}^{N} a_{ik} q_{i0}^{1/2} q_{k1}^{1/2} \tag{6.68}$$

Therefore, the quantity index QI^r can be expressed as

$$QI^r = \frac{u(\mathbf{q}_1)}{u(\mathbf{q}_0)} \tag{6.69}$$

This indicates that the quantity index defined in (6.31) becomes equivalent to the ratio of the utility functions when $r = 1$.

6.12 Mathematical Appendix B: Derivation of the Törnqvist Index

From the definition of the expenditure function, we have

$$C(\mathbf{p}_0, u_0) = \sum_{i=1}^{N} p_{i0} q_{i0}, \tag{6.70}$$

$$C(\mathbf{p}_1, u_1) = \sum_{i=1}^{N} p_{i1} q_{i1}. \tag{6.71}$$

By Shepherd-McKenzie's lemma:

$$w_{i0} = \frac{p_{i0} q_{i0}}{\sum_{i=1}^{N} p_{i0} q_{i0}} \tag{6.72}$$

$$= \frac{\partial \ln C\left(\mathbf{P}_0, u_0\right)}{\partial \ln p_{i0}} \tag{6.73}$$

Differentiating the translog expenditure function:

$$\frac{\partial \ln C\left(\mathbf{P}_0, u_0\right)}{\partial \ln p_{i0}} = w_{i0} \tag{6.74}$$

$$= a_i + \sum_{k=1}^{N} a_{ik} \ln p_{k0} + b_i \ln u_0 \tag{6.75}$$

Finally, let's derive an important formula for a quadratic function. Consider a function f defined as

$$f\left(z_1, z_2, \ldots, z_n\right) = a_0 + \sum_{i=1}^{N} a_i z_i + \frac{1}{2} \sum_{i=1}^{N}\sum_{k=1}^{N} a_{ik} z_i z_k, \tag{6.76}$$

$$a_{ik} = a_{ki}. \tag{6.77}$$

This is a quadratic function in z. Therefore, the difference between any two points should match the value of the second-order Taylor expansion at one of the points. Hence:

$$f(\mathbf{z}_1) - f(\mathbf{z}_0) = \sum_{i=1}^{N} \frac{\partial f(\mathbf{z}_0)}{\partial z_i}(z_{i1} - z_{i0}) + \frac{1}{2}\sum_{i=1}^{N}\sum_{k=1}^{N} \frac{\partial^2 f(\mathbf{z}_0)}{\partial z_i \partial z_k}(z_{i1} - z_{i0})(z_{k1} - z_{k0}) \tag{6.78}$$

Up to this point, we have applied the standard Taylor expansion naturally. Additionally, Diewert (1976) demonstrated that the following formula holds true for any quadratic function:

$$f(\mathbf{z}_1) - f(\mathbf{z}_0) = \left(\frac{1}{2}\right)\sum_{i=1}^{N}\left\{\frac{\partial f(\mathbf{z}_0)}{\partial z_i} + \frac{\partial f(\mathbf{z}_1)}{\partial z_i}\right\}(z_{i1} - z_{i0}) \tag{6.79}$$

This implies that the average of the slopes at two points accurately describes the difference between these points. This relation is known as the quadratic approximation formula and is equivalent to the function $f(\mathbf{z}_{i1})$ being quadratic. This is a critically important formula in index theory. Proving that this formula holds when f is a quadratic function is straightforward.[11] When the function is represented in matrix form, it can be organized as follows:

$$f(\mathbf{z}_1) - f(\mathbf{z}_0) = a^T \mathbf{z_1} + \frac{1}{2}\mathbf{z_1}^T A\mathbf{z_1} - a^T \mathbf{z_0} - \frac{1}{2}\mathbf{z_0}^T A\mathbf{z_0} \tag{6.80}$$

$$= a^T(\mathbf{z_1} - \mathbf{z_0}) + \frac{1}{2}\mathbf{z_1}^T A(\mathbf{z_1} - \mathbf{z_0}) + \frac{1}{2}\mathbf{z_0}^T A(\mathbf{z_1} - \mathbf{z_0})$$

$$= \frac{1}{2}[\nabla f(\mathbf{z_1}) + \nabla f(\mathbf{z_0})]^T(\mathbf{z_1} - \mathbf{z_0}) \tag{6.81}$$

6.13 Mathematical Appendix C: Derivation of Törnqvist Index Using Quadratic Approximation Formula

Since the logarithmic expenditure function is quadratic, we can use the quadratic approximation formula. However, as utility levels differ between two points, we have

$$\ln C(\mathbf{P}_1, u_0) - \ln C(\mathbf{P}_0, u_1) = \left(\frac{1}{2}\right)\sum_{i=1}^{N}\left[\frac{\partial \ln C(\mathbf{P}_1, u_1)}{\partial \ln p_i} + \frac{\partial \ln C(\mathbf{P}_0, u_0)}{\partial \ln p_i}\right](\ln p_{i1} - \ln p_{i0}) \tag{6.82}$$

$$+ \frac{1}{2}b_{00}(\ln u_1)^2 - b_{00}(\ln u_0)^2 \tag{6.83}$$

[11] For a proof that only quadratic functions satisfy the quadratic approximation formula, refer to Diewert (1976).

The term of difference in utility levels remains due to the non-homothetic preferences. Therefore, let's consider the geometric mean of utility levels at two points as

$$u^* = \sqrt{u_0 u_1} \tag{6.84}$$

Then, the term of utility differences vanishes. Noting the logarithmic derivative of the expenditure function at each period, we have

$$\frac{\partial \ln C\left(\mathbf{P}_1, u^*\right)}{\partial \ln p_i} = a_i + \sum_{k=1}^{N} a_{ik} \ln p_k + b_i \ln\left(\sqrt{u_0 u_1}\right) \tag{6.85}$$

$$= a_i + \sum_{k=1}^{N} a_{ik} \ln p_k + \frac{1}{2} b_i \ln u_0 + \frac{1}{2} b_i \ln u_1 \tag{6.86}$$

Adding the logarithmic partial derivatives at $\mathbf{P_1}$ and $\mathbf{P_0}$:

$$\frac{\partial \ln C\left(\mathbf{P}_1, u^*\right)}{\partial \ln p_i} + \frac{\partial \ln C\left(\mathbf{P}_0, u^*\right)}{\partial \ln p_i} \tag{6.87}$$

$$= \frac{\partial \ln C\left(\mathbf{P}_1, u_1\right)}{\partial \ln p_i} + \frac{\partial \ln C\left(\mathbf{P}_0, u_0\right)}{\partial \ln p_i} \tag{6.88}$$

Therefore, the cost-of-living index can be written as

$$\ln C\left(\mathbf{P}_1, u^*\right) - \ln C\left(\mathbf{P}_0, u^*\right) \tag{6.89}$$

$$= \frac{1}{2} \sum_{i=1}^{N} \left[\frac{\partial \ln C\left(\mathbf{P}_1, u^*\right)}{\partial \ln p_i} + \frac{\partial \ln C\left(\mathbf{P}_0, u^*\right)}{\partial \ln p_i} \right] \left(\ln p_{i1} - \ln p_{i0}\right) \tag{6.90}$$

$$= \frac{1}{2} \sum_{i=1}^{N} \left[w_{i0} + w_{i1}\right] \left(\ln p_{i1} - \ln p_{i0}\right) \tag{6.91}$$

References

Barnett, W., & Choi, K. (2008). Operational identification of the complete class of superlative index numbers: An application of Galois. *Theory. Journal of Mathematical Economics, 44*(7–8), 603–612.

Christensen, L. R., Jorgenson, D. W., & Lau, L. J. (1971). Conjugate duality and the transcendental logarithmic production function. *Econometrica, 39*(4), 255–256.

de Haan, J. (2020). The CES price index, index number theory and official price measurement. In *Presented at EMG Workshop 2019*.

Diewert, W. E. (1976). Exact and superlative index numbers. *Journal of Econometrics, 4*(2), 115–145.

Diewert, W. E. (1978). Superlative index numbers and consistency in aggregation. *Econometrica, 46*(4), 883–900.

Hill, R. (2006). Superlative index numbers: Not all of them are super. *Review of Income and Wealth, 52*(2), 309–325.
Lent, J., & Dorfman, A. (2009). Using a weighted average of base period price indexes to approximate a superlative index. *Journal of official Statistics, 25*(1), 139–149.
Lippe, P. V. D. (2007). *Index theory and price statistics*. Peter Lang Pub Inc.
Lloyd, P. J. (1975). Substitution effects and biases in nontrue price indices. *American Economic Review, 65*(3), 301–313.
Moulton, B. (1996). *Constant Elasticity Cost-of-Living Index in Share-Relative Form*. Bureau of Labor Statistics Manuscript: Unpublished U.S.
Redding, S. J., & Weinstein, D. E. (2020). Measuring aggregate price indices with taste shocks: Theory and evidence for CES preferences. *Quarterly Journal of Economics, 135*(1), 503–560.
Reinsdorf, M. B., & Dorfman, A. H. (1999). The Sato-Vartia index and the monotonicity axiom. *Journal of Econometrics, 90*(1), 45–61.
Samuelson, P. A. (1983). *Foundations of economic analysis*. Harvard University Press.
Shapiro, M. D., & Wilcox, D. W. (1997). Alternative strategies for aggregating prices in the CPI. *Louis Review, 79*(3), 113–125. Federal Reserve Bank of St.

Divisia Index

7

Abstract

The Divisia index, introduced by François Divisia in 1925, is a unique economic index that treats time as a continuous variable, contrasting with standard indices which rely on discrete-time points. It defines price and quantity indices through logarithmic differentiation, enabling integration over time, which enables us to conduct various economic analysis easily. Key properties include transitivity, factor reversal, aggregation consistency, and homogeneity of degree one, making it particularly relevant for productivity analysis under continuous-time models. Despite its theoretical strengths, practical application of the Divisia index faces difficulties due to the discrete nature of real-world data, necessitating approximations that often lose desirable properties. Chain indices, such as the chain Törnqvist index, serve as discrete approximations but are less accurate with high-frequency data, often displaying unrealistic trends. The Divisia index also encounters issues with path dependency and fails to satisfy identity and monotonicity without assumptions of homothetic preferences or linear homogegneous production technology.

7.1 Fundamentals of the Divisia Index

The Divisia index, developed by French economist François Divisia, is a price and quantity index introduced in Divisia (1925). Unlike standard price indices, which are formulated using data from two points in time (e.g., 1 year or 1 month ago) or two different locations (e.g., countries or prefectures), the Divisia index treats time as a continuum. It assumes that prices and quantities are continuous and time-differentiable functions. Integrals over continuous time offer several advantages over summations ($\sum$) over discrete time, enabling the derivation of indices with beneficial properties unattainable by standard indices. This index exhibits properties markedly

N. Abe, *Price Index Numbers*, Springer Texts in Business and Economics,
https://doi.org/10.1007/978-981-97-6305-4_7

distinct from those of the price and quantity indices discussed so far in this book, influencing both index number theory and macroeconomics significantly.[1]

The price index (PI^{DV}) and quantity index (QI^{DV}) of the Divisia index are defined through logarithmic differentiation as follows:

$$\frac{d\ln PI^{DV}}{dt}=\sum_{i=1}^{N}w_{it}\frac{d\ln p_{it}}{dt}, \tag{7.1}$$

$$\frac{d\ln QI^{DV}}{dt}=\sum_{i=1}^{N}w_{it}\frac{d\ln q_{it}}{dt} \tag{7.2}$$

$$\frac{d\ln p_{it}}{dt}=\frac{1}{p_{it}}\frac{dp_{it}}{dt},\quad \frac{d\ln q_{it}}{dt}=\frac{1}{q_{it}}\frac{dq_{it}}{dt} \tag{7.3}$$

$$w_{it}=\frac{p_{it}q_{it}}{\sum_{i=1}^{N}p_{it}q_{it}} \tag{7.4}$$

In essence, the logarithmic time derivative of the Divisia index aggregates the rate of change over time (logarithmic differentiation with respect to time) of prices and quantities, weighted by the expenditure (revenue) share at each point in time. Integrating both sides of Eqs. (7.1) and (7.2) over time yields the level of the Divisia index as follows:

$$\ln PI^{DV}(t,t')=\int_{t}^{t'}\sum_{i=1}^{N}w_{i\tau}\frac{d\ln p_{i\tau}}{d\tau}d\tau,\quad \ln QI^{DV}(t,t')=\int_{t}^{t'}\sum_{i=1}^{N}w_{i\tau}\frac{d\ln q_{i\tau}}{d\tau}d\tau \tag{7.5}$$

Although defined using integrals, the Divisia index is conceptually straightforward and mathematically elegant. In real-world data applications, price and quantity data are available at discrete-time points, making this formulation primarily theoretical. Nonetheless, similar to economic growth theories developed since the 1950s, the Divisia index can be naturally integrated into continuous-time models. Notably, it was employed in Robert Solow's seminal 1957 paper on modern economic growth theory (Solow 1957).[2] Additionally, the research conducted by Dale Jorgenson (1933–2022) and colleagues, notably in Jorgenson and Griliches (1967), highlights the critical importance of the discretized approximation of the Divisia index in analyzing real terms. The Divisia index has also facilitated the development of logarithmic-type price indices, like the Törnqvist index and chain indices, as

[1] For an extensive overview of the Divisia index in the early twenty-first century, refer to Balk (2005).

[2] However, while Solow (1957) includes an index number formula identical to the Divisia index, Divisia's name is not mentioned.

discrete-time approximations, significantly impacting various aspects of economic and index number research analysis.

The Divisia index, defined by integration (line integral) over continuous time, possesses properties different from those of standard price and quantity indices between two points in time. As discussed in Chap. 4, transitivity rarely holds in standard indices, and factor reversal and transitivity are essentially conflicting requirements. However, the Divisia index, defined in continuous time, satisfies both transitivity and factor reversal, in addition to possessing very important properties such as aggregate consistency and homogeneity of degree one.[3] Additionally, while standard indices must assume a specific functional form to coincide with the cost-of-living index, the Divisia index is known to become a COLI, independent of functional form, when preferences are homothetic or production technology is homogeneous of degree one (and under perfect competition). In other words, the Divisia index possesses almost all desirable properties of a price index from both axiomatic and economic approaches.

Despite its theoretically excellent properties, the Divisia index faces two problems. The first problem is that since real-world data are not functions over continuous time, it is impossible to calculate the Divisia index directly, and we must rely on its approximation. When approximated, most of the aforementioned excellent properties are lost. In the 1970s, extensive analysis was conducted on how much the various discrete approximations of the Divisia index deviate from the ideal index and which discrete approximation methods are preferable. A representative study is Star and Hall (1976), which generally reports positive findings, suggesting that the Divisia index can be sufficiently approximated by chain indices of log-change index numbers such as the Törnqvist index. However, as explained in the next chapter, chain indices do not satisfy many important axioms that standard indices should meet. Recently, with the use of high-frequency scanner data, it has become possible to create chain indices for even shorter periods, such as weekly or daily, closer to continuous time than a month or a quarter. However, it is known that chain indices based on high-frequency data often exhibit intense, sometimes unrealistic negative trends, more so than those created from annual data. As will be discussed in Chap. 8, it is known that a series of data such as expenditure shares, prices, and quantities becomes more volatile as it becomes high frequency due to factors such as bargain sales or seasonality. On the other hand, in the theory of the Divisia index, prices and quantities are assumed to be continuous and differentiable functions of time. Recent analyses based on high-frequency data indicate that this assumption is inconsistent with real-world data. Therefore, the discourse from the first half to the mid-twentieth century, treating chain indices as a "ideal" discrete approximation of the Divisia index, is hardly seen in current price index number theory, at least in analyses based on high-frequency data.

The second problem with the Divisia index is that the price between two points in time depends on the price and quantity information outside those two points, i.e., it

[3] However, it does not satisfy identity and monotonicity, which will be discussed in a later section.

is path dependent. Even if the prices are identical at two points, the value of the price index changes depending on the path that prices and quantities have taken in between. For this reason, the Divisia index does not satisfy identity and monotonicity. This is also a problem that occurs with chain indices, which will be discussed in the next chapter. However, it is also known that such problems do not occur if quantities are determined according to an economic model and the utility function or production function is homogeneous of degree one. While assuming homothetic preferences, i.e., when the utility function is described as a monotonic increasing transformation of a homogeneous function of degree one, is a strong assumption, the assumption of homogeneity of degree one for production functions is quite common, especially not a strong constraint in productivity analysis. Therefore, in productivity analysis, the Divisia index is considered particularly useful.

7.2 Derivation and Factor Reversal Property of the Divisia Index

First, consider the following value index for two periods, $[t, t']$, $(t < t')$:

$$V\left(t, t'\right) = \frac{\sum_{i=1}^{N} p_{it'} q_{it'}}{\sum_{i=1}^{N} p_{it} q_{it}}, \tag{7.6}$$

$$\ln V\left(t, t'\right) = \ln\left(\sum_{i=1}^{N} p_{it'} q_{it'}\right) - \ln\left(\sum_{i=1}^{N} p_{it} q_{it}\right) \tag{7.7}$$

The right-hand side of (7.7), assuming that prices and quantities are differentiable functions of time, can be expressed as the following integral:

$$\ln\left(\sum_{i=1}^{N} p_{it'} q_{it'}\right) - \ln\left(\sum_{i=1}^{N} p_{it} q_{it}\right) = \int_{t}^{t'} \frac{d\ln\left(\sum_{i=1}^{N} p_{i\tau} q_{i\tau}\right)}{d\tau} d\tau \tag{7.8}$$

Through simple algebra, we obtain

$$\frac{d\ln\left(\sum_{i=1}^{N} p_{i\tau'} q_{i\tau'}\right)}{d\tau} = \sum_{i=1}^{N} \left(w_{i\tau}\right) \frac{d\ln p_{i\tau}}{d\tau} + \sum_{i=1}^{N} \left(w_{i\tau}\right) \frac{d\ln q_{i\tau}}{d\tau} \tag{7.9}$$

Integrating both sides, we get

$$\ln PI^{DV}\left(t, t'\right) = \int_{t}^{t'} \sum_{i=1}^{N} w_{it} \frac{d\ln p_{i\tau}}{d\tau} d\tau, \ln QI^{DV}\left(t, t'\right) = \int_{t}^{t'} \sum_{i=1}^{N} w_{it} \frac{d\ln q_{i\tau}}{d\tau} d\tau \tag{7.10}$$

Therefore,

$$\ln V\left(t, t'\right) = \ln PI^{DV}\left(t, t'\right) + \ln QI^{DV}\left(t, t'\right) \tag{7.11}$$

$$V\left(t, t'\right) = PI^{DV}\left(t, t'\right) \times QI^{DV}\left(t, t'\right) \tag{7.12}$$

Thus, the value index becomes the product of the Divisia price index and quantity index. This demonstrates that the Divisia index satisfies the property of factor reversal.

7.3 Divisia Index and Axioms

Here, following Balk (2008), we discuss the Divisia index and some of its axiomatic properties.

7.3.1 Homogeneity of Zero Degree and Commensurability

What happens if we multiply all the prices of goods at any given time by a constant, $\lambda\,(> 0)$? Naturally, we have

$$\frac{d \ln \lambda p_{it}}{dt} = \frac{1}{\lambda p_{it}} \frac{d\lambda p_{it}}{dt} = \frac{d \ln p_{it}}{dt} \tag{7.13}$$

Therefore, the Divisia index is homogeneous of zero degree with respect to prices. This corresponds to homogeneity of minus one degree with respect to base prices and homogeneity of one degree with respect to comparison prices.

Also, if we change the scale of quantities, multiplying prices by λ and quantities by $1/\lambda$, the Divisia index remains unaffected, satisfying independence from measurement units, or commensurability.

7.3.2 Transitivity

Consider a time t'' such that $t < t'' < t'$. Will the following always hold true?

$$\ln PI^{DV}\left(t, t'\right) = \ln PI^{DV}\left(t, t''\right) + \ln PI^{DV}\left(t'', t'\right) \tag{7.14}$$

Generally, definite integrals can be partitioned. That is, for any integrable function $f(x)$:

$$\int_0^{t'} f(x)\,dx = \int_0^{t''} f(x)\,dx + \int_{t''}^{t'} f(x)\,dx \tag{7.15}$$

Therefore, the Divisia index satisfies transitivity.

7.3.3 Aggregation Consistency

Now, let's divide N types of goods into N_k $(k = 1, 2, 3, ..., K)$ groups. The Divisia index for group k is given by

$$\ln PI_k^{DV}\left(t, t'\right) = \int_t^{t'} \sum_{i=1}^{N_k} w_{i\tau}^k \frac{d \ln p_{i\tau}^k}{d\tau} d\tau, \tag{7.16}$$

$$w_{i\tau}^k = \frac{p_{i\tau}^k q_{i\tau}^k}{\sum_{i=1}^{N_k} p_{i\tau}^k q_{i\tau}^k} \tag{7.17}$$

Due to the linearity of integration, the Divisia index can be divided:

$$\ln PI^{DV}\left(t, t'\right) = \int_t^{t'} \sum_{i=1}^{N} w_{i\tau} \frac{d \ln p_{i\tau}}{d\tau} d\tau \tag{7.18}$$

$$= \int_t^{t'} \sum_{k=1}^{K} \left(\frac{\sum_{i=1}^{N_k} p_{i\tau}^k q_{i\tau}^k}{\left(\sum_{i=1}^{N} p_{i\tau} q_{it}\right)} \frac{d \ln PI_k^{DV}}{d\tau} \right) d\tau \tag{7.19}$$

Thus, it can be seen that the Divisia index satisfies aggregation consistency.

7.3.4 Monotonicity and Identity

The Divisia index, being a variant of the log-change index, inherits complexity due to its reliance on expenditure shares as weights. Nevertheless, this complexity persists even under the assumption that expenditure shares are independent of prices. In other words, the Divisia index encounters challenges with two fundamental axioms: monotonicity and identity. These challenges are significant as they impact the index's foundational properties and its application in economic analysis.

Suppose that over all periods between t and t', all product prices increase. That is,

$$\frac{d \ln p_{it}}{dt} \geq 0 \quad \text{for all } i \text{ and } t. \tag{7.20}$$

Revisiting the definition of the Divisia index,

$$\frac{d \ln PI^{DV}}{dt} = \sum_{i=1}^{N} w_{it} \frac{d \ln p_{it}}{dt} \geq 0 \tag{7.21}$$

Thus, the right-hand side is always non-negative (positive). Integrating a function that always takes positive values should result in a positive value. Therefore, if all prices continuously rise, the Divisia index satisfies monotonicity.[4] Similarly, assuming identity over all periods, i.e., prices are constant over time,

$$\frac{d \ln p_{it}}{dt} = 0 \quad \text{for all } i \text{ and } t \tag{7.22}$$

leads to

$$\frac{d \ln PI^{DV}}{dt} = 0 \tag{7.23}$$

and thus the Divisia index satisfies identity. However, these are very strong conditions. Relaxing the condition to

$$p_{it'} = p_{it} \quad \text{for all } i \tag{7.24}$$

and assuming prices are identical only at two points, does the Divisia index satisfy identity? Since the Divisia index is a line integral, and line integrals generally depend on the path, identity is not satisfied. Let's verify this with a numerical example. Consider a two-goods case from period 0 to 2, assuming the following price differential equations:

$$\begin{aligned} p_1(t) &= 2 - (t-1)^2, \\ \frac{dp_1(t)}{dt} &= -2(t-1), \\ p_2(t) &= 1 + (t-1)^2, \\ \frac{dp_2(t)}{dt} &= 2(t-1) \end{aligned}$$

In this case, the price vectors at periods 0 and 2 are both

$$\begin{aligned} (p_1(0), p_2(0)) &= (p_1(2), p_2(2)) \\ &= (1, 2). \end{aligned}$$

That is, prices at both points are identical. If the expenditure shares are constant at $w, (1-w)$, then the Divisia index would be

$$\begin{aligned} PI^{DV}(0,2) &= \exp\left(\int_0^2 \left(w \times \left(\frac{-2(t-1)}{2-(t-1)^2}\right) + (1-w) \times \left(\frac{2(t-1)}{1+(t-1)^2}\right)\right) dt\right) \\ &= \exp\left(w \left[\ln(t^2 - 2t - 1)\right]_0^2\right) \exp\left((1-w)\left[\ln(t^2 - 2t + 2)\right]_0^2\right) \\ &= \exp(w \times 0) \exp((1-w) \times 0) \\ &= 1. \end{aligned}$$

[4] It's important to clarify that in our analysis, the expenditure shares, denoted as w_{it}, are presumed to remain constant despite variations in prices.

Generally, if the expenditure shares are constant,

$$\frac{d \ln PI^{DV}}{dt} = \int_0^t \sum_{i=1}^{N} w_i \frac{d \ln p_{i\tau}}{d\tau} d\tau \tag{7.25}$$

$$= \sum_{i=1}^{N} w_i \int_0^t \frac{d \ln p_{i\tau}}{d\tau} d\tau \tag{7.26}$$

$$= \sum_{i=1}^{N} w_i (\ln p_{it} - \ln p_{i0}) \tag{7.27}$$

Thus, under constant expenditure shares, the Divisia index generally satisfies identity. This assumes very strong conditions where prices are identical at two points, and expenditure shares remain constant over the entire period, which is not realistic. Suppose, for argument's sake, we adopt the following time-varying expenditure shares:

$$w_1(t) = \frac{1}{2} + \left(\frac{t-1}{4}\right), \quad w_2(t) = \frac{1}{2} - \left(\frac{t-1}{4}\right) \tag{7.28}$$

Then, the Divisia index would be calculated as follows:

$$PI^{DV}(0,2) = \exp\left(\int_0^2 \left(\left(\frac{1}{2} + \frac{t-1}{4}\right) \times \frac{-2(t-1)}{2-(t-1)^2} + \left(\frac{1}{2} - \frac{t-1}{4}\right) \times \frac{2(t-1)}{1+(t-1)^2}\right) dt\right)$$
$$\approx 0.63062 \quad (\neq 1) \tag{7.29}$$

From the above example, it is evident that the Divisia index does not satisfy identity when considering the prices at the beginning and end of the period. Furthermore, the example demonstrates that the value of the Divisia index depends on the path taken between two points. Additionally, as the equation for prices in the second period is continuous, even a slight increase in any price does not significantly alter the value of the Divisia index. Thus, even if prices increase, the value of the Divisia index can remain below 1, creating scenarios that contradict the principle of monotonicity.

7.4 Homothetic Preferences and Path Dependency

As discussed in the previous section, the Divisia index does not necessarily become 1 even if prices at two points of times are the same, failing to satisfy identity. However, it is known that if there is an economic relationship between prices and quantities and if the functional form is homogeneous of degree one, then the path dependency is eliminated. Assume there is rational decision-making in households between quantities and prices, and an expenditure function for each period is defined as

$$C_t = C(\mathbf{p_t}, u_t) \tag{7.30}$$

If preferences are homothetic, the expenditure function can be expressed as

$$C\left(\mathbf{p_t}, u_t\right) = c\left(\mathbf{p_t}\right) u_t \tag{7.31}$$

Simple calculations show that for any u_0, u_t:

$$\begin{aligned} \frac{\partial \ln C\left(\mathbf{p_t}, u_0\right)}{\partial \ln p_{it}} &= \frac{\partial \ln c\left(\mathbf{p_t}\right)}{\partial \ln p_{it}} && (7.32) \\ &= \frac{\partial \ln C\left(\mathbf{p_t}, u_t\right)}{\partial \ln p_{it}} && (7.33) \\ &= w_{it} && (7.34) \end{aligned}$$

This implies that under homothetic preferences, the expenditure share, w_{it}, is independent of the utility level. Recalling Konüs's cost-of-living index which, at utility level at time 0, is defined as

$$COLI\left(0, t, u_0\right) = \frac{C\left(\mathbf{p_t}, u_0\right)}{C\left(\mathbf{p_0}, u_0\right)} \tag{7.35}$$

Taking the logarithmic time derivative of (7.35) and using (7.34), we get

$$\begin{aligned} \frac{d \ln COLI\left(0, t, u_0\right)}{d\tau} &= \frac{d \ln C\left(\mathbf{p_t}, u_0\right)}{d\tau} && (7.36) \\ &= \sum_{i=1}^{N} w_{it} \frac{d \ln p_{it}}{d\tau} && (7.37) \end{aligned}$$

which becomes the Divisia index. That is, the time derivative of the Divisia index is the time derivative of the true COLI for any homothetic utility function. By integrating it over time, we obtain Konüs's cost-of-living index:

$$\begin{aligned} \int_t^{t'} \sum_{i=1}^{N} w_{i\tau} \frac{d \ln p_{i\tau}}{d\tau} d\tau &= \int_t^{t'} \frac{d \ln C\left(\mathbf{p_ø}, u_0\right)}{d\tau} d\tau && (7.38) \\ &= \ln C\left(\mathbf{p_{t'}}, u_0\right) - \ln C\left(\mathbf{p_t}, u_0\right) && (7.39) \\ &= \ln c\left(\mathbf{p_{t'}}\right) - \ln c\left(\mathbf{p_t}\right) && (7.40) \end{aligned}$$

This depends only on the two-point price vectors and is not dependent on the integration path. Therefore, the Divisia index, when quantities and prices are consistent with household optimization behavior and preferences are homothetic, becomes independent of the path. Moreover, as long as the preferences are homothetic, regardless of the functional forms of utility functions,[5] the Divisia index aligns with Konüs's COLI.[6]

If prices and quantities are strictly consistent with utility maximization or profit maximization, it's not surprising that the cost-of-living and price indices coincide and possess various desirable properties. For instance, since the COLI is defined as a ratio of expenditure functions, it satisfies transitivity, monotonicity, and homogeneity of the first degree. Indices like the Sato–Vartia index for CES functions and the superlative index such as the Törnqvist index lack transitivity and monotonicity. Although these superlative indices are good approximations of the true cost-of-living index, they are still approximations. The remarkable property of the Divisia index is that under any homothetic preferences, it precisely matches the cost-of-living index. If we substitute preferences with production technology and assume a perfectly competitive market, the marginal product value aligns with the factor prices, allowing the logarithmic change in total revenue to be expressed as a weighted average of the time derivatives of each component's cost share. In this scenario, it becomes possible to decompose revenue changes into Divisia's price and quantity indices. Thus, the Divisia index becomes a very important formula in productivity analysis. Of course, such results are obtained assuming time is continuously defined, and the Törnqvist index, a natural discrete approximation of the Divisia index, aligns with the cost-of-living index only when the production or expenditure function is of the translog form. In this case, the Törnqvist index satisfies transitivity and monotonicity. However, if preferences are not of the translog form, even if there is an optimization-consistent relationship between quantities and prices, the Törnqvist index generally does not satisfy transitivity and monotonicity. The outstanding properties of the Divisia index are therefore only valid under very limited circumstances when approximated discretely.

7.4.1 Summary of Continuous-Time Divisia Index

Let us summarize the results of this chapter as follows:

(1) The Divisia index satisfies factor reversal property, transitivity, first-degree homogeneity, zero-degree homogeneity, unit indifference, and aggregation consistency.

(2) The Divisia index becomes 1 when prices are constant over all periods, and exceeds 1 when prices continuously rise over all periods.

(3) The Divisia index does not satisfy monotonicity and identity with respect to prices at two points.

---

[5] Assuming the existence of the expenditure function and the validity of the Shephard-McKenzie Lemma, with necessary conditions like convexity and rationality being met.

[6] Feenstra and Reinsdorf (2000) show that, even if preferences are not homothetic, the Divisia index can be interpreted as a cost-of-living index when evaluated as a weighted average over the time path of utility, in cases where the path of prices and income is log-linear.

(4) Generally, the value of the Divisia index depends on the integration path between two points.

(5) The Divisia index coincides with Konüs's cost-of-living index, regardless of the utility function's form, when preferences are homothetic (or input price index when production technology is homogeneous of degree one) and quantities and prices are determined according to utility maximization (or profit maximization).

(6) When preferences are homothetic and quantities and prices are determined according to preferences, the Divisia index does not depend on the integration path and satisfies monotonicity and identity with respect to prices at two points.

7.5 Discrete Approximation

If the Divisia index satisfies factor reversal and transitivity, could its discrete approximation also satisfy these properties, at least to a certain degree of accuracy? In particular, might the Törnqvist index, a natural discrete approximation of the Divisia index, be a candidate for such a good index? With this in mind, many studies in the 1970s were conducted on the approximation of the Divisia index. Trivedi (1981) showed that the Törnqvist index is the best approximation formula, achieving high accuracy. Star and Hall (1976) demonstrated that even approximating continuous time with long-term annual data, chain indices can be highly accurate approximations if weights are cleverly chosen. These approximation calculations are based on the assumption that (unobservable) true prices, quantities, and expenditure shares are differentiable functions of time. However, in actual transaction data, prices and quantities do not always behave as continuous functions of time. Particularly when looking at short-term scanner data, expenditure shares and prices exhibit much greater fluctuations than longer term data. Assuming inherently discontinuous or non-differentiable functions as continuous and approximating them discretely based on this assumption might lead to results vastly different from actual data. In the next chapter, we will discuss that chain indices based on high-frequency data have been found to produce unrealistic large negative trends, known as chain drift, resulting in a serious lack of transitivity. The analyses of the accuracy of the discrete approximations of the Divisia index made from the 1970s to the 1980s are now questioned for their validity in light of the availability of higher frequency transaction data today.

7.6 Some Recent Investigations

The Divisia index is fundamentally reliant on the assumption of continuous time, making it inapplicable to real-world situations where only discrete-time data is available. However, the axiomatic and economic properties of the Divisia index are still attractive to many researchers today. Especially in macrodynamic models that assume continuous time, the affinity with the Divisia index is high. It is a natural idea to use the Divisia index in constructing indicators of economic welfare in models, as in

Cysne (2003). However, the constraint of continuous time is a severe one when actually measuring prices. Furthermore, when preferences are not homothetic, the problem is complicated by the price values depending on the path of integration.

Feenstra and Reinsdorf (2000) and Oulton (2008) both propose deriving the cost-of-living index from the Divisia index approximated in discrete time when preferences are non-homothetic. Feenstra and Reinsdorf (2000) assume that prices and incomes are piecewise log-linear and impose special assumptions on the level of utility used in calculating the cost-of-living index, asserting that the Divisia index calculated using Simpson's formula becomes the cost-of-living index. On the other hand, Oulton (2008) proposes an algorithm to obtain the cost-of-living index by first estimating the demand system and then calculating the expenditure shares corresponding to compensatory demand, as the expenditure shares used in the Divisia index do not correspond to compensatory demand when preferences are non-homothetic, leading to path dependence. The former is easily executable but requires relatively strong assumptions. The latter requires the estimation of many parameters.

Baqaee and Burstein (2023) have incorporated preference changes into the Divisia index and are modeling and estimating long-term changes in prices and economic welfare. Here, the feature is that preference changes are not based on cardinal utility as in Redding and Weinstein (2020), but on money metric.

Divisia index has been noted, since its inception, as highly regarded by Schumpeter (1939). Even today, especially among economic theorists, research on its potential continues to accumulate.

References

Balk, B. M. (2005). Divisia price and quantity indices: 80 years after. *Statistica Neerlandica, 59*(2), 119–158.

Balk, B. M. (2008). *Price and quantity index numbers*. Cambridge University Press.

Baqaee, D. R., & Burstein, A. (2023). Welfare and output with income effects and taste shocks. *The Quarterly Journal of Economics, 138*(2), 769 783.

Cysne, R. P. (2003). Divisia index, inflation, and welfare. *Journal of Money, Credit and Banking, 35*(2), 221–238.

Divisia, F. (1925). L'indice Monétaire et la Théorie de la Monnaie, Revue d'Économie Politique, XXXIX, Nos. 4, 5, 6: pp. 842-61, 980-1008, 1121-1151.

Feenstra, R. C., & Reinsdorf, M. B. (2000). An exact priceiindex for the almost ideal demand system. *Economics Letters, 66*(2), 159–162.

Jorgenson, D. W., & Griliches, Z. (1967). The explanation of productivity change. *Review of Economic Studies, 34*(3), 249–283.

Oulton, N. (2008). Chain indices of the cost-of-living and the path-dependence problem: An empirical solution. *Journal of Econometrics, 144*(1), 306–324.

Redding, S. J., & Weinstein, D. E. (2020). Measuring aggregate price indices with taste shocks: Theory and evidence for CES preferences. *Quarterly Journal of Economics, 135*(1), 503–560.

Schumpeter, J. A. (1939). *Business cycles: A theoretical*. And Statistical Analysis of the Capitalist Process, McGraw-Hill Book Co: Historical.

Solow, R. (1957). Technical change and the aggregate production function. *Review of Economics and Statistics, 39*(3), 312–320.

Star, S., & Hall, R. (1976). An approximate divisia index of total factor productivity. *Econometrica, 44*(2), 257–263.

Trivedi, P. K. (1981). Some discrete approximations to divisia integral indices. *International Economic Review, 22*(1), 71–77.

Chain Index

8

Abstract

The chain index, introduced by Alfred Marshall in 1887, calculates indices over multiple periods or regions by sequentially shifting the base period and multiplying the indices from each intermediate period. This method, praised by Irving Fisher in the early twentieth century, addresses issues with commodities changing over time and is expected to help narrow the gap between Laspeyres and Paasche indices. Chain indices, such as the chain Laspeyres and chain Paasche indices, can result in significant chain drift, especially with high-frequency data, leading to discrepancies between direct and chain indices. This drift occurs due to non-transitivity in standard indices and is exacerbated by product turnover and seasonal variations. While chain indices offer advantages in dealing with changing products, they also face theoretical and practical challenges, such as losing desirable properties like identity and monotonicity. Recent approaches like the GEKS method, which ensures transitivity by using the geometric mean of bilateral indices, aim to mitigate chain drift. However, when combined with rolling windows, even GEKS can exhibit chain drift. The use of chain indices requires careful consideration of their limitations and the specific context of their application.

8.1 Basics of Chain Index

In this book, we have so far treated price and quantity indices as measures of changes in prices or quantities between two points in time, such as the changes between period 1 and period 2. Now, let us consider the existence of a third period and calculate the changes in prices and quantities between periods 1 and 3. In this case, there are two methods of calculation. The first method uses the index number formulas discussed so far, specifically calculating using the price and quantity information from periods 1 and 3. Let's call this index the direct index. The second method involves calculating

N. Abe, *Price Index Numbers*, Springer Texts in Business and Economics,
https://doi.org/10.1007/978-981-97-6305-4_8

the indices between periods 1 and 2 and between periods 2 and 3, and then multiplying them. The index calculated using this method is called the chain index.

Suppose there are multiple time points between period 0 and period t, arranged as 0, 1, 2, 3,...,$\tau - 1$,τ, $\tau + 1$, ..., t. If we denote the price index between two time points, $\tau - 1$ and τ, as $P(\tau - 1, \tau)$, the chain price index $P^c(0, t)$) is defined as

$$P^c(0, t) = \prod_{\tau=1}^{t} P(\tau - 1, \tau) \tag{8.1}$$

Here, $P(\tau - 1, \tau)$ can be any price index we have discussed so far, such as the Laspeyres index, Sato–Vartia, or the Stuvel index. That is to say, depending on the base index formula, chain indices can become various forms like chain Laspeyres, chain Paasche, chain Fisher, etc.

The chain index was proposed by Alfred Marshall in Marshall (1887) primarily to address the issue of commodities changing over time. For instance, if there are no common products between period 1 and period 3, it's impossible to directly compare their prices and quantities, making it infeasible to calculate the direct price index between period 1 and period 3. However, if there are common products between periods 1 and 2 and between periods 2 and 3, the chain index allows for the calculation of the price changes between periods 1 and 3. Irving Fisher highly praised the chain index in his major work (Fisher 1922).[1]

Another benefit of the chain index is the expected narrowing of the gap between the Laspeyres and Paasche indices when using chain indices. It is generally expected that the more distant the base and comparison periods are, the larger the divergence between the direct Laspeyres and direct Paasche indices tends to be.[2] The likelihood of a divergence in expenditure shares between the base period and the comparison point increases as the distance between these periods grows. Although many countries currently use the Laspeyres index as their consumer price index formula, it is often believed that by frequently changing the base period using the chain index or a similar method, the divergence from the Paasche index can be decreased. In the 1993 System of National Accounts (93SNA), which was released in 1993,[3] it was recommended to use the chain index when constructing gross domestic products and deflators in the System of National Accounts (SNA).[4] Therefore, many countries now use the chain index in their national accounts. However, as will be seen later in this chapter, the gap between the Laspeyres and Paasche indices does not always shrink with chain index. In high-frequency data, it may even expand, so it is important to understand that the aforementioned discussion merely suggests a potential for reduction.

[1] For an evaluation of the chain index by Fisher and Walsh, see Diewert (2005).

[2] However, this gap does not always widen as the base and comparison periods become more distant. Moreover, with high-frequency data, the chain index may often result in a larger gap.

[3] For details, refer to Hill (1993).

[4] In 2008 SNA, the chain index is also recommended. See Chap. 15 of System of National Account 2008.

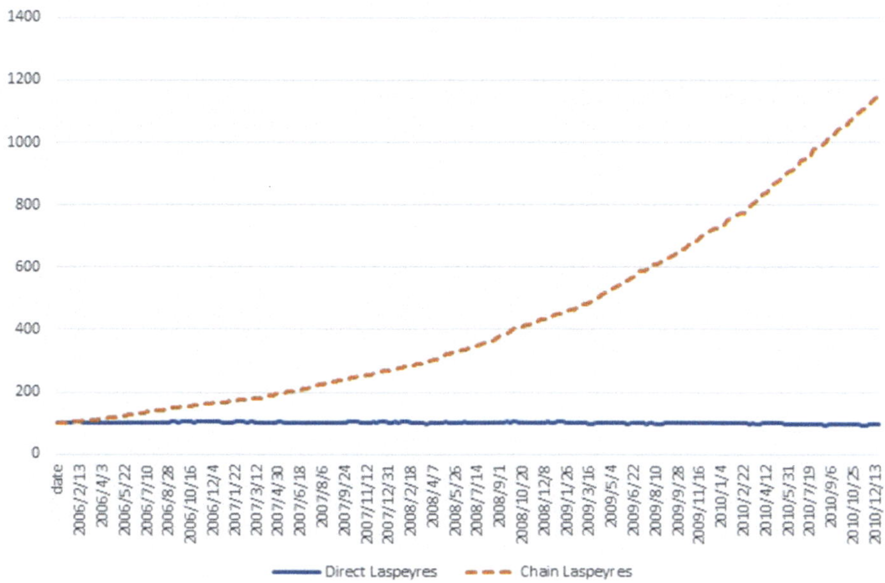

Fig. 8.1 Direct and Chain Laspeyres indices

Using high-frequency data, the adoption of the chain index can sometimes drastically widen the Laspeyres–Paasche gap. (fixed base) Laspeyres and Paasche indices based on retail sales data of cereals in Japan (weekly scanner data provided by a marketing research company in Japan, INTAGE Inc.).

In Fig. 8.1, the chain Laspeyres index shows a drastic upward trend, with cereal prices increasing 4 years. On the other hand, the direct index remains flat. In Fig. 8.2, there's a pronounced downward bias in the chain Paasche index, with cereal prices nearly reaching zero over 4 years. Hence, the Laspeyres–Paasche gap becomes considerably large with the adoption of the chain index.

From a theoretical perspective, Ragnar Frisch's seminal paper (Frisch 1936) extensively discussed the divergence or so-called "chain drift" between the chain index and the standard index. As noted in Chap. 4, except for the Jevons and Lowe indices, price indices are not inherently transitive, which leads to chain drift. Conversely, as introduced in Chap. 7, the Divisia index is transitive. Similarly, as discussed in Chap. 5, the cost-of-living index proposed by Konüs is also transitive. Therefore, one might argue that the natural approximation of the Divisia index, the chain Törnqvist index, is close to transitive. In addition, since the Törnqvist index is a superlative index—a good approximation of the cost-of-living index—it can be expected to exhibit properties close to transitivity. Diewert (2021) refers to this as "Approximate Transitivity" of the superlative index.[5] In other words, some might argue that by

[5] See page 27, footnote 74 of Diewert (2021).

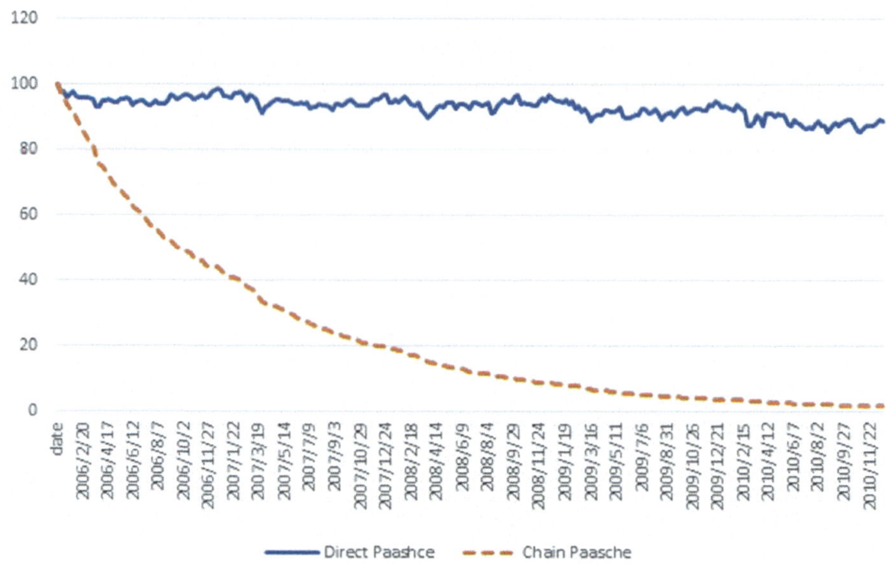

Fig. 8.2 Direct and Chain Paasche indices

using the Törnqvist index, the chain drift might be very small. Unfortunately, this is not the case in general.

If the above argument is correct, as the data frequency increases, the Törnqvist index is expected to approximate the Divisia index more closely. Figure 8.3 illustrates the chain indices of two superlative indices and the Sato–Vartia index using in-store cereal sales data from Japan, provided by INTAGE Inc. The blue line represents the direct Törnqvist index, while the yellow line represents the chain Törnqvist index. From 2006 to 2008, the direct Törnqvist index shows a price decrease of about 5%, but the chain Törnqvist index shows a decrease of nearly 30%, indicating a significant deviation. The trend is similar for the Fisher index and the Sato–Vartia index.[6]

If there is only one product, the price index simply reflects the price trend of that single product. By defining the price index as the price relatives of the product, it satisfies transitivity. However, with two or more products, chain drift, a discrepancy between the direct and chain indices, generally occurs. There are two primary reasons for this phenomenon when dealing with multiple products. Firstly, as Marshall and others have initially pointed out, goods change over time. In extreme cases, like the one presented at the beginning of this chapter, there are no common products between periods 1 and 3, making direct price comparisons impossible, and standard price

[6] In the direct price index, the Fisher index and the Sato–Vartia index almost coincide with the Törnqvist index, so they are omitted from the figure. However, when transformed into chain indices, a significant difference emerges even among the superlative indices.

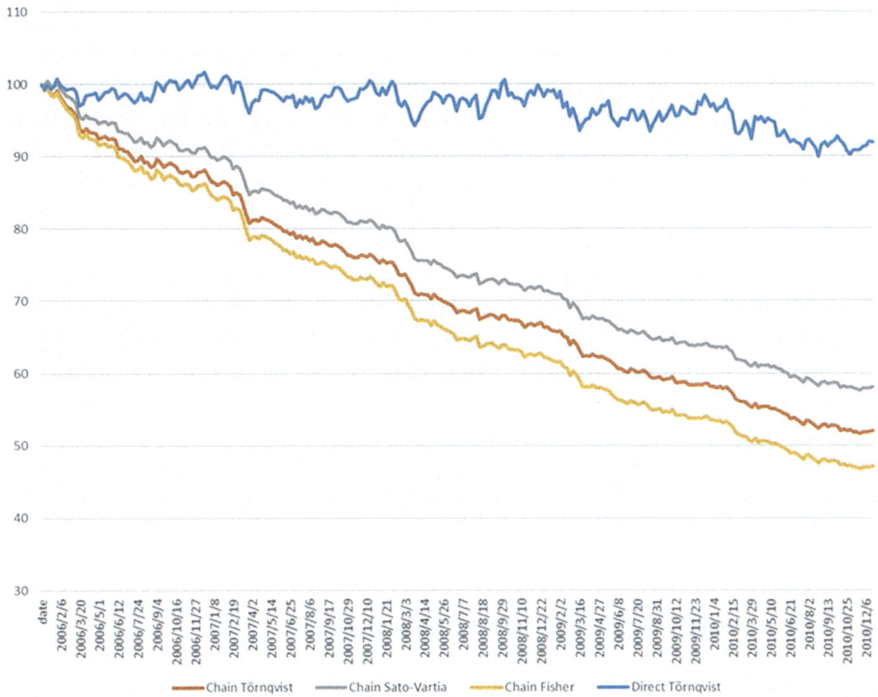

Fig. 8.3 Direct and Chain superlative indices

indices such as the Laspeyres index cannot be computed.[7] Even if not as extreme, when there are fewer common products between periods 1 and 3, it is natural for chain indices, which facilitate the comparison of more product prices, to diverge from direct indices. Addressing this issue remains at the forefront of current price index number theory and presents a daily challenge for statistical agencies worldwide. The second reason for chain drift, which occurs even if the product set is constant across all periods, lies in the inherent structures of index numbers, with a few exceptions. If the commodity set is constant over time, the Jevons index and the more general Cobb–Douglas-type index are transitive, thus no chain drift occurs. However, nearly all indices, including the Fisher and Törnqvist indices, known as superlative indices, exhibit chain drift. This drift becomes a significant problem when, as illustrated in Fig. 8.1, a trend difference emerges between the direct index and the chain index. The factors causing significant chain drift are now largely understood, and this chapter will explore this mechanism in detail.

Chain indices are practically the only index number formulas in scenarios where products change frequently. However, chain indices face many theoretical and practical difficulties. Beyond chain drift, another issue is that many ideal properties of

[7] The various issues and considerations in index making when the set of goods differs between two points in time will be discussed in detail later in this chapter and the next.

direct indices on which it is based are lost when they are converted into chain indices. For example, while the Fisher index satisfies identity and monotonicity, the chain Fisher index satisfies neither. From an axiomatic perspective, justifying the use of chain indices is not easy. One of the leading scholars in index number theory, Peter von der Lippe, has critically addressed chain indices in his work, Lippe (2007). The mathematical difference between the chain index and the direct index number formula is straightforward. The chain index is defined by the product of price indices over various periods, whereas the direct price index can be considered a special case without any chains. However, the differences in their index number properties and the actual calculated values, chain drift, can be significant. For instance, even with the Laspeyres index, there is a noticeable difference between the standard Laspeyres index and the chain Laspeyres index. Bert Balk, one of the leading researchers on index number theory, describes choosing between these two index formulas as choosing between two paradigms (Balk 2008, p.125).

Chain indices are central issues in today's index number theory. In this chapter, we will consider various issues surrounding chain indices, based on recent research findings.

8.2 Axiomatic Features of Chain Indices

As Hill (1993) emphasizes, the reason chain indices are adopted in practical situations like the SNA is to better reflect the actual economic activity in the price index by shortening the distance from the base period, for instance, bridging the Laspeyres–Paasche gap. Therefore, emphasizing the axiomatic properties of chain indices, and arguing that they are inferior to direct indices, might be uncomfortable for those advocating the adoption of chain indices. Nevertheless, chain indices have significantly different axiomatic characteristics than direct indices and can sometimes cause serious problems. In this section, we will summarize the axiomatic properties of chain indices for representative indices.

Considering the chain index, which includes the direct index as its special case, we limit our consideration to indices that contain information on times other than the base and comparison times, i.e., indices using information from different three or more points in time. We also consider the nine index formulas: Laspeyres, Paasche, Fisher, Törnqvist, Walsh, Sato–Vartia, Jevons, Carli, and Dutot. The axioms **(A-2) Linear Homogeneity, (A-4) Dimensionality** clearly hold for the chain index, since it's defined as the multiplication of indices at each point in time. Except for the Dutot index, all eight types of price indices have the property **(A-5) Commensurability**, meaning they are independent of measurement units, and the chain index also has this property. The Jevons index, when there is no change in the commodity sets over time satisfies **(A-8) Transitivity**. That is, the direct Jevons index and its chain index are identical as long as the product set does not vary over time or among regions. Therefore, when the set of goods does not change, the chain Jevons index is transitive. Additionally, the axiom **(A-9) Determinateness** clearly holds for chain indices for the indices Laspeyres, Paasche, Fisher, Carli, and Dutot. Another important property that holds true for chain indices is that the product of the Laspeyres quantity index and the Paasche price index results in the value index. The value index always possesses the property of transitivity. Therefore, it's possible to compute the value index from time point 0 to time point 2 using a chain calculation as follows:

$$V_{02} = V_{01} \times V_{12}$$
$$= \frac{\sum_j p_{j1}q_{j1}}{\sum_k p_{k0}q_{k0}} \times \frac{\sum_j p_{j2}q_{j2}}{\sum_k p_{k1}q_{k1}} \tag{8.2}$$

When decomposing the value index of each period into the Laspeyres index and the Paasche quantity index, we have

$$V_{02} = V_{01} \times V_{12}$$
$$= P^P(0,1) \times Q^L(0,1) \times P^P(1,2) \times Q^L(1,2)$$
$$= P^{CP}(0,2) \times Q^{CL}(0,2) \tag{8.3}$$

Thus, the value index can also be broken down into the chain Laspeyres quantity index $Q^{CL}(0,2)$ and the chain Paasche price index $P^{CP}(0,2)$. By using the chain Laspeyres quantity index, we can calculate the real GDP and real household consumption expenditure, and by dividing it by the nominal GDP or nominal household consumption expenditure, we can obtain the chain Paasche price index as an implicit deflator. Lastly, concerning the **(A-10) Factor Reversal Test** that both the Fisher and the Sato–Vartia indices satisfy, we can easily verify that the chain index also retains the factor reversal property, just as in the above example.[8]

These are useful properties that are also retained in chain indices. However, as axioms of the index number formula, especially the crucial ones like **(A-1) Monotonicity and (A-3) Identity**, are not satisfied in chain indices. **(A-6) Intermediate Value Property, (A-7) Proportionality**, and **(A-14) Aggregation Consistency** also aren't met in chains, even if direct indices satisfy them. To derive a result similar to identity in chain indices, we must make a special assumption that prices are identical across all periods included in the chain. If the objective of a price index is to quantify price differences between two points in time or space, the lack of identity is a very serious issue. The same applies to the Divisia index; the final value of the price index depends on how the two points in time or space are connected, that is, path dependency arises in chain indices. The potential absence of the intermediate value property, meaning that the price index might not fall between the minimum and maximum of the observed price ratios, would be a serious problem if it indeed occurs.

Just because chain indices don't meet crucial axioms doesn't make them problematic in practice if these issues are limited to extremely rare cases. However, Bohdan Szulc, who researched price indices for many years at Statistics Canada, reported in

[8] Many countries adopt the chain Paasche index in their SNA. The exceptions are the United States and Canada, which use the chain Fisher index. See Chap. 8 of the Quarterly National Accounts Manual by Lee (2018) for details.

a paper published in Szulc (1986) that in the chain consumer price index for Canada released in March 1978, the index for goods was 171.1, the index for services was 171.4, but the combined index for goods and services was 170.8. This was lower than the minimum of the category values. It was an actual example where the chain Laspeyres index didn't meet the consistency in aggregation and intermediate value property in official statistics. Of course, such phenomena aren't frequent, but the possibility that a lack of consistency in aggregation might lead to seemingly odd outcomes should always be kept in mind.

8.3 The Drift Function

Following Frisch (1936),[9] let's consider the formula below, referred to as the drift function:

$$D(0, t) = \frac{P^c(0, t)}{P(0, t)} \tag{8.4}$$

Considering the three periods of $\tau = 0, 1, 2$, the chain index and drift function can be described as follows:

$$P^c(0, 2) = P(0, 1) \times P(1, 2) \tag{8.5}$$

$$D(0, 2) = \frac{P(0, 1) \times P(1, 2)}{P(0, 2)} \tag{8.6}$$

The denominator of the drift function is the direct index between period 0 and period 2, while the numerator is the chain index. If $D(0, 2) = 1$ always holds, then the chain index and the direct index coincide. In other words, this is a necessary and sufficient condition for the index to possess transitivity.

As seen in the previous section, even in chain form, the Laspeyres index and the Paasche quantity index, when multiplied, resulted in the value index. Using this property, the drift of the chain Laspeyres quantity index is

$$\begin{aligned} D^{LQ}(0, 2) &= \frac{Q^L(0, 1) \times Q^L(1, 2)}{Q^L(0, 2)} \\ &= \frac{\left(V_{01}/P^P(0, 1)\right) \times \left(V_{12}/P^P(1, 2)\right)}{\left(V_{02}/P^P(0, 2)\right)} \\ &= \frac{1}{D^P(0, 2)} \end{aligned} \tag{8.7}$$

This indicates that the drift of the chain Laspeyres quantity index is the reciprocal of the drift of the chain Paasche price index. Therefore, if the drift of the Paasche price index is greater than 1, the drift of the Laspeyres quantity index will be less than 1.

[9] Frisch (1936) has named $D(0, t)$ as Triangle Divergency.

8.4 Chain Indices and the Laspeyres–Paasche Gap

One of the main reasons the chain index is currently used in the SNA is that it is expected to reduce the divergence between the Laspeyres index and the Paasche index compared to standard indices.[10] However, just as there isn't always a negative or positive divergence between the Laspeyres and Paasche indices, the gap between the chain Laspeyres and Paasche indices is not necessarily always decreased by using chain indices. Here, following Hill (2006), let's look at the mechanism by which chain drift is produced in Laspeyres and Paasche indices.

8.4.1 The Chain Drift of the Laspeyres Index

Transforming the drift function of the chain Laspeyres, we get

$$\frac{P_{01}^{L}P_{12}^{L}}{P_{02}^{L}} = \frac{\sum p_{j1}q_{j0}}{\sum p_{j0}q_{j0}} \cdot \frac{\sum p_{j2}q_{j1}}{\sum p_{j1}q_{j1}} \cdot \frac{\sum p_{j0}q_{j0}}{\sum p_{j2}q_{j0}} \tag{8.8}$$

$$= \frac{\sum p_{j2}q_{j1}}{\sum p_{j1}q_{j1}} \cdot \frac{\sum p_{j1}q_{j0}}{\sum p_{j2}q_{j0}} \tag{8.9}$$

This can be transformed as follows[11]:

$$\frac{P_{01}^{L}P_{12}^{L}}{P_{02}^{L}} = \frac{\sum w_{j1}\left(\frac{q_{j0}}{q_{j1}}\right)\sum w_{j1}\left(\frac{p_{j2}}{p_{j1}}\right)}{\sum w_{j1}\left(\frac{p_{j2}}{p_{j1}}\right)\left(\frac{q_{j0}}{q_{j1}}\right)} \tag{8.10}$$

Let the price and quantity ratios be denoted by[12] x, y.

$$x_j = \frac{q_{j0}}{q_{j1}}, y_j = \frac{p_{j2}}{p_{j1}}, \alpha_j = w_{j1} \tag{8.11}$$

Now, define

$$\begin{aligned} \overline{x} &= \sum \alpha_j x_j \\ \overline{y} &= \sum \alpha_j y_j \\ \sum \alpha_j &= 1 \\ \sigma_{xy} &= \sum_j \alpha_j \left(x_j - \bar{x}\right)\left(y_j - \bar{y}\right) \end{aligned}$$

[10] Refer to Hill (1993) p. 487, Sect. 16.51.
[11] Please refer to the Mathematical Appendix A of this chapter.
[12] Please note that the time periods for price and quantity differ.

then the mean of x, y are Laspeyres price and quantity indices as follows:

$$\overline{x} = Q^L(1,0), \overline{y} = P^L(1,2) \tag{8.12}$$

Therefore, we get

$$P^L_{01} P^L_{12} / P^L_{02} = \frac{1}{1 + \frac{\sigma_{xy}}{\overline{x}\,\overline{y}}} \tag{8.13}$$

The necessary and sufficient condition to have a positive change drift is given by

$$P^L_{01} P^L_{12} / P^L_{02} > 1 \quad \text{if and only if } \sigma_{xy} < 0 \tag{8.14}$$

8.4.2 The Chain Drift of the Paasche Index

The drift function of the Paasche index is given by

$$\frac{P^P_{01} P^P_{12}}{P^P_{02}} = \frac{\sum p_{j1} q_{j1}}{\sum p_{j0} q_{j1}} \cdot \frac{\sum p_{j2} q_{j2}}{\sum p_{j1} q_{j2}} \cdot \frac{\sum p_{j0} q_{j2}}{\sum p_{j2} q_{j2}} \tag{8.15}$$

$$= \frac{\frac{\sum p_{j0} q_{j2}}{\sum p_{j1} q_{j2}}}{\sum w_{j1} \left(\frac{p_{j0}}{p_{j1}} \right)} \tag{8.16}$$

Following the similar procedure in the case for Laspeyres index and defining the following variables, which switch the time points for quantity and price as compared to the Laspeyres index, we get

$$x_j = \frac{q_{j2}}{q_{j1}}, \quad y_j = \frac{p_{j0}}{p_{j1}}, \quad \alpha_j = w_{j1} \tag{8.17}$$

$$\frac{P^P_{01} P^P_{12}}{P^P_{02}} = \frac{\frac{\sum p_{j0} q_{j2}}{\sum p_{j1} q_{j2}}}{\sum w_{j1} \left(\frac{p_{j0}}{p_{j1}} \right)} \tag{8.18}$$

$$= 1 + \sigma_{xy} \frac{1}{\overline{x}\,\overline{y}} \tag{8.19}$$

Thus, the necessary and sufficient condition to have a negative chain drift for the Paasche index is given by

$$P^P_{01} P^P_{12} / P^P_{02} < 1 \quad \text{if and only if} \quad \sigma_{xy} < 0 \tag{8.20}$$

Due to the differing time points for x and y in the Laspeyres and Paasche indices, it's important to note that a positive drift in the Laspeyres index doesn't always mean a negative drift in the Paasche index. However, consider a scenario where a bargain sale occurs in the first period, causing a price drop, and in the second period, the price returns to the level of period 0. From period 0 to 1, the quantity would increase, and from period 1 to 2, the quantity would decrease. Meanwhile, the price would decrease from period 0 to 1 and increase from period 1 to 2. In such a case, both Eqs. (8.14) and (8.20) would hold true. When the fluctuations in quantity and price due to a sale reverse within one period (i.e., the sale ends in one period), a positive drift arises in the Laspeyres index and a negative drift in the Paasche index.

8.4.3 Laspeyres–Paasche Gap

Using the fact that the Laspeyres quantity index and the Paasche price index are co-factors, the Laspeyres–Paasche gap can be expressed as follows:

$$P^L(0,1)/P^P(0,1) = P^L(0,1)\,Q^L(0,1)/V(0,1) \tag{8.21}$$

Now, let

$$x_j = \frac{q_{j1}}{q_{j0}},\ y_j = \frac{p_{j1}}{p_{j0}},\ \alpha_j = w_{j1} \tag{8.22}$$

If we assume this, we obtain a result similar to the Bortkiewicz decomposition introduced in Chap. 3.

$$\frac{P^L(0,1)}{P^P(0,1)} = \frac{Q^L(0,1)P^L(0,1)}{V(0,1)} \tag{8.23}$$

$$= \frac{\left(\sum w_j^0 \frac{p_{j1}}{p_{j0}}\right)\left(\sum w_j^0 \left(\frac{q_{j1}}{q_{j0}}\right)\right)}{\sum w_j^0 \left(\frac{q_{j1}}{q_{j0}}\right)\frac{p_{j1}}{p_{j0}}} \tag{8.24}$$

$$= \frac{\overline{x}\,\overline{y}}{\overline{x}\,\overline{y} + \sigma_{xy}} \tag{8.25}$$

Therefore, we get

$$P^L(0,1)/P^P(1,1) > 1 \quad \text{if and only if} \quad \sigma_{xy} < 0 \tag{8.26}$$

The summary of the results can be written as

$$P^L_{01}P^L_{12}/P^L_{02} > 1 \quad \text{if and only if } Cov\left(\frac{q_{j0}}{q_{j1}}, \frac{p_{j2}}{p_{j1}}\right) < 0 \tag{8.27}$$

$$P^P_{01}P^P_{12}/P^P_{02} < 1 \quad \text{if and only if} \quad Cov\left(\frac{q_{j2}}{q_{j1}}, \frac{p_{j0}}{p_{j1}}\right) < 0 \tag{8.28}$$

$$P^{L}(0,1)/P^{P}(0,1) > 1 \quad \text{if and only if} \quad Cov\left(\frac{q_{j1}}{q_{j0}}, \frac{p_{j1}}{p_{j0}}\right) < 0 \tag{8.29}$$

Let's define the Laspeyres–Paasche gap resulting from chaining as follows:

$$PLG_{02}^{C} = \frac{\max\left[P^{P}(0,1)\,P^{P}(1,2)\,,\,P^{L}(0,1)\,P^{L}(1,2)\right]}{\min\left[P^{P}(0,1)\,P^{P}(1,2)\,,\,P^{L}(0,1)\,P^{L}(1,2)\right]} \tag{8.30}$$

Note that the gap of the direct index is

$$PLG_{02}^{D} = \frac{\max\left[P^{P}(0,2)\,,\,P^{L}(0,2)\right]}{\min\left[P^{P}(0,2)\,,\,P^{L}(0,2)\right]} \tag{8.31}$$

When would the gap of the chain index be smaller than the gap of the direct index? In other words, when would the following inequality hold?

$$PLG_{02}^{C} < PLG_{02}^{D} \tag{8.32}$$

Upon expanding as described in Mathematical Appendix B, we can derive two sets of inequalities concerning the magnitude of four covariances as sufficient conditions for the Laspeyres–Paasche gap of the chain index to be smaller than that of the regular index.

$$Cov\left(\frac{q_{j0}}{q_{j1}}, \frac{p_{j2}}{p_{j1}}\right) > 0,\ Cov\left(\frac{q_{j2}}{q_{j1}}, \frac{p_{j0}}{p_{j1}}\right) > 0,\ Cov\left(\frac{q_{j1}}{q_{j0}}, \frac{p_{j1}}{p_{j0}}\right) < 0,\ Cov\left(\frac{q_{j2}}{q_{j1}}, \frac{p_{j2}}{p_{j1}}\right) < 0 \tag{8.33}$$

$$Cov\left(\frac{q_{j0}}{q_{j1}}, \frac{p_{j2}}{p_{j1}}\right) < 0,\ Cov\left(\frac{q_{j2}}{q_{j1}}, \frac{p_{j0}}{p_{j1}}\right) < 0,\ Cov\left(\frac{q_{j1}}{q_{j0}}, \frac{p_{j1}}{p_{j0}}\right) > 0,\ Cov\left(\frac{q_{j2}}{q_{j1}}, \frac{p_{j2}}{p_{j1}}\right) > 0 \tag{8.34}$$

Conversely, as sufficient conditions for the gap to widen, we can derive the following two conditions concerning the same covariances:

$$Cov\left(\frac{q_{j0}}{q_{j1}}, \frac{p_{j2}}{p_{j1}}\right) > 0,\ Cov\left(\frac{q_{j2}}{q_{j1}}, \frac{p_{j0}}{p_{j1}}\right) > 0,\ Cov\left(\frac{q_{j1}}{q_{j0}}, \frac{p_{j1}}{p_{j0}}\right) > 0,\ Cov\left(\frac{q_{j2}}{q_{j1}}, \frac{p_{j2}}{p_{j1}}\right) > 0 \tag{8.35}$$

$$Cov\left(\frac{q_{j0}}{q_{j1}}, \frac{p_{j2}}{p_{j1}}\right) < 0,\ Cov\left(\frac{q_{j2}}{q_{j1}}, \frac{p_{j0}}{p_{j1}}\right) < 0,\ Cov\left(\frac{q_{j1}}{q_{j0}}, \frac{p_{j1}}{p_{j0}}\right) < 0,\ Cov\left(\frac{q_{j2}}{q_{j1}}, \frac{p_{j2}}{p_{j1}}\right) < 0 \tag{8.36}$$

Of these four covariances, the last two represent the sign of prices and quantities at the same point in time and are thus expected to be negative. However, for the first two, which involve prices and quantities from different periods, there isn't much inherently implied from the usual shape of the demand curve. Yet, if there's a bargain sale that lasts only for one period or a strong short-term seasonal variation, there's a price drop followed by a price rise in the next period, while quantities first rise and then fall. In this situation, $Cov\left(\frac{q_{j0}}{q_{j1}}, \frac{p_{j2}}{p_{j1}}\right)$ is likely to be negative. In this case, Eq. (8.36) holds, making both the Laspeyres and Paasche chain drifts larger, and thus the chain index Laspeyres–Paasche gap becomes larger than in the direct index case. It's important to note that such scenarios are not merely special cases. They are widely and generally observed in short-term data and in data with strong seasonal variations.

8.5 Chain Drift When the Product Set Changes

Up until now, we have only considered situations where the set of products remains consistent across time and locations. However, since the days of the nineteenth-century Marshall era, one of the primary objectives of the chain index has been to address the changing nature of products over time. What kind of relationship arises between the direct index and the chain index when products differ between points in time or locations? The shifting nature of products, and the increase and decrease in their varieties, presents a considerable difficulty in index number theory, as well as for economic theory. This represents the frontier of current research based on index number theory and economic approaches. While we will investigate this topic deeper in the next chapter, let us briefly introduce the challenges associated with index calculations as products interchange.

8.5.1 Chain Drift in the Jevons Index

Consider a scenario spanning three periods—0, 1, and 2—where three goods are introduced. As illustrated in Table 8.1, the price of the first good drops from 1 to 0.5 from period 0 to 1 and then disappears by period 2. In period 1, a new product is introduced at a price of 1, and its price decreases in period 2. The third good maintains a consistent price of 0.3 throughout all periods.

In this case, the direct Jevons index is given by $J(0, 1) = J(1, 2) = 0.7071$, and $J(0, 2) = 1$. The chain Jevons index, on the other hand, is $JC\,(0, 2) = J(0, 1) \times J(1, 2) = 0.5$, indicating a significant chain drift.

Table 8.1 Examples of prices with product turnover

		Commodities		
		1	2	3
Time	0	1		0.3
	1	0.5	1	0.3
	2		0.5	0.3

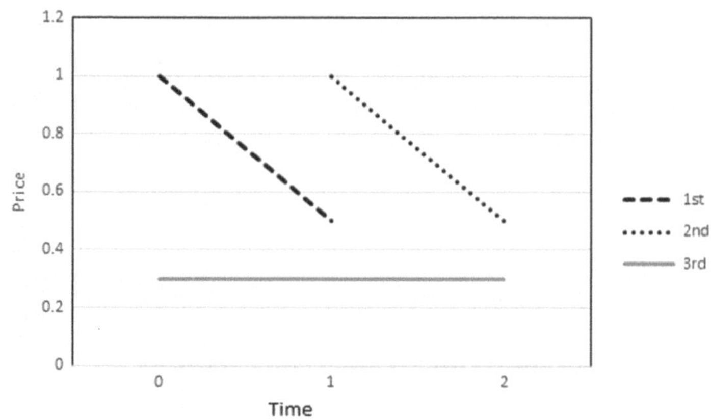

Fig. 8.4 Examples of prices with product turnover

Let's try to intuitively understand this chain drift based on Fig. 8.4. The chain Jevons index captures the price decline of products that are phasing out. Meanwhile, the direct index between periods 0 and 2 does not include any information on these products, reflecting only the information on constant prices. The reason the chain index is much smaller than the direct index is that while the chain index captures the price drop of disappearing products just before they disappear, it doesn't account for the price information when new products are introduced. If these products were homogeneous, they would be calculated using the Dutot index. In that case, the results would be $D(0, 1) = 0.923$, $D(1, 2) = 0.6667$, and $D(0, 2) = 0.615$. Meanwhile, the chain Dutot index would be $CD(0, 2) = 0.923 \times 0.6667 = 0.615$, equal to the direct Dutot index. This means that the Dutot index retains transitivity even when the sets of commodities change over time.

However, a problem arises when using the Dutot index. If these three products are homogeneous, it raises the question: why do goods with different prices coexist? One possible explanation is that for some consumers, only the first product is accessible, and they cannot purchase the cheaper third product—for instance, a person living in the United States might not have access to products from Australia—or perhaps the stores selling the first product provide attractive amenities such as comfortable air conditioning or baby care services. But in such cases, even if the products are identical as goods, they are not homogeneous from a purchasing perspective. The Dutot index would overlook these differences.

One way to explicitly incorporate the introduction of new products and the extinction of products into the index number formula is by using an economic model. In the example in Table 8.1, the first good has disappeared by the second period. If consumers wanted to purchase the first good in the second period but it has vanished, this situation can be equated to the price of the first good rising to infinity, or at least to a level where demand drops to zero. Viewing the extinction of a product as a drastic price increase is one way to understand product disappearance. This approach, using the reservation price method, was proposed by Diewert and Fox (2022) as an analytical technique for the disappearance of goods during the COVID-19 pandemic. This issue will be discussed in detail in Chap. 9.

8.6 Chain Drift in the Upper Level Aggregation

While high-frequency scanner data presented chain drift as a serious issue when making an elementary index for lower level aggregation, is chain drift actually problematic with monthly data or in the upper level aggregation? Using the soft drink data from Chap. 6, if we plot both the chain Törnqvist index and the standard direct Törnqvist index, the result will look like Fig. 8.5. In this instance, the Törnqvist index shows minimal chain drift. Therefore, the decision between using a chain or direct index has little impact on the actual value of the index based on monthly data.

However, for goods with strong seasonality like fruit, severe chain drift can occur, not just in the Laspeyres or Paasche indices, but even in the Jevons index. Figure 8.6 shows the upper level aggregation for the category, fruits in the consumer price index in Japan. Note that for seasonal products, using a direct index limits the products that can be compared. As a way to address this, in official statistics, the price of non-existent goods, like strawberries in the summer, is assumed to move in the same way as the prices of other fruits that are traded in the summer. While this is a practical approach, the basis for such assumptions is weak.

When aggregating at the upper level, using all the categories (excluding imputed rent) and plotting various indices, the result of the headline CPI will look like Fig. 8.7. Similarly, the chain indices are shown in Fig. 8.8. Thus, we can observe wide gap

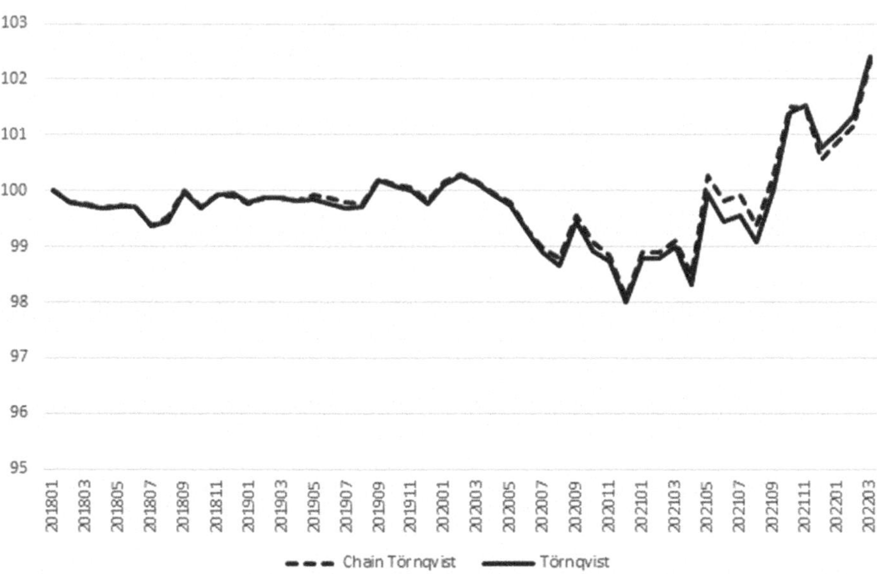

Fig. 8.5 Direct and Chain Törnqvist indices for soft drinks

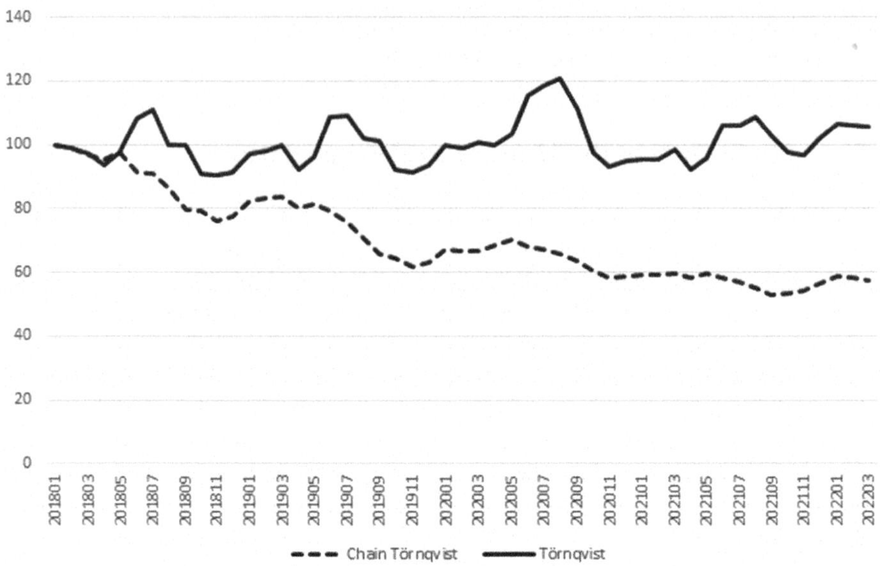

Fig. 8.6 Direct and Chain Törnqvist indices for fruits

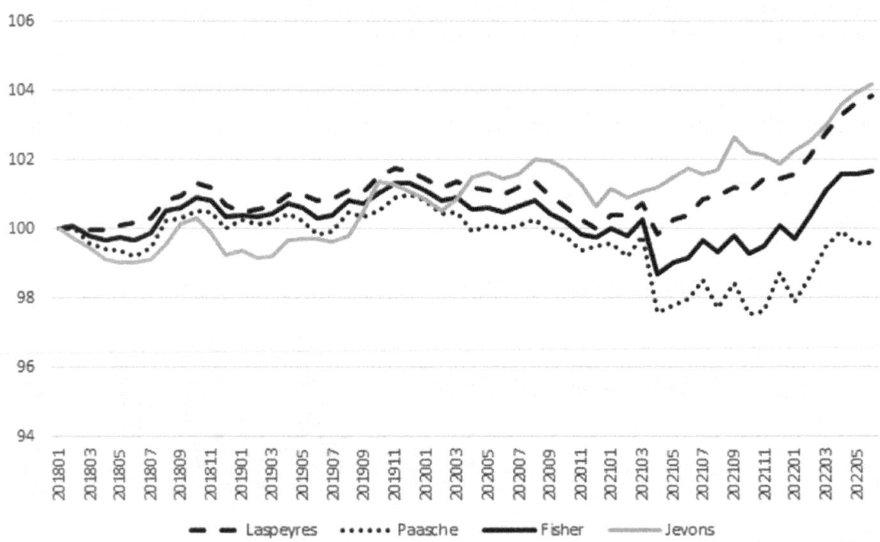

Fig. 8.7 Direct indices for all the products excl. imputed rents

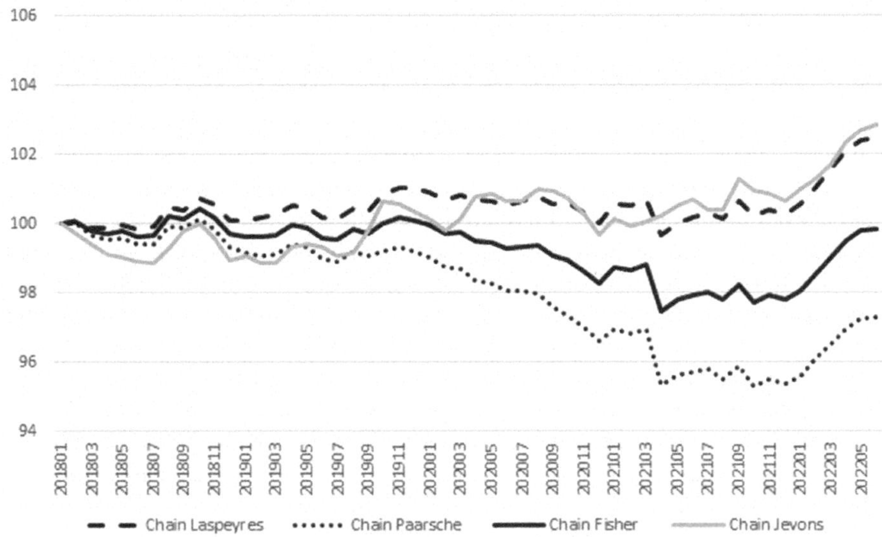

Fig. 8.8 Chain indices for all the products excl. imputed rents

between direct and chain indices even for the Jevons index. Using January 2018 as the base, by June 2022, it can be observed that the direct Fisher index is close to 102, while the chain index remains below 100. From this observation, chain drifts occur to a large degree for the upper level aggregation based on monthly data.

8.7 Chain Drifts and Chain Index

When presented with the choice between a direct index and a chain index, which should we adopt? The background for the introduction of the chain index was the need to address situations where products are replaced and the number of directly comparable goods decreases. Also, there is no theoretical justification for having a base year earlier than the previous year, especially when one is interested in year-on-year values. Therefore, it would be natural to believe that, if one is interested in year-on-year comparisons, it's more desirable to set the reference period to the same period of the previous year. In cases like Japan, where the Laspeyres index is revised once every 5 years, the further one gets from the base year, the more the weights used will deviate from actual consumer behavior. For instance, from October 2019, nursery school in Japan became free for children aged 3 years and older. However, the expenditure weight for nursery school remains fixed at the pre-free level, causing a significant divergence between the actual expenditures and the weights. Also, in 2020, during the COVID-19 pandemic, phenomena such as foreign travel and sports viewing, which were not even available due to lockdown, were given a positive expenditure share despite the absence of supply.[13] Although the Paasche index might be able to address rapid changes in weights, it can't resolve the problem when there are no comparable products. Neither can the Fisher index, of course.

When products change over time, it's true that the chain index is less affected than the direct index. However, at the point where products disappear or new products emerge, even in a chain index, there are items whose prices cannot be compared. When information about such non-comparable products is dropped from the chain index, it can lead to the serious problem of neglecting items that influence the real economy during price measurement. This phenomenon can be observed in durable goods like television sets and microwaves that introduce new models yearly. While it might be possible to equate old and new products by adjusting for quality when there's a clear successor, comparing the price of revolutionary products, like the iPhone in 2007, to their predecessors can be extremely challenging. For durable goods, specs are explicit, but for countless new potato chips or ice creams launched annually, guessing differences based on available ingredients is very difficult. Moreover, identifying which new product succeeded which older product is often unclear. The number of goods themselves isn't constant over time. For instance, Toshiba produced over 50 different TVs in 2010, but only around 20 by 2022. Many new ice creams sold in summer vanish by winter. When the number of products changes, even after quality adjustments, some items have no counterpart, which the chain index can't fix. These issues regarding product turnover and variation will be discussed in depth in the next chapter.

Recent academic papers, especially those using scanner data, predominantly adopt the chain index. Prominent examples include Broda and Weinstein (2010) and Redding and Weinstein (2020). However, they mainly report on the changes in the index numbers and do not investigate the progression of its levels. If one is only interested in the year-on-year change, it is more efficient to observe the year-on-year change directly rather than creating a price index that connects the changes in prices from the previous month. Chain indices can leverage this, but they tend to be smaller compared to direct indices due to the negative chain drifts that often occur in high-frequency scanner data. Whether this can be ignored is debatable.

For scenarios like the cereal example introduced at the start of this chapter, chain indices are unsuitable for long-term price comparisons due to severe drifts. However, when the number of directly comparable products decreases rapidly over time, and connecting new and old products using methods like the hedonic approach (which will be introduced in the next chapter) becomes difficult, the current index number theory provides only two options: either use the Dutot index assuming all products are homogeneous or adopt the chain index. Addressing or mitigating the effects of chain drift is a significant challenge in current index theory.

[13] Regarding the issues in Japan's price measurement during the COVID-19 pandemic, Abe (2022) introduces several cases.

8.8 GEKS (Gini–Eltető–Köves–Szulc)

The main method that has recently become popular to rectify chain drift is the GEKS (Gini–Eltető–Köves–Szulc) method. Originally, based on research by three scholars in the 1960s, this method was called the EKS (Eltető–Köves–Szulc) method. However, the same formula was proposed in a paper by Corrado Gini (1884–1965), Gini (1931), as a method to generate transitive indices from bilateral indices that do not satisfy transitivity. Therefore it has recently been more commonly referred to with the added "G," making it the GEKS method. Currently, the GEKS method is being used in the subindices of consumer price indices in countries like Australia, as well as by the World Bank in its compilation of purchasing power parities (PPP).

First, let us assume our interest lies in the price comparison between period 0 and period t. Now, for any two arbitrary points, j and k, in time between period 0 and period t, let's denote the Fisher index between j and k as PI_{jk}^{F}. In this case, the price index between points 0 and t as defined by the GEKS method is given as follows:

$$P_{0t}^{GEKS} = \prod_{l=0}^{t} \left(P_{0l}^{F} \times P_{lt}^{F} \right)^{\frac{1}{t+1}} \tag{8.37}$$

Namely, the price index over the interval from 0 to t becomes the geometric mean of the linked indices that encompass all possible third periods, denoted as l. The GEKS price index clearly satisfies transitivity. Adopting the Fisher index as the basis for GEKS ensures that since the Fisher index satisfies the factor reversal property, so does GEKS. The GEKS index is not limited to the Fisher index. It is possible to apply GEKS to all the indices discussed so far, including the Törnqvist and the Sato–Vartia indices. Since GEKS satisfies transitivity, it does not result in odd chaining drifts. However, being a type of chain index, it shares many of the problems of chain indices, such as the lack of identity, monotonicity, intermediate value properties, and consistency in aggregation. The biggest problem is that this index has little economic meaning. Even if based on the Fisher index, by taking (8.37), the exact property of the Fisher index regarding the cost-of-living index is lost. Chapter 11 will discuss more on GEKS.

8.9 Rolling Window GEKS

In many OECD countries, when constructing consumer price indices, extensive data based on transaction information from supermarkets, called scanner data, has been used in recent years. Specifically Switzerland, Netherlands, Denmark, Sweden, Belgium, Italy, Luxembourg, and New Zealand, scanner data is being increasingly used for many categories such as processed foods and daily necessities. Notably, the Australian Bureau of Statistics creates and publishes consumer price indices using the GEKS introduced in the previous section.

However, a significant issue with GEKS is that as new price and quantity information becomes available, past price values also get revised, leading to discrepancies between historical and current data. To address this, the Australian Bureau of Statistics adopts the Rolling Window GEKS (RWGEKS) method, as proposed by Diewert et al. (2011). This method utilizes data from a fixed recent time span, such as 5 years, for each period's calculation. As time progresses, the oldest data in the window is discarded, and new data is included. This requires the use of splicing methods such as Movement Splicing and Window Splicing to connect the indices of different periods in GEKS. These splicing methods have been proposed to address the need for continuity in the GEKS calculation across different periods.

Consider a window of period W, and focus on the connection from period $T-1$ to T. Let $P^{T}_{T-1,T}$ be the price index from period $T-1$ to T calculated based on the window used at time T. Meanwhile, let $P_{0,T-1}$ be the price index up to period $T-1$, based on period 0. In the Movement Splice method, this is defined as

$$P_{0,T} = P_{0,T-1} \times P^{T}_{T-1,T} \tag{8.38}$$

The following figure applies Movement Splicing to Rolling Window GEKS using weekly scanner data on detergents in Japan provided by INTAGE Inc.

The base period is the first week of 2017, with window length of 5 weeks, 10 weeks, 53 weeks, 106 weeks, and the entire period. A 2-week window length results in a standard chain index with significant negative drift. Even a long window period of 106 weeks shows substantial negative drift over 6 years. Notably, while the direct Fisher index indicates a rising trend from 2020 to 2021, GEKS does not show this increase, and Rolling Window GEKS does not observe a price increase after 2020. Given the rapid turnover of detergents, relying solely on a limited amount of product information for direct indices is not always preferable compared to GEKS or Rolling Window GEKS. Additionally, the chain Fisher index exhibits excessive drift, which complicates the interpretation of this trend as a reflection of detergent price movements.

The Australian Bureau of Statistics uses Window Splicing in its GEKS calculations, employing two price indices: the price change from period $T-W-2$ to $T-1$, denoted as $P^{T-1}_{T-2-W,T-1}$, and from $T-W-2$ to T, denoted as $P^{T}_{T\;2\;W,T}$. Specifically, it is defined as

$$P_{0,T} = P_{0,T-1} \times \frac{{P_{T-W-2,T}}^{T}}{{P_{T-W-2,T-1}}^{T-1}} \tag{8.39}$$

In the figure, Window Splicing in Rolling Window GEKS is nearly identical to Movement Splicing; therefore, it is not separately plotted in the figure.

Figure 8.9 demonstrates that even though GEKS does not inherently produce chain drift, its implementation in monthly price index calculations can still result in chain drift, rendering it unsuitable for observing long-term price trends. Figure 8.10 compares Direct, Chain, and GEKS indices, highlighting the discrepancies between the GEKS and the Direct index. Note that the whole period GEKS does not exhibit chain drift. The primary reason to use the otherwise economically unintelligible GEKS is to ensure transitivity, i.e., to avoid chain drift. However, adopting "rolling" methods that induce chain drift contradict the rationale for using GEKS. An alternative

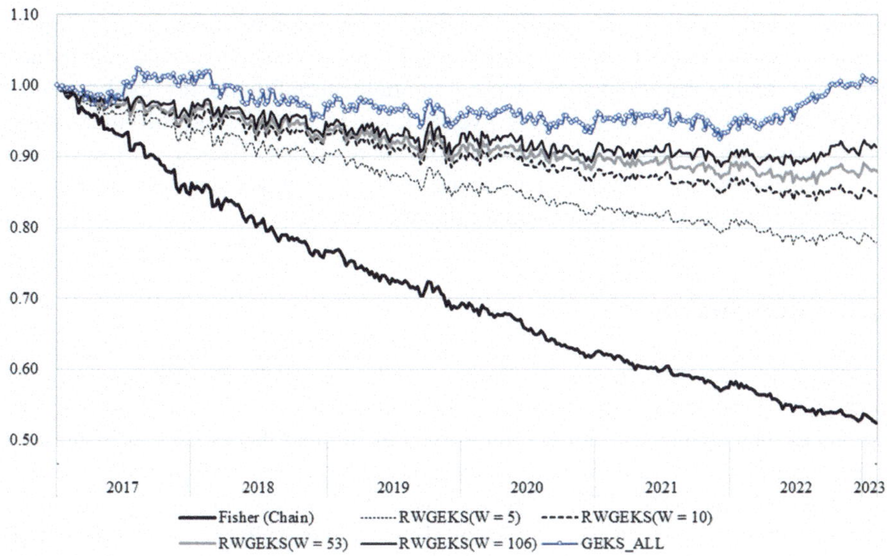

Fig. 8.9 Rolling Window GEKS

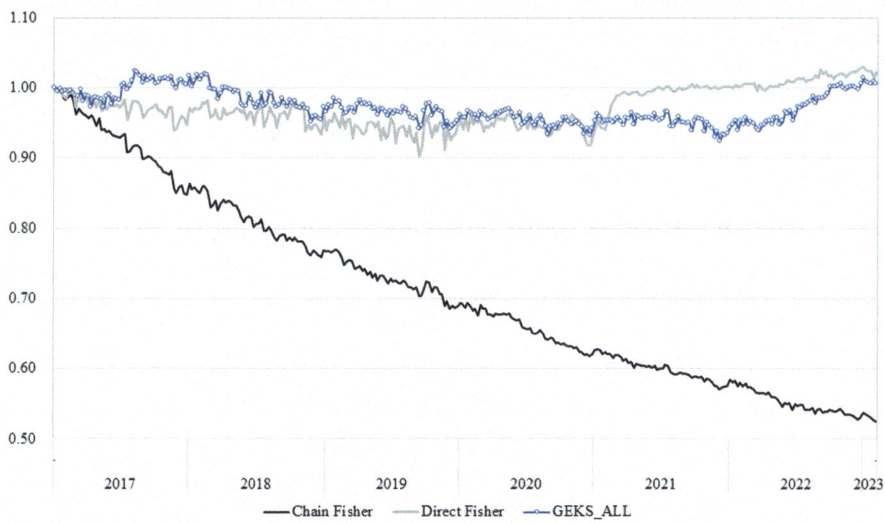

Fig. 8.10 Direct and Chain Fisher index

approach would be to fix the starting point and incrementally increase the window length with each period. However, continuing this for an extended period may reduce the number of directly comparable items, potentially destabilizing the results. Therefore, periodically, for example, every 3 years, it will be necessary to shift the starting period forward by 3 years and recalculate the GEKS index. These issues surrounding the Rolling Window approach are at the forefront of index number research and present significant challenges in actual price measurement.

8.10 Conclusion

In times when products frequently change or when people's demand patterns shift rapidly, chain indices are often considered suitable index number formulas that correspond to such changes. Leading figures in index number theory such as Fisher and Walsh gave positive evaluations to chain indices. However, both theoretically and empirically, it cannot be definitively said that chain indices are superior to direct indices. Sometimes, chain indices can produce serious drifts. Even if indices like GEKS satisfy transitivity, when adopted as official statistics and combined with a Rolling Window, chain drift still occurs. Chain drifts caused by seasonal fluctuations, issues arising from "new products" that appear once a year, like televisions and other durable consumer goods, and problems with special sales promotions are all related to chain indices. It's not a simple problem solved by adopting a particular index number formula. Regarding official statistics, including the current rule that does not allow revisions once published, a new perspective might be required.

8.11 Mathematical Appendix A: Derivation of Eq. (8.20)

Expand the chain Paasche index as follows:

$$
\begin{aligned}
P_{01}^{P} P_{12}^{P} / P_{02}^{P} &= \frac{\sum p_{j1} q_{j1}}{\sum p_{j0} q_{j1}} \frac{\sum p_{j2} q_{j2}}{\sum p_{j1} q_{j2}} \frac{\sum p_{j0} q_{j2}}{\sum p_{j2} q_{j2}} \\
&= \frac{\sum p_{j1} q_{j1}}{\sum p_{j0} q_{j1}} \frac{\sum p_{j0} q_{j2}}{\sum p_{j1} q_{j2}} \\
&= \frac{\frac{\sum p_{j0} q_{j2}}{\sum p_{j1} q_{j2}}}{\frac{\sum p_{j0} q_{j1}}{\sum p_{j1} q_{j1}}} \\
&= \frac{\frac{\sum p_{j0} q_{j2}}{\sum p_{j1} q_{j2}}}{\sum w_{j1} \left(\frac{p_{j0}}{p_{j1}} \right)}
\end{aligned}
$$

Similar to the case for Laspeyres Index, we can expand the equations as

$$\frac{\sum p_{j0}q_{j2}}{\sum p_{j1}q_{j1}} = \sum \frac{p_{j1}q_{j1}}{\sum p_{j1}q_{j1}} \left(\frac{q_{j2}}{q_{j1}}\right) \frac{p_{j0}}{p_{j1}}$$

$$\begin{aligned}
\frac{\sum p_{j0}q_{j2}}{\sum p_{j1}q_{j2}} &= \frac{\sum p_{j0}q_{j2}}{\sum p_{j1}q_{j2}} \frac{\sum p_{j1}q_{j2}}{\sum p_{j1}q_{j1}} \frac{\sum p_{j1}q_{j1}}{\sum p_{j1}q_{j2}} \\
&= \frac{\sum p_{j1}q_{j1}}{\sum p_{j1}q_{j2}} \frac{\sum p_{j0}q_{j2}}{\sum p_{j1}q_{j1}} \\
&= \frac{\frac{\sum p_{j0}q_{j2}}{\sum p_{j1}q_{j1}}}{\frac{\sum p_{j1}q_{j2}}{\sum p_{j1}q_{j1}}} \\
&= \sum w_{j1} \left(\frac{p_{j0}}{p_{j1}}\right) \frac{q_{j2}}{q_{j1}} / \sum w_{j1} \left(\frac{q_{j2}}{q_{j1}}\right)
\end{aligned}$$

Thus,

$$x_j = \frac{q_{j2}}{q_{j1}}, y_j = \frac{p_{j0}}{p_{j1}}, \alpha_j = w_{j1}$$

then,

$$\begin{aligned}
P_{01}^P P_{12}^P / P_{02}^P &= \frac{\frac{\sum p_{j0}q_{j2}}{\sum p_{j1}q_{j2}}}{\sum w_{j1} \left(\frac{p_{j0}}{p_{j1}}\right)} \\
&= \frac{\sum w_{j1} \left(\frac{p_{j0}}{p_{j1}}\right) \frac{q_{j2}}{q_{j1}}}{\sum w_{j1} \left(\frac{p_{j0}}{p_{j1}}\right) \sum w_{j1} \left(\frac{q_{j2}}{q_{j1}}\right)} \\
&= \frac{\overline{x}\,\overline{y} + \sigma_{xy}}{\overline{x}\,\overline{y}} \\
&= 1 + \sigma_{xy} \frac{1}{\overline{x}\,\overline{y}}
\end{aligned}$$

Thus, we can obtain the following necessary and sufficient condition for having a negative chain drift in the Paasche index:

$$P_{01}^P P_{12}^P / P_{02}^P < 1 \quad \text{if and only if}$$

$$\sigma_{xy} < 0$$

8.12 Mathematical Appendix B: The Derivations of the Laspeyres–Paasche Gap

Let's consider the sufficient condition for having the following inequality:

$$PLS_{02}^{C} < PLG_{02}^{D}$$

First, let's assume that the following relationships hold:

$$Cov\left(\frac{q_{j0}}{q_{j1}}, \frac{p_{j2}}{p_{j1}}\right) > 0, Cov\left(\frac{q_{j2}}{q_{j1}}, \frac{p_{j0}}{p_{j1}}\right) > 0, Cov\left(\frac{q_{j1}}{q_{j0}}, \frac{p_{j1}}{p_{j0}}\right) < 0, Cov\left(\frac{q_{j2}}{q_{j1}}, \frac{p_{j2}}{p_{j1}}\right) < 0$$

Furthermore, the last covariance is the necessary and sufficient condition for the Laspeyres index to exceed the Paasche index from period 1 to period 2. Namely, the following holds based on the signs of the last two covariances:

$$P^{L}(1,2) > P^{P}(1,2),$$
$$P^{L}(0,1) > P^{P}(0,1)$$

Also, from the signs of the first two covariances:

$$P_{01}^{L} P_{12}^{L} < P_{02}^{L},$$
$$P_{01}^{P} P_{12}^{P} > P_{02}^{P}$$

Therefore,

$$PLS_{02}^{D} = \frac{\max\left[P^{P}(0,2), P^{L}(0,2)\right]}{\min\left[P^{P}(0,2), P^{L}(0,2)\right]} = \frac{P^{L}(0,2)}{P^{P}(0,2)}$$

$$PLS_{02}^{C} = \frac{P^{L}(0,1)\, P^{L}(1,2)}{P^{P}(0,1)\, P^{P}(1,2)} < \frac{P^{L}(0,2)}{P^{P}(0,2)}$$

Thus, the sufficient condition for the chain Laspeyres–Paasche gap to be smaller than the regular index is

$$Cov\left(\frac{q_{j0}}{q_{j1}}, \frac{p_{j2}}{p_{j1}}\right) > 0, Cov\left(\frac{q_{j2}}{q_{j1}}, \frac{p_{j0}}{p_{j1}}\right) > 0, Cov\left(\frac{q_{j1}}{q_{j0}}, \frac{p_{j1}}{p_{j0}}\right) < 0, Cov\left(\frac{q_{j2}}{q_{j1}}, \frac{p_{j2}}{p_{j1}}\right) < 0$$

Similarly, it can easily be shown that

$$Cov\left(\frac{q_{j0}}{q_{j1}}, \frac{p_{j2}}{p_{j1}}\right) < 0, Cov\left(\frac{q_{j2}}{q_{j1}}, \frac{p_{j0}}{p_{j1}}\right) < 0, Cov\left(\frac{q_{j1}}{q_{j0}}, \frac{p_{j1}}{p_{j0}}\right) > 0, Cov\left(\frac{q_{j2}}{q_{j1}}, \frac{p_{j2}}{p_{j1}}\right) > 0$$

is also a sufficient condition.

On the other hand, if all the covariances have the same sign, namely,

$$Cov\left(\frac{q_{j0}}{q_{j1}}, \frac{p_{j2}}{p_{j1}}\right) > 0, Cov\left(\frac{q_{j2}}{q_{j1}}, \frac{p_{j0}}{p_{j1}}\right) > 0, Cov\left(\frac{q_{j1}}{q_{j0}}, \frac{p_{j1}}{p_{j0}}\right) > 0, Cov\left(\frac{q_{j2}}{q_{j1}}, \frac{p_{j2}}{p_{j1}}\right) > 0$$

or

$$Cov\left(\frac{q_{j0}}{q_{j1}}, \frac{p_{j2}}{p_{j1}}\right) < 0, Cov\left(\frac{q_{j2}}{q_{j1}}, \frac{p_{j0}}{p_{j1}}\right) < 0, Cov\left(\frac{q_{j1}}{q_{j0}}, \frac{p_{j1}}{p_{j0}}\right) < 0, Cov\left(\frac{q_{j2}}{q_{j1}}, \frac{p_{j2}}{p_{j1}}\right) < 0$$

then it can also be easily shown that the chain Paasche gap will be larger than the regular index.

8.13 STATA Code for Rolling Window GEKS

In this Appendix, we explain the STATA Code for calculating Rolling Window GEKS.

- To compute the GEKS, a square matrix of bilateral indices is created. For instance, using the Fisher index, the first column consists of Fisher indices with the first row as the base, and the second column with the second row as the base. This leads to all diagonal elements being 1, and each element in the upper triangle being the reciprocal of the corresponding lower triangle element. In other words, $P_{ij} \times P_{ji} = 1$.
- If the window length is 10, then the GEKS for each period is calculated from a 10×10 matrix centered on the diagonal elements. The following code utilizes Windows Splicing (Table 8.2).

Table 8.2 Example of a matrix of Fisher indices

full_mat1	full_mat2	full_mat3	full_mat4	full_mat5	full_mat6	full_mat7	…	
1.00	1.01	1.01	1.02	1.01	1.01	1.01	…	
0.99	1.00	1.00	1.01	1.00	1.00	1.01	…	
0.99	1.00	1.00	1.02	1.00	1.01	1.01	…	
0.98	0.99	0.98	1.00	0.99	0.99	0.99	…	
0.99	1.00	1.00	1.01	1.00	1.01	1.01	…	
0.99	1.00	0.99	1.01	0.99	1.00	1.01	…	
0.99	0.99	0.99	1.01	0.99	0.99	1.00	…	
…	…	…	…	…	…	…	…	

```
// Clear the current STAT environment
clear all

// Change the working directory to the specified path
cd D:\research\detergent\

// Load the dataset named 'full_fishermatrix'
use full_fishermatrix

// Convert variables full_mat1 to full_mat516 into a matrix named 'fisher'
mkmat full_mat1-full_mat516, mat(fisher)

// Initialize local variables for matrix dimensions and window length
local r = rowsof(fisher)
local n = rowsof(fisher)
local w = 50 // Window length

// Create matrices for GEKS computation
matrix rgeks_`w' = J(`n', 1, 1)
matrix geks_fisher = J(`w', `w', 1)

// Compute GEKS for the first window using all periods
forv i = 1/`w' {
    forv j = 1/`w' {
        scalar geks1_1 = (fisher[`i', 1] * fisher[`j', `i']) ^ (1/`w')
        matrix geks_fisher[`j', 1] = geks1_1 * geks_fisher[`j', 1]
        scalar drop geks1_1
    }
}

forv i = 1/`w' {
    matrix rgeks_`w'[`i', 1] = geks_fisher[`i', 1]
}

// Determine the number of rolling iterations
scalar k = `n' - `w' + 1
local k = `n' - `w' + 1 // Necessary for proper looping

// Initialize a matrix for growth rate calculation
matrix growthrate = J(`n', 1, 1)
```

```
// Compute GEKS for subsequent windows
forv i = 2/`k' {
    scalar gekswl = 1

    // Calculate for the previous window
    scalar m = `i' // Start of the previous window
    scalar l = `i' + `w' - 2 // End of the previous window

    forv j = 1/`w' {
        scalar gekswr = (fisher[`i' + `j' - 2, m] *
        fisher[l, `i' + `j' - 2]) ^ (1/`w')
        scalar gekswl = gekswr * gekswl
        scalar drop gekswr
    }

    scalar geksw2 = 1

    // Calculate for the latest window
    scalar m = `i' // Start of the latest window
    scalar l = `i' + `w' - 1 // End of the latest window

    forv j = 1/`w' {
        scalar geksw = (fisher[`i' + `j' - 1, m] *
        fisher[l, `i' + `j' - 1]) ^ (1/`w')
        scalar geksw2 = geksw2 * geksw
        scalar drop geksw
    }

    // Calculate and store the growth rate for the latest period
    matrix rgeks_`w'[l, 1] = rgeks_`w'[l - 1, 1] * geksw2 / gekswl
    matrix growthrate[l, 1] = geksw2 / gekswl
    scalar drop geksw2 gekswl
}

// Save the matrices 'rgeks_`w'' and 'growthrate' to the dataset
svmat rgeks_`w'
svmat growthrate
```

References

Abe, N. (2022). Measuring inflation under pandemic conditions': A comment. *Journal of Official Statistics, 38*(1), 295–300.

Balk, B. M. (2008). *Price and quantity index numbers*. Cambridge University Press.

Broda, C., & Weinstein, D. E. (2010). Product creation and destruction: Evidence and price implications. *American Economic Review, 100*(3), 691–723.

Diewert, W. E. (2005). Some Issues Concerning Index Number Theory. Paper Presented at the ESRI 'Conference on the Next Steps for the Japanese System of National Accounts: Towards More Accurate Measurement and More Comprehensive Accounts," Held in Tokyo, March 24-25, 2005.

Diewert, W. E. (2021b). The Chain Drift Problem and Multilateral Indexes. *Consumer Price Index Theory*, Chapter 7.

Diewert, W. E., & Fox, K. J. (2022). Measuring inflation under pandemic conditions. *Journal of Official Statistics, 38*(1), 255–285.

Diewert, W. E., Fox, K. J., & Ivancic, L. (2011). Scanner data, time aggregation and the construction of price indexes. *Journal of Econometrics, 161*(1), 24–35.
Fisher, I. (1922) *The making of index numbers*. Houghton Mifflin Company.
Frisch, R. (1936). Annual survey of general economic theory: The problem of index numbers. *Econometrica, 4*(1), 1–38.
Gini, C. (1931). On the circular test of index numbers. *Metron, 2*, 3–24.
Hill, T. P. (1993) Price and volume measure. Chapter 16 in System of National Accounts 1993 (pp. 379–406). Eurostat, IMF, OECD, UN and World Bank.
Hill, R. (2006). When does chaining reduce the Paasche–Laspeyres spread? An application to scanner data. *Review of Income and Wealth, 52*(2), 309–325.
Lee, K. (2018). *Quarterly national accounts manual (2017 edition)*. International Monetary Fund.
Lippe, P. V. D. (2007) *Index theory and price statistics*. Peter Lang Pub Inc.
Redding, S. J., & Weinstein, D. E. (2020). Measuring aggregate price indices with taste shocks: Theory and evidence for CES preferences. *Quarterly Journal of Economics, 135*(1), 503–560.

Price Comparisons with Time-Varying Commodity Sets

9

Abstract

This chapter explores the difficulties and methodologies associated with constructing price indices when the set of goods changes over time. It acknowledges that no two products are "exactly" identical, even within the same category, and the emergence and disappearance of goods complicate price comparisons. Seasonal goods, technological innovations, and disruptions like the COVID-19 pandemic further challenge traditional price measurement methods. The chapter discusses the hedonic method, which adjusts for quality differences by considering various attributes of goods, and highlights its limitations, including the difficulty of measuring new attributes and dealing with multicollinearity. The matching method, which compares only concurrently available goods, is straightforward but prone to bias due to non-random product exits and introductions. The chapter also introduces the concept of variety effects, where changes in the variety of goods impact consumer welfare and the cost-of-living index (COLI). Feenstra's COLI, which incorporates variety effects, is widely used but can exhibit significant chain drift over time, complicating long-term price comparisons. The chapter concludes by highlighting the ongoing research and practical issues in addressing these challenges, emphasizing the need for innovative approaches and new methodologies.

9.1 Difficulty of Price Comparisons When the Commodity Set Differs over Time

In the axiomatic and economic approaches discussed in earlier chapters, the sets of commodities are assumed to remain the same across two time periods or regions. However, upon closer examination, the concept of "the same" goods is somewhat relative. For instance, even if one were to dine at the same restaurant, say a Chinese restaurant, on two consecutive days and order the same dish, there might be slight variations in taste or portion. Moreover, considering the overall dining experience, including aspects like congestion and service, the utility derived from the meal could

N. Abe, *Price Index Numbers*, Springer Texts in Business and Economics,
https://doi.org/10.1007/978-981-97-6305-4_9

vary daily. Similarly, for perishable goods such as salmon or grapes, even if compared from the same origin or brand, each piece of salmon or grape cannot be said to be identical in size or taste. It is reasonable to state that no two products are "exactly" the same in the world. Even less extreme examples, such as comparing the assortment of goods in a supermarket now to those from 10 years ago, would likely show considerable differences. Furthermore, looking further back in time, it's not uncommon for the categories of goods themselves to have changed. Fifty years ago, there were no digital cameras or LCD TVs, and smartphones like the iPhone, upon their introduction, spanned various categories, posing a significant categorization challenge for statisticians at the time. Even today, as new services and products are developed, outdated ones disappear from the market. Home appliances, for instance, see new products introduced almost monthly, each touted for having features or performance that differ in some way from existing products.

Even beyond technological innovations, the availability of fresh food items often varies by season. For example, cherries are abundant in early summer but are seldom found in stores during winter. Seasonal goods, which see significant changes in the types of goods available depending on the season, make it challenging to compare prices over different seasons. Additionally, the COVID-19 pandemic in 2020 prompted lockdowns worldwide, halting most economic activities and travel in cities and leading to the disappearance of many services, such as overseas travel and sports viewing. It is unusual for entire categories of products to disappear so suddenly on a global scale, and these abrupt changes posed significant challenges for statistical offices worldwide in measuring the prices of vanished goods.

The development of new goods and services is a crucial driver of economic growth, while structural changes, such as demographic shifts, also lead to alterations in various goods and services. Furthermore, the availability of products in the market fluctuates significantly over time due to seasonal changes or the popularity of certain items. This poses a well-known and critical issue for econometricians: how should price and quantity indices be constructed when a corresponding product from the past cannot be found? When it is possible to match new and old products, standardization is achieved by setting a criterion, measuring the distance between the new and old products based on that criterion, and adjusting the price accordingly. Various approaches are possible, but the hedonic method is commonly used, with the overlap method, volume adjustment method, and direct comparison method being considered special cases of the hedonic approach. The challenge lies in the difficulty of quantitatively assessing the quality differences between new and old products.

Figure 9.1 displays the price index for information processing equipment, such as personal computers and tablets, across Eurozone countries. These countries share a common currency and do not impose tariffs on the movements of goods between them. Despite this, there is a significant divergence in trends over 10 years. Figure 9.2 illustrates the price index for televisions in the United States and Japan. As the currencies differ between these two countries, some of the price differences may reflect fluctuations in currency values; however, the difference in price trends is considerable. These discrepancies could indicate differences in quality adjustment

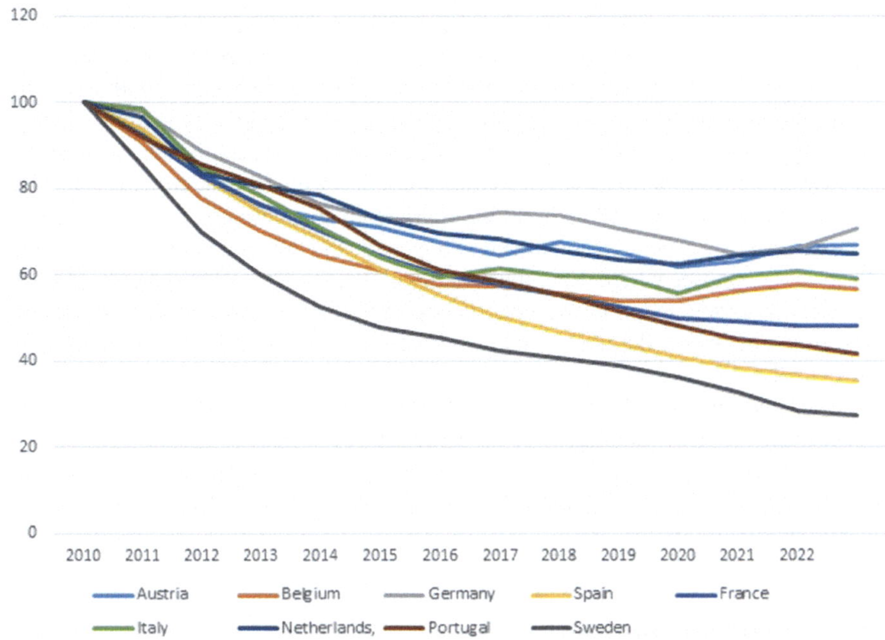

Fig. 9.1 Price index for information processing equipment. *Sources* European Central Bank Data Portal. The Base is set at Year 2010

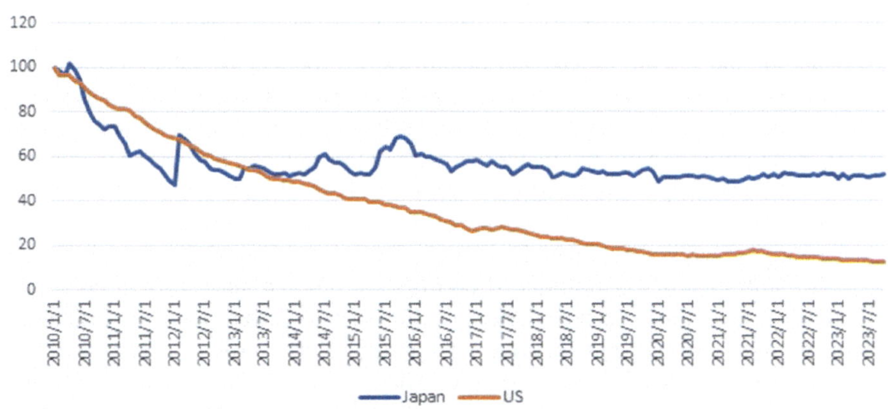

Fig. 9.2 Price index for television set. *Sources* BLS Consumer Price Index for All Urban Consumers (CPI-U); Statistical Bureau of Japan, Consumer Price Index

methods used by each country rather than actual price movements of the goods in these countries.

When a new product is introduced or an old product exits the market, a direct counterpart may not always be available. If a direct counterpart cannot be found between two points in time, or if the category of goods itself changes, conventional methods such as the overlap method and the hedonic method, which will be introduced later in this chapter, may not solve the problem. Addressing this issue is at the forefront of current index number theory and poses a significant challenge. The current standard method is the Variety Effects proposed by Robert Feenstra, but this method has difficulty addressing phenomena such as the disappearance of entire categories, like foreign travel services during the COVID-19 pandemic, for reasons that will be explained later. Furthermore, there is no consensus on how to economically compare prices between countries where pork and beef are not sold for cultural reasons and countries where these meats are widely available. This is a cutting-edge topic in aggregation and index number theory and practice, characterized by various innovations, including the use of advanced methods such as machine learning, in a rapidly evolving field.

Addressing new and disappearing products is one of the most critical issues in current index number making, with a vast amount of research and reports written on the subject. It is impossible to comprehensively describe their content in this chapter. Here, before introducing a formal economic model, let us discuss several conventional methods.

9.2 Matching Method

First of all, let us discuss what would happen if we ignore the changes in the commodity set, and use the commodities that exist both in base and comparison periods. Such a method is called as the matching method, which is often used with scanner data where detailed information on product quality is limited. This method, which calculates the index using prices and quantities of products available at both time points, avoids dealing with new products, making the calculation significantly easier. However, the matching method has faced substantial criticism, such as by Pakes (2003). A major issue with the matching method arises when product exits are not random but occur for specific reasons, introducing bias into price and quantity measures. Specifically, quantities of a product about to exit tend to significantly decrease, nearing zero, which gets reflected in the quantity index. Meanwhile, the substantial quantities sold of a newly introduced product are ignored since there's no corresponding product in the previous period, leading to a downward bias in the quantity index. The same can happen with prices; if a product's price drops due to a clearance sale before exiting, then that decrease is recorded in the price index. Conversely, the high introductory price of a new product is ignored due to the absence of a match in the previous period, potentially introducing a downward bias in the price index as well.

Although the matching method is widely used, especially with scanner data, it's primarily applied to price indices, with quantity indices being less common. However, when price indices are used as deflators, the potential for a negative bias in the corresponding quantity indices poses a significant issue. One approach to address this issue, albeit with acknowledged bias, is to use unit value prices, assuming that quality is determined solely by the quantity (e.g., volume or weight) for relatively homogeneous products. This unit value price index results in a similar outcome as the Dutot index, reflecting prices and quantities of new products in the index. The obvious drawback is that it ignores actual quality differences between new and old products. In many cases, prices and quantities of new products are disregarded, but in sectors with active product development, ignoring information on new product introductions can pose significant difficulties, warranting further analysis.

One method to mitigate issues with the matching method is to bridge between exiting and new products by finding corresponding items. While it's straightforward to connect products when a producer declares a successor, finding one-to-one matches is often challenging. Abe and Shinozaki (2018) propose using machine learning to identify the "closest" new product to a discontinued one from potential successors, based on various information such as names and specs, and consider half the price difference between the new and old products as quality improvement and the other half as price revision. The rationale for allocating 50% to quality improvement and price revision is based on previous research, but this may vary case by case and should be understood as a simplified approach. However, this method does not account for scenarios where no successor product exists, i.e., when a product category is discontinued, and might mechanically select the closest match. Despite these limitations, this machine learning-based approach is seen as a method to reduce the problems of simple matching and is expected to continue being utilized due to its ease of implementation. The matching method, which ignores the introduction of new products or changes in the commodity set, is widely used in constructing price indices with scanner data, such as GEKS. However, this approach has serious problems. If information on product attributes is available, it is undoubtedly desirable to incorporate as much information about new products as possible. The hedonic approach, which is used when the types of products are limited, such as durable consumer goods, will be explained next.

9.3 Hedonic Approach

9.3.1 Hedonic Regression

To construct a price index, price relatives for each item, i.e., price changes between two points in time, are typically used. However, when new products are introduced, it is impossible to calculate their price relatives because there are no past prices for these products. The price relatives for new products can only be calculated in the period following their introduction. Regardless of how many new products are purchased in the period they are introduced, they are not reflected in the price index at the time of their introduction. The hedonic approach circumvents this problem by pooling all products traded in the two periods and assuming that differences between products are fully controlled by observable quality information. Therefore, if a relatively expensive new product for its quality is introduced, it will be recognized as an increase in general prices.

The hedonic approach can be shown as the following simple regression model when using information on two time periods, say t and $t-1$:

$$\ln p_{it} = \alpha + \beta D_t + \sum_k \gamma_k \cdot z_{ik} + \varepsilon_{it} \tag{9.1}$$

where z_{ik} is the characteristics of the commodity i[1]. D_t is a dummy variable for time t. For example, if we are making price index of laptop computer, the vector of commodity, **z**, consists of the size of memory, the size of the display, the clock speed of the central processing unit, etc. β captures the general movement of prices after controlling for the differences in the quality of commodities.

Using the estimated coefficient $\widehat{\beta}$ as the (log) price index between $t-1$ and t, we can compute the chain price index PI_t as:

$$PI_t = PI_{t-1} \times \exp(\widehat{\beta}) \tag{9.2}$$

Using short-term data such as 2 months allows for controlling the effects of attribute value changes over time, i.e., the obsolescence of various features. If z_{ik} sufficiently captures the differences in quality of laptop computers and the error term ε_{it} is uncorrelated with explanatory variables, the method can measure changes in general price changes of laptop computers.

9.3.2 Theoretical Model of the Hedonic Method

The hedonic method, proposed by Court (1918) as a model to describe consumer behavior across goods with different attributes, was later established by scholars such as Gorman (1956), Griliches (1961), Lancaster (1966), and Rosen (1974). Today, it is widely used by statistical practitioners as a standard method for quality adjustment between different goods. In many countries, the hedonic method is adopted for home electrical appliances and personal computers. The theoretical aspects of the hedonic method in price measurement have been extensively discussed in seminal papers by Silver (1999), with significant contributions also from Triplett (2004), Menz et al. (2023), Pakes (2003), and de Haan and Diewert (2017). Here, we introduce the theory of the hedonic method, drawing on recent outstanding research by Crawford and Neary (2023).

Consider the representative consumer's behavior in a market with K types of goods, characterized by J attributes. For instance, in the market for laptop computers, we assume that there are K different commodities (laptop computers), and the performance of each computer is determined by J attributes such as screen size, clock speed, and memory size. Assuming the number of attributes J is not greater than the number of commodities ($J \leq K$), let z_{jt} denote the total amount of attribute j in period t, x_{kt} the total quantity of good k, and p_{kt} its corresponding price. The

[1] Here, we assume that the characteristics of good i are the same in period t and period $t-1$. However, if they change, it is necessary to add the subscript t.

representative consumer derives his/her utility from the total amount of attribute j in good k at time t, denoted as $a_t^{k,j}$, and it is assumed that

$$z_{jt} = \sum_k a_t^{k,j} x_{kt} \tag{9.3}$$

For example, z_{jt} could represent the total amount of memory in computers, and $a_t^{k,j}$ the memory size installed in computer k. Assuming the representative household in the market derives utility from the total amount of attributes, the utility maximization problem can be formalized as

$$\max_{\{x_{kt}\}} V = v\left(z_{1t}, z_{2t}, z_{3t}, \ldots, z_{Jt}\right) \tag{9.4}$$

$$\text{s.t. } z_{jt} = \sum_{k=1}^{J} a_t^{k,j} x_{kt}, \quad \forall j \in \{1, \ldots, J\} \tag{9.5}$$

$$y_t = \sum_{k=1}^{J} p_{kt} x_{kt}$$

where V and y_t are the utility function and the total income of the representative consumer at time t, respectively, while p_{kt} is the price of the commodity k at time t.

The first-order condition is

$$\sum_j a_t^{k,j} v_{jt} = \lambda p_{kt} \tag{9.6}$$

where λ is the Lagrange multiplier, while v_{jt} is the partial derivative of the utility function with respect to the attribute j.

Rearranging the above yields

$$p_{kt} = \sum_j a_t^{k,j} \frac{v_{jt}}{\lambda} \tag{9.7}$$

The ratio of marginal utility to the multiplier on the right-hand side can be considered the shadow price of attribute j, denoted as π_{jt}. This leads to

$$p_{kt} = \sum_j a_t^{k,j} \pi_{jt} \tag{9.8}$$

This equation can be interpreted as the hedonic equation.[2]

[2] In practice, we often use the natural logarithms of prices instead of the level of the price in a hedonic model. Note that to derive the hedonic model with the natural log of prices, some approximations of the first-order condition are necessary.

When formulated as a utility maximization problem, it's important to note that since the attribute parameters of goods $a_t^{k,j}$ are time dependent, the "quantity" of attributes derived from the goods can change over time even if the quantity of each good x_{kt} remains the same between two time points, making the utility level dependent on time. x_{kt} and x_{kt+1} are considered not just as the same products at different time points, but as similar yet slightly different goods or services.

The challenge lies in the fact that shadow prices or the parameter $a_t^{k,j}$ cannot be directly observed. However, if information on $a_t^{k,j}$ is available, it becomes possible to estimate:

$$p_{kt} = \sum_j a_t^{k,j} \widehat{\pi}_{jt} \tag{9.9}$$

from cross-sectional data for each period. This (or its log linearized version) forms the basis of hedonic estimation. During estimation, prices of products are regressed on product attributes, requiring strong assumptions about the presence of unobserved error terms, unobservable qualities, and their covariance structures.

Implementing the hedonic method requires selecting attributes and gathering information on $a_t^{k,j}$, which represents the relationship of those attributes to each good. This task is generally labor intensive. For laptop computers, quantifiable measures such as screen size, hard disk and memory capacity, and processing speed can serve as important indicators of quality. However, for new restaurants, qualitative aspects like service quality and taste become crucial, which are difficult to measure in general. The quality of books, magazines, and newspapers is also challenging to quantify, limiting the range of products suitable for hedonic estimation.

One extreme form of the hedonic method considers only volume as an attribute. If different brands of milk are introduced to the market but can be described solely by their volume, then prices of new and old milk can be compared based on price per unit volume. This idea leads to the concept of the unit value price index, proposed by Drobisch in the nineteenth century, and is applied in real-world price statistics compilation for many processed food products. For instance, if a new ice cream is sold in smaller portion, the price increase due to reduced volume connects the new and old products. This connection arises from the difficulty in quantifying information about ice cream quality, especially its "taste."

Another extreme case arises when we have no information on the values of the parameters $a_t^{k,j}$. Suppose there are only two products, new and old, with unknown quality differences but known price differences. With only one product per period, the first-order conditions become

$$\begin{aligned} p_{kt} &= a_t^{k,j} \pi_{jt}, \\ p_{kt+1} &= a_{t+1}^{k,j} \pi_{jt+1} \end{aligned}$$

From these equations, we derive the following relationship:

$$\frac{p_{kt+1}}{p_{kt}} = \frac{a_t^{k,j} \pi_{jt}}{a_{t+1}^{k,j} \pi_{jt+1}} \tag{9.10}$$

Without information on $a_t^{k,j}$, assumptions must be made about either the shadow prices or $a_t^{k,j}$ itself. For example, assuming constant shadow prices implies that the utility derived per unit price from new and old products remains unchanged. This leads to

$$\frac{p_{kt+1}}{p_{kt}} = \frac{a_t^{k,j}}{a_{t+1}^{k,j}} \tag{9.11}$$

In this scenario, all price differences are attributed to quality differences, and the overlap method, which treats price differences between new and old products as negligible, is applied in creating price statistics. Conversely, assuming constant $a_t^{k,j}$ implies that all price differences arise from differences in shadow prices, suggesting that the price of a product of the same quality has changed, i.e.,

$$\frac{p_{kt+1}}{p_{kt}} = \frac{\pi_{jt}}{\pi_{jt+1}} \tag{9.12}$$

This means treating new and old products as identical, regardless of name or price differences; a price increase in the new product is considered a price hike. Without additional information, it is impossible to determine whether the constant is the shadow prices, the quality parameters, or a combination of both.

Consider the trend in the price index for televisions in Japan's national consumer price index depicted in Fig. 9.2. A change in the surveyed TV in February 2012 led to a sharp price increase.[3] This unique phenomenon, which significantly impacted the headline CPI, is not commonly observed in other items. At that time, the Statistics Bureau of Japan adopted the direct comparison method, treating all price increases for new TVs compared to old ones as price hikes due to fixed quality parameters. Such price movements, especially sudden changes due to product replacements, are not ideal when using the consumer price index as a deflator, as it's unlikely that prices of other TVs not part of the basic brand changed simultaneously. New products typically command a premium for being new, which could be interpreted as part of their quality. If the utility derived from a TV increases simply because it's a new model, then the price increase associated with the new product's introduction could be considered part of a quality change, which would then depreciate like housing or durable goods. Nonetheless, when using the current consumer price index as a deflator, it's important to be mindful of such extreme movements.

[3] The basic model for televisions was a 32-inch high-definition LCD with LED backlighting, but from February 2012, the requirement was added to include two terrestrial digital tuners.

A limitation of the hedonic method is its inability to account for the impact of newly introduced attributes previously unknown. Forty years ago, the Internet did not exist, and a hundred years ago, neither did television. The attributes we expect from a TV might be compared to those of a cinema or theater, but it is quite a stretch to apply the hedonic method to equate the services of a cinema with a home television. While theoretically clear and practically the only method for addressing changes in goods, the limitations of the hedonic method must also be acknowledged.

9.3.3 Some Practical Issues

When we apply the hedonic model to consider the effects of new goods, there are several issues to be considered. The first is the selection of the variables included in the hedonic equation. The second is the functional form of the hedonic equation.

In Japan, the Statistics Bureau conducts hedonic estimation for televisions as follows.[4] Based on point-of-sales (POS) data, the price of television model i in period t, denoted as $p_{i,t}$, and its attributes $z_{i,k}$ (such as screen size, number of HDMI ports, etc.) are pooled with sales price and quantity information over 2 months to estimate the hedonic equation using weighted least squares, where sales volume is used as weights.

Note that it's not self-evident whether weights in weighted regression should be based on sales. We could use information on quantities for the weights. de Haan and Diewert (2017) use expenditure shares, whereas Diewert (2003) employs quantity shares for the hedonic model.

Secondly, careful consideration is needed on how to convert attribute information into numerical data. In the model above, we use a simple linear model. In reality, for example, the impact of screen size on log price might not be proportional to the screen area but follow a nonlinear relationship. In cases where the functional form is unknown, a Box-Cox transformation is commonly applied to both the dependent and independent variables, and maximum likelihood estimation is used to estimate the Box-Cox transformation parameters λ_p and λ_k[5]:

$$\frac{p_{i,t}^{\lambda_p} - 1}{\lambda_p} = \alpha + \beta \cdot Time + \sum_k \gamma_k \cdot \frac{z_{i,k}^{\lambda_k} - 1}{\lambda_k} + \varepsilon_{i,t} \tag{9.13}$$

Variable selection presents a deeper issue. In the case of televisions, higher end models tend to have higher values for various performance and quality metrics, leading to strong correlations among variables, i.e., multicollinearity. This makes variable selection difficult. Automatic selection based on statistical criteria like Akaike's Information Criterion can yield difficult-to-interpret or unstable results in the presence of multicollinearity. For national statistical bureaus that need to produce credible

[4] For details, see the official document, https://www.stat.go.jp/info/kenkyu/cpi/pdf/020-1-1.pdf.

[5] If the Box-Cox transformation parameter is 1, it is equivalent to taking the natural logarithm.

public statistics, conducting unstable and difficult-to-interpret hedonic estimations may be problematic. Thus, hedonic estimation, including noise removal, can heavily depend on the analyst's expertise, marking a significant difference from the mechanical computation of standard index number formulas.

Using data between two points in time to calculate the price index through equations like (9.1) or (9.13) and chaining them presents the challenging interpretation of the quality variable parameters $z_{i,k}$, i.e., the value of quality changing over time. For example, the hedonic equation parameter γ_k indicates the additional value for a 65-inch screen size over a 32-inch baseline. This value would likely differ significantly between 2010 and 2022. When comparing television prices between 2010 and 2020, which year's γ_k should we use? Should we take an average of both or pool the data between the two points and re-estimate? Will the resulting price index match the chained results of hedonic estimates performed annually? Generally, price indices derived from hedonic equations with different specs yield different values, leading to chain drift in the indices derived from hedonic method. However, sufficient insights into the characteristics of this chain drift are not yet gathered.

A recent development in hedonic estimation to mitigate multicollinearity involves the practical application of sparse estimation techniques. While the technical details are omitted here, this innovative approach is expected to significantly alleviate hedonic estimation problems.[6] However, being a new method, it's unclear whether it will be widely adopted across all hedonic endeavors. Yet, with the advancement of computational power and the expansion of data sizes, new computational methods are being developed globally, and it's anticipated that a new standard method for hedonic method will eventually be established.

9.4 Treatment of Seasonal Products

Differences in commodity sets also occur for perishable food items like fruits and fish that are predominantly available in the market only during specific times of the year, with little to no expenditure observed during other periods. Figure 9.3 shows the expenditures and prices of persimmon in Japan. Every year, the price of persimmons is surveyed in the retail price statistics only during the months of October, November, and December, and the CPI for persimmons is also calculated during these 3 months. However, expenditures are recorded, albeit small, in August, September, January, and February as well, leading to a mismatch between price information and expenditure amounts. Such seasonal products are not uncommon. Moreover, even if expenditures do not drop to zero, expenditures outside the peak season tend to be very small, and prices tend to rise. How should the price index be calculated in such cases?

Persimmons are hardly found in the market during spring and summer and are sold at very high prices in high-end stores for gift purposes. The expenditure on persimmons during spring and summer is assumed to be on these high-priced gift

[6] Bank of Japan adopts this methods. See Fruta et al. (2021) for detail.

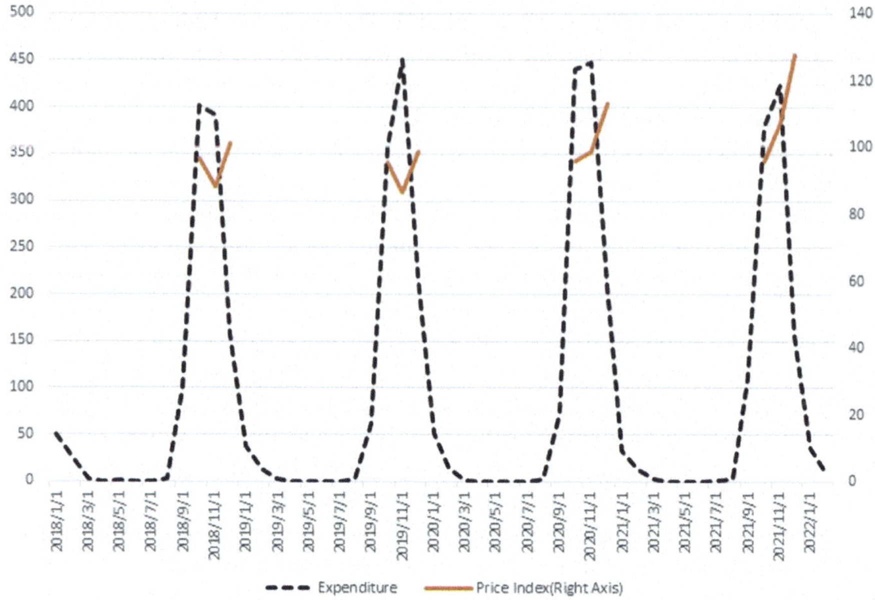

Fig. 9.3 Persimmon: Expenditure and Prices. *Sources* Retail Price Data & Family Income and Expenditure Survey by the Statistics Bureau of Japan

persimmons. However, theoretically, it would be desirable to survey and record the price of persimmons corresponding to any expenditure, even if minor. The issue arises during periods when persimmon expenditure is almost zero, trading volumes are low, and price surveys are not easy. Moreover, under such circumstances, persimmons cannot be considered representative fruits. Whether the persimmons available in fall and those presumed for gifting in spring and summer can be considered the same product is not straightforward.

From the perspective of the cost-of-living index, the disappearance of fruits like persimmons or peaches from the market can be interpreted as these products becoming unattainable, meaning the price of peaches or persimmons has become infinitely high, or the demand has dropped to zero. Adopting this stance, Diewert and Fox (2022) argued that when products disappear from the market, the reservation price should be calculated and used. Diewert and Fox (2022) were particularly considering the impact of the COVID-19 pandemic in 2020 when services like overseas travel and sports viewing ceased worldwide, leading to expenditures near zero and making price observations difficult or impossible. Although an exceptional event, their logic is applicable to many cases, including seasonal products and durable consumer goods. The argument by Diewert and Fox (2022) naturally emerges from the theory of the COLI. However, practical implementation faces significant difficulties: (1) estimating the latent price, (2) applying it to the Laspeyres index, and (3) addressing issues with the underlying assumptions of the COLI. To calculate the reservation price, one needs to know the shape of the demand function. For example, with a CES utility function, the reservation price would be infinite. Even slight changes in demand function parameters can lead to significant variations in reservation price levels. In the case of the Laspeyres index, widely used, even a minor expenditure share coupled with an infinite price increase would render the entire price index infinite, making the index useless. Therefore, while Diewert and Fox (2022) advocate for the Fisher index, its adoption would be impractical without monthly, high-precision household expenditure surveys. Lastly, the theoretical premise of the COLI assumes constant preferences over time, but the demand for out-of-season persimmons or peaches, or the utility derived from overseas travel during the COVID-19 pandemic compared to pre-pandemic times, is subject to debate.[7]

One method of adopting Diewert and Fox (2022)'s proposal is to assume the elasticity of substitution is greater than one and use an exact index like the Sato–Vartia index. If the elasticity of substitution is greater than one, a 1% price increase would result in more than a 1% decrease in quantity, reducing the expenditure share. As price increases become infinite, the expenditure share for that good converges to zero, making the overall price index calculated using indices like the Paasche, Fisher, or Törnqvist finite. This idea fundamentally aligns with the Variety Effects discussed by Feenstra (1994) in the next section. The issue in this case is the substantial impact on the overall price index and instability in the index value when the elasticity of substitution is close to one. These details will be discussed in the following section.

In practice, seasonal products like persimmons and peaches are only reflected in the price index during periods when retail prices are surveyed, treating the expenditure amount as zero when price information is missing and relying only on information from other items. During periods with missing prices for persimmons and peaches, the price index for categories like fruits and fresh foods is calculated based on information from other fruits with observed prices at that time. This method saves computational effort but, as shown in Fig. 9.3, leaves room for arbitrariness in deciding how long prices should be surveyed. For persimmons, the price in December is higher than in November. Expenditures on persimmons continue into January, and if surveyed, January prices would likely be higher than December's. The decision on when to stop surveying persimmon prices affects the values of the fruit and fresh food price index number and the overall price index, making the arbitrariness a significant issue, especially for the Laspeyres index. For indices like the Fisher or Sato–Vartia, which also use expenditure information at the comparison point, the choice of cut-off period has less impact on the overall index since expenditures during high-price periods are small.

The treatment of seasonal products poses a challenge to the concept of the COLI and is an annual issue for statistical practitioners. The current approach adopted by statistical bureaus in many countries, ignoring missing prices, i.e., assuming the

[7] For those interested, the March 2022 issue of *the Journal of Official Statistics* includes critical papers on Diewert and Fox (2022)'s proposal and several comment papers such as Abe (2022).

price movement of the missing good mirrors that of the higher level category index, provides easy and stable index numbers but lacks a solid economic foundation. The theoretical framework for handling missing goods primarily follows the analyses by Diewert and Fox (2022) or Feenstra (1994), which present challenges yet remain the most convincing theories to date.

9.5 Variety Effects

The concept of "Variety Effects," as introduced in this section, has been utilized in numerous recent studies as the primary model for calculating the COLI when there is a change in the variety of goods, distinct from the hedonic approach. In the Constant Elasticity of Substitution (CES) utility function, the number of goods, denoted as N, was previously fixed. This section explores what occurs when N changes. We denote the number of goods at time t as N_t and consider the following utility function:

$$U_t = \left(\sum_{i=1}^{N_t} (\varphi_{it} q_{it})^{\frac{\sigma-1}{\sigma}} \right)^{\frac{\sigma}{\sigma-1}} \tag{9.14}$$

where $\sigma > 1$ and $\varphi_{it} > 0$, with φ_{it} being a parameter that captures the effect of quality or taste on commodity i.

The corresponding indirect utility function is then given by

$$V(\mathbf{p}, Y) = Y_t \left(\sum_{i=1}^{N_t} \left(\frac{p_{it}}{\varphi_{it}} \right)^{1-\sigma} \right)^{\frac{1}{\sigma-1}} \tag{9.15}$$

where Y_t is the income at time t. Assuming all goods have identical and time invariant quality parameters and prices, i.e., $\varphi_{it} = \varphi$ and $p_{it} = 1$, the indirect utility function simplifies to

$$\begin{aligned} V(\mathbf{p}, Y) &= Y_t \left(\sum_{i=1}^{N_t} \left(\frac{1}{\varphi} \right)^{1-\sigma} \right)^{\frac{1}{\sigma-1}} \\ &= Y_t \left(N_t \varphi^{\sigma-1} \right)^{\frac{1}{\sigma-1}} \\ &= Y_t N_t^{\frac{1}{\sigma-1}} \varphi \end{aligned} \tag{9.16}$$

This approach provides a clearer understanding of the utility functions and the effects of changing the variety of goods within the CES utility framework. The indirect utility level is an increasing function of the variety of goods, N_t, indicating that people's welfare increases with more variety. As the elasticity of substitution, σ, approaches 1, the indirect utility diverges to infinity. Increasing the variety of goods, while income and prices remain constant, means reducing the quantity purchased of each good. The increase in welfare with more variety, i.e., consuming a small amount of many goods, is referred to as the Love of Variety.[8]

Nobel laureate Paul Krugman utilized this feature in Krugman (1980) to show that Love of Variety could be a source of international trade by assuming differences between domestic and foreign-produced goods. Similarly, Nobel laureate Paul Romer in Romer (1987) also used this functional form in the production function, showing that an increase in the variety of goods can enhance productivity and induce endogenous growth. Variety Effects have been applied across various economic fields, making a significant impact.

Regardless of the CES form, it is natural to assume that an increase in the variety of goods and products raises utility levels and a decrease reduces achievable utility levels, implying the presence of goods effects not unique to the CES form but related to the breadth of opportunity sets.

How to depict the increase in consumer choices in economic models is also a question of econometrics. A famous example in the multinomial logit model is the "Red Bus, Blue Bus" problem raised by McFadden (1974), where the market has two modes of transportation: taxis and buses, with the latter being painted red. Now, imagine a bus with identical functionality, performance, schedule, and fare to the existing red bus, but painted blue. For many passengers, the color of the bus, red or blue, is inconsequential, so it's natural to think that the market for the red bus is simply split by the introduction of the blue bus. However, assuming the Independence of Irrelevant Alternatives (IIA) required by the logit model, the choice between the red bus and a taxi does not depend on the presence of the blue bus, so the share ratio of taxis to red buses must remain the same as before the blue bus was introduced. This leads to a problem where the red and blue buses are considered complete substitutes, yet are treated as different goods, ignoring their substitutability. When considering the variety effects, careful consideration is needed on what differences between products or goods are being considered and how appropriate the assumption of constant elasticity, as assumed by the CES utility function, is. For example, skiing in winter mountains and beach activities in summer offer two distinct choices that enhance people's welfare. However, the presence of a popular pop star's photo on the lid of a cup noodle may represent a different product for fans of that pop star, but a perfect substitute for those who are indifferent. This issue relates to many products, like smartphones with new features used by some and ignored by others, or various functionalities added to TVs and PCs. Upon closer examination, it becomes clear that the substitutability between products is not a straightforward matter.

[8] Dixit and Stiglitz (1977) did not consider Love of Variety, assuming a fixed number of goods. However, they also explored models allowing for different elasticities of substitution between goods, highlighting that the assumption of constant elasticity of substitution across goods is quite strong.

The justification for the Love of Variety in the CES model could be viewed as an approximation of more complex models. The economic analysis of product differentiation has a long history, including Hotelling (1929) and subsequent studies on differentiation through location. For instance, it's more efficient for residents of North America to consume locally produced goods than those imported from South Africa if the markets are not integrated, leading to monopolistic competition and product differentiation. The challenge with these models is dealing with heterogeneous consumers and their application to various fields like macroeconomics or international trade. On the other hand, the Love of Variety produced by the CES utility function by Dixit and Stiglitz (1977), minimizing the elements of heterogeneous individuals or firms, has the significant advantage of allowing analysis with a simple model and numerous applications.

While Love of Variety has its limitations, it has become the de facto standard framework in current macroeconomics and international trade research when assuming different goods. The following will introduce the COLI by Feenstra (1994).

9.6 Variety Effects and Feenstra's Cost-of-Living Index

Assuming the existence of a representative individual in the economy with preferences modeled by a Constant Elasticity of Substitution (CES) utility function, the unit expenditure function can be expressed as

$$C(\mathbf{p_t}, 1) = P_t = \left(\sum_{i=1}^{N_t}\left(\frac{p_{it}}{\varphi_{it}}\right)^{1-\sigma}\right)^{\frac{1}{1-\sigma}} \tag{9.17}$$

Here, we consider the change in prices between two periods, t and $t-1$. Let I_t represent the set of goods available in period t, and $I(\neq \emptyset)$ the set of goods available in both periods, with φ_{it} being constant over time, i.e., $\varphi_{it} = \varphi_i$. The unit cost function, depending on the set of goods available in I_t, is then

$$P_t(\mathbf{p_t}, I_t) = \left(\sum_{i=1}^{N_t} \varphi_{it}^{\sigma-1} p_{it}^{1-\sigma}\right)^{\frac{1}{1-\sigma}} \tag{9.18}$$

The COLI between the two periods is

$$COLI = \frac{P_t(\mathbf{p_t}, I_t)}{P_{t-1}(\mathbf{p_{t-1}}, I_{t-1})} \tag{9.19}$$

Feenstra (1994) demonstrated that

$$PI^{FS} = \frac{P_t(\mathbf{p_t}, I_t)}{P_{t-1}(\mathbf{p_{t-1}}, I_{t-1})} = PI^{sv} \times \left(\frac{\lambda_t}{\lambda_{t-1}}\right)^{\frac{1}{\sigma-1}} \tag{9.20}$$

$$\lambda_r = \frac{\sum_{i \in I} p_{i,r}x_{i,r}}{\sum_{i \in I_r} p_{i,r}x_{i,r}}$$

where PI^{sv} is the Sato–Vartia index limited to the common goods, i.e., continuing products. Thus, Feenstra's COLI can be represented as the product of the Sato–Vartia index for continuing products and a function of the λ-Ratio. λ_t represents the sales ratio of continuing products out of all available products in period t. A surge in new products leads to a decrease in this ratio. If the expenditure share of continuing products decreases due to an influx of new products, λ_t/λ_{t-1} would decrease. Assuming $\sigma > 1$, this typically results in a decrease in PI^{FS}. In other words, an increase in the variety of goods leads to a decrease in COLI.

Addressing the change in the space of goods using an axiomatic approach is extremely challenging. On the other hand, incorporating structure into the utility function allows for the recording of price changes even in such situations, showcasing the advantage of the economic approach. The challenge lies in the necessity of elasticity information to compute COLI, beyond just price and quantity data. While the Sato–Vartia index can be considered an exact index or COLI for CES utility functions without the need to estimate elasticity, in this case, elasticity must be estimated.

Estimating the elasticity of substitution is not straightforward. Even with a large number of observed price and quantity data, it's difficult to distinguish whether the variations reflect changes in demand or supply. If appropriate instrumental variables can be found, or if it's possible to isolate shifts that only affect the supply curve, then it's feasible to estimate demand elasticity from observed data. However, it's generally impossible to find such convenient instrumental variables or supply shifts for all goods markets. Feenstra (1994) has proposed a relatively straightforward method for estimating this elasticity, applicable when elasticity remains constant over time.[9]

Feenstra's (1994) COLI is widely used in international trade and macroeconomics. Broda and Weinstein (2010) applied it to product-level POS data, assuming a utility function with nested CES preferences, and demonstrated that variety effects are significant in COLI in the United States. Specifically, they assumed three different elasticities between products, manufacturers, and categories. While categories are constant over time, the variety of product brands and types can change. They divided the λ-Ratio into two levels. Broda and Weinstein's (2010) COLI is as follows:

[9] Note that we can estimate the elasticities of substitutions using linear regression models if panel data on prices and expenditures are available. For more details, see Feenstra (1994).

$$PI^{BW} = \prod_{g \in G} \left(\prod_{b \in g} \left[PI^{sv} \left(\frac{\lambda_{bt}}{\lambda_{bt-1}} \right)^{\frac{1}{\sigma w(b)-1}} \right]^{\Phi_{tw}(b)} \cdot \left(\frac{\lambda_{gt}}{\lambda_{gt-1}} \right)^{\frac{1}{\sigma b(g)-1}} \right)^{\Phi_{tb}(g)} \tag{9.21}$$

Here, $\lambda_{st}(s = g, b)$ represents the expenditure share of continuing products at the brand and product level, $\sigma w(b)$ is the elasticity within a brand, and $\sigma b(g)$ is the elasticity between brands. $\Phi_{tb}(s)$ and $\Phi_{tw}(s)$ are weights within and between brands, respectively, used in the Sato–Vartia index. Unlike Feenstra (1994), this estimation requires a large number of elasticity estimates but can also be determined through linear regression.

Based on Feenstra's (1994) method, numerous papers have been published, including Hambry and Weinstein (2015) and Hottman et al. (2016), spreading awareness of the importance of variety effects. Redding and Weinstein (2020) also include variety effects in line with Feenstra (1994), and in recent years, Feenstra's COLI has been applied to countries other than the United States, such as in Ueda et al. (2019) and Cavallo et al. (2023). This approach plays a central role in measuring price changes when the variety of goods changes in economic modeling.

However, there's a significant issue with the variety effects model of Feenstra (1994) when viewed as a price index number. An example is shown in a comparison of direct and chain indices derived from weekly scanner data on detergents in Japan, using the first week of 2006 as a baseline. The turnover of detergent products is rapid, with a significant percentage changing within a year. Therefore, with a direct index, only a small fraction of the information on detergents actually traded is used after 2 or 3 years, eventually leading to a situation where no common products exist.

Figure 9.4 reveals that the Sato–Vartia index experienced chain drifts of nearly 20 percentage points over just under 3 years, while Feenstra's index shows even more severe chain drifts of up to 50 percentage points. The Feenstra-type index, being a sum of the (logarithmic) Sato–Vartia index and the λ ratio, implies that a strong negative chain drift occurs in the λ ratio. Many studies utilizing Feenstra's index tend to report rates of change, such as the year-over-year rate or the rate from the previous period, reflecting the difficulty of long-term price comparisons due to the strong chain drifts inherent in Variety Effects.

When a direct index only reflects information from a few products and becomes computationally unfeasible over the long term, Feenstra's index also becomes inapplicable. Returning to the definition of the COLI for CES utility functions when the variety of goods changes, we find

$$CUPI(s,t) = \left(\frac{\sum_{i=1}^{N_t} \left(\frac{p_{it}}{\varphi_i} \right)^{1-\sigma}}{\sum_{i=1}^{N_s} \left(\frac{p_{is}}{\varphi_i} \right)^{1-\sigma}} \right)^{\frac{1}{1-\sigma}} \tag{9.22}$$

This shows that it's not that the COLI cannot be defined when the variety of goods changes; rather, the issue arises when expressing it as an exact index. Variety Effects based on Feenstra (1994) are widely used in academia today, but the debate

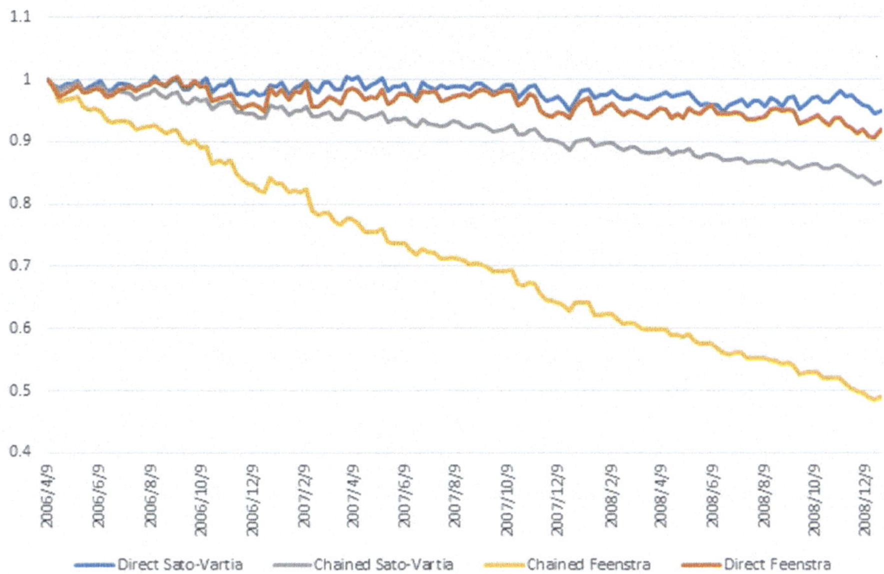

Fig. 9.4 Chain Drifts in Feenstra's Index. *Sources* Weekly scanner data for detergent, from SRI provided by INTAGE Inc.

on chain drifts is not yet resolved. However, the author believes that the issue of chain drifts cannot be avoided when considering long-term price comparisons, especially in terms of the variety effects of goods and services in economic development.

9.7 Concluding Remarks

In conclusion, constructing price indices when goods differ across times or locations is not only a paramount challenge for current index number theory but also an issue constantly faced by statistical offices worldwide. Although the availability of big data and proposals for methods using hedonic methods and machine learning have increased the options, solutions remain elusive. The standard method in current academic circles, Feenstra's (1994) variety effects, requires the strong assumption that the elasticity of substitution is constant and greater than one, limiting its applicability. The handling of seasonal goods, quality improvements in durable consumer goods, the emergence of new products like the iPhone that create new categories, and the disappearance of goods and services by category due to special circumstances like the COVID-19 pandemic present challenges from everyday tasks to theoretical frameworks. Currently, a lot of research is being conducted energetically using new tools such as sparse estimation and machine learning. Recent theoretical research based on the cost-of-living index includes works by Ueda et al. (2019), Ehrlich et al. (2023), and Carluccio et al. (2023), among others.[10]

9.8 Mathematical Appendix: Derivation of (9.20)

The expenditure share of good i is given by

$$w_{it} = \left(\frac{p_{it}}{\varphi_i P_t} \right)^{1-\sigma} \tag{A9.23}$$

Therefore, we have

$$P_t = \left(\frac{p_{it}}{\varphi_i} \right) w_{it}^{\frac{1}{\sigma-1}} \tag{A9.24}$$

This can be transformed into

$$\frac{P_t \left(\mathbf{p}_t, I_t\right)}{P_{t-1} \left(\mathbf{p}_{t-1}, I_{t-1}\right)} = \frac{p_{it} w_{it}^{\frac{1}{\sigma-1}}}{p_{it-1} w_{it-1}^{\frac{1}{\sigma-1}}}, \tag{A9.25}$$

$$= \left(\frac{p_{it}}{p_{it-1}} \right) \left(\frac{w_{it}}{w_{it-1}} \right)^{\frac{1}{\sigma-1}} \tag{A9.26}$$

Considering the relationship between the expenditure share $w_{it}(I)$ for good i limited to continued goods and the regular expenditure share $w_{it} = w_{it}(I_t)$, we get

$$w_{it}\left(I_t\right) = \frac{p_{i,r} x_{i,t}}{\sum_{j \in I_t} p_{j,t} x_{j,t}}, \tag{A9.27}$$

$$= w_{it}(I) \frac{\sum_{j \in I} p_{j,t} x_{j,t}}{\sum_{j \in I_t} p_{j,t} x_{j,t}}, \tag{A9.28}$$

$$= w_{it}(I) \lambda_t \tag{A9.29}$$

Thus, we have

$$\frac{P_t(\mathbf{p}_t, I_t)}{P_{t-1}(\mathbf{p}_{t-1}, I_{t-1})} = \left(\frac{p_{it}}{p_{it-1}} \right) \left(\frac{w_{it}(I)}{w_{it-1}(I)} \right)^{\frac{1}{\sigma-1}} \left(\frac{\lambda_t}{\lambda_{t-1}} \right)^{\frac{1}{\sigma-1}} \tag{A9.30}$$

[10] Additionally, various practical issues in quality adjustment are reported at the biennial Ottawa Group conference, where numerous research papers are presented. See the website of the Ottawa Group: https://www.ottawagroup.org/.

Calculating the geometric mean for continued goods using s_i on the right-hand side gives

$$\frac{P_t(\mathbf{p}_t, I_t)}{P_{t-1}(\mathbf{p}_{t-1}, I_{t-1})} = \left(\frac{\lambda_t}{\lambda_{t-1}}\right)^{\frac{1}{\sigma-1}} \prod_{i \in I} \left(\frac{p_{it}}{p_{it-1}}\right)^{s_i} \left(\frac{w_{it}(I)}{w_{it-1}(I)}\right)^{\frac{s_i}{\sigma-1}} \tag{A9.31}$$

$$s_i = \frac{(w_{it} - w_{it-1}) / (\ln w_{it} - \ln w_{it-1})}{\sum_{i=1}^{n} (w_{it} - w_{it-1}) / (\ln w_{it} - \ln w_{it-1})} \tag{A9.32}$$

As previously shown, the Sato–Vartia index is given by

$$PI^{sv} = \prod_{i \in I} \left(\frac{p_{it}}{p_{it-1}}\right)^{s_i} \tag{A9.33}$$

What remains is

$$\prod_{i \in I} \left(\frac{w_{it}(I)}{w_{it-1}(I)}\right)^{\frac{s_i}{\sigma-1}}$$

Taking the natural logarithm results in

$$\sum_{i \in I} \left(\frac{s_i}{\sigma - 1}\right) (\ln w_{it}(I) - \ln w_{it-1}(I)) \tag{A9.34}$$

$$= \left(\frac{1}{\sigma - 1}\right) \sum_{i \in I} \frac{(w_{it} - w_{it-1}) / (\ln w_{it} - \ln w_{it-1})}{\sum_{i=1}^{n} (w_{it} - w_{it-1}) / (\ln w_{it} - \ln w_{it-1})} (\ln w_{it}(I) - \ln w_{it-1}(I)) \tag{A9.35}$$

$$= \left(\frac{1}{\sigma - 1}\right) \sum_{i \in I} \frac{(w_{it} - w_{it-1})}{\sum_{i=1}^{n} (w_{it} - w_{it-1}) / (\ln w_{it} - \ln w_{it-1})} \tag{A9.36}$$

Here, the numerator is

$$\sum_{i \in I} (w_{i1} - w_{i0}) = \sum_{i \in I} w_{i1} - \sum_{i \in I} w_{i0} = 1 - 1 = 0 \tag{A9.37}$$

Therefore, we have

$$\prod_{i \in I} \left(\frac{w_{it}(I)}{w_{it-1}(I)}\right)^{\frac{s_i}{\sigma-1}} = 1 \tag{A9.38}$$

This allows us to demonstrate the following:

$$\frac{P_t(\mathbf{p_t}, I_t)}{P_{t-1}(\mathbf{p_{t-1}}, I_{t-1})} = \left(\frac{\lambda_t}{\lambda_{t-1}}\right)^{\frac{1}{\sigma-1}} PI^{sv}.$$

References

Abe, N., & Shinozaki, K. (2018) Compilation of Experimental Price Indices Using Big Data and Machine Learning: A Comparative Analysis and Validity Verification of Quality Adjustments. Bank of Japan Working Paper Series 18-E-13, Bank of Japan.

Abe, N. (2022). Measuring inflation under pandemic conditions': a comment. *Journal of Official Statistics, 38*(1), 295–300.

Broda, C., & Weinstein, D. E. (2010). Product creation and destruction: evidence and price implications. *American Economic Review, 100*(3), 691–723.

Carluccio, J., Gautier, E., & Guilloux-Nefussi, S. (2023). Dissecting the impact of imports from low-wage countries on inflation. *European Economic Review, 160*, 104613.

Cavallo, A., Feenstra, R. C., & Inklaar, R. (2023). Product variety, the cost of living, and welfare across countries. *American Economic Journal: Macroeconomics, 15*(4), 40–66.

Crawford, I., & Neary, J. P. (2023). New characteristics and hedonic price index numbers. *Review of Economics and Statistics, 105*(3), 665–682.

Court, A. T. (1939) Hedonic price indexes with automotive examples. In *The Dynamics of Automobile Demand*, The General Motors Corporation, New York, pp. 99–117.

de Haan, J., & Diewert, W. E. (2017). *Quality Change*. Deutsche Bundesbank: Hedonic Regression and Price Index Construction.

Diewert, W. E. (2003). Hedonic regressions: a consumer theory approach. In R. C. Feenstra & M. D. Shapiro (Eds.), *Scanner Data and Price Indexes, 61* (pp. 317–348). University of Chicago Press.

Diewert, W. E., & Fox, K. J. (2022). Measuring inflation under pandemic conditions. *Journal of Official Statistics, 38*(1), 255–285.

Dixit, A. K., & Stiglitz, J. E. (1977). Monopolistic competition and optimum product diversity. *American Economic Review, 67*(3), 297–308.

Ehrlich, G., Haltiwanger, J. C., Jarmin, R. S., Johnson, D., Olivares, E., Pardue, L. W., Shapiro, M. D., & Zhao, L. (2023). Quality Adjustment at Scale: Hedonic vs. Exact Demand-Based Price Indices. NBER Working Papers 31309, National Bureau of Economic Research, Inc.

Feenstra, R. C. (1994). New product varieties and the measurement of international prices. *American Economic Review, 84*(1), 157–177.

Furuta, S., Hatayama, Y., Kawakami, A., & Oh, Y. (2021). New hedonic quality adjustment method using sparse estimation. *Monetary and Economic Studies, Institute for Monetary and Economic Studies, Bank of Japan, 39*, 109–142.

Gorman, W. M. (1956). A possible procedure for analysing quality diferentials in the eggs market. *Review of Economic Studies, 47*(5), 843–856.

Griliches, Z. (1961). Hedonic price indexes for automobiles: an econometric of quality change. In *The Price Statistics of the Federal Government*, Chapter 3, Government Printing Office, pp. 173–196.

Hotelling, H. (1929). Stability in competition. *Economic Journal, 39*(153), 41–57.

Hottman, C. J., Redding, S. J., & Weinstein, D. E. (2016). Quantifying the sources of firm heterogeneity. *Quarterly Journal of Economics, 131*(3), 1291–1364.

Krugman, P. (1980). Scale economies, product differentiation, and the pattern of trade. *American Economic Review, 70*(5), 950–959.

Lancaster, K. J. (1966). A new approach to consumer theory. *Journal of Political Economy, 74*(2), 132–157.

McFadden, D. (1974). Conditional logit analysis of qualitative choice behavior. *Zarembka* (P, pp. 105–142). Frontiers in Econometrics: Academic Press.

Menz, J. O., Wieland, E., & Mehrhoff, J. (2023). Estimating the Impact of Quality Adjustment on Consumer Price Inflation. ECB Working Paper No. 2023/2773.

Pakes, A. (2003). A Reconsideration of Hedonic Price Indexes with an Application to PC's. *American Economic Review, 93*(5), 1578–1596.

Redding, S. J., & Weinstein, D. E. (2020). Measuring aggregate price indices with taste shocks: Theory and evidence for CES preferences. *Quarterly Journal of Economics, 135*(1), 503–560.

Romer, P. (1987). Growth based on increasing returns due to specialization. *American Economic Review, 77*(2), 56–62.

Rosen, S. (1974). Hedonic prices and implicit markets: product differentiation in pure competition. *Journal of Political Economy, 82*(1), 34–55.

Silver, M. (1999). An evaluation of the use of hedonic regressions for basic components of consumer price indices. *Review of Income and Wealth, 45*(1), 41–56.

Triplett, J. E. (2004). Handboodk on Hednic Indexes and Quality Adjustments in Price Indexes: Special Application to Information Technology Product. OECD Science, Technology and Industry Working Papers 2004/09.

Ueda, K., Watanabe, K., & Watanabe, T. (2019). Product turnover and the cost of living index: quality vs. fashion effects. *American Economic Journal: Macroeconomics, 11*(2), 310–347.

Stochastic Approach

10

Abstract

This chapter discusses the stochastic approach to price indices, exploring its historical development, methodologies, and applications. Initially proposed by Jevons and Edgeworth in the nineteenth and early twentieth centuries, this approach treats price movements as stochastic variables, reflecting uncertain fluctuations. Despite early support, the approach fell out of favor until its revival in the 1980s, driven by renewed interest in core inflation estimation and international price comparisons. The classical stochastic approach focuses on identifying common price change factors across goods, while the new stochastic approach, advanced by Selvanathan and Rao (1994), employs techniques like Generalized Least Squares to estimate price indices with standard errors. The chapter also covers criticisms of the new stochastic approach, particularly regarding the variance of residual terms, changes in estimated indices with varying sample periods, and despite these difficulties the approach has proven valuable for core inflation measurement and spatial price indices, utilizing methods such as Structural Vector Autoregression (SVAR) and Dynamic Stochastic General Equilibrium (DSGE) models. The chapter concludes by emphasizing the growing importance of the stochastic approach in econometric analysis and its potential to become a standard tool for index number theory.

10.1 Introduction

During the late nineteenth and early twentieth centuries, as the theory of price indices was being developed, discussions revolved around two main properties that price indices should satisfy. The first concerned the monotonicity of prices, questioning whether a price index should increase if, among numerous goods, the price of just one item rises while the prices of all other goods remain constant. The second point of discussion was whether price indices are stochastic variables, meaning whether the concept of "prices" or the value of a price index involves unpredictable fluctuations or ambiguities that are not well understood.

N. Abe, *Price Index Numbers*, Springer Texts in Business and Economics,
https://doi.org/10.1007/978-981-97-6305-4_10

In the twenty-first century, there is a considerable consensus on these two questions. The answer to the first depends on the purpose for which the price index is being calculated. If it is considered from the perspective of the cost-of-living index (COLI), then an increase in the price of one good, even if all others remain constant, should lead to an increase in the price index because it represents a rise in costs for consumers. However, if the price index is targeted for monetary policy, i.e., as an indicator of value of money, then fluctuations in prices of goods like fresh food and energy, are often excluded from the indicators of core inflation. Therefore, in terms of measuring monetary value, the answer would be "no."

Regarding the second question, in today's macroeconomics, price indices are commonly treated as stochastic variables, much like other macroeconomic variables such as GDP, household consumption, and capital investment, due to the widespread adoption of Dynamic Stochastic General Equilibrium (DSGE) models. Thus, the answer to the second question would likely be "yes." Even outside of macro-models, few researchers would deny that price indices contain various measurement errors. However, in the early twentieth century, the prevailing answer was "yes" to the first question and "no" to the second. Jevons and Edgeworth were two individuals who, even then, provided answers that align with current views. Their work is considered the beginning of the stochastic approach to price indices, which is discussed in this chapter.

In contrast, significant figures like Walsh, who had immense influence on index number theory at the time, the highly renowned economist Keynes, and Frisch, who played a crucial role in the development of index number theory and won the first Nobel Prize in Economics, had an opposing view. By the mid-twentieth century, the stochastic approach had disappeared from index number theory, only to re-emerge in the 1980s. Many studies from this period, particularly those focused on core inflation, revisited the ideas proposed by Jevons and Edgeworth over a century earlier. These ideas were rediscovered and developed independently from the earlier research. It wasn't until 1995 that Diewert pointed out the similarities between the discussions on core inflation at that time and those by Edgeworth and others, indicating that many researchers on core inflation lacked sufficient knowledge of this historical context.

The stochastic approach to price indices, which leads to the current scientific study of prices, was discussed in Jevons (1863). In a comprehensive work analyzing various factors affecting price movements and fluctuations, Jevons's arguments, if simplified for modern understanding, might be summarized as follows: Consider five types of goods, A, B, C, D, and E, where A is money, and its relative price with other goods determines their nominal prices. The relative prices between goods B and C are determined by their demand and supply, with their fluctuations resulting from a variety of factors. Similarly, the relative price between goods A and B is determined by their respective demand and supply. If our interest lies in the fluctuations of the supply and demand for good A, i.e., money, it should have a common effect on the prices of all other goods. Since the factors causing price fluctuations for various goods are not fully understood, their prices become stochastic variables. The fluctuation in monetary value affects all these prices, which are stochastic variables, and measuring monetary value involves extracting this common factor. Returning to the initial problem posed at the beginning of this chapter, a fluctuation in the price of a commodity, no matter how significant, would not be reflected in the price index or its measure if it is unrelated (independent) to the fluctuation in monetary value.

The essence of the stochastic approach mentioned above can be illustrated with a simple model. Let us assume that the price change of a good i can be decomposed into a common factor π_t among all goods and an idiosyncratic factor ε_{it} for each good. In the simplest case, it can be expressed as follows:

$$\ln\left(\frac{p_{it}}{p_{it-1}}\right) = \pi_t + \varepsilon_{it} \tag{10.1}$$

Our primary interest lies in identifying the common factor π_t. If we know the distribution of the unique factor ε_{it}, it would be easy to estimate π_t. For instance, if ε_{it} has a mean of zero and is independent of π_t, then the simple average of $\ln\left(\frac{p_{it}}{p_{it-1}}\right)$ becomes the unbiased estimator of π_t, expressed as

$$\widehat{\pi}_t = \frac{1}{N}\sum_{i=1}^{N}\ln\left(\frac{p_{it}}{p_{it-1}}\right) \tag{10.2}$$

Furthermore, by treating each good's price as a stochastic variable, it is possible to calculate the standard error of π_t. Assuming the variance of ε_{it} is identical for each good and denoted as σ^2, the variance of this estimator can be expressed as follows:

$$\begin{aligned} Var\left(\widehat{\pi}_t\right) &= Var\left(\frac{1}{N}\sum_{i=1}^{N}\left(\frac{p_{it}}{p_{it-1}}\right)\right) \\ &= Var\left(\frac{1}{N}\sum_{i=1}^{N}\left(\pi_t + \varepsilon_{it}\right)\right) \\ &= \frac{1}{N}\sigma^2 \end{aligned} \tag{10.3}$$

The unbiased estimator for σ^2 can be obtained as

$$\widehat{\sigma^2} = \frac{\sum_{i=t}^{N}\left(\frac{p_{it}}{p_{it-1}} - \widehat{\pi}_t\right)^2}{N-1} \tag{10.4}$$

If we assume there is a certain constant trend, t_i, in price changes unique to each good, the equation becomes

$$\ln\left(\frac{p_{it}}{p_{it-1}}\right) = \pi_t + t_i + \varepsilon_{it} \tag{10.5}$$

In this case, π_t can be obtained as the coefficient of the time dummy when regressing the log price ratio on goods and time dummies. The estimation method varies depending on the stochastic process considered for each price series. However, what remains consistent is that, in the stochastic approach, the computation of index numbers involves extracting the common factor, i.e., the signal, from various fluctuations in goods prices.

In the twenty-first century, the discussion above does not seem particularly off the mark. However, despite being proposed by Jevons and Edgeworth, who have earned immortal fame in the history of economics, it was entirely disregarded by index number researchers such as Walsh and Fisher, who systematically and almost exhaustively organized index number theory. As introduced in Chap. 2, it was severely criticized by Keynes and was essentially given the death knell by Frisch, who established the economic approach to index number theory and played a decisive role in its further development.

This chapter introduces the classical stochastic approach and the so-called "New Stochastic approach" by Kenneth Clements, Anthony Selvanathan, and Prasada Rao, concluding with an introduction to various core inflation estimates. Core inflation measurement is one of the most critical issues in current macroeconomics, with numerous ongoing researches. Therefore, the analysis employs some technical methods like the Kalman filter, vector autoregression, and dynamic general equilibrium models incorporating various stickiness, requiring considerable space just for introductions. Thus, only the key points about core inflation will be briefly introduced. Spatial price indices will be discussed in the next chapter. Regarding the general stochastic approach, the textbook by Selvanathan and Rao (1994), although slightly dated, is well known. For more recent reviews, see Clements et al. (2006). Additionally, Lippe (2007) discusses the stochastic approach from a critical perspective. Concerning core inflation, Wynne (2008) provides an academic perspective, while Silver (2006) offers a survey from a practical viewpoint.

10.2 New Stochastic Approach

As introduced in Chap. 2, after the criticism by Keynes and others, the stochastic approach to price indices experienced a revival in the 1980s. Two of the key figures in this revival are the authors of the textbook on index number theory, Selvanathan and Rao (1994). They emphasize that the stochastic approach allows for the estimation of price indices with standard errors, thereby quantifying the reliability of the indices. A smaller standard error indicates higher reliability of the estimate. The overall R^2 of the regression could also be considered an indicator of the fit of the regression to the data, i.e., the reliability of the regression itself. The stochastic approach by Jevons and Edgeworth is now regarded as the classical approach, while the approach by Rao and others is termed the New Stochastic Approach. Here, we will introduce the method using Generalized Least Squares (GLS), following Selvanathan and Rao (1994).

Consider the model initially introduced:

$$\ln\left(\frac{p_{it}}{p_{it-1}}\right) = \alpha_t + \varepsilon_{it} \tag{10.6}$$

Following the notation of a standard econometrics textbook, let us denote the above as the following model where y_{it} is the log of price relatives while x_{it} is a constant term:

$$y_{it} = \beta_t x_{it} + \varepsilon_{it} \tag{10.7}$$

In this case, when using the weight matrix $\mathbf{\Omega}$, the GLS is given by

$$\begin{aligned} \widehat{\beta}_t^{GLS} &= \left(X_t'\mathbf{\Omega}^{-1}X_t\right)^{-1} X_t'\mathbf{\Omega}^{-1}Y_t \\ X_t &= (1, 1, 1, 1, ..., 1)' \\ Y_t &= \left(\ln\left(\frac{p_{1t}}{p_{1t-1}}\right), \ln\left(\frac{p_{2t}}{p_{2t-1}}\right), \ln\left(\frac{p_{3t}}{p_{3t-1}}\right), ..., \ln\left(\frac{p_{Nt}}{p_{Nt-1}}\right)\right) \end{aligned} \tag{10.8}$$

Here, assume that the error terms are not independent and identically distributed (i.i.d), and let us introduce the following variables:

$$u_{it} = \frac{\varepsilon_{it}}{\sqrt{\rho_{it}}} \tag{10.9}$$

$$\rho_{it} = \frac{1}{2}\left(w_{it} + w_{it+1}\right) \tag{10.10}$$

where w_{it} is the expenditure share of commodity i at time t.

In this case, Ordinary Least Squares (OLS) is inefficient and heteroscedasticity occurs. The denominator becomes the weight in the Törnqvist index. Assuming the variance of ε_{it} is σ^2, the covariance matrix is

$$\mathbf{\Omega} = \begin{pmatrix} \frac{\sigma^2}{\rho_{1t}} & 0 & \cdots & 0 \\ 0 & \frac{\sigma^2}{\rho_{2t}} & \ddots & \vdots \\ \vdots & \ddots & \ddots & 0 \\ 0 & \cdots & 0 & \frac{\sigma^2}{\rho_{Nt}} \end{pmatrix}. \tag{10.11}$$

$$\mathbf{X}_t'\mathbf{\Omega}^{-1} = \frac{1}{\sigma^2}\left(1\ 1\ 1 \cdots 1\right)\begin{pmatrix} \rho_{1t} & 0 & \cdots & 0 \\ 0 & \rho_{2t} & \ddots & \vdots \\ \vdots & \ddots & \ddots & 0 \\ 0 & \cdots & 0 & \rho_{Nt} \end{pmatrix} \tag{10.12}$$

$$= \frac{1}{\sigma^2}\left(\rho_{1t}, \rho_{2t}, \ldots, \rho_{Nt}\right) \tag{10.13}$$

$$\mathbf{X}_t'\mathbf{\Omega}^{-1}\mathbf{X}_t = \frac{1}{\sigma^2}(\rho_{1t}, \rho_{2t}, \dots, \rho_{Nt})(1, 1, .., 1)'$$
$$= \frac{1}{\sigma^2} \tag{10.14}$$
$$\mathbf{X}_t'\mathbf{\Omega}^{-1}\mathbf{Y}_t = \frac{1}{\sigma^2}\sum_{i=1}^{N}\rho_{it}\ln\left(\frac{p_{it}}{p_{it-1}}\right) \tag{10.15}$$

Therefore, we get following:

$$\hat{\beta}_t^{GLS} = \sigma^2\frac{1}{\sigma^2}\sum_{i=1}^{N}\rho_{it}\ln\left(\frac{p_{it}}{p_{it-1}}\right)$$
$$= \sum_{i=1}^{N}\frac{1}{2}(w_{it} + w_{it})\ln\left(\frac{p_{it}}{p_{it-1}}\right) \tag{10.16}$$

Thus, we can derive the Törnqvist index using GLS, with standard errors also easily computed. Besides the Törnqvist index, many other price indices, such as the Laspeyres index, can be obtained as GLS estimators by modifying the weight matrix. Selvanathan and Rao (1994) demonstrate that various price indices can be estimated in this manner. Additionally, the standard error of GLS estimators is readily calculable, facilitating the evaluation of the degree of error in the estimated price indices.

10.3 Identification of the Common Trend

Here, let us consider that while there is a common trend in commodity prices, there are differences in the levels of price change rates among commodities, namely,

$$\ln\left(\frac{p_{it}}{p_{it-1}}\right) = \alpha_t + \beta_i + \varepsilon_{it} \tag{10.17}$$

It is, of course, not possible to estimate all the parameters of this equation. The reason is that if there were some estimates, reducing all commodity-specific effects by 1/2 and increasing α_t by 1/2 would result in exactly the same residuals. Therefore, an identification condition must be imposed externally. For instance, setting the specific effect of a particular commodity to zero could work, but more naturally, Selvanathan and Rao (1994) set the condition that

$$\sum w_{i0}\beta_i = 0 \tag{10.18}$$

which means the average of commodity-specific effects, when weighted by expenditure shares at the base period, is zero. Under this constraint, the price index is estimated, which is feasible with OLS under linear constraints on coefficients. Specifically, with coefficient constraints as

$$\mathbf{R}\beta = 0, \text{ where } \mathbf{R} = (w_{10}, w_{20}, \ldots, w_{N0}) \tag{10.19}$$

Setting the estimation equation as

$$\mathbf{Y} = \mathbf{X}\beta + \varepsilon \tag{10.20}$$

and deriving the constrained OLS estimator, after some cumbersome calculations[1]:

$$\widehat{\beta}^{cons} = \widehat{\beta}^{ols} - \left(\mathbf{X}'\mathbf{X}\right)^{-1}\mathbf{R}'\left[\mathbf{R}\left(\mathbf{X}'\mathbf{X}\right)^{-1}\mathbf{R}'\right]^{-1}\mathbf{R}\widehat{\beta}^{ols} \tag{10.21}$$

Selvanathan and Rao (1994) showed that when the variance of ε_{it} is given by σ_2/w_{i0} (with all off-diagonal elements being zero), the constrained estimator of the common component becomes the Laspeyres index.

10.4 Economic Interpretation of the Stochastic Approach

A direct criticism of the new stochastic approach to index number might be that the estimation equations are not derived from any theory but are instead arbitrarily provided by researchers. A counterargument to this is found in Feenstra and Reinsdorf (2007). The unit cost function of the CES utility function can be expressed as follows:

$$c\left(\mathbf{p_t}, \mathbf{b_t}\right) = \left(\sum_{i=1}^{N} b_{it}\, p_{it}^{1-\sigma}\right)^{\frac{1}{1-\sigma}} \tag{10.22}$$

Using the Shepherd–McKenzie Lemma and organizing this logarithmic derivative, we get

$$\begin{aligned}\frac{\partial \ln c\left(\mathbf{p_t}, \mathbf{b_t}\right)}{\partial \ln p_{it}} &= \frac{p_{it}q_{it}}{c\left(\mathbf{p_t}, \mathbf{b_t}\right)} = w_{it} \\ &= c\left(\mathbf{p_t}, \mathbf{b_t}\right)^{\sigma-1} b_{it}\, p_{it}^{1-\sigma}\end{aligned} \tag{10.23}$$

which becomes the expenditure share on good i. Therefore, taking the logarithmic difference, we have

$$\Delta \ln w_{it} = (\sigma - 1)\,\Delta \ln c\left(\mathbf{p_t}, \mathbf{b_t}\right) + \Delta \ln b_{it} + (1 - \sigma)\,\Delta \ln p_{it} \tag{10.24}$$

[1] See the mathematical appendix for the derivation.

Here, if we set

$$\varepsilon_{it} = \Delta \ln b_{it}, \alpha_t = (\sigma - 1) \Delta \ln c (\mathbf{p_t}, \mathbf{b_t}) \tag{10.25}$$

then we get

$$\Delta \ln w_{it} = \alpha_t + (1 - \sigma) \Delta \ln p_{it} + \varepsilon_{it} \tag{10.26}$$

Further transforming, we obtain

$$\begin{aligned}\Delta \ln p_{it} &= \Delta \ln c (\mathbf{p_t}, \mathbf{b_t}) + \frac{\Delta \ln w_{it}}{(1 - \sigma)} + \frac{\varepsilon_{it}}{(\sigma - 1)} \\ &= \ln PS^{sv} + \frac{\Delta \ln w_{it}}{(1 - \sigma)} + \frac{\varepsilon_{it}}{(\sigma - 1)}\end{aligned} \tag{10.27}$$

Let us compare this equation to the following fundamental equation of the new stochastic approach:

$$\Delta \ln p_{it} = \alpha_t + \beta_i + \varepsilon_{it} \tag{10.28}$$

Note that the following identification condition

$$\sum w_{it} \beta_i = 0 \tag{10.29}$$

corresponds to setting some kind of mean of $\Delta \ln w_{it}$ to be zero. Consider the following weights employed in the Sato–Vartia index:

$$s_i = \frac{(w_{it} - w_{it-1})/(\ln w_{it} - \ln w_{it-1})}{\sum_{i=1}^{n} (w_{it-1} - w_{it})/(\ln w_{it-1} - \ln w_{it})} \tag{10.30}$$

Then, we get the following:

$$\sum s_i \frac{\Delta \ln w_{it}}{(1 - \sigma)} = 0 \tag{10.31}$$

Feenstra and Reinsdorf (2007) argue that this justifies the estimation equations of the new stochastic approach from an economic standpoint. Of course, as Feenstra (1994) himself points out, since the error term ε_{it} is a function of the preference parameter b_{it} and closely related to expenditure weights, the OLS estimation equations would be biased, necessitating the use of methods such as GMM. Moreover, strong assumptions about the distribution of changes in preference parameters need to be made, leaving several difficulties in this justification. However, from the discussion in Feenstra and Reinsdorf (2007), it can be seen that the new stochastic approach also possesses the properties of an exact index from an economic approach.

10.5 Some Criticism

The new stochastic approach faces criticism, particularly from Diewert (1995), who offers stringent critiques. Specifically, he points out three main issues: (1) the variance of the residual terms obtained after estimation differs from the assumed variance, (2) the estimated indices change when the sample periods differ, and (3) real changes leading to relative price shifts become noise in the trend change.

While all these criticisms are severe, (1) and (3) are particularly significant. The fundamental result of the new stochastic approach is that various indices can be generated by altering the variance of the error terms. However, the variance of the error terms should ideally be estimated and justifying strong assumptions without any basis is problematic. If the GLS by the new stochastic approach is correct, then the Feasible GLS (FGLS), which calculates the variance–covariance matrix using the OLS in the first step and then applies weighted least squares using this matrix in the second step, should almost match. However, in many cases, the results of FGLS do not coincide with standard indices. Issue (2) criticizes that when estimating using regression analysis, the estimated value of price changes from 1990 to 1991 changes whether or not data from 2000 is included. During estimation, rather than using all sample periods, it becomes necessary to pre-set specific window periods like 1 year or 3 years and fix the estimation period. Otherwise, it would be necessary to revise all past index values every time the index is updated monthly. Issue (3) is also a severe problem, leading to fundamental questions about what constitutes common fluctuations and why relative prices fluctuate. In regression analysis or maximum likelihood methods, the distribution information of the error terms becomes crucially important, presenting problems due to the lack of theory.

Lippe (2007) questions the treatment of expenditure weights, which include stochastic variables such as prices, as exogenous in the New Stochastic Approach. Indeed, if prices fluctuate, weights should normally change, and the assumption that the variance of the error terms does not depend on prices is difficult to justify. Moreover, Lippe (2007) conducts numerical calculations and points out that while the average values of various indices like Laspeyres and Paasche differ significantly, the standard errors derived from the new stochastic approach show little difference. One of the main advantages of the new stochastic approach is the inclusion of standard errors, but if there is little variation in these, they do not provide particularly useful information when comparing various indices.

The new stochastic approach excels in estimating core inflation and in calculating price indices between different regions, as introduced next. As discussed in the previous chapter, calculating price indices becomes a challenging issue when commodities differ between two points. In completely different regions, such as the poorest and wealthiest countries, finding identical goods might be more difficult. When very similar goods are scarce, and there is no information on quality, measuring the price index itself becomes impossible. However, it is possible to describe and statistically remove differences between goods using econometric models. The Country-Product-Dummy (CPD) method, frequently used in measuring international price indices today, is a crucial step in index calculation. This will be introduced in more detail in the next chapter, discussing regional price indices.

10.6 Core Inflation

In current monetary policy, core inflation serves as an important policy target. Concepts of core inflation are diverse, including core, supercore, American-style core, and Japanese-style core. But what exactly is core inflation? Various definitions have been proposed, such as excluding fresh food, excluding energy-related items, excluding items that show large fluctuations (trimmed mean), and using median values. However, is there an economic or academic basis for these definitions? The concept of core inflation was formally introduced by Eckstein (1981), but it was Bryan and Cecchetti (1994) who significantly influenced today's estimation of core inflation. Since then, numerous studies on core inflation have been published, all sharing the notion that core inflation, a target for monetary policy, differs from a cost-of-living index aimed at measuring consumer welfare.

This section introduces the methodology for constructing core inflation following Bryan and Cecchetti (1994). They define core inflation based on macroeconomic models as follows: firstly, assume that numerous homogeneous firms set prices at the beginning of the period. Since firms are homogeneous, the prices set at the beginning should change at a rate consistent with the money growth rate compared to the previous period. Next, assume that each firm faces independent and identically distributed stochastic shocks during the period that are uncorrelated across firms and over time. Also, assume that firms incur menu costs for price adjustments. Consequently, firms experiencing significant shocks and considering it worthwhile to pay the menu costs will adjust their prices, whereas others will not. If policymakers can only observe end-of-period prices, they will face a distribution of various commodity price changes, with each firm's price change rate differing. The prices of each firm's products, when appropriately setting the model parameters, can be expressed as

$$\ln\left(\frac{p_{it}}{p_{it-1}}\right) = \pi_t + \varepsilon_{it} \qquad (10.32)$$

This equation is identical to the basic equation of the classical stochastic approach introduced by Jevons at the beginning of this chapter.[2] Unlike Jevons and others, the approach by Bryan and Cecchetti (1994) is based on a simple macroeconomic model, making it easier to impose further structure on the above equation. The aspect criticized by Keynes and Frisch, that the concept of monetary value defined stochastically lacks substance, is theoretically covered. The perception of econometric models among economists in the early twentieth century, when Frisch was active, and in the late twentieth to twenty-first century fundamentally differs. Frisch, one

[2] However, Bryan and Cecchetti (1994) do not cite Jevons or Edgeworth.

of the founders of the Econometric Society and a pioneer in establishing macroeconomics and econometrics, expressed strong doubts about treating inflation rates as stochastic variables. However, today, few would hesitate to treat macro-variables such as GDP and household consumption as stochastic variables. It's evident that almost all observed macro-data include influences of factors not accounted by simple macroeconomic models, and there's little dispute that robust estimation against such factors is desirable when estimating models.

Theoretical linkage of commodity prices with general price levels, formulated as econometric models with stochastic variables, implies that different estimation models and methods are dictated by the underlying economic theory. A vast body of research on core inflation continues to grow. For details, refer to survey papers like Silver (2006) and Wynne (2008). Recent important papers include Crone et al. (2013) and Ball et al. (2024). This approach can be classified into two categories: an approach that does not strictly adhere to economic models and a model-specific approach. The first category, which relies minimally on economic models, involves dropping information on commodity prices deemed difficult to manipulate by monetary policy, specifically excluding fresh food prices for core inflation and further excluding energy prices in some countries. Non-model-based approaches might include conducting principal component analysis on commodity price fluctuations and taking the first component or assuming persistence in common components and applying dynamic factor analysis, which do not rely on a specific economic model. Blinder (1997) discusses excluding food and energy, and Bryan and Cecchetti (1994) investigate dynamic factor analysis.

Estimates of core inflation using economic models can be divided into those based on Structural Vector Autoregression (SVAR or Identified Vector Autoregression) and those derived from calibration or structural estimation. A representative study using VAR is Quah and Vahey (1995), who assume that output and price levels have stochastic trends but are not cointegrated. They postulate the existence of two types of shocks in the economy: demand shocks, which are assumed not to affect output in the long run, and supply shocks. They consider price fluctuations caused by demand shocks as core inflation and estimated them.

Since the 1990s, the quantification of macroeconomic models has rapidly progressed, and a series of studies known as the New Keynesian Dynamic Stochastic General Equilibrium (NKDSGE) models have been extensively conducted. In these studies, structural parameters of economic models are assumed or estimated, and dynamic general equilibrium models are solved to align simulations with actual observed economic data. In the realm of NKDSGE models, the stickiness of prices is particularly emphasized as a mechanism through which monetary policy influences the real economy. Aoki (2001) theoretically demonstrated that when an economy consists of sectors with both flexible and sticky prices, the target of monetary policy should be the inflation rate in the sticky-price sector. Generalizing this result suggests that the inflation rate targeted by central banks, namely, the core inflation rate, not only involves extracting signal and noise as emphasized by Edgeworth and Bryan and Cecchetti (1994) but also crucially depends on the stickiness of individual commodity prices. Eusepi et al. (2011) assumed an economy with many goods of differing price stickiness and derived the core inflation rate that central banks should target through calibration. These models are coherent, including estimation, within a single model framework, and excel in terms of consistency. However, they also possess the drawback of being entirely dependent on model assumptions. For instance, Eusepi et al. (2011) assume that price adjustments for each commodity follow the so-called Calvo pricing rule, where the possibility of price changes is determined by rolling a die at each point in time. Moreover, solving nonlinear models through linear approximation makes it very difficult to incorporate nonlinear constraints like zero interest rates, rendering them incompatible with quantitative easing policies adopted in recent years. Whether the Calvo pricing rule accurately reflects reality or even serves as a valid first approximation is highly debatable. Core inflation measurement relying entirely on DSGE assumptions shares both the advantages and disadvantages of micro-founded macro-model analysis, and adopting its results as indicators of core inflation crucial for daily monetary policy decisions is not straightforward.

10.7 Conclusions and Current Progresses in the Stochastic Approach

The stochastic approach to price indices, while having a very old history in the theory of price indices, had once completely halted in its development, only to be rediscovered as a completely new method after several decades. Economics, as a field that builds upon previous research like stacking bricks to construct a house, demonstrates through this example that its development is not linear but rather spirals. This leads to the current major theme in macroeconomic analysis, the estimation of core inflation, where a vast amount of research is being actively conducted. In this context, it's natural for the works of Jevons and Edgeworth to be re-evaluated by scholars like Diewert (1995). In today's world, where econometrics has become essential knowledge for almost all economists, focusing on the stochastic structure of indices and advancing analysis in this direction is also natural. The stochastic approach, which examines various fluctuating factors contained in data and pursues desirable index formulas while keeping in mind the fundamental issue of why we are interested in prices, using econometric methods, is expected to gain further importance in the theory and calculation of indices in the future. Many studies collect various price data, treat the common component as the prices, and attempt to measure it through regression analysis. Research like that of Handbury and Weinstein (2015) is conducted as part of standard empirical analysis, independent of the stochastic approach tradition in price index number theory.[3] As discussed in this chapter, many challenges remain in the stochastic approach to index number theory. However, with econometric analysis becoming a standard tool for many economists today, viewing price indices as stochastic variables and employing various estimation methods, similar to hedonic

[3] For recent theoretical analyses, see Hajargasht and Rao (2019) and Gorajek (2024). For application to the purchasing power parity, see Deaton and Dupriez (2011).

estimation discussed in the previous chapter, the stochastic approach is expected to become a common tool for many theories of indices, not just an independent branch of index number theory, as the author anticipates.

10.8 Mathematical Appendix: Derivation of (10.12)

Consider the following constrained minimization problem:

$$\min_{\beta} (\mathbf{Y} - \mathbf{X}\beta)' (\mathbf{Y} - \mathbf{X}\beta) - 2\lambda \mathbf{R}\beta$$

The first-order condition is

$$-\mathbf{X}'\mathbf{Y} + \mathbf{X}'\mathbf{X}\beta - \mathbf{R}'\lambda = 0 \tag{10.33}$$

$$\widehat{\beta}^{\text{cons}} = (\mathbf{X}'\mathbf{X})^{-1} \mathbf{X}'\mathbf{Y} + (\mathbf{X}'\mathbf{X})^{-1} \mathbf{R}'\boldsymbol{\lambda} \tag{10.34}$$

$$\mathbf{R}\widehat{\beta}^{\text{cons}} = \mathbf{R}(\mathbf{X}'\mathbf{X})^{-1} \mathbf{X}'\mathbf{Y} + \mathbf{R}(\mathbf{X}'\mathbf{X})^{-1} \mathbf{R}'\boldsymbol{\lambda} \tag{10.35}$$

$$0 = \mathbf{R}\widehat{\beta}^{\text{ols}} + \mathbf{R}(\mathbf{X}'\mathbf{X})^{-1} \mathbf{R}'\boldsymbol{\lambda} \tag{10.36}$$

Hence,

$$\lambda = -\left[\mathbf{R}\left(\mathbf{X}^{\mathbf{X}}X\right)^{-1}\mathbf{R}'\right]^{-1}\mathbf{R}\widehat{\beta}^{ols}$$

Substituting this into (10.34) yields (10.12)

$$\begin{aligned}\widehat{\beta}^{cons} &= (\mathbf{X}'\mathbf{X})^{-1} \mathbf{X}'\mathbf{Y} - (\mathbf{X}'\mathbf{X})^{-1} \mathbf{R}' \left[\mathbf{R}(\mathbf{X}'\mathbf{X})^{-1} \mathbf{R}'\right]^{-1} \mathbf{R}\widehat{\beta}^{ols} \\ &= \widehat{\beta}^{ols} - (\mathbf{X}'\mathbf{X})^{-1} \mathbf{R}' \left[\mathbf{R}(\mathbf{X}'\mathbf{X})^{-1} \mathbf{R}'\right]^{-1} \mathbf{R}\widehat{\beta}^{ols}\end{aligned}$$

References

Aoki, M. (2001). Optimal monetary policy responses to relative-price changes. *Journal of Monetary Economics, 48*(1), 55–80.

Ball, L., Carvalho, C., Evans, C., & Ricci, L. (2024). Weighted median inflation around the world: a measure of core inflation. *Journal of International Money and Finance., 142*, 103017. https://doi.org/10.1016/j.jimonfin.2024.103017

Blinder, A. (1997). Commentary 1 on 'Measuring short-run inflation for central bankers' by Stephan Cecchetti, Federal Reserve Bank of St. *Louis Review,79*(3), 157–160.

Bryan, M. F., & Cecchetti, S. G. (1994) Measuring core inflation. In N. Gregory Mankiw (Ed.), Monetary policy (pp. 195–215). University of Chicago Press.

Clements, K. W., Izan, H. Y., & Selvanathan, E. A. (2006). Stochastic index numbers: a review. *International Statistical Review, 74*(2), 235–270.

Crone, T. M., Khettry, N. N. K., Mester, L. J., & Novak, J. A. (2013). Core measures of inflation as predictors of total inflation. *Journal of Money, Credit and Banking, 45*(2/3), 505–519.
Deaton, A., & Dupriez, O. (2011). Purchasing power parity exchange rates for the global poor. *American Economic Journal: Applied Economics, 3*, 137–166.
Diewert, W. E. (1995). On the stochastic approach to index numbers. University of British Columbia, Department of Economics Discussion Paper No. 95-31.
Eckstein, O. (1981). *Core inflation*. Prentice Hall.
Eusepi, S., Hobijn, B., & Tambalotti, A. (2011). CONDI: A cost-of-nominal-distortions index. *American Economic Journal: Macroeconomics, 3*(3), 53–91.
Feenstra, R. C., & Reinsdorf, M. B. (2007). Should Index Numbers Have Standard Errors? Theory and Application to Asian Growth. In E. R. Berndt & C. R. Hulten (Eds.), *Hard-to-Measure Goods and Services: Essays in Honor of Zvi Griliches* (pp. 483–513). University of Chicago Press.
Feenstra, R. C. (1994). New product varieties and the measurement of international prices. *American Economic Review, 84*(1), 157–177.
Hajargasht, G., & Rao, D. S. P. (2019). Multilateral index number systems for international price comparisons: properties, existence and uniqueness. *Journal of Mathematical Economics, 83*, 36–47.
Gorajek, A. (2024). Generalizing the stochastic approach to price indexes. *Review of Income and Wealth, 70*, 80–101.
Handbury, J., & Weinstein, D. E. (2015). Goods prices and availability in cities. *Review of Economic Studies, 82*(1), 258–296.
Jevons, W. S. (1863). A serious fall in the value of gold ascertained and its social effects set forth. Edward Stanford.
Lippe, P. V. D. (2007). Index theory and price statistics. Peter Lang Pub Inc.
Quah, D., & Vahey, S. P. (1995). Measuring core inflation. *Economic Journal, 105*(432), 1130–44.
Selvanathan, E. A., & Rao, D. S. P. (1994). *Index numbers: a stochastic approach*. Springer.
Silver, M. (2006). Core inflation: measures and statistical issues in choosing among them. IMF Working Papers, No. 2006/097.
Wynne, M.A. (2008). Core inflation: a review of some conceptual issues. Federal Reserve Bank of St. Louis, 90(3, Part 2), pp. 205–228.

Comparisons of Price Levels Across Regions: Theory and Practice

11

Abstract

This chapter discusses the theory and practice of regional price index numbers, particularly focusing on exchange rates and Purchasing Power Parity (PPP). The chapter begins by highlighting the limitations of using exchange rates for price comparisons due to their volatility and the Balassa–Samuelson effect, which causes market exchange rates to undervalue currencies of developing countries. It suggests using price indices to measure prices across countries, adapting the theoretical framework used for temporal comparisons to spatial ones. The concept of Purchasing Power Parity (PPP), introduced by Gustav Cassel in 1918, is discussed in depth. It emphasizes that while comparing prices between two countries using a basket of goods is straightforward, involving more countries complicates calculations due to non-transitivity issues. To address these complexities, the chapter introduces three main methods used for constructing PPP: Gini–Eltető–Köves–Szulc (GEKS), Geary-Khamis (GK), and the Country Product Dummy (CPD). Each method has its strengths and weaknesses, with GEKS ensuring transitivity and GK satisfying aggregation consistency. The CPD method employs regression analysis to account for differences in goods across countries, making it suitable for international comparisons where homogeneous goods are difficult to find. The chapter also introduces the Minimum Spanning Tree (MST) method, which aims to reflect the "distance" between countries in price index calculations. Despite advancements, the chapter acknowledges the challenges in constructing accurate regional price indices, such as differences in consumption baskets and the quality of goods and services between countries. It concludes by highlighting the ongoing research and the importance of PPP for international economic comparisons.

11.1 Exchange Rates and Purchasing Power Parity

When comparing prices between countries, using exchange rates is a natural approach given the presence of different currencies. Although market exchange rates offer valuable insights into price variations across countries, they also pose certain

N. Abe, *Price Index Numbers*, Springer Texts in Business and Economics,
https://doi.org/10.1007/978-981-97-6305-4_11

problems when used to measure price levels. Firstly, exchange rates are volatile and are influenced by factors beyond immediate commodity prices, including expectations for future policies. Secondly, there is the issue of the Balassa–Samuelson effect by Balassa (1964) and Samuelson (1964). Converting 100 US dollars into the local currency of a developing country using the market exchange rate typically allows for purchasing significantly more goods than the same amount in developed countries. It is widely recognized that market exchange rates tend to underestimate the price levels in developing countries. In their papers, Béla Balassa and Paul Samuelson showed that productivity disparities between tradable and non-tradable goods lead to the undervaluation of developing countries' currencies, a phenomenon now known as the Balassa–Samuelson effect. This effect is still observed today and has been substantiated by extensive research.[1]

If exchange rates are not utilized as indicators of price levels or monetary values, there arises a need to measure price levels across countries. The theoretical framework for price indices developed in this book, typically used to compare different times, can be adapted for regional comparisons by simply replacing the time index (t) with a country index (s), without changing the underlying mathematical structure. Consequently, indices such as the Fisher, Törnqvist, or Sato–Vartia indices can be established between countries like the USA and Germany. Additionally, cost-of-living indices and quantity indices can be constructed using an economic approach. Price indices derived from country-specific quantity and price data are known as Purchasing Power Parity (PPP).

11.2 Challenges of Constructing PPP

This concept of PPP was introduced by a Swedish economist Gustav Cassel over a century ago, in Cassel (1918). Cassel proposed a theory of exchange rate determination, advocating that the exchange rate between two countries should align such that their currencies' purchasing powers are equalized. The purchasing power of a currency measures the quantity of goods that can be bought with one unit of that currency. If only one type of good existed, assessing purchasing power would be much simpler. For example, if Big Macs were the only product available worldwide, the PPP between two countries could be determined by comparing the price of a Big Mac in each country. If a Big Mac costs 6 dollars in the United States and 3 pounds in the United Kingdom, the PPP would suggest that 1 dollar is equivalent to 0.5 pound. However, with a variety of goods available, it becomes necessary to select a basket of goods to accurately measure purchasing power across different economies. When evaluating prices across multiple countries using a standard basket of goods from country A, employing the Laspeyres index with country A as the base serves

[1] The Balassa–Samuelson effect is a phenomenon that continues to be observed today, with a substantial body of research supporting it. Tica and Družić (2006) conducted a survey of empirical analyses, many of which demonstrate the existence of this effect.

as an example of Purchasing Power Parity (PPP). Depending on the specific basket chosen, other PPP measures such as the Paasche or Walsh indices might also be applicable, paralleling standard inter-temporal price index number theory. Additionally, the log difference price index, like the Sato-Vartia index, can be used for PPP calculations. This approach is straightforward when comparing prices between two countries using index number theory. However, introducing a third country into the analysis significantly increases the complexity of the calculations.

Consider the case with three countries: A, B, and C. When measuring changes in prices over time, there is a natural order, such as $t, t+1, t+2$. The period following t is $t+1$, and then $t+2$. Although many price indices do not satisfy transitivity, the lack of transitivity in measuring price changes over time may not be considered significant if comparisons over long periods are not of interest. However, when comparing countries, it's not always straightforward to determine whether country A is closer in economic terms to country B or C. Furthermore, the choice of the base country can significantly impact the PPP calculations between countries other than the base. This issue highlights the critical need for meticulous selection and analysis in employing Purchasing Power Parity (PPP) to compare economic conditions across nations. When measuring a country's income (value added) through per capita real GDP, the non-transitivity of the deflator, or price index, means that altering the base country can significantly change the perceived income of other countries. For example, let's consider the United States as the base country and construct the price indices for various countries using, for instance, the Fisher index. If we have the price indices of the United States and the United Kingdom, as well as the United States and China, it is possible to determine the price ratio between the United Kingdom and China by taking the ratio of these indices. However, if there is no transitivity, this ratio will differ from the value obtained by directly calculating the price index between the United Kingdom and China using the Fisher index. Additionally, if a country other than the United States is adopted as the base country, the price indices between countries will also vary. With more than three countries involved, international price indices need to satisfy transitivity to ensure reliable and consistent comparisons.

As discussed in Chap. 4, if price indices depend only on the price and quantity vectors of two points or regions without assuming any specific relationship between prices and quantities, the only transitive price indices are problematic ones like the Dutot index, which lacks independence from measurement units, or Cobb–Douglas-type indices.[2] Adopting Cobb–Douglas indices requires assuming that the expenditure shares on various goods and services are identical across different regions, an assumption that diverges too much from reality in international comparisons. Therefore, in international comparisons, instead of standard bilateral price indices that depend only on information from two points, multilateral index numbers are used. The chain indices discussed in Chap. 8 are multilateral in that they use prices and quantities from periods between the two points to compare prices. Similarly, in

[2] Additionally, when using the Lowe index, if the quantities used as weights are adjusted to reflect changes in measurement units, it is possible to consider it as a transitive index.

international comparisons, calculations use prices and quantities from other points when comparing prices between two countries.

Currently, there are three main methods used for constructing the PPP, transitive multilateral price indices, by international organizations and research institutions: (1) Gini–Eltető–Köves–Szulc (GEKS), (2) Geary-Khamis (GK), and (3) the Country Product Dummy (CPD).[3] Additionally, a method based on graph theory called Minimum Spanning Tree (MST) has been proposed to uniquely determine the "direction," or order, of price comparisons between regions. The GEKS method is used by the World Bank in its International Comparison Program (ICP), while the GK method is employed in the Penn World Table.[4] Although the Fisher, Törnqvist, and Sato-Vartia indices differ significantly in their index number formulas, their calculated results are generally close enough that their differences can be nearly ignored. However, in the case of regional price indices, GEKS and GK can produce significantly different results, drastically affecting a country's real income and production values depending on which is used. Therefore, the construction method for regional price indices has been a subject of intense debate both theoretically and policy-wise over the past 20 years, with vigorous ongoing research. However, the current state of international price index number theory and statistical practice can be well summarized by the words of Alan Heston, a leading figure in macroeconomic statistics, and Nobal laureate in Economics, Angus Deaton:

> In the rest of this paper, we shall follow the national income accountants' practice of thinking in terms of price indexes, not cost-of-living indexes. Critics of this approach argue that it leaves the welfare basis of the calculations unclear. We agree, but do not know how to do better, and therefore endorse a statistical rather than a welfare interpretation of the price indexes from the ICP. (p.6 in Deaton and Heston (2010)[5]

Thus, when constructing international price indices, it is difficult to employ an economic approach similar to Konüs's cost-of-living index. The three methods of price indices mentioned earlier, GEKS, GK, and CPD, require very strong constraints to be economically justified. Specifically, the cost-of-living index assumes identical preferences between the two time points or locations being compared. However, applying this assumption to countries like India and the United States, or China and Canada, is unrealistic. These countries often have significantly different consumption patterns, with the goods and services consumed varying greatly between them. This discrepancy makes the assumption of identical preferences particularly problematic in accurate international economic comparisons. The situation becomes even more severe when comparing low- and high-income countries. Developing index number

[3] Neary (2004) proposes the "Geary-Allen Additive International Accounts (GAIA) multilateral system," which extends the GK method to align with consumer theory. For potential issues associated with this method, refer to Deaton and Heston (2010).

[4] GK method was the main method for aggregation until the 2005 round of the ICP.

[5] In the same issue as Deaton and Heston (2010), critical commentaries are also published. For more details, refer to Diewert (2010) and Ravallion (2010).

formulas that have economic meaning and can be used for international price comparisons is one of the foremost challenges in current index number theory, currently, no widely accepted solution has been found.

The theory of PPP has a history of over 100 years. Additionally, the United Nations Statistics Division began creating PPPs for various countries using a unified method with Alan Heston and Robert Summers from the University of Pennsylvania (originally called the International Comparison Project) in 1968, marking over 50 years of history.[6] However, measuring PPP across many countries has consistently proven to be highly difficult. In the 1980s, the University of Pennsylvania withdrew from the project, the number of countries participating in the PPP survey hardly increased, and many questions were raised about the accuracy of PPP statistics.[7] At the end of the twentieth century, the International Comparison Project was renamed the International Comparison Program (ICP), and significant organizational changes were made. Then, with the 2005 survey (ICP 2005), PPPs for 199 countries were finally compiled.[8] However, when the results of the next PPP survey conducted in 2011 (ICP 2011) were announced in 2014, a major debate erupted again. The estimated PPPs for 2011, extrapolated using each country's CPI from the 2005 survey results, differed significantly from the ICP 2011, and based on the new survey, the world's average income had increased by 25%. This discrepancy was particularly notable in developing countries; for example, Indonesia's per capita GDP was $4,620 based on extrapolations from the ICP 2005, but it nearly doubled to $8,539 according to the ICP 2011. The number of people living below the international poverty line of $1.25 a day dropped from 1.2 billion based on the 2005 survey to 570 million in the 2011 survey, suddenly suggesting a dramatic reduction in global poverty. This indicates significant issues with either the 2005 survey, the 2011 survey, or both.[9] Regional price indices are still developing both theoretically and empirically. Interest in global poverty and inequality remains strong, and many organizations, including the World Bank and OECD, are actively trying to create and improve statistical indicators for measuring the Sustainable Development Goals (SDGs), and monitoring the Millennium Development Goals (MDGs). PPP is at the very heart of such statistics.

[6] The Asian Development Bank (2021), which provides a detailed report on the measurement methods of ICP 2017 in Asia, explains the history of the ICP and the Penn World Table in detail in its Chap. 8.

[7] The criticisms at the time and proposals for necessary reorganization are summarized in the Ryten Report (1999).

[8] See Deaton and Heston (2010) for the detail of the ICP 2005.

[9] Several studies have been conducted on the differences between ICP 2005 and ICP 2011. Notable ones include Deaton and Aten (2014) and Inklaar and Rao (2017).

11.3 Gini–Eltető–Köves–Szulc (GEKS) Method

This method, sometimes referred to as the EKS method, is based on the research conducted by three scholars in the 1960s,[10] but in recent years, it is often referred to as the GEKS method, considering the classical study by Corrado Gini published in the 1930s as its precursor.[11] The GEKS method is a multilateral index approach that ensures transitivity in bilateral. It is one of the standard PPP measurement methods today, along with the GK method mentioned later, and is currently adopted by the World Bank for PPP creation.

Assuming there are M countries in the world and denoting the Fisher price index between any two countries, j, k, within M as P_{jk}^F, the price index between countries j and k according to the GEKS method is defined as follows:

$$P_{jk}^{GEKS} = \prod_{l=1}^{M} \left(P_{jl}^F \times P_{lk}^F \right)^{\frac{1}{M}} \tag{11.1}$$

In other words, the GEKS price index between countries j and k is simply the geometric mean of indirect comparisons between the two countries j and k through a link country l, $(l = 1, 2, ..., M)$, covering all possibilities of third countries l (including j, k countries). The GEKS price index clearly satisfies transitivity.[12] By using the Fisher price index, which is considered the superlative index, as the base formula, the GEKS method possesses desirable properties in index number theory, such as factor reversal and independence from units of measurement, and seems to be justifiable economically. However, GEKS is also a type of chain index and does not satisfy (1) identity, (2) monotonicity, and (3) the intermediate value property. Note that the GEKS method in (11.1) is not limited to the Fisher index; GEKS can be applied to almost all indices discussed so far as long as the index satisfies time or country reversal test, including Törnqvist, Sato-Vartia, and Walsh indices.[13]

While having significant axiomatic issues, one reason GEKS is widely adopted by international institutions today is that it is the "closest" transitive index to the bilateral price comparisons based on the Fisher index. Specifically, the following

[10] Eltető and Kőves(1964) (in Hungarian) and Szulc (1964) (in Polish).

[11] Gini's paper (Gini 1931) is short, but clearly discusses what adjustments are necessary to ensure transitivity, presenting various ideas that directly lead to the current analysis.

[12] Instead of the Fisher index, Caves et al. (1982) argue that the Törnqvist index is preferable. However, the choice between Fisher and Törnqvist makes little difference in PPP creation by the World Bank.

[13] While the GEKS transformation can be applied to any bilateral index number formula, applying it to indices that lack the time (country) reversal property, such as Laspeyres and Paasche indices, may result in problematic index numbers.

result is known: let $\left\{P_{jk}^F\right\}_{j=1,2,\ldots,M}^{k=1,2,\ldots,M}$ be the Fisher indices. Consider minimizing the function by varying P_{jk}:

$$\text{Min} \sum_{j=1}^{M} \sum_{k=1}^{M} \left[\ln P_{jk}^F - \ln P_{jk}\right]^2 \quad \text{subject to} \quad P_{jl} \cdot P_{lk} = P_{jk}, \forall j, k, l = 1, 2, \ldots, M \tag{11.2}$$

The solution to the above problem is given by

$$P_{jk}^{F-GEKS} = \prod_{l=1}^{M} \left[P_{jl}^F \cdot P_{lk}^F\right]^{\frac{1}{M}} \tag{11.3}$$

Furthermore, if the base index is changed from Fisher to another index, the solution to the above minimization problem will still be the GEKS of that index. Those interested in the proof should refer to Rao and Banerjee (1986).

One issue with the GEKS method is that it is a simple geometric mean of all indirect comparisons giving same weight irrespective of the size of the economies and the reliability of the bilateral comparisons involved. This can be seen as a democratic index that takes small countries into consideration, but, on the other hand, when analyzing the relative prices between China and the United States, for example, the GEKS method uses price indices between countries which may have very dissimilar price structures—say between Japan and Zimbabwe and USA. Whether this is appropriate or not is debatable. Another issue with the GEKS method, unlike the Geary-Khamis method discussed later, is that it does not satisfy aggregation (additive) consistency. This means there is a lack of consistency between the price indices at the item level and the overall price index. In the case of indices without aggregation consistency, the overall index and the price indices for each item need to be calculated separately, and various problems may arise, such as the overall index not falling between the minimum and maximum values of the item-specific indices.

However, the most significant issue with GEKS is the lack of any economic rationale. Neary (2004) points out that GEKS becomes an economic cost-of-living index (COLI) only when GEKS coincides with the original Fisher index, i.e., when there is no need to apply GEKS. If the Fisher index strictly becomes a COLI, it implies transitivity. Since GEKS is the index closest to the original index with transitivity, Neary (2004)'s result is natural. Moreover, in economic theory, there is usually no room for information from a third location to enter the welfare comparison between two points, meaning that the GEKS operation itself deviates from economic theory.

11.4 Geary-Khamis (GK) Method

Alongside the GEKS method, the Geary-Khamis (GK) method is frequently used as an aggregation method and is known to satisfy aggregation consistency.[14] The GK method is currently adopted in the Penn World Table (PWT)[15] and was also utilized in the 1990s by European countries and the International Comparison Program (ICP) within the World Bank.

First, let's assume that for each country j, there exists a composite price index PPP_j, and for each good i, there exists an international average price P_i, which is normally the average price per unit quantity, i.e.,

$$P_i = \frac{\sum_{j=1}^{M} p_{ij} q_{ij}}{\sum_{j=1}^{M} q_{ij}} \tag{11.4}$$

However, if the monetary units differ between countries or if the composite price index (PPP_j) varies, it becomes necessary to account for these differences. In other words, dividing the product prices in each country by the composite price index might be more appropriate:

$$P_i = \frac{\sum_{j=1}^{M} \frac{p_{ij} q_{ij}}{PPP_j}}{\sum_{j=1}^{M} q_{ij}} \tag{11.5}$$

The problem is that we do not know the composite price index PPP_j for each country, and thus cannot compute the right-hand side. Therefore, let's assume we know the international average price P_i for each good. It then becomes natural to consider PPP_j as a weighted sum of the ratio between the international average price P_i and the price of good i in country j, similar to the Paasche index using the quantities q_{ij} in country j:

$$PPP_J = \frac{\sum_{i=1}^{N} p_{ij} q_{ij}}{\sum_{i=1}^{N} P_i q_{ij}} \tag{11.6}$$

Note that we assume there are N commodities. Calculating PPP_j requires P_is, while calculating P_is requires PPP_j. To obtain both P_i and PPP_j, we must solve a system of $M + N$ nonlinear equations involving P_i and PPP_j. It is generally impossible to analytically solve this system of equations. However, Khamis (1970, 1972) has proven that under general assumptions, the system uniquely determines

[14] See Khamis (1970), Khamis (1972), and Geary (1958).

[15] Specifically, in PWT, GEKS is used within sectors, such as Household Consumption, Investment and Government Expenditure, while GK is employed for inter-sector aggregation. Refer to Feenstra et al. (2015) for details.

positive values (one country or one commodity needs to be used as a reference).[16] With the capabilities of modern computers, solving this problem can be accomplished in seconds through matrix inversion or by employing an iterative scheme, even when dealing with over 100 types of goods and more than 100 countries.

A frequently mentioned advantage of the GK method, as previously mentioned, is that it satisfies aggregation consistency. Let's examine this in detail. Define a country's "real" GDP as its total final expenditure divided by the country's composite price index PPP_j. It's clear from the definition of the GK that

$$\frac{\sum_{i=1}^{N} p_{ij} q_{ij}}{PPP_j} = \sum_{i=1}^{N} P_i q_{ij} \tag{11.7}$$

This implies that the total expenditure converted to real terms matches the aggregated real quantities, a property not found in the GEKS method. This feature is useful because it allows for consolidating multiple countries into one or dividing a country's activities into several sub-aggregates. In national accounts, real values of various expenditure items, such as household consumption, capital investment, and government spending, are calculated and aggregated to derive real GDP. The weighted average of the composite price index and the price indices of each component aligns when the Paasche index is used as the deflator. Similarly, using the GK method, the price index calculated from aggregated quantities matches the aggregated price indices calculated for each component. However, with GEKS, aggregating the price indices of the components does not result in the price index of the aggregate.

Another advantage of the GK method is that it satisfies factor reversal test—product of price and quantity indices defined in (11.8) and (11.9) equal value index. Define the GK quantity index as

$$QI_{jk}^{GK} = \frac{\sum_{i=1}^{N} P_i q_{ik}}{\sum_{i=1}^{N} P_i q_{ij}} \tag{11.8}$$

i.e., the ratio of quantities evaluated at international average prices, and define the price index as

$$PI_{jk}^{GK} = \frac{PPP_k}{PPP_j} \tag{11.9}$$

16 Various conditions exist, for example, if all quantities are positive, the Perron–Frobenius theorem can be applied. Note that multiplying the calculated PPP by 10 and dividing P by 1/10 still satisfies the system of equations, making it necessary to establish a reference country whose PPP is set to unity.

Then,

$$PI_{jk}^{GK} \times QI_{jk}^{GK} = \frac{PPP_k}{PPP_j} \times \frac{\sum_{i=1}^{N} P_i q_{ik}}{\sum_{i=1}^{N} P_i q_{ij}} \tag{11.10}$$

$$= \frac{\sum_{i=1}^{N} p_{ik} q_{ik}}{\sum_{i=1}^{N} P_i q_{ik}} \times \frac{\sum_{i=1}^{N} P_i q_{ij}}{\sum_{i=1}^{N} p_{ij} q_{ij}} \times \frac{\sum_{i=1}^{N} P_i q_{ik}}{\sum_{i=1}^{N} P_i q_{ij}} \tag{11.11}$$

$$= \frac{\sum_{i=1}^{N} p_{ik} q_{ik}}{\sum_{i=1}^{N} p_{ij} q_{ij}} \tag{11.12}$$

which matches the value index, or the ratio of expenditures, implying factor reversal test is satisfied. A problem with the GK method is that the impact on PPP depends on the size of the country, meaning that the prices of larger economies significantly influence the international average price. Also, whether quantities and expenditures are per capita or for the entire country can alter the results of the GK method, a phenomenon not encountered with the Fisher or Törnqvist index-based GEKS method, representing a serious issue.

11.4.1 Comparison of the GEKS and GK Methods

As mentioned earlier, the GEKS method is adopted by the World Bank's ICP, while the GK method is used in the Penn World Table.[17] The two indices employ entirely different calculation methods, leading to potentially significant differences in PPP values. Therefore, the choice of method can alter the estimated real income and poverty levels globally. The GK method enables the calculation of real total expenditure as the sum of real quantities, thereby satisfying aggregation consistency. This means it effectively aggregates data across different items and sectors, allowing for comprehensive economic analysis. However, despite these strengths, the GK method has recently come under increasing scrutiny and criticism, primarily due to its lower substitution bias. Real GDP in the GK method becomes $\sum_{i=1}^{N} P_i q_{ij}$, evaluating quantities at international average prices rather than actual prices, leading to potential overestimation, similar to the issue with the Paasche quantity index. Even if there's a shift in demand toward cheaper consumer goods, they are evaluated at international average prices, resulting in values higher than actual expenditures. This suggests that GDP in poorer countries, which often face lower prices, may be overestimated. This effect, known as the Gerschenkron effect in homage to Alexander Gerschenkron's mid-twentieth-century work on index and base year selection,

[17] The Penn World Table (PWT) is regularly updated, and these updates are significant rather than minor. As a result, it's important to acknowledge that different versions of the PWT can lead to varying outcomes in economic analyses. Johnson et al. (2013) highlighted that many studies employing the PWT, including influential research published in top journals, have shown differing results when the version of the PWT used was changed. This variability underscores the necessity of specifying the version used in analyses to ensure clarity and reproducibility in economic research.

indicates that the GK method's overestimation of quantities can be severe (Ackland et al. 2013). They find that the GK method's estimates tend to underestimate global poverty by about 30% compared to the GEKS method, particularly underestimating poverty in Asian countries. This finding casts doubt on the accuracy of the PPP based on the GK, and strongly suggests potential biases in data for poorer countries, making it a noteworthy study. While the GK method was once used by institutions like the World Bank, it has been replaced by the GEKS method since the 2005 ICP cycle.[18]

11.5 Country-Product-Dummy (CPD) Method

Alongside GEKS and GK methods, the Country-Product-Dummy (CPD) method, which employs regression analysis, is also frequently used in current PPP creation. This method, which performs regression during index calculation, belongs to the category of stochastic approaches. Although it was long neglected within index number theory, it was utilized in part for PPP calculations below the basic heading level or the elementary index level by Kravis, Heston, and Summers in the early phases of the ICP. Summers (1973) outlines the basic elements of the CPD method. Later, the theoretical relationship between GK, GEKS, and CPD was elaborated in the works of Prasada Rao (such as Rao 2005), leading to its widespread adoption in many countries for PPP creation, with the exception of the EU and OECD comparisons.

As discussed in Chap. 10, the stochastic approach to index number theory views index making as signal extraction from information containing noise. Specifically, in the CPD, the price p_{ij} of good i in country j is assumed to be determined as follows:

$$p_{ij} = P_i \times PPP_j \times u^*_{ij} \tag{11.13}$$

where P_i is the average price of good i, PPP_j is the PPP of country j, and u^*_{ij} is an error term. It's assumed that we cannot observe all product prices, only a sampled subset. When estimating the above equation, we take logarithms and consider the following regression formula with product and country dummies:

$$\ln p_{ij} = \eta_1 D_1 + \eta_2 D_2 + \ldots + \eta_n D_n + \pi_1 D^*_1 + \pi_2 D^*_2 + \ldots + \pi_M D^*_M + u_{ij} \tag{11.14}$$

[18] There have been many attempts to improve the GK method while maintaining its additivity. The most famous of these is the Iklé–Dikhanov–Balk (IDB) method, adopted for PPP estimates in African countries by the ICP in 2005. The KS-S index by Yoshiharu Kurabayashi and Itsuo Sakuma and the SRK index developed by them and Prasada Rao have also been proposed. For more details, see Balk (2008).

Here, D_i are product dummies and D_i^* are country dummies. If the error term u_{ij} is orthogonal to the explanatory variables, it's possible to obtain the coefficients of each dummy variable through linear regression. Defining

$$PPP_j = \exp\left(\widehat{\pi}_j\right) \tag{11.15}$$

where $\widehat{\pi}_j$ is the estimate of π_j, the price index between two countries j and k can be defined as

$$P^{jk} = \frac{PPPk}{PPP_j} \tag{11.16}$$

This approach has the advantage of being easily extendable, such as by adding regressors or using various weights to control for subtle differences between products in each country. Additionally, the price index between two countries becomes a simple ratio of two real numbers, satisfying transitivity.

Summers (1973) argued that regression analysis is effective when it is difficult to find comparable and representative goods that are comparable across multiple countries. Ideally, when measuring PPP, there should exist goods that are both homogeneous and representative in all countries, allowing for a comparison of their prices. However, in reality, even between geographically close countries like the Unites States and Canada, dietary habits significantly differ, making it challenging to find common, representative, and homogeneous goods between the two countries. This task becomes even more difficult when comparing developed countries in Europa with developing countries. Moreover, even if identical goods are found, their prices could vary significantly depending on whether they are purchased online, in large stores within major shopping malls, or in small individual shops. In such cases, the CPD method allows for controlling differences in goods, services, or stores as a type of hedonic model by adjusting them as regression variables.

When the ICP calculates PPPs for each country, it first provides a list of 155 basic headings (222 basic headings for European countries) and a list of goods to be surveyed within each basic heading for each country. The 155-item list includes rice, sugar, and education, known as Basic Headings, which serve as the smallest units for aggregation.

Consider the case of "rice" basic heading. Japonica rice, commonly consumed in Japan, is not necessarily commonly eaten in other countries. Instead, Indica or Basmati rice may be more common in many countries. To compare prices between countries, it is necessary to compare the prices of quality of rice. However, in the ICP's PPP measurements, Japonica rice was not included in the survey list for a long time, and thus the price of rice in Japan's PPP was based on the price of glutinous rice. It was only very recently, starting with PPP2017, that Japonica rice (non-glutinous) was included in the survey list. Similar issues are presumed to occur in various countries. When aggregating rice within Basic Headings, different types of rice will be included, and the CPD, which can statistically mitigate the impact of the choice of surveyed goods to some extent, is more suitable for measuring the level differences between different types of rice between countries than the usual Fisher or Törnqvist

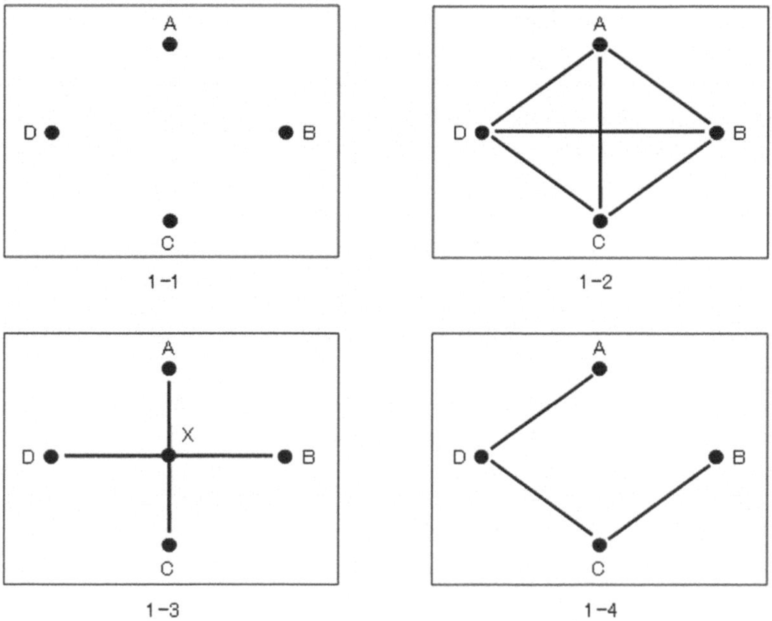

Fig. 11.1 Various Approaches to Comparing Prices between Countries

index. On the other hand, in European countries where it is relatively easy to find homogeneous goods, the price indices of basic headings are calculated using the variants of the GEKS method but not the CPD.

11.6 Minimum Spanning Tree (MST)

Assuming there are 100 countries in the world, the GEKS method creates Fisher indices for all possible combinations of these countries, namely, 4950 (= 100 × 99/2) types, and then takes their simple geometric mean of all indirect comparisons through a link country, for any given pair of countries. In contrast, the GK method calculates price levels in each country after comparisons with hypothetical international average prices. The GEKS method, covering all combinations, and the GK method, focusing on deviation from a "mean," can be considered two extremes. When calculating price indices among four countries, as shown in Fig. 11.1, GEKS corresponds to Fig. 11-1-2, while GK to Fig. 11-1-3. Both methods treat each country equally. However, for example, Canada is closer to the United States both geographically and linguistically than Japan or China. Could we somehow reflect such "distance" between countries when calculating price indices? For instance, if the gap between the Laspeyres index PI_{AB}^{L} and the Paasche index PI_{AB}^{P} between two countries (A and B) is small, it might be inferred that their price and/or quantity structures are similar. Could we construct price indices using information only from similar countries and connect them to calculate global PPP? One approach that is currently gaining attention is the use of the Minimum Spanning Tree (MST) in price indices, proposed by Hill (2004). A spanning tree is a concept used in graph theory. While detailed explanations can be found in a series of papers by Hill (1999a, 1999b, 2004), a spanning tree connects all countries with lines, ensuring no cycles, i.e., no subsets of countries that are closed off from the rest. When calculating MST, for any two countries A and B, a distance metric between them, such as the deviation between the Laspeyres index PI^L_{AB} and the Paasche index PI^P_{AB} defined below, is assigned:

$$D(A, B) = \left| \ln \frac{PI^L_{AB}}{PI^P_{AB}} \right| \tag{11.17}$$

The spanning tree with the smallest total distance among all spanning trees becomes the MST. MST can be thought of as corresponding to Fig. 11-1-4. For example, there might be an MST where everything is connected in a straight line, or one where everything radiates out from a central country. Unlike GEKS, which is difficult to justify economically, this provides some rationale for the connections between countries. However, the MST obtained might not always make persuasive connections between countries. For instance, in Hill (1999a), the MST for OECD countries shows Japan connected to the United States via Norway, Switzerland, Germany, Ireland, Australia, and finally Canada. While Norway is undoubtedly significant, it might feel unnatural to have to go through these countries to connect the United States and Japan.[19] Another serious issue is the instability in MSTs. That is, the index number values by MSTs may not be stable when we use different dataset. Many issues remain with MST, and the ICP has yet to adopt it. MST is currently undergoing many improvements and has a significant number of supporters.[20] The assessment of this method might change significantly in the future.

11.7 Current Status and Future Challenges of Regional Price Index Research

Regional price indices, especially those comparing price levels between countries, present numerous challenges. Comparing prices between countries with significantly different consumption baskets is both theoretically and practically difficult. For instance, consider comparing the prices in countries that consume only bread with those that consume only rice. This difference in consumption sets, as discussed in the previous chapter, may reflect differences in preferences highlighted by Deaton and Heston (2010). The question is whether to defend traditional methods, as Diewert (2010) and Ravallion (2010) do. Lewbel (1989) attempted to calculate price indices

[19] Figure 2.4 in P. 118, Hill (1999a).

[20] Hill (1999b), Hill (2004) are representative studies, and for subsequent developments, Hill and Hill (2009) provide detailed information.

across different households by measuring equivalence scales, providing important guidelines for future PPP analysis.

Moving away from the problems with the economic approach, creating indices, such as the standard Fisher index, poses its challenges. Differences in the quality of goods and services between countries, especially differences in imputed rents and service quality, make measurement difficult. Nonetheless, PPP is crucial for international comparisons of national strength and is widely used not only for academic and policy purposes. For further discussions on international price comparisons papers by Feenstra et al. (2009, 2015) as well as resources available on the ICP website can be informative.

Recent advances not extensively discussed in this chapter include research on measurement errors in inter-regional price indices. As introduced earlier, the World Bank's PPP measurements have faced many issues since their inception, but recent years have seen more rigorous analysis of measurement errors, starting with Deaton (2012). Interested readers may find Rao and Hajargasht (2016), Hajargasht and Rao (2019), and Hajargasht et al. (2019) useful.[21] Additionally, alternatives to the GEKS index, such as the QU index currently used in the Netherlands, have been developed to ensure transitivity in index number formula.[22] PPP is a crucial concept in international trade, macroeconomics, and development economics. Many macroeconomists, particularly those analyzing with the PWT, face significant challenges in creating comparable macro-variables across countries. Despite these difficulties, best efforts are being made to produce many statistics, which may significantly evolve with technological advancements. The analysis of spatial price indices poses many difficulties but is of high importance, and future advancements are anticipated.

References

Ackland, R., Dowrick, S., & Freyens, B. (2013). Measuring global poverty: Why PPP methods matter. *Review of Economics and Statistics, 95*(3), 813–824.

Asian Development Bank (2021) 2017 International Comparison Program for Asia and the Pacific: Purchasing Power Parities and Real Expenditures-Results and Methodology, : Asian Development Bank.

Balassa, B. (1964). The purchasing-power parity doctrine: a reappraisal. *Journal of Political Economy, 72*(6), 584–596.

Balk, B. M. (2008). *Price and quantity index numbers*. Cambridge University Press.

Cassel, G. (1918) Abnormal deviations in international exchanges. *Economic Journal, 28*(112), 413–415.

Caves, D. W., Christensen, L. R., & Diewert, W. E. (1982). The economic theory of index numbers and the measurement of input, output, and productivity. *Econometrica, 50*(6), 1393–1414.

Chessa, A. G. (2015). Towards a generic price index method for scanner data in the Dutch CPI. In *Ottawa Group Meeting, 20–22 May 2015*. Japan: Urayasu City.

[21] For recent developments in CPD, see Rao and Hajargasht (2016).

[22] For further details, refer to Chessa (2015).

Deaton, A., & Aten, B. (2014). Trying to Understand the PPPs in ICP2011: Why are the Results so Different? NBER Working Papers, No. 20244.
Deaton, A., & Heston, A. (2010). Understanding PPPs and PPP-based national accounts. *American Economic Journal: Macroeconomics, 2*(4), 1–35.
Deaton, A. (2012). Calibrating measurement uncertainty in purchasing power parity exchange rates. Research Program in Development Studies, mimeographed, Princeton.
Diewert, E. (2010). Understanding PPPs and PPP-Based National accounts: comment. *American Economic Journal: Macroeconomics, 2*(4), 36–45.
Éltet, O., & Köves, P. (1964). On an index computation problem in international comparisons, (in Hungarian). *Statistztikai Szemle, 42*, 507–18.
Feenstra, R. C., Heston, A., Timmer, M. P., & Deng, H. (2009). Estimating real production and expenditures across nations: a proposal for improving the Penn World Tables. *The Review of Economics and Statistics, 91*(1), 201–212.
Feenstra, R. C., Inklaar, R., & Timmer, M. (2015). The next generation of the Penn world table. *American Economic Review, 105*(10), 3150–3182.
Geary, R. C. (1958). A note on the comparison of exchange rates and purchasing power between countries. *Journal of the Royal Statistical Society, Series A: General, 121*(1), 97–99.
Gini, C. (1931). On the circular test of index numbers. *Metron, 2*, 3–24.
Hajargasht, G., Rao, D. S. P., & Valadkhani, A. (2019). Reliability of basic heading PPPs. *Economics Letters,180*(C), 102–107.
Hajargasht, G., & Rao, D. S. P. (2019). Multilateral index number systems for international price comparisons: properties, existence and uniqueness. *Journal of Mathematical Economics, 83*, 36–47.
Hill, R. (1999). International comparisons using spanning trees. In A. Heston & R. E. Lipsey (Eds.), *International and interarea comparisons of income, output, and prices* (pp. 109–120). University of Chicago Press.
Hill, R. (1999). Comparing price levels across countries using minimum-spanning trees. *Review of Economics and Statistics, 81*(1), 135–142.
Hill, R. (2004). Constructing price indexes across space and time: the case of the European Union. *American Economic Review, 94*(5), 1379–1410.
Hill, R., & Hill, T. P. (2009). Recent developments in the international comparison of prices and real output. *Macroeconomic Dynamics, 13*(S2), 194–217.
Inklaar, R., & Rao, D. S. P. (2017). Cross-country income levels over time: did the developing world suddenly become much richer. *American Economic Journal: Macroeconomics, 9*(1), 265–290.
Johnson, S., Larson, W., Papageorgiou, C., & Subramanian, A. (2013). Is newer better? Penn World Table revisions and their impact on growth estimates. *Journal of Monetary Economics, 60*(2), 255–274.
Khamis, S. H. (1970). Properties and conditions for the existence of a new type of index numbers. *Sankhyd: The Indian Journal of Statistics, Series B,32*(1/2), 81–98.
Khamis, S. H. (1972). A new system of index numbers for national and international purposes. *Journal of the Royal Statistics Society, Series A: General, 135*(1), 96–121.
Lewbel, A. (1989). Household equivalence scales and welfare comparisons. *Journal of Public Economics, 39*(3), 377–391.
Neary, J. (2004). Rationalizing the penn world table: True multilateral indices for international comparisons of real income. *American Economic Review, 94*(5), 1411–1428.
Rao, D. S. P., & Banerjee, K. S. (1986). A multilateral index number system based on the factorial approach. *Statistical Papers, 27*(1), 297–313.
Rao, D. S. P. (2005). On the equivalence of weighted Country-Product-Dummy (CPD) method and the rao-system for multilateral price comparisons. *Review of Income and Wealth, 51*(4), 571–580.
Rao, D. S. P., & Hajargasht, G. (2016). Stochastic approach to computation of purchasing power parities in the International Comparison Program (ICP). *Journal of Econometrics, 191*(2), 414–425.
Ravallion, M. (2010). Understanding PPPs and PPP-based National accounts: comment. *American Economic Journal: Macroeconomics, 2*(4), 46–52.

Ryten, J. (1999) Evaluation of the International Comparison Programme. Document E/CN.3/1999/8 of the U. N. Economic and Social Council, dated 16 November 1998.

Samuelson, P. A. (1964). Theoretical notes on trade problems. *Review of Economics and Statistics, 46*(2), 145–154.

Summers, R. (1973). International price comparisons based upon incomplete data. *Review of Income and Wealth, 19*(1), 1–16.

Szulc, B. (1964). Index numbers of multilateral regional comparisons (in Polish). *Przeglad Statystyczny, 3*, 239–254.

Tica, J., & Družić, I. (2006). The Harrod-Balassa-Samuelson Effect: A Survey of Empirical Evidence. University of Zagreb, Faculty of Economics and Business, FEB-Working Paper Series 06-7/686.

Measurement of Price Indices Based on the Engel Curve

12

Abstract

This chapter explores the measurement of price indices using the Engel curve, which reflects the relationship between food expenditure and total expenditure (Engel coefficient). Ernst Engel's 1857 study found that as income increases, the proportion of income spent on food decreases. Recent studies leverage this relationship to measure price index biases, suggesting significant biases in existing indices. The chapter details the Almost Ideal Demand System (AIDS), introduced by Deaton and Muellbauer (1980), as a central model for such measurements. The AIDS model provides a second-order approximation to any expenditure function, making it a robust tool for analyzing consumption patterns and estimating price indices. Nakamura (1996), Hamilton (2001), and Costa (2001) found significant biases in historical consumer price statistics in the US, using the Engel curve to analyze changes in food expenditure relative to income and prices. Almås (2012) extended this approach internationally, revealing substantial biases in purchasing power parity, particularly for developing countries. Despite the method's simplicity and the substantial body of literature supporting it, official price indices have not adopted the Engel curve approach. The chapter highlights criticisms, including the model's reliance on invariant preference parameters across time and regions, and the omission of factors like savings and home production. These issues cast doubt on the method's reliability for official statistics, even as it gains traction in academic research.

12.1 Introduction

The proportion of food expenditure in total expenditure, known as the Engel coefficient, is often discussed as a decreasing function of income (or total expenditure level), indicating that the poorer a household is, the higher its Engel coefficient tends to be. Ernst Engel, a nineteenth-century German statistician, found in Engel (1857) paper based on household expenditure data in Belgium that the proportion of total

N. Abe, *Price Index Numbers*, Springer Texts in Business and Economics,
https://doi.org/10.1007/978-981-97-6305-4_12

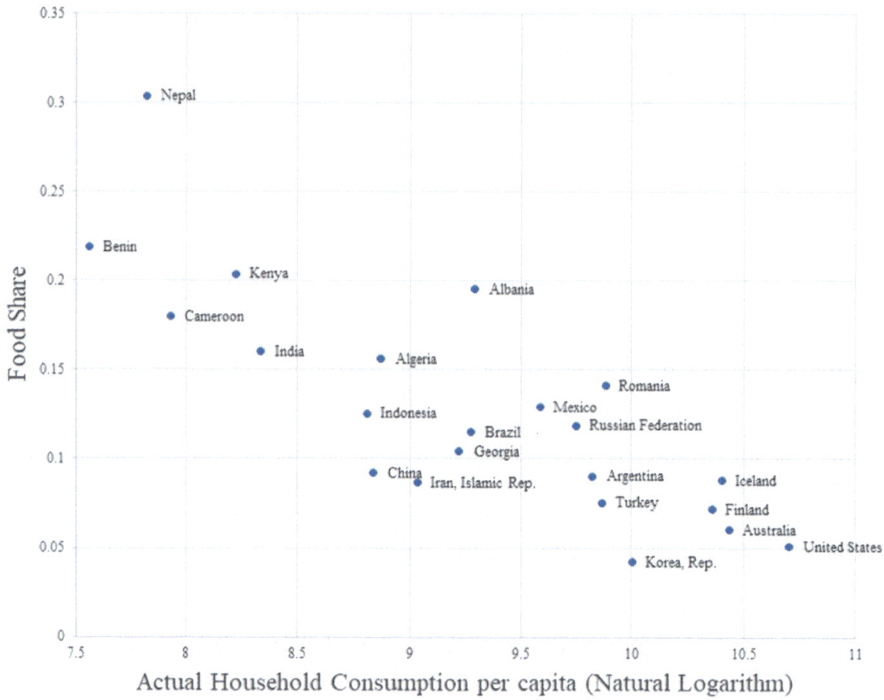

Fig. 12.1 Engel's coefficient for various countries *Sources* ICP 2017, World Bank

consumption spent on food[1] decreases as households become wealthier.[2] Figure 12.1 illustrates the relationship between per capita Actual Household Consumption and Food Share, using data from the World Bank's International Comparison Program (ICP 2017).[3] Clearly, there is a negative correlation between food share and total consumption expenditure, with wealthier countries tending to have lower Engel coefficients.

In recent years, numerous studies have attempted to measure price indices or the bias in existing price indices using the relationship between consumption levels and the food share, known as Engel's law. These studies have reported startling findings that existing price indices, whether at the national or international level,

[1] More precisely, on "nourishment," which includes alcohol and tobacco, thus covering a broader range than just food.

[2] The original text reads as follows: "je ämer eine Familie ist, einen desto groeseren Antheil von der Gesammtausgabc muss zur Beschaffung' der Nahrung aufgewendet" (Engel 1857 in p. 26). As far as the author knows, there are no English translations of Engel's famous paper, but excellent introductory articles are available. Zimmerman (1932) and Chai and Moneta (2010) are particularly informative.

[3] Although ICP 2017 includes data for a large number of countries, only a few are shown here to avoid overlapping country names.

contain significant biases, potentially amounting to several percent annually and even several hundred percent between countries.

This chapter discusses a series of studies on price measurement using Engel's law and organizes the various issues involved.

Consider the following "demand function" for food:

$$\omega_{it} = \alpha + \beta(\ln P_{it}^{F} - \ln P_{it}^{NF}) + \gamma \ln\left(\frac{Y_{it}}{P_{it}}\right) + D_t + e_{it} \tag{12.1}$$

where ω_{it} represents the proportion of food expenditure in total consumption expenditure, i.e., the Engel coefficient, for region (household) i at time t. P_{it}^{F} and P_{it}^{NF} denote the price indices for food and non-food items, respectively, Y_{it} is the nominal total consumption expenditure, and P_{it} is the general price index in region i. e_{it} is the error term, and D_t represents dummy variables for time, region, or attributes such as age. Let us assume that the constant term α and the elasticities β and γ are constant across time and region, and that the expected value of the error term e_{it} is always zero within any subset of the sample. Furthermore, assume there is no measurement error in the nominal total consumption expenditure and that the Engel coefficient is a linear function of the relative prices of food to non-food and real income. Under these assumptions, the effect of the time dummies, D_t, should always be zero. If D_t is not zero, and all the previous assumptions hold, the only reason for D_t to be non-zero would be systematic measurement errors in either or all of the price indices, P_{it}^{F}, P_{it}^{NF}, and P_{it}. For instance, if there is an error in the general price index causing it to understate the "true" price index, real income $\left(\frac{Y_{it}}{P_t}\right)$ would be overestimated, thereby deviating the proportion of food expenditure from the predicted value by the demand function. This deviation would manifest as the value of the dummy variable.

Nakamura (1996) used official statistics of the United States to discover the following facts. From 1959 to 1974, the proportion of food expenditure decreased from 27.3% to 23.1%, while per capita GDP increased from \$12,494 to \$18,178. Conversely, from 1974 to 1994, the Engel coefficient decreased from 23.1% to 16%, and real per capita GDP increased from \$18,178 to \$25,352. The decrease in the Engel coefficient was significantly larger in the latter half (7.1% points) compared to the former half (4.2% points), but the change in income was not as large as the change in the Engel coefficient suggested. Thus, Nakamura (1996) concluded that real income for the latter period was underestimated, i.e., the consumer price index was overestimated. Price measurement was conducted using the relationship between the Engel coefficient and income, i.e., the Engel curve. Subsequently, Hamilton (2001) reached similar conclusions using a more sophisticated econometric model, and Costa (2001) applied it to historical statistics in the US, concluding that there were significant errors in historical consumer price statistics in the US. Almås (2012) measured the bias in international price indices by the ICP using the Engel curve, arguing that significant biases occur, especially in developing countries.

Equation (12.1) is a very simple demand function (for expenditure shares). The price and income elasticities are constant, appearing as a simple linear model. So, why is this simple demand function frequently used in numerous leading journals?

Is it indeed an appropriate method for estimating measurement errors in prices? This section will explore recent price measurement methods using the Engel curve.

12.2 Almost Ideal Demand System

The demand function (12.1), which plays a central role in price measurement using the Engel curve, is very famous in consumption analysis and is referred to as the Almost Ideal Demand System (AIDS). This is based on Deaton and Muellbauer (1980), and employs a logic similar to that used by Diewert (1976) in the discussion of the superlative index, which provided a second-order approximation to the COLI for any twice continuously differentiable expenditure function. As a functional form that gives a second-order approximation, consider the translog type as follows, from which the Törnqvist index is derived:

$$\ln C(\mathbf{p}, u) = a_0 + \sum_k \alpha_k \ln p_k + \frac{1}{2}\sum_k \sum_m \gamma^*_{km} \ln p_k \ln p_m + u\beta_0 \prod_k p_k^{\beta_k}$$

$$\gamma^*_{km} = \gamma^*_{mk}, \sum_{i=1}^{n} a_i = 1, \sum_{m=1}^{n} \gamma^*_{km} = 0, \beta_0 > 0, \sum_k \beta_k = 0 \tag{12.2}$$

Here, p_i is the price of good i, and u is the level of utility, with constraints on various parameters imposed to ensure homogeneity of degree one in prices and symmetry in prices for the expenditure function. Calculating the cost-of-living index (COLI) from this expenditure function, as introduced in Chap. 6, yields

$$\begin{aligned} COLI &= \ln C(\mathbf{p_1}, u_0) - \ln C(\mathbf{p_0}, u_0) \\ &= \sum \alpha_k \Delta \ln p_k + \frac{\Delta}{2}\sum_k \sum_m \gamma^*_{km} \ln p_k \ln p_m + u_0\beta_0\Delta \prod_k p_k^{\beta_k} \end{aligned} \tag{12.3}$$

It is notable that the COLI depends on the utility level, covering cases where preferences are not homothetic. Whether the fixed utility level is set at period 0 or period 1, the value of the COLI differs. When deriving the Törnqvist index from the cost-of-living index, the utility level to be evaluated was fixed at the simple geometric mean of the utility levels at the two time points. Generally, in the case of non-homothetic preferences, the COLI will vary with income level, possessing different characteristics from a general price index.

Now, from Shepherd's lemma, differentiating (12.2) with respect to log prices yields

$$\begin{aligned}\omega_i &= \frac{\partial \ln C(\mathbf{p}, u)}{\partial \ln p_i} \\ &= \alpha_i + \frac{1}{2}\sum_k \gamma_{ki}^* \ln p_k + \frac{1}{2}\sum_k \gamma_{ik}^* \ln p_k + \beta_i u \beta_0 \prod_k p_k^{\beta_k} \\ &= \alpha_i + \sum_k \gamma_{ki} \ln p_k + \beta_i u \beta_0 \prod_k p_k^{\beta_k} \end{aligned} \tag{12.4}$$

where $\gamma_{ki} = \frac{1}{2}\left(\gamma_{ki}^* + \gamma_{ik}^*\right)$. The challenging part here is the third term on the right side, but it can be expressed from (12.2) as

$$u\beta_0 \prod_k p_k^{\beta_k} = \ln C(\mathbf{p}, u) - \left(a_0 + \sum \alpha_k \ln p_k + \frac{1}{2}\sum_k \sum_m \gamma_{km}^* \ln p_k \ln p_m\right) \tag{12.5}$$

Therefore, defining the price-level index P as

$$\ln P = a_0 + \sum_k \alpha_k \ln p_k + \frac{1}{2}\sum_k \sum_m \gamma_{km}^* \ln p_k \ln p_m \tag{12.6}$$

leads to

$$u\beta_0 \prod_k p_k^{\beta_k} = \ln C(\mathbf{p}, u) - \ln P \tag{12.7}$$

where $\ln C(\mathbf{p}, u)$ is the observed log nominal total consumption level, which equals the log nominal income, $\ln Y$, if savings are not considered. Thus, (12.4) can be written as

$$\omega_i = \alpha_i + \sum_k \gamma_{ki} \ln p_k + \beta_i (\ln Y - \ln P) \tag{12.8}$$

Taking the difference between two time periods t and 0 for the price-level index (12.6) yields

$$\ln P_t - \ln P_0 = \sum_k \alpha_k \Delta \ln p_k + \frac{\Delta}{2}\sum_k \sum_m \gamma_{km}^* \ln p_k \ln p_m$$

which matches with the condition of utility level set to zero, i.e., $u = 0$, in (12.3). That is, from the price-level index in AIDS, we can obtain Koüns's COLI when the utility level is fixed to zero.[4]

[4] This is evident from the shape of the expenditure function, but for further details, see Oulton (2008).

If there are only two types of goods, food, and non-food, then

$$\omega_F = \alpha_F + \gamma_F \ln p_F + \gamma_{NF} \ln p_{NF} + \beta_i(\ln Y - \ln P) \quad (12.9)$$

Furthermore, from the coefficient constraint

$$\sum_{m=1}^{N} \gamma_{km}^* = 0$$

we have

$$\sum_{m=1}^{N} \gamma_{km} = \frac{1}{2}\sum_{m=1}^{N}(\gamma_{km}^* + \gamma_{mk}^*) = 0 \quad (12.10)$$

Therefore,

$$\gamma_{NF} = -\gamma_F \quad (12.11)$$

From this, we get

$$\omega_F = \alpha_F + \gamma_F(\ln p_F - \ln p_{NF}) + \beta_i(\ln Y - \ln P) \quad (12.12)$$

This equation is derived from the translog expenditure function, which is a second-order approximation of any expenditure function, by imposing the constraint of homogeneity of degree one, and derived from Shepherd's lemma, with the only imposed constraints being (1) second-order differentiability, (2) local approximation, and (3) the price index formula as (12.6). For specific individual or household expenditure shares, under the condition of local approximation, this equation serves as a very good approximation. While only food expenditure is used here, if there are other consumption categories, it leads to a system of simultaneous equations for numerous expenditure shares. This system, corresponding to any expenditure function, is called the Almost Ideal Demand System (AIDS) due to its close approximation to the ideal, and is used in many studies as a demand function applicable to general cases, including those where preferences are not homothetic.[5]

12.3 Estimating CPI Bias Using the AIDS Model

The measurement of CPI bias using the Engel curve began with Nakamura (1996), but significant impacts in the field of economics were made by Hamilton (2001) and Costa (2001). Hamilton (2001) used the Panel Study of Income Dynamics (PSID), a

[5] AIDS is utilized in a wide range of fields, and numerous empirical studies can be found. For the theoretical foundation, refer to Deaton and Muellbauer (1980), and for an extension to nonlinear models, see Banks et al. (1997).

representative household-level panel dataset in the United States, to measure the magnitude of year dummies based on (12.1). Estimating (12.1) requires cross-sectional price differences. However, due to the lack of data on regional differences in price levels, estimates were derived using regional differences in price change rates. From 1974 to 1991, the proportion of food expenditure in income decreased from 16.64% to 12.04%. However, only about half of the observed decline can be explained by food and non-food prices, real income, and household attributes in the AIDS model. A 2.5% point drop must be explained by year dummies, indicating a significant CPI bias. The CPI bias measured from year dummies and income elasticity averaged 3% per year from 1974 to 1981 and about 1% thereafter, pointing to a considerable presence of CPI bias.

Costa (2001) conducted estimations using data over a long period from 1888 to 1994. The data used include various surveys on living costs conducted by the Department of Labor in the nineteenth century and the Bureau of Labor Statistics in the early twentieth century. However, like Hamilton, due to the absence of statistics on regional price-level differences, estimates were made using differences in regional price change rates. The estimation equation is the same as Hamilton's (12.1), and the method for estimating CPI bias is similar. The results show that CPI bias was small, around –0.1% per year, from 1888 to 1919, but increased to 0.7% per year from 1919 to 1935 and to 2.7% per year from 1972 to 1982, indicating a very large CPI bias. These results are generally consistent with those of Nakamura (1996) and Hamilton (2001).

Almås (2012) used estimates of Engel curves between countries to measure the bias in purchasing power parity generated by the World Bank. The formula used is similar to Hamilton (2001) and Costa (2001), but country dummies are used instead of time dummies. Specifically, by limiting to two-parent, two-child households from individual data of 10 countries,[6] a pooled AIDS model with country dummies was estimated to obtain various elasticities and country dummies. Then, the estimated parameters were applied to consumption, income, and price data of each country contained in the Penn World Table (PWT) to measure the CPI bias between countries. Unlike Hamilton (2001) and Costa (2001), the estimates used information on differences in price levels between regions.[7] The analysis based on 10-country data showed that the international price indices estimated using the Engel curve are higher than those estimated using the Geary-Khamis method in the PWT, with deviations from the PWT being larger for poorer countries. This implies that real incomes calculated by the PWT are higher than those estimated using the Engel curve, especially in developing countries like Nepal and Tanzania, where the deviation can be three to four times as large. Real incomes estimated using the Engel curve are closer to incomes converted at nominal exchange rates in poor countries. Applying the coefficients obtained from the 10-country AIDS estimates to another 32 countries in the

---

[6] The 10 countries include the UK, Spain, Hungary, Brazil, Bulgaria, Peru, Azerbaijan, Ivory Coast, Nepal, and Tanzania.

[7] Many adjustments were made to account for quality differences in food prices between countries during estimation. For more details, see Almås 2012.

PWT, Nakamura et al. (2016) analyzed that, similar to the 10-country estimates, the PWT price indices are underestimated for poorer countries.[8]

12.4 Advantages and Disadvantages of Using the Engel Curve

Hamilton (2001) highlights the advantages of estimating CPI bias using the Engel curve, including (1) its distinct methodology from standard CPI measurement techniques, (2) the absence of a need for extensive databases, and (3) the ease of measuring changes in the COLI across different social strata. Indeed, this method allows for the estimation of CPI measurement errors using relatively simple datasets, offering a stark contrast to the substantial efforts expended by national statistical offices and international organizations in measuring prices. Compared to existing methods that involve selecting numerous comparable goods across regions, continuously surveying prices and expenditures, and adjusting for the quality of goods and services, this approach of estimating the price index solely based on (12.1) could revolutionize price index measurement if proven reliable. This approach has indeed rapidly gained attention across fields such as macroeconomics, labor economics, economic development, international trade, and economic history.

Since the first publication on price measurement using the Engel curve in 1996, over two decades have passed. Despite the rapid increase in related literature, I have yet to encounter any official price indices employing the Engel curve, nor is there any mention of Engel curve-based analyses in the latest CPI manual, which exceeds 500 pages and was published in 2020. Therefore, it appears that index creators have not yet recognized the use of the Engel curve in price measurement as a viable alternative to existing index creation methodologies. From the perspective of index number theory, this method is fraught with problems.

Firstly, the price index used in AIDS, (12.6), not only differs from existing price indices but also does not coincide with the cost-of-living index within AIDS, as given by (12.3). The latter depends on income or utility levels. Almås et al. (2019) pointed out this inconsistency and developed a method to reconcile the two, arguing that many CPI biases remain even with different price indices for each income stratum and that this inconsistency does not result in significant quantitative differences. Similarly, Nakamura et al. (2016) found that significant biases remain in China's CPI even after accounting for different CPIs for each income stratum. A more fundamental issue is the necessary condition of invariance in parameter values such as the constant term and elasticities for considering the time or regional dummies in AIDS as CPI bias. For instance, in Almås (2012), analysis, households in the UK and Tanzania, consisting of two parents and two children and facing identical prices and income levels, are assumed to have the same proportion of food expenditure in their income (total consumption) and the same changes in food expenditure elasticity

[8] Outside the US, studies on CPI bias using the Engel curve have been conducted. See Beatty and Larsen (2005) for Canada and by Higa (2013) for Japan.

when food prices or income levels change. In Costa (2001), it is assumed that the preferences of people in the United States remain unchanged over a century. These assumptions play a crucial role in identification, and not accepting them could significantly undermine the validity of their estimates. These assumptions of invariant or common preference parameters might seem like strong assumptions. However, to estimate AIDS parameters, there must be regional differences in prices. Reliable data on regional price differences are not always abundant, and verifying whether preference parameters change with regional and temporal differences is a difficult task. Moreover, in discussions on price indices, preferences are mostly assumed to be constant, and attempts to measure prices assuming different preferences across regions and nations are not numerous. Therefore, the assumption that the structural parameters in the Engel curve are common across regions, individuals, and time points may seem strong, but it is consistent with standard price index analysis. Logan (2009) criticized the studies by Costa (2001) for attributing all model specification errors to CPI bias and noted that most of the significant biases found by Costa (2001) disappear when allowing for changes in the impact of family composition on food expenditure over time.

Criticizing the AIDS model, (12.1), is not difficult. First, although the AIDS model is indeed a demand function derived from a second-order approximation of any expenditure function, the approximation is merely local and not global. Therefore, while it may be suitable for analyzing similar households or short-term time series, the deviation from the "true" expenditure function can become non-negligible in analyses with significantly different income levels or over long periods. Part of this criticism is mitigated by Banks et al. (1997), which added a quadratic term for income, but price elasticity remains a local approximation. A more fundamental criticism is that very important information, such as consumption-saving choices, home production, and imputed rent, is often omitted when estimating the AIDS model. For example, suppose a consumption tax rate increase is unexpectedly announced to take effect next month. Households would increase their purchases of durable goods and storable food items before the tax rate increase, temporarily increasing total expenditure. Then, even if relative prices and income levels remain constant, the Engel coefficient using total consumption expenditure would decrease. This decrease in the Engel coefficient due to pre-tax rate increase demand would appear as if it resulted from an overestimation in official price statistics due to the Engel coefficient-based approach. Many pieces of information that significantly affect household consumption behavior but are missing in the data are likely to exist. Shifts in the Engel coefficient caused by these factors are all considered as resulting from CPI measurement errors, a reasoning that is likely to be unacceptable to those compiling official statistics. A step to estimate the components of systematic residuals in estimations that are due to CPI measurement errors is necessary, but analyzing them with existing data is almost insurmountably difficult.

Hamilton (2001) and Almås (2012) were both published in *the American Economic Review*, and Costa (2001) in *the Journal of Political Economy*, truly top journals referred to as the "top five" in the field of economics. The impact of multiple papers being published in these top journals is significant, and numerous studies are currently being conducted. While there are now a vast number of papers on price measurement using the Engel curve, the names of leading researchers who have specialized in analyzing price indices, such as Erwin Diewert, Prasada Rao, Bert Balk, Robert Hill, and Mick Silver, are absent, and their papers rarely cite these studies. The time dummies in the estimation of the Engel curve represent shifts in the constant term, essentially the time variation of residuals, or what's left over from the estimation. The approach of interpreting specification errors in the estimation of the Engel curve as CPI measurement errors, adopted by these researchers, is understandably hard for price index researchers, who have collected numerous commodity prices and analyzed their aggregation methods with great effort, to accept. However, the fact that their research has been published in numerous top journals strongly suggests a significant divergence between traditional index number theory researchers and other economists. While it is unlikely that price measurement using the Engel curve will become the mainstream method in national statistical offices in the near future, the issues it raises are significant.

References

Almås, I., Beatty, T. K. M., & Crossley, T. F. (2019). Lost in Translation: What Do Engel Curves Tell Us about the Cost of Living? ESCoE Discussion Paper, 2019-09.

Almås, I. (2012). International income inequality: Measuring PPP bias by estimating Engel curves for food. *American Economic Review, 102*(2), 1093–1117.

Banks, J., Blundell, R., & Lewbel, A. (1997). Quadratic Engel curves and consumer demand. *Review of Economics and Statistics, 79*(4), 527–539.

Beatty, T. K. M., & Larsen, E. R. (2005). Using Engel curves to estimate bias in the Canadian CPI as a cost of living index. *The Canadian Journal of Economics, 38*(2), 482–499.

Chai, A., & Moneta, A. (2010). Retrospectives engel curves. *Journal of Economic Perspectives, 24*(1), 225–240.

Costa, D. (2001). Estimating real income in the United States from 1888 to 1994: Correcting CPI bias using Engel curves. *Journal of Political Economy, 109*(6), 1288–1310.

Deaton, A., & Muellbauer, J. (1980). An almost ideal demand system. *American Economic Review, 70*(3), 312–326.

Diewert, W. E. (1976). Exact and superlative index numbers. *Journal of Econometrics, 4*(2), 115–145.

Engel, E. (1857). Die Productions- und Consumtionsverhaltnisse des Königreichs Sachsen. In F. von Holtzendorff & L. Brentno (Eds.), Zeitschrift des Statistischen Buireaus des Königlich-Sachsischen, Ministerium des Innern, 8(9), pp. 1–54, Reprinted as an Appendix to Engel, E. (1895) "Die Lebenskosten Belgischer Arbeiter Familien Frfther und Jetzt," Bulletin de l'Institut International de Statistique, Tome IX, Premiere Livraison.

Hamilton, B. W. (2001). Using Engel's Law to estimate CPI bias. *American Economic Review, 91*(3), 619–630.

Higa, K. (2013). Estimating Upward Bias in the Japanese CPI Using Engel's Law. Global COE Hi-Stat Discussion Paper Series, No. 295, Hitotsubashi University.

Logan, T. (2009). Are Engel curve estimates of CPI bias biased? *Historical Methods, 42*(3), 97–110.

Nakamura, L. (1996). Is U.S. Economic Performance Really That Bad? Federal Reserve Bank of Philadelphia Working Paper, No. 95- 21/R.

Nakamura, E., Steinsson, J., & Liu, M. (2016). Are Chinese growth and inflation too smooth? Evidence from Engel curves. *American Economic Journal: Macroeconomics, 8*(3), 113–144.

Oulton, N. (2008). Chain indices of the cost-of-living and the path-dependence problem: An empirical solution. *Journal of Econometrics, 144*(1), 306–324.
Zimmerman, C. C. (1932). Ernst Engel's law of expenditures for food. *Quarterly Journal of Economics, 47*(1), 78–101.

13 Future Directions

Abstract

This final chapter discusses the future prospects and expectations for index and aggregation theory analysis, highlighting the gap between academic researchers and official statistics producers. It emphasizes the need for indices grounded in economic theory and addresses the challenges in their practical implementation. Traditional cost-of-living indices assume homothetic preferences, but recent studies stress the importance of non-homothetic preferences, which consider varying income elasticities and are crucial for analyzing income inequalities. The chapter also explores significant quality improvements in durable goods in the long run and the difficulties in measuring these improvements using traditional methods, suggesting the potential role of Artificial Intelligence and machine learning. Furthermore, it highlights the unrealistic assumption of fixed consumer preferences in standard cost-of-living indices, advocating for indices that account for changing preferences. It proposes creating different price indices for various households or regions to accurately measure income and consumption disparities, noting the significance of detailed household consumption data. The chapter concludes by emphasizing the importance of index number theory in the practical world and the need for more researchers specializing in this field. It calls for integrating economic theory with data aggregation and encourages researchers to become not only users but also makers of indices. This ongoing research and collaboration between academia and statistical offices are essential for developing accurate and theoretically sound indices.

13.1 Challenges in Index Number and Aggregation Theory

When conducting economic analyses, especially those involving models with economic agents' decision-making such as utility maximization or profit maximization, the corresponding data often comes in aggregated form. Even in household-level or firm-level analyses, variables like food expenditure or labor input are typically

N. Abe, *Price Index Numbers*, Springer Texts in Business and Economics,
https://doi.org/10.1007/978-981-97-6305-4_13

aggregated to prevent the model from becoming too unwieldy to be practical. Like other fields, economics has become specialized. Those who analyze models and those who construct economic index numbers are often separate in today's context. The gap between index makers and index users is likely to persist. Typically, national statistical offices or international organizations undertake the role of the former. In these settings, economic theory seldom takes precedence, and indices with an economic foundation, like the cost-of-living index, are rarely produced. This poses a potentially serious problem because if academic researchers, as index users, employ data created through non-economic aggregation methods for refined model analysis, a significant discrepancy between the data and the model might arise.

As emphasized in this book, numerous unresolved issues remain in current index and aggregation theory. Even superlative indices, considered excellent in the 1970s, require caution in their use with today's high-frequency data. What kind of indices should we create? Can they be implemented in the statistical practices of various countries? What problems arise with traditional indices? These are critical issues for academic researchers involved in index creation. In academic analysis, researchers can freely explore without considering social implementation, i.e., adoption by national statistical offices as official statistics. They can employ complex nonlinear solutions and iterative processes that take time to converge for refined analysis. On the other hand, for statistical offices which are required to produce official statistics monthly, it is natural to hesitate to continuously run nonlinear models with uncertain convergence. A perpetual divergence exists between analyses aimed at practical implementation and those expanding the frontiers of academia.

Fortunately, there is active exchange between those engaged in official statistics and academic researchers in the field of price index number theory and construction. Various conferences and research meetings, such as the biennial Ottawa meeting on price statistics, organized around price indices by international institutions like the United Nations, the World Bank, and the International Statistical Institute (ISI), continue efforts to minimize gap between academia and official statistics.

This chapter provides a brief explanation of index research topics not fully covered in this book but currently being actively analyzed, along with the author's aspirations for future index research.

13.2 Introduction of Non-Homothetic Preferences

The economic theory of price indices presented in this book assumes homothetic preferences in most cases. The Törnqvist index becomes an index for special circumstances with non-homothetic preferences, but generally assumes the same price index between high- and low-income earners. The assumption of homothetic preferences imposes a very strong assumption that the income elasticity of each good is 1. As seen in Chap. 12, the food expenditure ratio is usually a decreasing function of income (Engel's law), contradicting the assumption of homothetic preferences. Therefore, considering non-homothetic preferences is crucial, especially when analyzing inequalities. Recent publications in *Econometrica* by Handbury (2021) and in *the Quarterly Journal of Economics* by Baqaee and Burstein (2023), though different in approach, both emphasize price aggregation with non-homothetic preferences. Handbury (2021) divides people's purchasing behavior into several stages, further separating grocery spending from other expenditures. For grocery spending, a CES-type utility function as developed in this book is assumed, but non-homothetic preferences introduced for non-grocery purchasing behavior, using income as a proxy, successfully make the price index dependent on income levels. Although complex nonlinear estimation is required, the analysis aims to closely align with standard cost-of-living indices and rely on observable data, attracting attention among index researchers. On the other hand, Baqaee and Burstein (2023) rely on the Divisia index, focusing primarily on welfare comparisons. As discussed in this chapter, the Divisia index can be defined under non-homothetic preferences and has potential applications across various fields. However, the extent to which it retains the properties of a true cost-of-living index when approximated discretely remains questionable. For now, implementing either of these proposals into official statistics may take time, but considering non-homothetic preferences when analyzing price increases and income disparities seem natural, and research is expected to continue.

13.3 Quality Evaluation of Durable Consumer Goods

The quality improvement in durable consumer goods, especially recent innovations in home appliances, is remarkable. New products that significantly reduce household chores while enhancing the quality of life, such as drum washing machines, automatic vacuum cleaners, dishwashers, microwaves, and automatic cookers, are introduced almost yearly. Greenwood et al. (2021) argue that durable consumer goods prices in the United States have decreased by an annual rate of 5% from 1880 to 2020, significantly impacting domestic production activities in American households. The impact of introducing electricity to homes, enabling long-term food preservation with refrigerators, or significantly reducing laundry time with electric washing machines is indeed significant, but such improvements in durable goods are usually measured as changes in the durable goods price index. How much improvement has there been in the quality of durable consumer goods? As discussed in Chap. 9, national statistical offices employ hedonic methods for quality adjustment of durable consumer goods, but these methods face many theoretical and practical challenges. Firstly, when quality-adjusted prices measured monthly using the hedonic method are chained, drift can occur. This would be particularly important when using long-term series, as in Greenwood et al. (2021). The next issue is handling entirely new products incomparable to traditional ones. The hedonic method is principally suited for comparisons between products with similar performance and is not intended for comparing state-of-the-art drum washing machines with ancient washboards. How should the quality of a drum washing machine introduced into a world with only washboards be measured? How should the welfare change in a household that purchases a television in a world with only radios be measured? Of course, this is not a new problem, but many studies are conducted yearly on price measurement of durable consumer goods, especially high-value items, proposing new methods. Particularly, recent methods utilizing Artificial Intelligence (AI) and machine learning are noteworthy. However, currently, these new methods mainly aim to mitigate existing methodological problems and do not enable the measurement of quality differences between washboards and drum washing machines. In essence, comparing economic welfare across different product spaces is not easy to discuss under standard microeconomics, and research is expected to continue in both academic and practical fields.

13.4 Differences in Preferences

Standard cost-of-living index theory assumes fixed consumer preferences. This assumption lacks persuasiveness when comparing seasonal fluctuations, long-term price comparisons, or comparisons between regions and nations. Although Redding and Redding and Weinstein (2020) have created a cost-of-living index for differing preferences, this index faces many challenges, particularly being undefined when the elasticity of substitution is less than 1, making it practically impossible to apply in cases of significant preference differences, such as between food and non-food items. Criticisms have been made by Martin (2022) and Kurtzon (2020) regarding the indeterminacy of index values due to Redding and Weinstein's assumption of cardinal utility functions. There is currently no consensus on the nature of the cost-of-living index for differing preferences. However, careful reading of Handbury (2021) and the now-classic paper by Feenstra (1994) reveal that their empirical analyses include preference shocks. While the model treats preferences as fixed, preference shocks are introduced as residuals in empirical analyses. It seems unlikely that anyone would dispute the inclusion of preference shocks in data. Thus, the remaining challenge is to define a convincing cost-of-living index, a task made difficult by factors like the replacement of goods. However, it is natural for many to feel discomfort with the assumption of identical preferences across all countries for price comparisons. The current question is how to solve or mitigate the many challenges faced by Redding and Weinstein (2020), or whether an entirely different approach is possible.

13.5 Other Aspects

Price indices should differ among households if preferences and incomes vary. When measuring income and consumption inequalities between households or regions, it would be ideal and consistent with microeconomic theory to create different price indices for each household or region and measure real income or consumption inequalities based on these. However, differences in prices between households are seldom considered in inequality research. Even in the representative consumption inequality study by Lise and Seitz (2011), a single price index is used to convert nominal consumption to real terms, without considering the possibility of different price changes for different income groups. However, with detailed household consumption data now available, it is not unlikely that price indices vary significantly between households, especially between low- and high-income households, potentially experiencing different inflation rates. Especially during the winter of 2022 to 2023, with surging energy prices, energy expenditures tend to increase globally, and like food expenditures, the proportion of energy spending tends to be higher in lower income households. This means that rising energy prices have a stronger impact on low-income households. Given the current availability of more detailed household consumption data and significant relative price movements between goods due to the COVID-19 pandemic and international conflicts, the differences in prices between households are likely to have increased. In macroeconomic analyses dealing with household consumption and labor or heterogeneous households, or in industrial organization theory analyzing competition between firms, researchers are expected to construct different consumption or production price indices for each household or firm and analyze real variables using these, rather than relying on macro-official statistics.

Column 7: The Relationship Between Academia and Practitioners in Index Research

In economics, particularly in macroeconomics, fiscal and public economics, there is a close connection with government economic policies, leading to active exchanges between university researchers and government agencies. However, the field of index number theory might be unique in having more than half of the participants in major conferences and workshops affiliated with government institutions. The International Working Group on Price Indices, known colloquially as the "Ottawa Group," meets biennially for a four-day conference on a wide range of topics related to price measurement. It attracts statisticians from government agencies worldwide and academic researchers, with discussions on pricing continuing into break times and evening meals. The conference is named after Ottawa, where the first meeting was held, but it has been hosted in various locations around the world, including Rome in 2022. According to Diewert (2004), such interaction between academia and practitioners was rare in the past and only became as we see it today after the late 1970s. The "Ottawa Group" meetings, starting with the first one in 1994, have significantly contributed to bridging the gap between academia and practitioners. When I attended the Ottawa Group meeting in 2022, I was impressed by the highly constructive discussions that unfolded, including the problems faced by statisticians from different countries, proposals from the academic community, and the exchange of questions. One concern, however, is the limited presence of Asian countries at the Ottawa Group meetings. Most reports are by statisticians from European and north American institutions or academic researchers. I hope for an increase in the number of research reports from countries in Africa, Asia, Oceania, and South America.

13.6 Final Remark

Few universities worldwide include index number theory in the curriculum at the undergraduate or graduate level. However, it remains a crucial field in practical applications. With the advent of so-called big data in the world of statistical practice, index and aggregation analysis are taken seriously by statistical bureaus in various countries. In the academic world, up until the mid-twentieth century, researchers like Samuelson and Clark, and later Diewert, Hall, and Deaton conducted many studies, but the number of researchers specializing in index number research in the twenty-first century is not as numerous as before. The gap between those who create index numbers and those who use them is widening. However, today's researchers have unprecedented access to microdata and retail transaction data. This allows for the aggregation of goods and prices in ways that align with economic theory, a feat that mid-twentieth-century researchers could not achieve. This access greatly enhances the accuracy of economic model analyses.

Despite sophisticated models and econometric methods, relying solely on aggregate data that is inconsistent with economic theory, such as household consumption expenditures deflated by the Laspeyres price index, can limit the potential for refined research. It is hoped that researchers, when analyzing economic models, will critically assess and use aggregation methods that best suit their analysis. The goal is for index users to eventually become index makers themselves.

References

Baqaee, D. R., & Burstein, A. (2023) Welfare and output with income effects and taste shocks. *The Quarterly Journal of Economics, 138*(2), 769–783.

Diewert, E. W. (2004). The Relationship of Academic Measurement Research and Official Statistics, 23rd Meeting of Nordic Statisticians.

Feenstra, R. C. (1994). New product varieties and the measurement of international prices. *American Economic Review, 84*(1), 157–177.

Greenwood, J., Guner, N., & Marto, R. (2021). The Great Transition: Kuznets Facts for Family-Economists. Working Papers wp2021_2105, CEMFI.

Handbury, J. (2021). Are poor cities cheap for everyone? Non-homotheticity and the cost of living across U.S. cities. *Econometrica, 89*(6), 2679–2715.

Kurtzon, G. (2020). The Problem with Normalizing Preferences that Change in a Cost-of-Living Index. BLS Working Paper, 534.

Lise, J., & Seitz, S. (2011). Consumption inequality and intra-household allocations. *The Review of Economic Studies, 78*(1), 328–355.

Martin, R. S. (2022) Revisiting taste change in cost-of-living measurement. *Journal of Economic and Social Measurement, 46*(2), 109–147.

Redding, S. J., & Weinstein, D. E. (2020). Measuring aggregate price indices with taste shocks: Theory and evidence for CES preferences. *Quarterly Journal of Economics, 135*(1), 503–560.

Bibliography

Abe, N. (2022). Measuring inflation under pandemic conditions': A comment. *Journal of Official Statistics, 38*(1), 295–300.

Abe, N. (2023). Bukka Shisu Gairon (The Theory of Price Index Number), in Japanese, Nihon Hyoron Sha.

Abe, N., Inoue, T., & Sato, H. (2022). Price index numbers under large-scale demand shocks: The Japanese experience of the COVID-19 pandemic. *Journal of Official Statistics, Sciendo, 38*(1), 301–317.

Abe, N., & Rao, D. S. P. (2019). Multilateral Sato-Vartia index for international comparisons of prices and real expenditures. *Economics Letters, 183*, 108535.

Abe, N., & Rao, D. S. P. (2020). Generalized logarithmic index numbers with demand shocks: Bridging the gap between theory and practice. RCESR Discussion Paper Series, DP20-1.

Abe, N., & Rao, D. S. P. (2022a). Transitivity, substitution bias and the fixed basket multilateral walsh index for international price and real expenditure comparisons, RCESR Discussion Paper Series, DP22-1.

Abe, N., & Rao, D. S. P. (2022b). The fixed basket multilateral walsh index for international price and real expenditure comparisons. *Economics Letters, 220*, 110857.

Abe, N., & Shiotani, K. (2014). Who faces higher prices an empirical analysis based on Japanese homescan data. *Asian Economic Policy Review, 9*(1), 94–115.

Ackland, R., Dowrick, S., & Freyens, B. (2013). Measuring global poverty: Why PPP methods matter. *Review of Economics and Statistics, 95*(3), 813–824.

Aczél, J. (1966). *Lectures on functional equations and their applications, 19*. Academic.

Aczél, J. (1987). *A short course for the functional equation*. Springer.

Aczél, J. (1990). Determining merged relative scores. *Journal of Mathematical Analysis and Applications, 150*(1), 20–40.

Afriat, S. N. (1977). *The price index*. Cambridge University Press.

Aguiar, M., & Hurst, E. (2007). Life-cycle prices and production. *American Economic Review, 97*(5), 1533–1559.

Allen, R. G. D. (1933). On the marginal utility of money and its application. *Economica, 40*, 186–209.

Allen, R. G. D. (1975). *Index numbers in economic theory and practice*. Routledge.

Allen, R. C., & Diewert, W. E. (1981). Direct versus implicit superlative index number formulae. *The Review of Economics and Statistics, 63*(3), 430–435.

Almås, I. (2012). International income inequality: Measuring PPP bias by estimating Engel curves for food. *American Economic Review, 102*(2), 1093–1117.

Almås, I., Beatty, T. K. M., & Crossley, T. F. (2019). Lost in translation: What do Engel curves tell us about the cost of living? ESCoE Discussion Paper, 2019-09.

N. Abe, *Price Index Numbers*, Springer Texts in Business and Economics,
https://doi.org/10.1007/978-981-97-6305-4

Aoki, M. (2001). Optimal monetary policy responses to relative-price changes. *Journal of Monetary Economics, 48*(1), 55–80.

Asian Development Bank (2021) 2017 International Comparison Program for Asia and the Pacific: Purchasing Power Parities and Real Expenditures - Results and Methodology. Asian Development Bank.

Atkinson, F. J. (1897). Silver prices in India. *Journal of the Royal Statistical Society, 60*(1), 84–147.

Australian Bureau of Statistics (2016). Making greater use of transactions data to compile the consumer price index. Information Paper 6401. 0. 60. 003.

Baqaee, D. R., & Burstein, A. (2023). Welfare and output with income effects and taste shocks. *The Quarterly Journal of Economics, 138*(2), 769–783.

Balassa, B. (1964). The purchasing-power parity doctrine: A reappraisal. *Journal of Political Economy, 72*(6), 584–596.

Balk, B. M. (1980). A method for constructing price indices for seasonal commodities. *Journal of the Royal Statistical Society A: General, 143*(1), 68–75.

Balk, B. M. (1989). Changing consumer preferences and the cost-of-living index: Theory and nonparametric expressions. *Journal of Economics, 50*(2), 157–169.

Balk, B. M. (1995). Axiomatic price index theory: A survey. *International Statistical Review / Revue Internationale de Statistique, 63*(1), 69–93.

Balk, B. M. (1996). Consistency-in-aggregation and Stuvel indices. *Review of Income and Wealth, 42*(3), 353–363.

Balk, B. M. (2005). Divisia price and quantity indices: 80 years after. *Statistica Neerlandica, 59*(2), 119–158.

Balk, B. M. (2008). *Price and quantity index numbers*. Cambridge University Press.

Balk, B. M., & Diewert, W. E. (2001). A Characterization of the Törnqvist Price Index. *Economics Letters, 72*(3), 279–281.

Ball, L., Carvalho, C., Evans, C., & Ricci, L. (2024). Weighted median inflation around the world: A measure of core inflation. *Journal of International Money and Finance., 142*, 103017. https://doi.org/10.1016/j.jimonfin.2024.103017

Banks, J., Blundell, R., & Lewbel, A. (1997). Quadratic Engel curves and consumer demand. *Review of Economics and Statistics, 79*(4), 527–539.

Barnett, W., & Choi, Ki. (2008). Operational identification of the complete class of superlative index numbers: An application of Galois, theory. *Journal of Mathematical Economics, 44*(7–8), 603–612.

Beatty, T. K. M., & Larsen, E. R. (2005). Using Engel curves to estimate bias in the Canadian CPI as a cost of living index. *The Canadian Journal of Economics, 38*(2), 482–499.

Białek, J. (2019). Remarks on Geo-logarithmic price indices. *Journal of Official Statistics, 35*(2), 287–317.

Białek, J. (2020). Basic statistics of Jevons and Carli indices under the GBM price model. *Journal of Official Statistics, 36*(4), 737–761.

Blinder, A. (1997). Commentary 1 on 'Measuring Short-Run Inflation for Central Bankers' by Stephan Cecchetti. *Federal Reserve Bank of St. Louis Review, 79*(3), 157–160.

Bodin, J. (1568). La Response de Maistre Jean Bodin Advocat en la Cour au Paradoxe de Monsieur de Malestroit, Touchant l'encherissement de ToutesChoses, & Le Moyen d'y Remedier. A Monsieur Prevost, Seigneur de Morsan, President pour le Roy en sa Cour de Parlemennt, Martin le Jeune. Paris, English Translation by Tudor, H., W. W. Dyson, and D. P O'Briedn (1997) Response to the Paradoxes of Malestroit. Primary Sources in Political Thought, 2, Bloomsbury Publishing Plc.

Bortkiewicz, L. V. (1923). Zweck und Struktur einer Preisindexzahl. *Nordisk Statistisk Tidsskrift, 2*, 369–408.

Boskin, M. J., Dulberger, E., Gordon, R., Griliches, Z., & Jorgenson, D. (1996). *Toward a more accurate measure of the cost of living*. Final Report to the Senate Finance Committee, December 4.

Broda, C., & Weinstein, D. E. (2010). Product creation and destruction: Evidence and price implications. *American Economic Review, 100*(3), 691–723.

Bryan, M. F., & Cecchetti, S. G. (1994). Measuring core inflation. In N. Gregory Mankiw (Eds.), *Monetary policy* (pp. 195–215). University of Chicago Press.

Bureau of Labor Statistics (BLS) (2001). The experimental CPI using geometric means (CPI-U-XG). Retrieved October 16, 2001 from https://web.archive.org/web/20081128080159/http://www.bls.gov/cpi/cpigmrp.htm

Carli, G. A. (1764). Del Valore e della Proporzione dei Metallic Monetati con i Generi in Italia Prima delle Scoperte dell'Indie col Confronto del Valore e della Proporzione de' Tempi Nostri, Lucca, Reprinted in a Series Dedicated to the Italian Economists in 1804.

Carluccio, J., Gautier, E., & Guilloux-Nefussi, S. (2023). Dissecting the impact of imports from low-wage countries on inflation. *European Economic Review, 160*, 104613.

Cassel, G. (1918). Abnormal deviations in international exchnages. *Economic Journak, 28*(112), 413–415.

Cavallo, A., Feenstra, R. C., & Inklaar, R. (2023). Product variety, the cost of living, and welfare across countries. *American Economic Journal: Macroeconomics, 15*(4), 40–66.

Caves, D. W., Christensen, L. R., & Diewert, W. E. (1982). The economic theory of index numbers and the measurement of input, output, and productivity. *Econometrica, 50*(6), 1393–1414.

Chai, A., & Moneta, A. (2010). Retrospectives Engel curves. *Journal of Economic Perspectives, 24*(1), 225–240.

Chessa, A. G. (2015). *Towards a generic price index method for scanner data in the Dutch CPI.* Ottawa Group Meeting, 20–22 May 2015. Japan: Urayasu City.

Christensen, L. R., Jorgenson, D. W., & Lau, L. J. (1971). Conjugate duality and the transcendental logarithmic production function. *Econometrica, 39*(4), 255–256.

Clark, G. N. (1936). The occasion of Fleetwood's 'Chronicon Preciosum'. *English Historical Review, 51*(204), 686–690.

Clements, K. W., & Izan, H. Y. (1987). The measurement of inflation: A stochastic approach. *Journal of Business and Economic Statistics, 5*(3), 339–350.

Clements, K. W., Izan, H. Y., & Selvanathan, E. A. (2006). Stochastic index numbers: A review. *International Statistical Review, 74*(2), 235–270.

Coondoo, D., Majumder, A., & Chattopadhyay, S. (2011). Estimating spatial consumer price indices through Engel curve analysis. *Review of Income and Wealth, 57*(1), 138–155.

Costa, D. (2001). Estimating real income in the United States from 1888 to 1994: Correcting CPI bias using Engel curves. *Journal of Political Economy, 109*(6), 1288–1310.

Court, A. T. (1939). Hedonic price indexes with automotive examples. *The dynamics of automobile demand* (pp. 99–117). New York: The General Motors Corporation.

Crawford, I., & Neary, J. P. (2023). New characteristics and hedonic price index numbers. *Review of Economics and Statistics, 105*(3), 665–682.

Crone, T. M., Khettry, N. N. K., Mester, L. J., & Novak, J. A. (2013). Core measures of inflation as predictors of total inflation. *Journal of Money, Credit and Banking, 45*(2/3), 505–519.

Cysne, R. P. (2003). Divisia index, inflation, and welfare. *Journal of Money, Credit and Banking, 35*(2), 221–238.

Darwin, G. (1875). Theory of exchange value. *Fortnightly Review, 243*.

de Haan, J. (2020). *The CES price index, index number theory and official price measurement.* Presented at EMG Workshop 2019.

de Haan, J., & Van der Grient, H. A. (2011). Eliminating chain drift in price indexes based on scanner data. *Journal of Econometrics, 161*(1), 36–46.

de Haan, J., & Diewert, W. E. (2017). Quality change, hedonic regression and price index construction. Deutsche Bundesbank.

de Haan, J., & Deaton, A. (2010). Price indexes, inequality, and the measurement of world poverty. *American Economic Review, 100*(1), 5–34.

Deaton, A., & Heston, A. (2010). Understanding PPPs and PPP-based national accounts. *American Economic Journal: Macroeconomics, 2*(4), 1–35.

Deaton, A., & Aten, B. (2014). Trying to understand the PPPs in ICP2011: Why are the results so different? NBER Working Papers, No. 20244.

Deaton, A., & Dupriez, O. (2011). Purchasing power parity exchange rates for the global poor. *American Economic Journal: Applied Economics, 3*, 137–166.

Deaton, A., & Muellbauer, J. (1980). An almost ideal demand system. *American Economic Review, 70*(3), 312–326.

Debreu, G. (1959). *Theory of value*. Wiley.

Deartment of Mint (1881). Report of the Director of the Mint on the Production of the Precious Metals.

Diewert, W. E. (1976). Exact and superlative index numbers. *Journal of Econometrics, 4*(2), 115–145.

Diewert, W. E. (1978). Superlative index numbers and consistency in aggregation. *Econometrica, 46*(4), 883–900.

Diewert, W. E. (1992). Fisher ideal output, input, and productivity indexes revisited. *Journal of Productivity Analysis, 3*(3), 211–248.

Diewert, W. E. (1993). The early history of price index research. In W. E. Diewert & A. O. Nakamura (Eds.), *Essays in index number theory* (Vol. 1, pp. 33–65).

Diewert, W. E. (1995). On the stochastic approach to index numbers. University of British Columbia, Department of Economics Discussion Paper No. 95-31.

Diewert, W. E. (2001). The consumer price index and index number purpose. *Journal of Economic and Social Measurement, 27*(3–4), 167–248.

Diewert, W. E. (2003). Hedonic regressions: A consumer theory approach. In R. C. Feenstra & M. D. Shapiro (Eds.), *Scanner data and price indexes, 61* (pp. 317–348). University of Chicago Press.

Diewert, E. W. (2004). The relationship of Academic measurement research and official statistics. In *23rd Meeting of Nordic Statisticians*.

Diewert, W. E. (2005) Some issues concerning index number theory. Paper Presented at the ESRI 'Conference on the Next Steps for the Japanese System of National Accounts: Towards More Accurate Measurement and More Comprehensive Accounts, Held in Tokyo, March 24–25, 2005.

Diewert, W. E. (2012). Consumer price statistics in the UK, Office for National Statistics, the Government Statistical Agency for the UK.

Diewert, W. E. (2018). Scanner data, elementary price indexes and the chain drift problem. Discussion Paper 18–06. Vancouver School of Economics: University of British Columbia.

Diewert, W. E. (2021a). *The axiomatic or test approach to index number theory* (p. 3). Chapter: Consumer Price Index Theory.

Diewert, W. E. (2021b). *The chain drift problem and multilateral indexes* (p. 7). Chapter: Consumer Price Index Theory.

Diewert, W. E., Fox, K. J., & Ivancic, L. (2011). Scanner data, time aggregation and the construction of price indexes. *Journal of Econometrics, 161*(1), 24–35.

Diewert, W. E., & Fox, K. J. (2022). Measuring inflation under pandemic conditions. *Journal of Official Statistics, 38*(1), 255–285.

Diewert, W. E., & Zelenyuk, V. (2023). On the Problem of the Purchasing Power of Money by A. A. Konus and S. S. Byushgens: Translation and Commentary. *Journal of Productivity Analysis*. https://doi.org/10.1007/s11123-023-00696-x

Divisia, F. (1925). L'indice Monétaire et la Théorie de la Monnaie. Revue d'Économie Politique, XXXIX, Nos. 4, 5, 6, pp. 842–61, 980–1008, 1121–1151.

Divisia, F. (1952). *Exposés d'Économique, 1*. Dunod.

Dixit, A. K., Stiglitz, J., & E. (1977). Monopolistic competition and optimum product diversity. *American Economic Review, 67*(3), 297–308.

Drobisch, M. W. (1871). Über Mittelgrossen und die Anwendbarkeit derselben auf die Berechnung des Steigens und Sinkens des Geldwerths. Berichte über die Verhandlungen der Königlich Sächsischen Gesellschaft der Wissebschaften zu Leipzig, Bd.XXIII (pp. 25–48).

Dutot, N. (1738). Reflexions Politiques sur les Finances et le Commerce, A La Haye: Vaillant and Nicolas Prévost, English Translation: Political Reflections Upon the Finances and Commerce of France, A. Millar, 1739.

Eckstein, O. (1981). *Core inflation*. Prentice Hall.

Edgeworth, F. Y. (1888). Some new methods of measuring variation in general prices. *Journal of the Royal Statistical Society, 51*(2), 346–368.

Edgeworth, F. Y. (1889). Measurement of change in value of money. In *The Third Memorandum Presented to the British Association for the Advancement of Science*; Reprinted as pp. 259–297 in Papers Relating to Political Economy, 1, New York: Burt Franklin, 1925.

Edgeworth, F. Y. (1896). A defense of index-numbers. *Economic Journal, 6*(21), 132–142.

Edgeworth, F. Y. (1923). The doctrine of index-numbers according to Mr. Correa Walsh. *Economic Journal, 33*(131), 343–351.

Edgeworth, F. Y. (1925). *Papers relating to political economy 1, London*. Ltd: Macmillan and Co.

Edgeworth, F. Y. (1925). The plurality of index-numbers. *Economic Journal, 35*(139), 379–388.

Edo, A. & Melitz, J. (2019). The primary cause of european inflation in 1500–1700: Precious metals or population? The English Evidence, CEPII Working Paper 2019-10.

Ehrlich, G., Haltiwanger, J. C., Jarmin, R. S., Johnson, D., Olivares, E., Pardue, L. W., Shapiro, M. D., & Zhao, L. (2023). Quality adjustment at scale: Hedonic vs. exact demand-based price indices. NBER Working Papers 31309, National Bureau of Economic Research, Inc.

Eichhorn, W. (1978). Functional equations in economics, Ser. Applied Mathematics and Computation; No.11, Addison-Wesley Publishing Co., London.

Eichhorn, W., & Voeller, J. (1976). *Theory of the price index: Fisher's test approach and generalizations*. Lecture notes in economics and mathematical systems (Vol. 140). Springer.

Éltet, O., & Köves, P. (1964). On an index computation problem in international comparisons, (in Hungarian). *Statistztikai Szemle, 42*, 507–18.

Engel, E. (1857). Die Productions- und Consumtionsverhaltnisse des Königreichs Sachsen. In F. von Holtzendorff, & L. Brentno (Eds.), Zeitschrift des Statistischen Buireaus des Königlich-Sachsischen, Ministerium des Innern, 8(9), pp. 1-54, Reprinted as an Appendix to Engel, E. (1895) "Die Lebenskosten Belgischer Arbeiter Familien Frfther und Jetzt," Bulletin de l'Institut International de Statistique, Tome IX, Premiere Livraison.

European Commission, International Monetary Fund, Organization for Economic Co-operation and Development, United Nations, and World Bank (2009) System of National Accounts 2008, New York.

Eurostat (1999) Compendium of HICP Reference Documents: Harmonisation of Price Indices, Eurostat, January.

Eurostat (2018) Harmonised Index of Consumer Prices (HICP) methodological manual.

Eusepi, S., Hobijn, B., & Tambalotti, A. (2011). CONDI: A cost-of-nominal-distortions index. *American Economic Journal: Macroeconomics, 3*(3), 53–91.

Fattore, M. (2010). Axiomatic properties of geo-logarithmic price indices. *Journal of Econometrics, 156*(2), 344–353.

Feenstra, R. C. (1994). New product varieties and the measurement of international prices. *American Economic Review, 84*(1), 157–177.

Feenstra, R. C. (1995). Exact Hedonic price indices. *Review of Economics and Statistics, 77*(4), 634–653.

Feenstra, R. C., Inklaar, R., & Timmer, M. (2015). The next generation of the Penn world table. *American Economic Review, 105*(10), 3150–3182.

Feenstra, R. C., & Reinsdorf, M. B. (2000). An exact priceiindex for the almost ideal demand system. *Economics Letters, 66*(2), 159–162.

Feenstra, R. C., & Reinsdorf, M. B. (2007). Should index numbers have standard errors? Theory and application to Asian growth. In E. R. Berndt & C. R. Hulten (Eds.), *Hard-to-measure goods and services: Essays in honor of Zvi Griliches* (pp. 483–513). University of Chicago Press.

Fisher, F. M., & Shell, K. (1971). Taste and quality change in the pure theory of the true cost of-living index. In Z. Griliches (Ed.), *Price indexes and quality change*. Harvard University Press.

Fisher, I. (1922). *The making of index numbers*. Houghton Mifflin Company.

Fisher, W. C. (1913). The tabular standard in Massachusetts history. *Quarterly Journal of Economics, 27*(3), 417–454.

Fleetwood, W. (1707). Chronicon preciosum: Or, an account of english money, the price of corn, and other commodities, for the last 600 years: In a Letter to a Student in the University of Oxford, Printed for Charles Harper.

Frisch, R. (1930). Necessary and sufficient conditions regarding the form of an index number which shall meet certain of Fisher's tests. *American Statistical Association Journal, 25*(172), 397–406.

Frisch, R. (1936). Annual survey of general economic theory: The problem of index numbers. *Econometrica, 4*(1), 1–38.

Funke, H., & Voeller, J. (1978). A note on the characterization of Fisher's 'ideal index. In W. Eichhorn, R. Henn, O. Opitz, & R. W. Shephard (Eds.), Theory and applications of economic indices. Physica-Verlag HD (pp 177–181).

Funke, H., Hacker, G., & Voeller, J. (1979). Fisher's circular test reconsidered. Schweizerische Zeitschrift fur Volkswirtschaft and Statistik, 1979-IV-2 (pp. 677–688).

Furuta, S., Hatayama, Y., Kawakami, A., & Oh, Y. (2021). New hedonic quality adjustment method using sparse estimation. *Monetary and Economic Studies, Institute for Monetary and Economic Studies, Bank of Japan, 39*, 109–142.

Gábor-Tóth, E., & Vermeulen, P. (2019). Elementary index bias: Evidence for the Euro area from a large scanner dataset. *German Economic Review, 20*(4), e618–e656.

Geary, R. C. (1958). A note on the comparison of exchange rates and purchasing power between countries. *Journal of the Royal Statistical Society, Series A: General, 121*(1), 97–99.

Gershenkron, A. (1951). *A dollar index for soviet machinary output, 1927–28 to 1937*. Rand Corporation.

Gibson, J., & Scobie, G. (2010). Using Engel curves to estimate CPI bias in a small, open, inflation-targeting economy. *Applied Financial Economics, 20*(17), 1327–1335.

Gibson, J., Stillman, S., & Le, T. (2008). CPI Bias and real living standards in Russia during the transition. *Journal of Development Economics, 87*(1), 140–160.

Gibson, J., Le, T., & Kim, B. (2017). Prices, Engel curves, and time-space deflation: Impacts on poverty and inequality in Vietnam. *The World Bank Economic Review, 31*(2), 504–530.

Gini, C. (1931). On the circular test of index numbers. *Metron, 2*, 3–24.

Goethe, J. W. von, (2007). Faust (Part II), Wordsworth Classics of World Literature, 2007 (first published in 1832)

Gorman, W. M. (1956). A possible procedure for analysing quality diferentials in the eggs market. *Review of Economic Studies, 47*(5), 843–856.

Great Britain. Royal Commission to Inquire into the Depression of Trade and Industry (1986) Third Report of the Royal Commission Appointed to Inquire into the Depression of Trade and Industry: with Minutes of Evidence and Appendix, Eyre and Spottiswoode.

Greenwood, J., Guner, N. & Marto, R. (2021). The great transition: Kuznets facts for family-economists. Working Papers wp2021_2105, CEMFI.

Griliches, Z. (1961). Hedonic price indexes for automobiles: An econometric of quality change. The Price statistics of the federal government, Chapter 3, Government Printing Office (pp. 173–196).

Groshen, E. L., & Moyer, B. C., Aizcorbe, A. M., Bradley, R., & Friedman, D. M. (2017). How government statistics adjust for potential biases from quality change and new goods in an age of digital technologies: A view from the trenches. *The Journal of Economic Perspectives, 31*(2), 187–210.

Haberler, G. (1927). Der Sinn der Indexzahlen: eine Untersuchung uber den Begriff des Preisniveaus und die Methoden seiner Messung, 134 S. Tübingen: J. C. B. Mohr (Paul Siebeck).

Hajargasht, G., & Rao, D. S. P. (2019). Multilateral index number systems for international price comparisons: Properties, existence and uniqueness. *Journal of Mathematical Economics, 83*, 36–47.

Hajargasht, G., Rao, D. S. P., & Valadkhani, A. (2019). Reliability of basic heading PPPs. *Economics Letters, 180*(C), 102–107.

Hamilton, B. W. (2001). Using Engel's law to estimate CPI bias. *American Economic Review, 91*(3), 619–630.

Hamilton, E. J. (1928). American treasure and Andalusian prices, 1503–1660: A study in the Spanish price revolution. *Journal of Economic and Business History, 1*, 1–35.

Handbury, J. (2021). Are poor cities cheap for everyone? Non-homotheticity and the cost of living across U.S. Cities. *Econometrica, 89*(6), 2679–2715.

Handbury, J., & Weinstein, D. E. (2015). Goods prices and availability in cities. *Review of Economic Studies, 82*(1), 258–296.

Hasan, F. (2016). The price of development: The Penn-Balassa-Samuelson effect revisited. *Journal of International Economics, 102*(C), 291–309.

Hicks, J. R., & Allen, R. G. D. (1934). A reconsideration of the theory of value: Part I. *Economica, 1*(1), 52–76.

Higa, K. (2013). Estimating upward bias in the Japanese CPI using Engel's law. Global COE Hi-Stat Discussion Paper Series, No. 295, Hitotsubashi University.

Hill, R. (1999). International comparisons using spanning trees. In A. Heston & R. E. Lipsey (Eds.), *International and interarea comparisons of income, output, and prices* (pp. 109–120). University of Chicago Press.

Hill, R. (1999). Comparing price levels across countries using minimum-spanning trees. *Review of Economics and Statistics, 81*(1), 135–142.

Hill, R. (2004). Constructing price indexes across space and time: The case of the European union. *American Economic Review, 94*(5), 1379–1140.

Hill, R. (2006). Superlative index numbers: Not all of them are super. *Review of Income and Wealth, 52*(2), 309–325.

Hill, R. (2006). When does chaining reduce the Paasche-Laspeyres spread? An application to scanner data. *Review of Income and Wealth, 52*(2), 309–325.

Hill, R. (2018). Peter Hill (1929–2017). In Memoriam. *Review of Income and Wealth, 64*(1), 239–242.

Hill, R., & Hill, T. P. (2009). Recent developments in the international comparison of prices and real output. *Macroeconomic Dynamics, 13*(S2), 194–217.

Hill, T. P. (1993). Price and volume measures. Chapter 16 in System of National Accounts 1993, Eurostat, IMF, OECD, UN and World Bank (pp. 379–406).

Hotelling, H. (1929). Stability in competition. *Economic Journal, 39*(153), 41–57.

Hottman, C. J., Redding, S. J., & Weinstein, D. E. (2016). Quantifying the sources of firm heterogeneity. *Quarterly Journal of Economics, 131*(3), 1291–1364.

Ichimura, S. (1951). A critical note on the definition of related goods. *Review of Economic Studies, 18*(3), 179–183.

Inklaar, R., & Rao, D. S. P. (2017). Cross-country income levels over time: Did the developing world suddenly become much richer. *American Economic Journal: Macroeconomics, 9*(1), 265–290.

International Labour Organization (ILO), IMF, OECD, Eurostat, United Nations and World Bank (2004a) Consumer Price Index Manual: Theory and Practice, International Labour Organization.

International Labour Organization (ILO), Eurostat, IMF, OECD, World Bank, UN (2004b) Producer Price Index Manual: Theory and Practice. International Monetary Fund.

International Monetary Fund (IMF) (2010) System of National Accounts Manual 2017 edition.

International Monetary Fund (IMF) (2018) Quarterly National Accounts 2008

International Monetary Fund (IMF), Eurostat, United Nations, OECD, and World Bank (2020) Consumer Price Index Manual: Concepts and Methods.

Ivancic, L., Diewert, W. E., & Fox, K. J. (2011). Scanner data, time aggregation and the construction of price indexes. *Journal of Econometrics, 161*(1), 24–35.

Jevons, W. S. (1861). LIV. On the deficiency of rain in an elevated Rain-gauge, as Caused by Wind. *London, Edinburgh, and Dublin Philosophical Magazine and Journal of Science, 22*(149), 421–433.

Jevons, W. S. (1863). A serious fall in the value of gold ascertained and its social effects set forth, Edward Stanford.

Jevons, W. S. (1865). On the variation of prices and the value of currency since 1728. *Journal of the Royal Statistical Society, 28*, 294–320 (+1-4).

Jevons, W. S. (1884). *Investigations in currency and finance*. London: Macmillan and Co.

Johnson, S., Larson, W., Papageorgiou, C., & Subramanian, A. (2013). Is newer better? Penn world table revisions and their impact on growth estimates. *Journal of Monetary Economics, 60*(2), 255–274.

Jorgenson, D. W., & Griliches, Z. (1967). The explanation of productivity change. *Review of Economic Studies, 34*(3), 249–283.

Kendall, M. G. (1969). Studies in the history of probability and statistics, XXI. The early history of index numbers. *Revue de l'Institut International de Statistique / Review of the International Statistical Institute, 37*(1), 1–12.

Keynes, J. M. (1909). The method of index numbers with special reference to the measurement of general exchange value. In The Collected Writings of John Maynard Keynes. Macmillan (pp. 50–156).

Keynes, J. M. (1930). *Treatise on money, 1*. Macmillan.

Keynes, J. M. (1936). *The general theory of employment, interest, and money*. Macmillan.

Khamis, S. H. (1970). Properties and conditions for the existence of a new type of index numbers. *Sankhyd: The Indian Journal of Statistics Series B, 32*(1/2), 81–98.

Khamis, S. H. (1972). A new system of index numbers for national and international purposes. *Journal of the Royal Statistics Society, Series A: General, 135*(1), 96–121.

Kitao, S., & Nakakuni, K. (2023). On the trends of technology, family formation, and women's time allocations. mimeo.

Kiyosue, T. (1975). The life of Bodin (1) (Bodan no Shogai 1) in Japanese). *Hokudai Hougaku Ronshu*, 03–26: *25*(4), 65–148.

Konüs, A. A. (1939). The problem of the true index of the cost of living. Translated from the Russian 1924. *Econometrica, 7*(1), 10–29.

Krsinich, F. (2016). The FEWS index: Fixed effects with a window splice. *Journal of Official Statistics, 32*(2), 375–404.

Krtscha, M. (1984). A characterization of the Edgeworth-Marshall Index. *Methods of Operations Research, 48*, 127–135.

Krugman, P. (1980). Scale economies, product differentiation, and the pattern of trade. *American Economic Review, 70*(5), 950–959.

Kurabayashi, Y., & Sakuma, I. (1990). *Studies in international comparisons of real product and prices*. Kinokuniya Company, LTD.

Kurtzon, G. (2020). The problem with normalizing preferences that change in a cost-of-living index. BLS Working Paper, 534.

Lancaster, K. J. (1966). A new approach to consumer theory. *Journal of Political Economy, 74*(2), 132–157.

Lancaster, K. J. (1979). *Variety, equity and efficiency*. Columbia University Press.

Laspeyres, E. (1864). Hamburger Waarenpreise 1850-1863 und die Kalifornisch-Australischen Geldentdeckung Seit 1848. Jahrbücher für Nationalökonomie. *Statistik, 3*, 81–118, 209–236.

Laspeyres, E. (1871). Die Berechnung einer mittleren Waarenpreissteigerung. *Jahrbucher für Nationalökonomie und Statistik, 16*, 296–315.

Laughlin, J. L. (1887). Gold and prices since 1873. *The Quarterly Journal of Economics, 1*(3), 319–355.

Laughlin, J. L. (1887). Prices in the United States. *The Quarterly Journal of Economics, 1*(3), 397–399.

Lehr, J. (1885). Beitrage zur Statistik der Preise: Insbesondere des Geldes und des Holzes, Frankfurt a. M.: J. D. Sauerlander Verlag.

Lent, J., & Dorfman, A. (2009). Using a weighted average of base period price indexes to approximate a superlative index. *Journal of official Statistics, 25*(1), 139–149.

Leontief, W. (1936). Composite commodities and the problem of index numbers. *Econometrica, 4*(1), 39–59.

Lerner, A. P. (1935). A note on the theory of price index numbers. *Review of Economic Studies, 3*(1), 50–56.

Levell, P. (2012). A winning formula? Elementary indices in the retail prices index. IFS Working Paper, W12/22.

Lippe, P. V. D. (2007). *Index theory and price statistics*. Peter Lang Pub Inc.

Lise, J., & Seitz, S. (2011). Consumption inequality and intra-household allocations. *The Review of Economic Studies, 78*(1), 328–355.

Lloyd, P. J. (1975). Substitution effects and biases in nontrue price indices. *American Economic Review, 65*(3), 301–313.

Logan, T. (2009). Are Engel curve estimates of CPI bias biased? *Historical Methods, 42*(3), 97–110.

Lowe, J. (1823). *The present State of England in regard to agriculture, trade and finance; with a comparison of the prospects of England and France* (2nd edn.). Hurst, Rees, Orme and Brown: Longman.

Lucas, R. E., Jr. (1996). Nobel lecture: Monetary neutrality. *Journal of Political Economy, 104*(4), 661–682.

Luce, R. D. (1964). A generalization of a theorem of dimensional analysis. *Journal of Mathematical Psychology, 1*(2), 278–284.

Malestroit, J. C. D. (1566). Les Paradoxes du Seigneur de Malestroit, Conseillor du Roy et Maistre Ordinaire de ses Comptes, sur le Faict des Monnoyes Présentez à sa Majesté, au Mois de Mars, MDLXVI. In J.-Y. Le Branchu (Eds.), *Ecrits Notables sur la Monnaire (XVIe siècle)*, De Copernic à Davanzati, 1, Félix Alcan (pp. 49–68).

Marshall, A. (1887). Remedies for fluctuations of general prices. *Contemporary Review, 1866–1900*(51), 355–375.

Martin, R. S. (2022). Revisiting taste change in cost-of-living measurement. *Journal of Economic and Social Measurement, 46*(2), 109–147.

McFadden, D. (1974). Conditional logit analysis of qualitative choice behavior. *Zarembka* (pp. 105–142). Frontiers in Econometrics: Academic Press.

Menz, J. O., Wieland, E., & Mehrhoff, J. (2023). Estimating the impact of quality adjustment on consumer price inflation. ECB Working Paper No. 2023/2773.

Mitchell, W. C. (1938). *The making and using of index numbers* (p. 656). No: The Bulletin of the United States Bureau of Labor Statistics.

Mizobuchi, H., & Zelenyuk, V. (2021). Quadratic-mean-of-order-r indexes of output, input and productivity. *Journal of Productivity Analysis, 56*(2–3), 133–138.

Moulton, B. (1996). *Constant elasticity cost-of-living index in share-relative form*. Bureau of Labor Statistics Manuscript: Unpublished U.S.

Nakamura, E., Steinsson, J., & Liu, M. (2016). Are Chinese growth and inflation too smooth? Evidence from Engel curves. *American Economic Journal: Macroeconomics, 8*(3), 113–144.

Nakamura, L. (1996). Is U.S. economic performance really that bad? Federal Reserve Bank of Philadelphia Working Paper, No. 95- 21/R.

Neary, J. (2004). Rationalizing the Penn world table: True multilateral indices for international comparisons of real income. *American Economic Review, 94*(5), 1411–1428.

Newmarch, W. (1859). On the electoral statistics of England and Wales, 1856–8: Memorandum with reference to certain portions of the paper read in February, 1858. *Journal of the Statistical Society of London, 22*(2), 297–305.

Northcote, S. H. (1886). Report of the royal commission appointed to inquire into the depression of trade and industry: Presented to Both Houses of Parliament by Command of Her Majesty.

O'Brien, D. P. (2000). Bodin's analysis of inflation. *History of Political Economy, 32*(2), 267–292.

OECD PPP Mannual (2012) EUROSTAT-OECD Methodological Manual on Purchasing Power Parities (PPPs) (2nd edn.)

Osborne, M. (2018). Approximating the cost-of-living index for a storable good. *American Economic Journal: Microeconomics, 10*(2), 286–331.

Oulton, N. (2008). Chain indices of the cost-of-living and the path-dependence problem: An empirical solution. *Journal of Econometrics, 144*(1), 306–324.

Outhwaite, R. B. (1982). Inflation in tudor and early Stuart England: Studies in economic and social history series (2nd edn.) Macmillan.

Paasche, H. (1874). Über die Preisentwicklung der Letzten Jahre Nach den Hamburger Börsennotirungen. *Jahrbücher für Nationalökonomie und Statistik, 12*, 168–178.

Pakes, A. (2003). A reconsideration of Hedonic price indexes with an application to PC's. *American Economic Review, 93*(5), 1578–1596.

Phelps-Brown, E. H., & Hopkins, S. V. (1956). Seven centuries of the prices of consumables, compared with Builders' Wage-Rates. *Economica, 23*(92), 296–314.

Philps, L. (1974). *Applied consumption analysis*. North-Holland.

Pierson, N. G. (1896). Further considerations on index-numbers. *Economic Journal, 6*(21), 127–131.

Pigou, A. C. (1912). *The economics of welfare*. London: Macmillan.

Pollak, R. A. (1971). The theory of the cost of living index. Research Discussion Paper No. 11, Research Division, Office of Prices and Living Conditions, U. S. Bureau of Labor Statistics.

Quah, D., & Vahey, S. P. (1995). Measuring core inflation. *Economic Journal, 105*(432), 1130–44.

Rao, D. S. P. (1990). A system of long-change index numbers for multilateral comparisons. *Contributions to Economic Analysis, 194*, 127–39.

Rao, D. S. P. (2004). The country-product-dummy method: A stochastic approach to the computation of purchasing power parities in the ICP. CEPA Working Papers Series WP032004, School of Economics, University of Queensland, Australia.

Rao, D. S. P. (2005). On the equivalence of weighted Country-Product-Dummy (CPD) method and the rao-system for multilateral price comparisons. *Review of Income and Wealth, 51*(4), 571–580.

Rao, D. S. P., & Banerjee, K. S. (1986). A multilateral index number system based on the factorial approach. *Statistical Papers, 27*(1), 297–313.

Rao, D. S. P., & Hajargasht, G. (2016). Stochastic approach to computation of purchasing power parities in the International Comparison Program (ICP). *Journal of Econometrics, 191*(2), 414–425.

Redding, S. J., & Weinstein, D. E. (2020). Measuring aggregate price indices with taste shocks: Theory and evidence for CES preferences. *Quarterly Journal of Economics, 135*(1), 503–560.

Reinsdorf, M. B., & Dorfman, A. H. (1999). The Sato-Vartia index and the monotonicity axiom. *Journal of Econometrics, 90*(1), 45–61.

Ricardo, D. (1822) Speech on Mr. Western's motion, for a committee to consider the effects produced by the "Resumption of Cash Payments," delivered on the 12th of June, 1822.

Romer, P. (1987). Growth based on increasing returns due to specialization. *American Economic Review, 77*(2), 56–52.

Romer, P. (1990). Endogenous technological change. *Journal of Political Economy, 98*(5-Part 2), S71–S012.

Rosen, S. (1974). Hedonic prices and implicit markets: Product differentiation in pure competition. *Journal of Political Economy, 82*(1), 34–55.

Ryten, J. (1999). Evaluation of the international comparison programme. Document E/CN.3/1999/8 of the U. N. Economic and Social Council, dated 16 November 1998.

Sackley, A. (1965). Coinage, commodities, and count Carli: An account of the inventor and the computation of the original index numbers. *Monthly Labor Review, 88*(7), 817–821.

Salop, S. (1979). Monopolistic competition with outside goods. *Bell Journal of Economics, 10*(1), 141–156.

Samuelson, P. A. (1964). Theoretical notes on trade problems. *Review of Economics and Statistics, 46*(2), 145–154.

Samuelson, P. A. (1983). *Foundations of economic analysis*. Harvard University Press.

Samuelson, P. A., & Swamy, S. (1974). Invariant economic index numbers and canonical duality: Survey and synthesis. *American Economic Review, 64*(4), 566–593.

Sato, K. (1974). Ideal index numbers that almost satisfy factor reversal test. *Review of Economics and Statistics, 56*(4), 549–552.

Sato, K. (1976). The ideal log-change index number. *Review of Economics and Statistics, 58*(2), 223–228.

Sauerbeck, A. (1896). Prices of commodities and the precious metals. *Journal of the Statistical Society of London, 49*(3), 581–648.

Schumpeter, J. A. (1939). *Business cycles: A theoretical, historical, and statistical analysis of the capitalist process* McGraw-Hill Book Co.

Schumpeter, J. A. (1954). *History of economic analysis*. Edited from Manuscript by E. B: Schumpeter. Oxford University Press.
Scrope, G. P. (1833). Principles of Political Economy, Longman, Rees, Orme, Brown, Green, & Longman.
Selvanathan, E. A., & Rao, D. S. P. (1994). *Index numbers: A stochastic approach*. Springer.
Shapiro, M. D., & Wilcox, D. W. (1997). Alternative strategies for aggregating prices in the CPI. *Federal Reserve Bank of St. Louis Review, 79*(3), 113–125.
Shiskin, J. (1974). Updating the consumer price index? *An overview. Monthly Labor Review, 97*(7), 3–20.
Shuckburgh-Evelyn, G. (1798). An account of some endeavours to ascertain a standard of weight and measure. *Philosophical Transactions of the Royal Society of London, 88*, 133–182.
Silver, M. (1999). An evaluation of the use of hedonic regressions for basic components of consumer price indices. *Review of Income and Wealth, 45*(1), 41–56.
Silver, M. (2006). Core inflation: Measures and statistical issues in choosing among them. IMF Working Papers, No. 2006/097.
Silver, M. (2009). The Hedonic country product dummy method and quality adjustments for purchasing power parity calculations. IMF Working Papers, No. 09/271.
Silver, M., & Heravi, S. (2007). Why elementary price index number formulas differ: Evidence on price dispersion. *Journal of Econometrics, 140*(2), 874–883.
Smith, A. (1776). An inquiry into the nature and causes of the wealth of nations, W. Strahan and T. Cadell.
Soetbeer, A. (1885). Materialien zur Erläuterung und Beurteilung der wirtschaftlichen Edelmettallverhältnisse und der Währungsfrage
Solow, R. (1957). Technical change and the aggregate production function. *Review of Economics and Statistics, 39*(3), 312–320.
Star, S., & Hall, R. (1976). An approximate divisia index of total factor productivity. *Econometrica, 44*(2), 257–263.
Stuvel, G. (1989). The index-number problem and its solution. Intl Specialized Book Services, Inc.
Summers, R. (1973). International price comparisons based upon incomplete data. *Review of Income and Wealth, 19*(1), 1–16.
Swamy, S. (1965). Consistency of Fisher's tests. *Econometrica, 33*(3), 619–623.
Szulc, B. (1964). Index numbers of multilateral regional comparisons (in Polish). *Przeglad Statysticzny, 3*, 239–254.
Theil, H. (1965). The information approach to demand analysis. *Econometrica, 33*(1), 67–87.
Theil, H. (1973). A new index number formula. *Review of Economics and Statistics, 55*(4), 498–502.
Theil, H. (1974). More on log-change index numbers. *Review Economics and Statistics, 56*(4), 552–554.
Thirsk, J. (Ed.) (1989). *The Agrarian history of England and Wales*, VI 1750–1850, Cambridge University Press.
Tica, J., & Družić, I. (2006). The Harrod-Balassa-Samuelson effect: A survey of empirical evidence. University of Zagreb, Faculty of Economics and Business, FEB-Working Paper Series 06-7/686.
Törnqvist, L. (1936). The bank of Finland's consumption price index. *Bank of Finland Monthly Bulletin, 10*, 1–8.
Törnqvist, L., Vartia, P., & Vartia, Y. O. (1985). How should relative changes be measured? *American Statistician, 39*(1), 43–46.
Triplett, J. E. (2001). Should the cost-of-living index provide the conceptual framework for a consumer price index? *The Economic Journal, 111*(472), F311–F334.
Triplett, J. E. (2004). Handboodk on Hednic indexes and quality adjustments in price indexes: Special application to information technology product. OECD Science, Technology and Industry Working Papers 2004/09.
Trivedi, P. K. (1981). Some discrete approximations to divisia integral indices. *International Economic Review, 22*(1), 71–77.
Tusset, G. (2020). Gian Rinaldo Carli (1720–1795): Diagnosis and treatment of a monetary plague. *History of Economic Thought and Policy, 9*(2), 39–65.

Ueda, K. (2020). Dynamic cost of living index for storable goods. *Economics Letters, 189*, 109013.
Ueda, K., Watanabe, K., & Watanabe, T. (2023). Product turnover and the cost-of-living index: Quality versus fashion effects. *American Economic Journal: Macroeconomics, 11*(2), 310–347.
Ueda, K., Watanabe, K., & Watanabe, T. (2024). Household inventory, temporary sales, price indices. *International Economic Review, 65*(1), 217–251.
United Nations. (2010). *International Recommendations for the Index of Industrial Production 2010* (p. 107). Series F: Department of Economic and Social Affairs Statistics Division Statistical Papers.
Vartia, Y. O. (1976). Ideal log-change index numbers. *Scandinavian Journal of Statistics, 3*, 121–126.
Vaughan, R. (1675). A discourse of coin and coinage, Th. Basset.
Velde, F. (2012). The life and tines of Nicolas Dutot. *Journal of the History of Economic Thought, 34*(1), 67–107.
Vogt, A. (1981). Characterizations of indices, especially of the Stuvel and the Banerjee index. *Statistishce Hefte, 22*(3), 241–245.
von Auer, L. (2008). Questioning some general wisdom in axiomatic index theory. mimeo.
von Auer, L., & Wengenroth, J. (2021). Consistent aggregation with superlative and other price indices. *Journal of the Royal Statistical Society Series A: Statistics in Society, 184*(2), 589–615.
Wald, A. (1937). Zur Theorie der Preisindexziffern. *Zeitschrift für Nationalökonomie, 8*(2), 179–219.
Wald, A. (1951). On some systems of equations of mathematical economics. *Econometrica, 19*(4), 368–403.
Walsh, C. M. (1901). *The measurement of general exchange value*. Macmillan.
Walsh, C. M. (1924). Professor Edgeworth's views on index-numbers. *Quarterly Journal of Economics, 38*(3), 500–519.
Weidman, J. (2012). Money creation and responsibility. In *Speech at the 18th Colloquium of the Institute for Bank-Historical Research (IBF)*, Frankfurt, September 2012.
Westergaard, H. (1890). Die Grundzüge der Theorie der Statistik, Gustav Fischer.
Wynne, M. A. (2008). Core inflation: A review of some conceptual issues. *Federal Reserve Bank of St. Louis, 90*(3, Part 2), 205–228.
Young, A. (1812). An enquiry into the progressive value of money in England, as marked by the price of agricultural products: with observations upon Sir G. Shuckburgh's table of appreciation: The whole deduced from a great variety of authorities, not before collected, MacMillan.
Zimmerman, C. C. (1932). Ernst Engel's law of expenditures for food. *Quarterly Journal of Economics, 47*(1), 78–101.

Index

N. Abe, *Price Index Numbers*, Springer Texts in Business and Economics,
https://doi.org/10.1007/978-981-97-6305-4

The manufacturer's authorised representative in the EU is Springer Nature Customer Service Centre GmbH, Europaplatz 3, 69115 Heidelberg, Germany. If you have any concerns regarding our products, please contact ProductSafety@springernature.com

Printed and bound by CPI Group (UK) Ltd, Croydon, CR0 4YY
21/09/2026
02219973-0005